A2
Psychology

Christine Brain

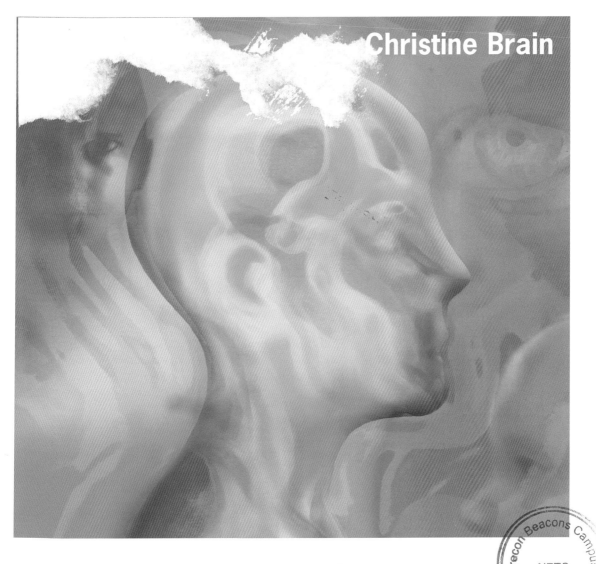

D0418356

Thank you Jenny, Katie and the team at Philip Allan Updates for all the support and guidance given, and thank you Alastair.

For Alex and Doug — best sons, best friends.

Philip Allan Updates, an imprint of Hodder Education, an Hachette UK company, Market Place, Deddington, Oxfordshire OX15 0SE

Orders

Bookpoint Ltd, 130 Milton Park, Abingdon, Oxfordshire OX14 4SB
tel: 01235 827827
fax: 01235 400401
e-mail: eduction@bookpoint.co.uk

Lines are open 9.00 a.m.–5.00 p.m., Monday to Saturday, with a 24-hour message answering service. You can also order through the Philip Allan Updates website: www.philipallan.co.uk

© Philip Allan Updates 2009

ISBN 978-0-340-96684-6

Impression number   6
Year   2013

This material has been endorsed by Edexcel and offers high quality support for the delivery of Edexcel qualifications.

Edexcel endorsement does not mean that this material is essential to achieve any Edexcel qualification, nor does it mean that this is the only suitable material available to support any Edexcel qualification. No endorsed material will be used verbatim in setting any Edexcel examination and any resource lists produced by Edexcel shall include this and other appropriate texts. While this material has been through an Edexcel quality assurance process, all responsibility for the content remains with the publisher.

Copies of official specifications for all Edexcel qualifications may be found on the Edexcel website: www.edexcel.com

Design by Juha Sorsa

Printed in Dubai

Hachette UK's policy is to use papers that are natural, renewable and recyclable products and made from wood grown in sustainable forests. The logging and manufacturing processes are expected to conform to the environmental regulations of the country of origin.

P2051

Contents

Chapter 3 Health psychology: substance misuse

Chapter 4 Sport psychology

Unit 4: How Psychology Works

Chapter 5 Clinical psychology

Chapter 6 Issues and debates

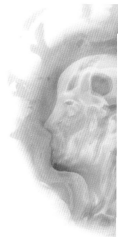

Introduction

This textbook is written specifically for students following the Edexcel A2 Psychology course.

The A2 course

Some features of the A2 course are that:

- four applications of psychology are offered, from which the student chooses two
- the AS approaches are used as explanations of various aspects of the applications
- there is continued emphasis on how psychology works, with the AS methodology being applied to the applications
- there is a fifth application, clinical psychology, which is compulsory because of the strong science element and the clear links to the AS approaches
- issues and debates within psychology, including methodological and ethical issues, are considered to help to draw the whole course together
- for each application, including clinical psychology, methodology and a key issue are studied and advice on a practical is offered

Unit 3 covers two applications from criminological, child, health and sport psychology:

- Criminological psychology examines explanations of criminal behaviour including social learning theory, and looks at three studies of eyewitness testimony. There is also an examination of ways of treating offenders.
- Child psychology looks at attachment theory, issues of deprivation and privation, developmental issues such as autism or ADHD, and the advantages and disadvantages of daycare.
- Health psychology focuses on substance misuse, and biological and learning explanations of substance abuse. Heroin and one other drug are examined in detail. Ways of treating substance misuse are also examined.
- Sport psychology focuses on explanations about sporting participation and sporting performance, including the effects of personality. Achievement motivation and the inverted U hypothesis are covered. The improvement of sporting performance is also considered.

Unit 4 covers clinical psychology and issues and debates:

- Clinical psychology questions how to define abnormality and considers issues around diagnosing mental disorders. Two disorders are examined in depth (schizophrenia and one other).
- The chapter on 'issues and debates' reviews the many issues of the course including methodology, ethics and key issues. There is also consideration of the contributions of the five AS approaches and the A2 applications to society,

in addition to the four main debates: a discussion of the effects of culture, how far psychology can be described as a science, how psychology is used as social control and the debate about nature–nurture.

Structure of each application

The A2 applications follow the same structure as the AS approaches. Indeed, the A2 structure is nearly the same as that for AS. However, there is one small difference: the key issue falls within the practical rather than in addition to the practical. Within each application there is:

- a definition of the application, including some key terms to learn
- methodology used in the application to see how psychology works and how AS research methods are applied
- content — which involves theories, explanations (from the approaches) and treatments or practical applications of the theories
- two studies in detail from the four Unit 3 applications and three studies for the Unit 4 application (clinical psychology)
- one practical, which can be either a content analysis focusing on a key issue for that application or an article analysis which has to focus on the content of the application

The unit tests

- The Unit 3 test is a written paper of 1 hour 30 minutes' duration. It is worth 60 marks and is 40% of the total A2 marks.
- The Unit 4 test is a written paper of 2 hours' duration. It is worth 90 marks and is 60% of the total A2 marks.
- Unlike the AS units there are no multiple-choice questions for either Unit 3 or Unit 4. For Unit 3 there are four main parts, one for each application. Each main part has a short-answer section and an extended writing section. Students have to answer questions for two of the applications out of the four. For Unit 4 there is one part on clinical psychology, within which there is a short answer section and an extended writing section. Then there is a second part on issues and debates, again with both a short answer section and an extended writing section.

Assessment objectives

You are being tested on three assessment objectives (AOs):

- AO1 — knowledge with understanding, good use of terminology and answers communicated clearly
- AO2 — application and evaluation of what you have learnt
- AO3 — knowledge and evaluation of psychology in practice, of the methodology you have studied and the methodology of studies carried out by others

Marking

There are two main types of marking for the A2 papers:

- Many answers are marked point by point, which means each point you make that answers the question clearly and effectively gains a mark. You can also gain marks by adding more about that point (elaboration). Sometimes an example can gain a mark if it helps to explain your answer or show that you understand the point(s) you are making.

■ Other answers are marked using 'levels'. Your answer will be put into a level according to criteria such as 'shows good understanding' or 'focuses on all parts of the question'. The criteria are likely to include how you write the answer, your spelling and grammar and also (importantly) your use of appropriate specialist terms. Essays and questions about practicals use this kind of marking. Two-mark questions can use 'levels' as well, in that 1 mark is given for a brief answer and 2 marks if the answer is clear and more thorough.

About this book

The first five chapters in this book cover an application each: criminological, child, health, sport and clinical psychology. Chapter 6 covers issues and debates. The 'issues and debates' section of the course is synoptic, which means drawing on the rest of the course. The chapter summarises the appropriate areas, but links with other parts of the course (including the AS) are suggested to review the required information.

Throughout the book advice is offered to guide you through the course:
■ 'Explore' boxes — suggestions for you to extend your study of particular areas.
■ 'Study hint' boxes — to help with preparing for the exams.
■ AS link boxes — to highlight links to AS material to support your learning. Where appropriate, page references are given to the Edexcel AS Psychology textbook, published by Philip Allan Updates.
■ Examination-style questions — to help you revise.
■ Extension questions — to help you learn the material by answering broader questions that will extend your learning; this will help you in the exams.

How to use this book

■ You will only be studying two of the four Unit 3 applications, which means you do not need to cover two of the first four chapters. Make sure you know which applications you are studying.
■ Each chapter is presented in the order of the specification for your course, so it is useful to read the chapter through in the order presented.
■ Chapters 5 and 6 cover compulsory material that you will need to know.
■ In the various applications there are choices to be made — such as which other mental health disorder you will study for the clinical approach (other than schizophrenia) and which other explanation for criminal behaviour in the chapter on criminological psychology (other than social learning theory). Your teacher will probably have set out these choices already, so make sure you use the appropriate material. Certain choices are made in this book and other material can be found in the online resources.

About practicals and key issues

You will carry out three practicals for A2 psychology. For the two Unit 3 applications you need to carry out one practical each. One must be a content analysis looking at a key issue you have chosen — this must be a key issue that you can explain using concepts, theories and/or research from the relevant application. The other practical must be an article analysis looking at an area of the content you have studied for that application. The third practical, within clinical psychology, asks you to prepare a leaflet about an issue. There is no separate key issue for each application, because the key issue is part of the analysis practical.

The Edexcel website

Edexcel has its own website (**www.edexcel.com**), with a section for psychology. Use it to find out more about your course, including the specification. The specification outlines everything you need to know for your course, and this textbook follows every aspect of Units 3 and 4.

- Use the specimen assessment materials, which include exam papers and mark schemes. The mark schemes will help you to see how to answer the question and score marks.
- You can ask questions using the website, through the 'Ask the Expert' service.

Take charge of your own learning and you will do very well.

Being synoptic — Chapter 6

Chapter 6 is the synoptic part of the course and requires you to bring in material that you covered at AS and the rest of A2. Think of this chapter as being about helping you remember what you have learnt rather than giving you new information. Take the time to check back to the areas signposted in Chapter 6, and check your understanding of them. It is tempting to ignore such suggestions and instructions, but the questions in the second part of Unit 4 — those that focus on issues and debates — will ask you to draw on different areas of your course, so you need to practise doing so.

Online resources

The website accompanying this textbook contains brief coverage of the studies, theories and explanations in the further options and key issues. This can be accessed by visiting **www.hodderplus.co.uk/philipallan**.

Enjoying the A2 course

One way of enjoying a course is to be motivated to pass it. Renew your motivation to achieve a good grade in A-level psychology, as this will help your learning. To do well you need organised notes and a good revision strategy. You should also link what you learn in the course to your own experiences. Where possible, think of examples in your own life or link your own experiences to what you are learning. For example, have you 'suffered' from a self-fulfilling prophecy? What do you think the outcome of being deprived of an attachment would be? How would you define abnormality?

Although you will not be a psychologist when you have completed your course, you could try to apply your learning to other people and events in society. For example, if you read about someone with schizophrenia, note whether they are being prescribed medication or if there is any mention of a family history. If you read about someone who is a witness, see if anything is mentioned about bias in their testimony. This approach will help you to enjoy the course and to be involved in your learning.

Unit 3
Applications of Psychology

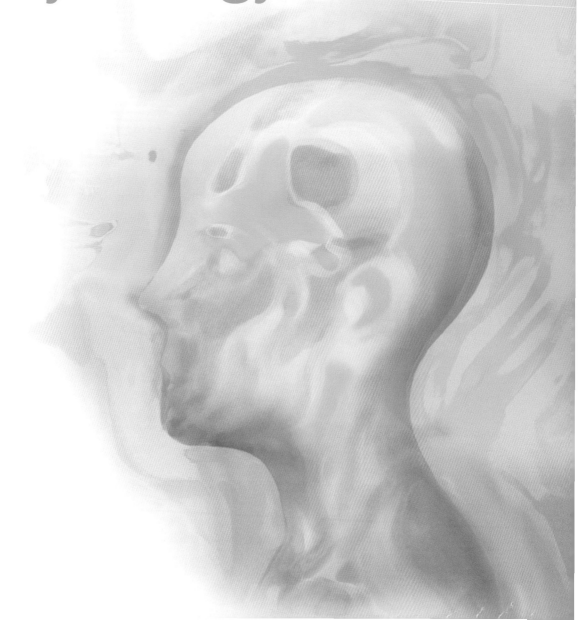

Chapter

Criminological psychology

This chapter is about criminological psychology, which is an **application** in psychology. This means that theories and studies are applied to issues of concern to society and the individual. Criminological psychology covers many areas, from finding criminals, to procedures in court, to treatment of offenders. In your course you will just touch on some of these issues. You will look at two explanations for what makes someone a criminal and two ways of treating criminals. You will also investigate eyewitness testimony issues, such as research methods to study such issues and studies that have been done to show how witness testimony can be unreliable. As with the AS, in the A2 applications you need to know two studies in detail as well as one key issue in the area you are studying. You will also carry out a practical based on the key issue.

Summary of learning objectives

Definitions
You have to be able to define the terms:

- crime
- recidivism
- token economy
- antisocial behaviour
- stereotyping
- modelling
- eyewitness testimony

Methodology
- the laboratory and field experiment research methods, as used to assess witness effectiveness
- evaluation of both the field and the laboratory experiment research methods, including their use in criminological psychology and issues of validity, reliability and ethics

Content

You have to be able to describe and evaluate:

- the social learning theory explanation of criminal/antisocial behaviour (the learning approach) — including considering the role of the media in modelling antisocial behaviour
- one other explanation of criminal/antisocial behaviour from two options — either labelling and self-fulfilling prophecy (the social approach) or one example of how personality explains criminal behaviour (the biological approach)
- three studies into eyewitness testimony, including one laboratory experiment and one field study (and one other)
- the way the token economy programme is used to treat offenders
- one other way of treating offenders

Studies in detail

You have to be able to describe and evaluate in detail:

- the laboratory experimental study of Loftus and Palmer (1974), studying the effect of leading questions on eyewitness testimony
- one other study from Yuille and Cutshall (1986), Charlton et al. (2000) and Gesch et al. (2003)

Key issues and practical

You have to carry out one practical that focuses on a key issue which you choose, that relates to criminological psychology. The practical can be a content analysis of articles, programmes or other material about the key issue, or a summary of two articles from which you then draw conclusions about the key issue.

Table 1.1 Checklist of what you need to know for criminological psychology and your progress

I need to know about	Done	More work	I need to know about	Done	More work
Defining: crime, antisocial behaviour and recidivism			Loftus and Palmer (1974) — a laboratory experiment looking at eyewitness testimony (and evaluation)		
Defining: eyewitness testimony, stereotyping, modelling and token economy			Yuille and Cutshall (1986) — a field study looking at eyewitness testimony (and evaluation)		
Laboratory and field experi-ments and examples/evaluation of their use to assess witness effectiveness			One other study into eyewitness testimony and evaluation		
Evaluating laboratory and field experiments including reliability and validity			Token economy programmes and treating offenders (and evaluation)		
Use of laboratory and field experiments with regard to ethics			One other way of treating offenders (and evaluation) e.g. anger management		
Social learning theory and explaining antisocial behaviour			One key issue and a practical relating to it		
Labelling and self-fulfilling prophecy and explaining antisocial behaviour *or* one personality theory to explain it					

Definitions

Crime, **antisocial behaviour** and **recidivism** are three terms used when defining criminological psychology in this section. The term **eyewitness testimony** is explained when looking at methodology, as well as in other places in this chapter. **Modelling**, **stereotyping** and **token economy** are terms defined and explained in the content section.

An introduction to criminological psychology

Criminological psychology is about all aspects of crime and antisocial behaviour, from defining and looking at causes of crime to identifying criminals, making judgements about them and treating them.

Crime is defined as an act that is against the law. Crime also implies a punishment — or at least some treatment to prevent recidivism. Criminological psychology is about applying psychological principles to all aspects of crime. For example, you will be relating the approaches you studied for AS to criminological psychology.

Recidivism is the term used when someone repeats a crime or a behaviour for which they have either been punished or received treatment. It means returning to and repeating behaviour that should have been extinguished. There are rates of recidivism but only criminals who are caught again, or who reveal their renewed criminal activity, will be counted, so reported rates are probably lower than the reality.

Antisocial behaviour may not be about an action that is an actual crime but is considered part of what criminological psychology looks at, because it involves actions that citizens dislike and which could become crime at some stage. Antisocial behaviour is any behaviour that affects other people negatively and, in psychology, is often used to mean aggressive behaviour.

Antisocial behaviour may not be criminal but is behaviour that has a negative effect on one or more people in society, and it is therefore studied within criminological psychology

TopFoto

Recently in the UK, antisocial behaviour orders (ASBOs) have been created, illustrating how close antisocial behaviour is to criminal activity. For example, just meeting in small groups in a certain area can lead young people to receive an ASBO — which has made meeting in groups in certain areas a crime.

Explore   Look up the government website 'Respect' (**www.respect.gov.uk**) to find out what is thought about antisocial behaviour and what is being done about it in the UK.

Study hint   When asked a question about criminal behaviour, it is usually accepted that you may include references to antisocial behaviour, or you might be asked specifically about antisocial behaviour.

Psychology and defining crime

Society and legal processes decide what is and is not a crime in a particular society. Some actions may be a crime in all countries but crime is often seen as **socially constructed**, which means that different countries and cultures understand the concept differently and, if what is a crime differs between countries and cultures, then crime is a construct. The importance of this is that it is hard to argue that an action is a crime without considering the context and the situation. Psychology considers such aspects when studying what crime is, including whether someone is 'of sound mind' or whether there was intention in their action(s).

Explore   Look up 'social constructionism' and compare the idea with scientific understanding. If something is scientifically 'proved' then it should be true of all people in all cultures and is likely to come from nature. It is a universal law of behaviour. If something is a construct, in that it differs between cultures, then it is likely to be about nurture. So the concepts of social constructionism, universal laws and science are useful when you discuss the nature–nurture debate later in your course.

Causes of crime

Causes of crime are often split into nature and nurture aspects of behaviour. For example, personality, genes, hormones and brain structure have all been said to be causes of criminal behaviour. These are biological aspects of crime, and crime then comes from someone's nature. However, an accident or head injury can affect someone's biology and their behaviour, so crime might not be 'born' but can be 'made' and is still biologically caused.`

Others say that crime is caused by environment and nurture. In child psychology (if you study that area of psychology for your course), you will look at the theory of Bowlby and others, who claimed that being deprived of mother love as an infant can lead to juvenile delinquency and worse when older. So maternal deprivation may be a cause of crime. Other similar theories include labelling and the self-fulfilling prophecy, both of which are about stereotyping — predicting behaviour and then, by expecting such behaviour, producing criminal behaviour. Most theories about nurture and crime are about the (bad) influence of families. Criminal behaviour might be copied, for example, or encouraged, or expected.

Study hint In this chapter you will look at the social learning explanation of criminal behaviour — that it is copied — and one other theory. In this textbook the other theory focused upon is labelling and the self-fulfilling prophecy, and a biological explanation (personality) is explained in more detail in the online material that accompanies this book. Draw on your later studies to expand your understanding of the causes of crime.

Identifying criminals, making judgements and treating offenders

In the following methodology and content sections, you will learn more about problems with eyewitness testimony and you can choose this as a key issue on which to carry out a practical. You will also look at two ways (of many) of treating offenders, which will add to your understanding. Other areas of criminological psychology, which are not covered in this chapter, include how a jury is affected by the defendant. For example, would you be more likely to think someone dressed in a suit and without a regional accent is innocent than someone dressed in jeans and speaking in a local accent? It appears that juries are affected by issues such as race, accent and attractiveness and these are issues studied within criminological psychology but not in your course.

Forensic psychologists cover many areas, from helping the police to find criminals to treating offenders in institutions. They are interested in **rehabilitation**, which is about preparing someone to become a productive and settled member of a community. Forensic psychologists also carry out research, so they are working within criminological psychology. A degree in criminology, however, would also cover sociological aspects of crime, including recidivism rates, and how gender, race or class might affect criminal activity.

Study hint If you are also studying sociology, it is probably best to keep your study of crime separate in the two subjects, although labelling and self-fulfilling prophecy (which you will study later in this chapter) are also part of sociology.

Examination-style questions

1 What is meant by recidivism? *(2 marks)*

2 What is the difference between crime and antisocial behaviour? *(2 marks)*

3 Explain three areas of study that are of interest to criminological/forensic psychologists. *(6 marks)*

Methodology

This section is about a particular area of criminological psychology — witness testimony. This area is studied using laboratory experiments and field experiments, and both these research methods are studied in this section. They are described and evaluated to see how useful they are for finding out about witness effectiveness. Aspects of reliability, validity and ethics are also examined with regard to these two research methods.

AS link Note that you might be asked to draw on AS material for both the Methodology and Content sections of this chapter.

Laboratory experiments

Laboratory experiments used to examine witness effectiveness look for cause-and-effect relationships by controlling as much as is possible about the situation, the setting and participants, while changing one variable (the independent variable — IV) to see the effect(s) of that change on another variable (the dependent variable — DV). They test a hypothesis that is generated from a theory and then the theory is amended or confirmed according to the results of the experiment.

AS link Review your learning about laboratory experiments, including checking your understanding of the terms 'hypothesis', 'independent variable', and 'dependent variable' (pp. 95–97).

Loftus's laboratory experiments

One laboratory experiment that is well known in the study of eyewitness effectiveness is that of Loftus and Palmer (1974). This is one of the two studies that you must know in detail, so it is explained thoroughly on pp. 39–41. Use your knowledge of the detail of their study in questions about laboratory experiments looking at witness testimony.

Elizabeth Loftus carried out many laboratory experiments in the field of eyewitness testimony and often used students as participants. **Eyewitness testimony** is an account people give of an incident they have witnessed. 'Witnessing' in this case means they have seen the incident — it is a legal term.

Loftus's basic method was to show students a film or give them a scenario and then ask them questions about what they had seen. The questions were sometimes 'leading' — by using particular words, and sometimes they were 'misleading' — by including incorrect information. The idea was to find out what it was about questioning that might lead a witness to give 'false' information, albeit not deliberately.

Loftus is a forensic psychologist and she acts as an expert witness in the area of eyewitness testimony. She has drawn attention to factors such as how a jury will place trust in witness testimony, especially if the witness is confident. If a witness is wrongly confident then this can have serious consequences for a defendant. If a witness reports in a biased way what he or she saw, then this too has serious consequences.

The misinformation effect

Loftus used laboratory studies to look at the effect of giving the wrong information to a 'witness'. The aim was to see if the witnesses involved would incorporate the wrong information into their 'witness statement', or if they would even notice. The idea is that memory is **reconstructive** and not like a tape recording. Witnesses will use past experiences and information, not only from the event but from those around and from any questioner, when they are telling their story.

When questions included misinformation, Loftus discovered a **misinformation effect**. This is the effect of using leading questions when the question includes inaccurate information. In laboratory experiments this wrong information affected what participants said they saw.

One example is when participants witnessed a car accident at a junction where there was a stop sign. After the participants had seen the film of the accident half were given information that the stop sign was a 'yield' (give way) sign (though it was a stop sign). Those who had seen the 'yield' sign information were much more likely to recall a 'yield' sign, whereas the other half of the participants were more likely to be accurate and remember a stop sign.

In another study participants recalled a 'barn' that they were asked about but which was not there. In the second part of the Loftus and Palmer (1974) study, which you will look at later in this book, participants were asked about broken glass when there was none in the scene they watched. Those who had been asked about a car 'smashing' into another remembered broken glass more often than when they had been asked about a car 'hitting' another. Presumably 'smash' suggests broken glass more than 'hit' does.

Loftus also found that, if there was a time lapse between the viewing of the film and being asked questions about what they had seen, participants were even more open to the misinformation effect and more likely to change their memories to include the misinformation.

Practice 1.1

Using the four studies outlined briefly above, answer the following questions. The four studies are the 'stop/yield sign' study, the 'barn' study, the 'broken glass' part of the Loftus and Palmer study (1974), and the 'time taken before recall' study.

1 For two of the studies, what is the hypothesis?

2 For two of the studies what is the IV and what is the DV?

3 For the 'stop/yield sign' study, what is the experimental design?

Answers are at the end of Chapter 1.

Creating false childhood memories

Loftus has also carried out research in planting false early memories to see if people accept those memories as accurate. It seems they do. Again, she used laboratory experiments. To be sure that any planted memory would not be too traumatic for participants — ethical considerations being important — she came up with the idea of having been lost in a shopping mall as a child. The participants were asked to try to remember incidents from their childhood; a relative helped with three real incidents and also the fake one about being lost (the researchers having first checked that each participant had not been lost in this way).

The scenario is that the child became lost in a shopping mall and started crying. The child was then comforted by an elderly woman, and was finally reunited with a family member. The participant read all four stories and had to say what they remembered about each event. They could write that they did not remember the event if they could not recall it. The question was, would they 'remember' the 'being lost' story, which was false?

The results were that 29% — 7 of the 24 participants — 'recalled' being lost. Then, after being interviewed again about the story at a later date, 25% (6 of them) still claimed they remembered. Of the events that actually took place, 68% were remembered. Loftus concluded that memories are reconstructed from present and past experiences, but also that some 'memories' might be completely false, which affects how we view eyewitness testimony. Loftus was actually interested in this issue because of the false memories that therapists can instil in their clients, but this work on false memories also has implications for witness testimony.

Drawing conclusions about Loftus's experimental work

You should now have a number of studies on which to draw to discuss the use of laboratory experiments in eyewitness testimony research. You should be able to discuss the procedures in sufficient detail to evaluate the studies, as is done later in this section.

Earwitness testimony

Although your course focuses on eyewitness testimony, research has also been carried out on 'earwitness' testimony — when witnesses report on what they have *heard* rather than on what they have *seen*. For example, Cook and Wilding (1996) carried out a study to see if people remember more when they hear something from a well known voice or a voice they have heard only once. They found little difference.

There is no need for you to know any details about earwitness testimony, but it is useful to be aware that research has taken place in this area.

How useful are laboratory experiments in studying witness effectiveness?

Laboratory experiments, especially since the 1970s, have been the main way of investigating witness effectiveness. This is because everything can be controlled except the IV, so that researchers can claim that the IV causes the change in the DV. If all participants who watch the same film, for example, were in the same situation and had many other similarities (such as that they were students), and then half of them were given information about a yield sign and half were not, then when more participants remembered a yield sign in that group it could be claimed that it was the misinformation that caused the 'memory'. A case study, observation or questionnaire asking about memory would not have given this information about a cause and an effect. Laboratory experiments are scientific, and a body of knowledge can be built using such firm foundations.

Field experiments used to look at witness effectiveness are examined later in this section. When you have studied these, discuss the relative advantages and disadvantages of laboratory experiments compared to field experiments.

The lack of validity in laboratory experiments is important in that any attempt to apply the findings of these studies to real eyewitnesses in real cases may not be appropriate because laboratory experiments are not like real life.

Evaluating laboratory experiments in terms of reliability and validity

Research methods are evaluated in terms of their reliability and validity. Reliable data are data that have been found more than once by repeating a study. If data are found only once and then not again when a study is repeated, you would not want to base real life policy and practice on them. Valid data are data about real life situations and behaviour.

> **AS link** Review or recall your study of validity and reliability. These were two evaluation areas you will have come across often when learning about psychology. The reliability and validity of laboratory experiments was discussed when you looked at cognitive psychology (p. 104).

Reliability

Laboratory experiments are replicable because of the strong controls. They are replicable because they are clearly detailed and someone else can repeat them exactly. They are usually repeated by the researchers to test the findings for reliability, and they may also be repeated by others. Researchers such as Loftus and her students have carried out so many studies that have come up with similar findings that their work appears to be reliable. If the results are scientifically gathered and reliable, they have greater weight. This is even more important if the results are going to be used in real situations, as Loftus's results have been.

Validity

Laboratory experiments are, however, not usually valid, because of the strong controls in place. The very controlled situation — watching a film, being asked questions about it, it possibly having no relevance to the participant, and using students as participants — means that validity is likely to be low. The whole set-up is not like a 'real' car accident or a 'real' situation that is witnessed.

> **AS link** Review evaluation of laboratory experiments from your AS studies (pp. 104–07).

Table 1.2	Strengths and weaknesses of laboratory experiments	
	Strengths	**Weaknesses**
	• Laboratory experiments are replicable because of strong controls, so they are testable for reliability	• Laboratory experiments are not ecologically valid, because they do not take place in the participant's natural setting
	• Laboratory experiments use scientific methodology, such as forming a hypothesis from a theory and controlling all aspects except the IV	• Laboratory experiments might not be valid with regard to the task — for example, watching a car accident on film is not the same as watching it in real life

Field studies and experiments

AS link Review your learning about field experiments, which you studied at AS when learning about the cognitive approach (pp. 103–07).

Another way in which witness effectiveness is tested is to use field experiments, because these are based in real situations — they can be carried out to avoid the accusation that laboratory experiments are not valid. Field experiments and field studies are not the same thing, because a field experiment has all the features of an experiment, whereas there are field studies that tend not to have control over the IV and DV.

Field studies

Field studies tend to use methods that gather descriptive (qualitative) data rather than numerical (quantitative) data. **Qualitative data** are where attitudes, opinions and stories are gathered. **Quantitative data** are based on numbers, such as percentages or the number of 'yes' or 'no' answers given. Field studies can use research methods such as ethnography, case studies or tests carried out in real-life settings.

In **ethnography** a researcher gets involved in the whole setting being studied, using many different research methods. This is similar to carrying out an in-depth case study. Field studies are not field experiments if there is no manipulation of an independent variable to see the effect on a dependent variable, and if there are no controls. However, field experiments can be called field studies because they are studies carried out in the field.

One field study that you will examine in detail later in this chapter is that of Yuille and Cutshall (1986), so refer to this when you are discussing the use of field studies in the study of witness effectiveness. Their study is a field study but not a field experiment (they used interviewing).

Study hint In this methodology section you are asked about field experiments. Make sure you do not get this confused with field studies. In practice, if you call a field experiment a field study you will not be wrong, but it might be incorrect to call a field study a field experiment (if there are no controls and no manipulation of the independent variable).

Field experiments

Field experiments are just like laboratory experiments in terms of their aim to find cause-and-effect conclusions by controlling what can be controlled, and varying the

IV to see what the effect is on the DV. The difference is that laboratory experiments take place in a controlled and artificial environment and field experiments take place in the field — which means using the natural environment of the participants.

Maass and Köhnken (1989)

A field experiment to look at witness effectiveness was undertaken by Maass and Köhnken in 1989. In their study, 86 non-psychology students in their own environment (in the field) were approached by a woman holding a pen or a syringe. She either said or did not say that she would give them an injection. The participants were then asked to identify the woman in a line-up, and those exposed to the syringe rather than the pen performed worse in their identification. Participants remembered less facial detail the greater their fear of injections. This study supports other research that claims that when a weapon is present in a situation, people will focus on the weapon rather than the person or what is happening. In Maass and Köhnken's study, participants seemed to have focused on the syringe more than the pen.

Experimental features of the Maass and Köhnken (1989) study

- Experimental hypothesis: participants will remember more details about a woman who approaches them holding a pen than if she approaches holding a syringe.
- Directional or non-directional: directional (they will remember more in the 'pen' condition).
- Independent variable: whether the woman holds a pen or a syringe.
- Dependent variable: how much they remember about the woman — measured by whether they pick her out in a line-up.
- Experimental design: independent groups (half had the 'pen' condition and half had the 'syringe' condition). In fact, half also had the 'administering an injection' statement.

In Maass and Köhnken's study, a woman walked towards the participant holding either a pen or a syringe

Greg Blomberg/Alamy

In 2004 Yarmey carried out an experiment in a public place, which makes it a field experiment. A young woman approached people individually and they spoke to her for about 15 seconds. Then, either 2 minutes later or 4 hours later, they were questioned about the woman and asked to identify her in a photo. When the woman was seen, she either had dark glasses and a baseball cap or she did not, and some witnesses were warned they would be tested and others were not. There were therefore a number of different conditions. This study is explained in more detail in the content section of this chapter.

Explore Look up this study to find out more, or investigate other field experiments carried out by Yarmey.

How useful are field experiments of witness effectiveness?

After a period of about 30 years of using laboratory experiments to study witness memory, more recently there has been a tendency to use field experiments instead. This is mainly to produce more valid results — for example, much research now focuses on police line-ups and identification of people by witnesses. Field experiments can reassure practitioners in police forces that findings about eyewitness memory are important, and that the guidance the police are asked to implement is sound. Features that are required in order for field experiments to be seen as valid are double-blind techniques and random assignment to groups, as these help to rule out confounding variables.

AS link Review what is meant by double-blind techniques (p. 98), random assignment to groups (p. 102) and confounding variables (p. 97).

However, the controls and procedures of the field experiments must be thorough, such as using double-blind techniques and randomisation. Well controlled and carefully planned field experiments are valuable because they have the reliability and scientific status of laboratory experiments, while also having validity because of being in a real-life setting and using real-life situations.

Evaluating field experiments in terms of reliability and validity

Reliability

Field experiments are reliable if the procedures are carefully controlled and planned. If they are repeated they tend to get the same results and are as reliable as laboratory experiments. However, there is a chance that, because they take place in the field, in some ways this is an uncontrolled environment, which could mean there are confounding variables and the findings are not reliable.

Validity

Field experiments are valid with regard to the setting, which means they have **ecological validity**, because they occur in the participants' natural setting or a setting that could be natural for the task (or both). However, the task is still manipulated to see the effect of different conditions on the dependent variable, so the task itself might not be valid. Usually, researchers try to use a task that is realistic even if set up. Therefore field experiments have more validity than laboratory experiments.

> **AS link** Review the evaluation of field experiments from your AS studies (pp. 106–07).

Table 1.3 *Strengths and weaknesses of field experiments*

Strengths	Weaknesses
• Field experiments are replicable to an extent because of strong controls, so they are testable for reliability • Field experiments are ecologically valid, because they take place in the participant's natural setting	• Field experiments might not allow enough control over variables to be reliable, because the setting is not controlled as it is in a laboratory experiment • Field experiments might not be valid with regard to the task either — for example, a line-up that has been set up is not the same as identifying a real-life criminal

Ethical issues

Both laboratory and field experiments involve manipulating an independent variable to see the effect of that manipulation on a dependent variable, and there are a lot of controls. When people are controlled (as participants in experiments tend to be), then there are various ethical issues involved.

> **AS link** Review the ethical issues you studied at AS. These include obtaining informed consent, debriefing, not using unnecessary deceit, providing the right to withdraw, being competent, and ensuring privacy and confidentiality.

The British Psychological Society sets out a code of ethics. These guidelines must be followed by students of psychology, no matter which research method is used. Laboratory and field experiments are not in themselves ethical or unethical — it all depends on the procedure and the decisions made by the researcher(s).

Informed consent and deceit

The participant should be told as much as possible so that he or she can give informed consent. Any deceit must be kept to a minimum. However, there will almost certainly be some deceit involved, because the manipulated variable will have to be kept secret so that participants do not deliberately change their behaviour. Any change in behaviour needs to be shown to be because of the independent variable rather than an awareness of the investigation. Both laboratory and field experiments are likely to require some level of deceit, so there is unlikely to be fully informed consent.

Distress

Participants are not supposed to be unduly distressed or have harm cause to them. They should leave a study in the same emotional state as that in which they started.

Practice 1.2

Review some of the studies that have been presented in this methodology section and, in each case, note down where there is a need for deceit and one other ethical issue in the study.

1 Loftus's barn study

2 Maass and Köhnken's study about the pen/syringe

3 Yarmey's study of asking participants to identify someone who had approached them

Answers are at the end of Chapter 1.

Debriefing

As there is usually some deceit involved in a study, and consent is not totally informed, there must be a thorough debrief to make sure that participants are happy with and understand what was done, and that they are happy to have their results used in the study.

Right to withdraw, privacy and confidentiality

Participants must be told they can withdraw at any time and they should be reminded of this at times throughout the study. They should be asked if they want to withdraw their involvement at the end, too, and this can be done as part of the debrief. The participants' identity must be kept secret, to preserve their privacy and to maintain confidentiality.

Competence

The researcher must be competent to carry out the study and, if in any doubt, must consult with a colleague or someone else who is competent.

Explore Find at least two other ethical principles that should be followed when doing research in psychology and relate them to field and laboratory experiments.

Comparing field and laboratory experiments in terms of ethics

One main difference that makes field experiments less ethical than laboratory experiments is that participants in some field experiments cannot be asked for consent at all, let alone informed consent. This is because participants are found in the field and in public places, so they are often not prepared beforehand to let them know they are in a study at all. Participants are asked for their consent afterwards, but this could be seen as less ethical than laboratory experiments, where participants usually know they are taking part in a study.

Study hint You will be studying two applications for A2, from criminological, child, health and sport psychology. In both applications you will be asked about methodological issues including reliability, validity and ethics. Once you have studied both applications, make some notes for yourself about ethical issues and how they relate to different research methods.

1

Examination-style questions

1 Outline three features of a laboratory experiment as a research method. *(6 marks)*

2 Explain one way in which a field experiment differs from a laboratory experiment. *(2 marks)*

3 Describe one way that a laboratory experiment has been used to study witness effectiveness. *(4 marks)*

Extension questions

1 Compare the field experiment and the laboratory experiment as ways of studying witness effectiveness. In your answer refer to validity, reliability and ethical issues. *(12 marks)*

2 With reference to two studies, explain how the experimental research method is used to study witness effectiveness. *(8 marks)*

Content

In this section of criminological psychology you will look at two explanations for criminal or antisocial behaviour, three studies into eyewitness testimony issues and two ways of treating offenders. In the methodology section of this chapter you will have looked in detail at eyewitness testimony, so there is less about such issues in this content section. Just one study is explained in detail, as the other two are found in the 'Studies in detail' section towards the end of this chapter. Therefore, the main focus in this section is on explaining criminal or antisocial behaviour and examining two ways of treating offenders. The structure of this section is to move from *reasons* for being a criminal, through a quick dip into *identifying* a criminal (looking at problems with eyewitness memory), and ending with looking at *how* criminals are treated.

> **AS link** Note that you might be asked to draw on AS material for both the Methodology and Content sections of this chapter.

The two explanations of criminal/antisocial behaviour given in your course are the social learning theory explanation and one from either a personality theory or the labelling/self-fulfilling prophecy explanation. In this section, the second chosen theory examined is the labelling/self-fulfilling prophecy explanation. A personality theory is explained in more detail in the online resources if you prefer to make that choice.

The social learning explanation of crime/ antisocial behaviour

Role models, social learning theory and crime

Social learning theory suggests that behaviour, to an extent at least, comes from observing role models and imitating their behaviour. This is known as **observational learning**. Role models are those with whom people identify in some way — often someone they look up to. Thus people tend to imitate those of the same gender, possibly of a similar age, or people they see as powerful or having something to be achieved, such as celebrities. Bandura, Ross and Ross (1961), for example, showed that children imitated an adult model who was aggressive. They found that

> **AS link** Review social learning theory from your AS course. Remind yourself about the modelling process and which role models are more likely to be imitated. Recall your study of Bandura, Ross and Ross's work (1961), which showed how young children copy aggressive behaviour (pp. 339–42).

boys imitated physical aggression more than girls, who showed more verbal aggression than physical aggression. They also discovered that both girls and boys were more likely to imitate the adult male model than the female model. This suggests that there is also an element of expectation involved, such as that males are imitated more if they are aggressive, because it is expected that aggression is found more in males. There are some complex issues involved, but the basic idea is that behaviour can come from imitation of role models.

The role of reinforcement in social learning theory and crime

Social learning theory suggests that people commit crimes because of an association with others. Not only is it possible to be exposed to criminal models, it is also possible to be 'reinforced' for crime. Crime becomes not only acceptable but also desirable.

Reinforcement of criminal behaviour can be positive or negative. **Positive reinforcement** might come from financial or material gain from the crime, or approval from one's peers. **Negative reinforcement** might come from the removal of something unpleasant by committing the crime, such as removing disapproval from peers or removing financial hardship. Social learning theory would predict that, if someone commits a second crime, it is likely to be the same as, or similar to, the first crime, since that would match the patterns of reinforcement. Punishment is likely to deter criminal behaviour. These are the principles of operant conditioning, and social learning theory adopts these principles as well as the idea of observational learning.

> **AS link** Review operant conditioning from the learning approach of the AS course (pp. 327–32).

The modelling process

Social learning theory suggests that people observe role models and model that behaviour, but usually under certain circumstances. So far, the importance of the role model has been underlined — and whether the role model is similar to the observer and someone with whom to be identified. The importance of whether the behaviour is reinforced or punished has also been explained. However, there are other requirements for behaviour to be learned and modelled. The modelled behaviour has to be noticed, which is called **attention**. What has been observed then has to be remembered, which is called **retention**. The next stage is being able to reproduce the behaviour, which is called **reproduction**. Finally, there has to be a good reason for wanting to take on the behaviour, and this is called **motivation**.

The modelling process involves the behaviour being demonstrated (which can be called modelling in itself), paid attention to, remembered, and reproduced (which again is often called modelling) if there is motivation to do so. Therefore, **modelling** refers to the behaviour being demonstrated as well as the behaviour being reproduced.

Sociology, crime, antisocial behaviour and social learning theory

Psychology often focuses on social learning theory as an explanation of antisocial behaviour, which is frequently defined as aggression. It is sociology that focuses on social learning theory and crime, with Ronald Akers as a main name in that field. In psychology, Bandura and his colleagues focused on social learning of aggression rather than crime. The principles are the same — there are role models, modelling takes place, and much depends on the reinforcement patterns that dictate whether the behaviour is repeated. In sociology, Akers' main point from his 1998 study was that crime occurs through social learning in a social structure. He did not look at individual differences but at social situations in general. Psychology looks more at how an individual learns aggressive behaviour.

Evaluation of social learning theory as an explanation of criminal behaviour

Table 1.4 *Strengths and weaknesses of social learning theory as an explanation of crime*

Strengths	Weaknesses
• There is a lot of experimental evidence to show that behaviour is imitated, including evidence to show that aggressive behaviour is imitated; some of this evidence is explained later in this section when looking at the role of the media • The theory has a practical application and can help to rehabilitate offenders, as appropriate role models can be used to help learn appropriate behaviour, alongside appropriate reinforcements	• The theory does not look at individual differences, only at how an individual is influenced by social factors; therefore, biological aspects are not considered • The theory does not account for criminal behaviour that is opportunistic and has not been observed first — it tends to account more for stealing, aggression and other crimes that are reasonably easily observed in society, rather than murders; therefore, the theory does not account for all crime

Social learning theory, aggression and the role of the media

There has been much interest in the role of the media in promoting aggressive behaviour, and an explanation of how people might learn violence or other behaviour from the media uses social learning theory principles. Some of the evidence is presented here.

Looking at the media and how it might be modelling aggression, which is then imitated, is often referred to as the study of 'violence in the media'. The term 'the media' can refer to television, magazines, DVDs, video games, games consoles and computer games. Many early studies looked at the effects of violence on television but newer studies have looked at the effects of computer and video games.

In general, the conclusion from studies is that there is an effect from violence in the media, but that it is not the main cause of violence in someone. There is a suggestion that people are predisposed to violence, which means violence is in their biology, and there are often other factors at work, such as how much other television they might be exposed to, and prosocial behaviour in television programmes. **Prosocial behaviour** is when 'good' and moral behaviour is shown on television, which is just as likely to be imitated as violent behaviour. There are three suggestions about the effects of violence in television programmes on children:

- Children may become **desensitised** to violence, which means they are less disturbed by violence than those who do not watch it on television.
- Children may be more likely to use violence themselves or show aggression towards others.
- Watching violence on television might make children more afraid in general.

None of these reactions is good for society or the individual, so such findings are taken seriously. One way this has been tackled is by the introduction of a 9 p.m. watershed on television in the UK, which restricts scenes of serious violence to after that time of night.

Reasons for such an interest in the effects of aggression in the media

A shocking event took place in April in 1999 at Columbine High School in Colorado. What occurred has been linked to the playing of violent video games.

Case Study

Eric Harris and Dylan Klebold, who enjoyed playing violent video games, devised their own version of the game 'Doom' and appeared to act it out at the school. They carried out a shooting spree, killing 12 students and a teacher, wounding 23 others and then killing themselves. The whole event was planned, including the setting off of a bomb to start a fire some way away to distract the emergency services. It has not been proved that playing video games caused the shootings, and indeed it would be hard to prove this, but many people believe there was a link.

Explore Look up the Columbine High School massacre for more details of this event, or find another such example — there have been several similar occurrences in recent years. See if there is a connection between such shootings and violence on television or playing violent video games.

Studies looking at the effect of observing violence in the media

Two main names in the study of television violence are Huesmann and Eron. Their investigation in 1986 looked at the number of hours of television watched by children at a young age, regardless of whether the content was violent or not. Then they looked at the behaviour of the same children as they grew up. It was found that those who watched more television when young (around 8 years old) were more likely to be aggressive as teenagers. They were also more likely to be arrested as adults for criminal behaviour. Therefore, there seems to be a link between watching television as a child, being aggressive in adolescence and later turning to crime as an adult.

However, it is difficult to show a causal link between television watching and later aggressive or criminal behaviour. Perhaps children with more aggression watch more television, rather than watching more television leading to more aggression. Huesmann and Eron also carried out studies examining rates of television watching and rates of violence across different countries and they did not find a link in most of the countries.

It has been found that in some countries where there is a lot of violence on television, there is a comparatively low violent-crime rate. There are also spikes in the rate of violent crime, such as in the USA, but no spikes in violence in the media, which has been steadily rising rather than having sudden changes. These pieces of evidence suggest that there is not a strong link between violence in the media and violent crime.

Explore Look up the work of Huesmann and of Eron and summarise their studies. Evaluate these , considering issues of validity, reliability and ethics.

Table 1.5 *Evaluation of Huesmann and Eron (1986)*

Strengths	Weaknesses
• Being a longitudinal study, the same children were returned to as adolescents and as adults so that personality and temperament factors were controlled; this can only be done using longitudinal methods and not many studies continue for that long, so this is a strength of the study • The measure of television viewing was in hours watched, which was a quantitative measure, so to an extent there was no need for interpretation; however, the time was not measured scientifically, just estimated by parents	• This was a longitudinal study and many factors could have affected the aggressive levels when the participants were teenagers and the criminal activities when they were adults; it was not possible to show that it was the extra television viewing that led to the differences in behaviour • This was also a correlational study and the link between hours of television watched and subsequent criminality cannot be proved, just suggested; perhaps it was more likely that some underlying aggression led to more television being watched rather than more television being watched leading to more aggression

More recent interest has focused on violent video games, and Craig Anderson has carried out studies in this area. In 2000 a study in which Anderson (with Karen Dill) was involved used two different research methodologies and found some evidence that playing violent video games caused aggressive responses. The researchers first used a survey to link the likelihood of playing violent video games with admitting to aggressive behaviour. Second, they carried out a laboratory experiment and found that those who played a violent video game were more aggressive when given the opportunity to be angry than those who did not play the game. It has been suggested that violent video games may be more harmful than violence on television because they are interactive and the player actually identifies with (or even 'becomes') the aggressive person in the video game. Anderson and others in 2003 also found that violent song lyrics tended to increase aggressive thoughts and emotions.

Explore Look up Anderson's work on violence in video games. Summarise one or two studies and note down some evaluation points.

Table 1.6 *Evaluation of Anderson and Dill (2000)*

Strengths	Weaknesses
• Part of the study was a laboratory experiment with the environment controlled and an IV and a DV, so results were scientifically gathered • The experiment is replicable and can be tested for reliability, which helps to build a scientific body of knowledge • Using two different research methods gave more reliability, as the same connection was found in two different ways	• It has been claimed that Anderson and Dill's experimental study used measures of aggression that had not been **standardised** and also did not find significant results in all their measures, only in one of them; the measures of aggression were artificial both in the experiment and the survey • Being a laboratory experiment, there was a lack of validity and the participants may have guessed the purpose of the study, so results might not reflect real life • Anderson and Dill's experiment looked at aggression immediately after playing the video games and was not able to see if any aggressive response from playing a violent video game would last longer than a very short time

Evaluating the methodology

Studies that have taken place to look at the effects of violence in the media are often carried out in the laboratory or in the field. Laboratory studies are artificial in that the situation and the task are set up and tend to lack validity, though they are often reliable. Bandura carried out laboratory experiments, as did Anderson. Field experiments are more valid with regard to the setting but the task is usually set up artificially, so they can still lack validity to an extent. However, the controls involved mean that field experiments can be tested for reliability.

Studies are also often correlational (e.g. Huesmann and Eron 1986), meaning that watching television and behaving aggressively might go together but that does not mean that one causes the other. There are also longitudinal studies (Huesmann and Eron 1986), where a person or group of people are followed as they age to look for possible long-term effects of exposure to violence in the media. A problem with longitudinal studies is that, because people are likely to drop out, the remaining sample can be biased. There are also so many factors changing over time that it is

1

difficult, if not impossible, to show that just the exposure to violent television is the cause of any possible later antisocial behaviour or criminal activity.

Summary of methodological problems

- Laboratory experiments lack validity both with regard to task and setting.
- Field experiments lack validity with regard to the task.
- Correlations show a link only, not a cause-and-effect relationship.
- Longitudinal studies tend to have a high drop-out rate, which biases the sample.
- Because longitudinal studies examine so many factors, it is hard to pinpoint exposure to violence in the media as a cause for later antisocial or criminal behaviour.

Evaluating social learning theory: another explanation

A more modern theory of the effects of violence on television (McQuail 2002) has considered cognitive aspects of the viewer's response, in that **schemata** for violence might be activated, which might then activate a violent response. Schemata are plans or scripts in the mind that are built up with experience, such as a restaurant script telling us what happens in a restaurant. This is moving on from social learning theory to incorporate more cognitive factors. Social learning theory takes some cognition into account, such as paying attention and having motivation, but modern theories take this further and also suggest that such **cognitions** in the brain can trigger biological reactions such as the **alarm reaction**, which prepares for flight or fight and can lead to an aggressive or violent response.

> **AS link** Review the idea of schemata being used in memory, if you studied the reconstructive theory of memory for your AS work in the cognitive approach (p. 116).

Other explanations for criminal behaviour include personality theories, like Eysenck's, and social theories such as labelling and the self-fulfilling prophecy. Eysenck's personality theory is explained in the online resources, and labelling and the self-fulfilling prophecy are explained in the section that follows.

Labelling and the self-fulfilling prophecy

Labelling and the self-fulfilling prophecy go together as an explanation of crime and anti-social behaviour — the process of the prophecy is that someone is first labelled and then 'becomes' the label.

> **AS link** Review your learning at AS about the social approach and how it is defined. For example, the social approach considers interactions between individuals as well as the effects of groups. Labelling and the self-fulfilling prophecy fall within the social approach (pp. 5–6).

Labelling

Labelling involves a majority group considering a minority group as inferior, and using inferior terms when talking about them. There is a negative connotation to being 'labelled', though in theory someone can be labelled positively as 'bright', for example. When applied to crime, labelling means referring to someone as 'a thief', for example; or, when applied to education, it means referring to someone's ability, for example, as 'not good at maths'. Labelling links to stereotyping and usually someone stereotypes someone else and the label comes from the stereotype. A label can start from something one person says, rather than coming from stereotyping.

Stereotyping

Stereotyping means thinking of a whole group as having certain characteristics, usually using evidence from one member of the group and assuming that this evidence is true of all members. Sometimes there is no direct evidence and people stereotype from what they hear about a group. A label derived from the stereotype would involve one or more of those characteristics. The self-fulfilling prophecy, which is explained below, develops from a label, which can be positive (such as 'clever') or negative (such as 'violent').

Self-fulfilling prophecy

The self-fulfilling prophecy (SFP) can be applied to criminal behaviour and other behaviours. The term came mainly from studies in schools that looked at how educational processes work. It has since been applied to other areas such as crime, and it tends to focus on how children develop. The theory is that, when individuals are labelled in some way, they begin to see themselves in the way the label portrays them and, as they are expected to act according to the label, they do so. The self-fulfilling prophecy claims that people fulfil the expectations of others and become what others think and say they will become. This is good if someone is labelled 'clever' but unhelpful and destructive if someone is labelled 'bad'.

This concept of a SFP is also known as the **Pygmalion effect**. George Bernard Shaw wrote the play *Pygmalion*, which was later adapted into the film *My Fair Lady*. The story is about a London flower seller, Eliza, who has a strong cockney accent. She is taken in by a professor of phonetics, who says he can turn her into a lady, which he does by training her. The idea is that, if someone is known as a lady, and treated as a lady, she becomes a lady, which Eliza did.

The SFP involves various stages. First, there is labelling, then there is treatment of the person based on the label. This is followed by the individual reacting to expectations by behaving according to the label. The individual's behaviour, therefore, fulfils the expectations, which confirms the label, and so the behaviour continues.

Rosenthal and Jacobson (1968)

Probably the best-known study of the SFP is not about crime but about education. Rosenthal and Jacobson (1968) carried out a study in which at the start of a school year they told teachers that certain pupils were 'about to bloom' and do well at school, though in fact they chose the pupils at random. They had given all the pupils an IQ test, so the teachers thought the predictions had come from the test,

1

though this was not true. At the end of that teaching year the researchers tested the pupils again. Those who had been labelled as 'about to bloom' had improved in IQ score more (in the case of younger pupils) than the other pupils, and the researchers concluded that they had evidence for a SFP. The teachers must have treated the pupils differently from the rest and, as a result of that additional attention, the pupils did better — or perhaps they gained more confidence because the teachers perceived them to be brighter.

Table 1.7 *Evaluation of Rosenthal and Jacobson (1968)*

Strengths	Weaknesses
• This is a well-controlled study in which the teachers did not know the IQ test results and the children said to be 'about to bloom' were randomly chosen; this deceit meant that nothing could have affected the children except for teacher attention of some sort, because they were not all 'about to bloom' • The study is replicable because it was carefully planned, so it can be tested for reliability; other studies in education have found similar results when studying teacher–child interactions	• The study is artificial and the teachers were given a false belief, which they then acted upon — perhaps they thought they were supposed to act on the information in some way, whereas in another situation, they may not have acted as they did; this is a validity problem • Perhaps it is not ethical to 'choose' some children, expecting that they will get special attention and 'bloom' when other children might not have been given special attention because of the study

The SFP and crime

The link between crime and being lower class is clear in statistics, and it is possible that a reason for this is a SFP. If a young person is known to come from a poor family, for example, he or she might — through stereotyping — be labelled as 'bad' in some way. Or the person may come from a family with criminal members, and again could be labelled as 'bad'. According to the prophecy, such individuals would be treated according to their label, would act as they were treated and eventually fulfil the prophecy. Other family members or others from that area might then also be labelled 'bad', and this could account for more criminals being found in the lower classes and poor areas.

Madon et al. (2003): the self-fulfilling influence of mother expectations on children's underage drinking

Self-fulfilling prophecies occur when beliefs for which there is no evidence or expectations about behaviour come true when the beliefs are fulfilled. In this study it is suggested that a mother's false expectations about her child's future drinking of alcohol may result in her expectations coming true. Parents can either overestimate or underestimate their children's future alcohol drinking behaviour.

Results of previous studies

Rosenthal and Jacobson (1968) showed that teacher expectations could lead to a self-fulfilling prophecy of a child's academic ability, but this was an unnatural study because the independent variable (whether a child was about to bloom) was set up. In naturalistic studies expectations develop naturally and these are important, because they can affect achievement and occupational opportunities as well as personal development.

In general, although it is found that incorrect teacher expectations do lead to self-fulfilling prophecies, the effect is small. This is mainly because teacher expectations are found to be largely accurate, as they are based on valid information (unlike in Rosenthal and Jacobson's study).

Outside educational settings, however, it might be that the self-fulfilling prophecy occurs and has more of an effect. Child self-esteem, family social class and parental expectations are seen as factors that might affect whether a self-fulfilling prophecy occurs. For example, it could be said that children with low self-esteem are more likely to be affected by persuasive messages, and so are more affected by false expectations, or that children with high self-esteem have had more support and approval from their parents, so they might be more influenced by parental judgements and expectations. These are the sorts of issues that are considered in this study.

Aims

Madon et al. set out to look at the self-fulfilling prophecy in a natural situation outside the educational setting and with naturally occurring false expectations. Questions included whether mothers' expectations about their children's future alcohol use would predict their future alcohol use. The researchers also looked at whether the accuracy of a mother's expectations limited the self-fulfilling prophecy. Another issue that was investigated was whether some children are more susceptible to a self-fulfilling prophecy than others — perhaps because of their self-esteem or social class.

Procedure

Participants

The study looked at 505 mother–child pairs. Only one child from the family was included, even if there were more. The pairs were found from families of seventh graders in 36 rural schools from 22 counties in a US state. There were 233 girls and 272 boys in the study.

Gathering data

The data were gathered from a longitudinal survey using both questionnaires and interviews, and were correlational. Researchers contacted the families to arrange an initial in-home visit, and then visited again the families who agreed to take part. There was an interview to gather general information and a written questionnaire. Family members completed the questionnaire individually and separately, and confidentiality was guaranteed. Questionnaires were carried out at the baseline (the start) and 18 months later. Family members were paid a small amount for taking part.

Study hint Note that this study is longitudinal, naturalistic, uses interviews and questionnaires, and produces correlational data. Therefore, it can be used as an example for all these features of methodology.

Assumptions within the study

The study relies on the belief that valid background variables influence children's future alcohol use and mothers' expectations about their children's future alcohol use. To this extent, a mother's expectations are accurate (if based on valid background variables). Background variables in this study include the child's behaviour, attitudes, intentions, norms, the family demographics and environments (peer, social and family). Such variables have been shown to affect early alcohol use.

A mother's expectations can also affect a child's future alcohol use through a self-fulfilling prophecy. Only inaccurate expectations can be self-fulfilling (by definition). A mother's expectations are inaccurate if not based on valid background variables about her child's future alcohol use. There are moderator variables such as self-esteem, social class and valence (the value in the sense of positive or negative) of the mother's expectations, and these can moderate the influence of a mother's expectations on her child's future alcohol use.

These beliefs come from the reflection–construction model (Jussim 1991).

Measures

The questionnaires assessed variables related to family, peers and substance abuse. Baseline measures included a mother's expectation of her child's future alcohol use, as well as family income, the gender of the child and his/her perception of friends' alcohol use. The 18-month follow-up included a measure of the child's alcohol use up to that time.

Examples of questions for the children include: 'How many of your friends do you think get drunk at least once a week?' and 'If you had the money and wanted to get beer, wine or liquor, do you think you could get some?' Mothers were asked: 'On a scale of 1 to 10, rate how likely you think it is that your child in the study will drink alcohol regularly as a teenager?'

A reliability check was carried out by asking the children who answered 'yes' to the question about having drunk alcohol for more information, and getting a new score from them. The researchers could check this new score against the questionnaire score to look for a correlation in respect of past and future alcohol use. This was in case children said they drank alcohol because of demand characteristics or peer desirability. At baseline, 89% said they had not drunk alcohol, so it was not thought that claiming to drink alcohol when they did not was a large problem.

Results

There was a need to know how much of a mother's expectation was wrong, because only an incorrect expectation can cause a self-fulfilling prophecy. Predictor variables were studied (such as school, type of parenting, past alcohol use and self-esteem of the child) to find out what proportion of expectations about future alcohol use are predicted from background variables and what proportion are incorrect. The accuracy of expectation can be shown by how far the expectation differs from the prediction according to the variables.

- If prediction of alcohol use is the same as predicted by background variables, there is no effect from the prediction.
- If prediction of alcohol use is greater than predicted by background variables, there is a positive difference and a negative effect (predicts more alcohol use), so a self-fulfilling prophecy would have a negative effect.
- If prediction of alcohol use is less than predicted by background variables, there is a negative difference and a positive effect (predicts less alcohol use), so a self-fulfilling prophecy would have a positive effect.

Overall, Madon et al. (2003) concluded that 52% of the relationship between a mother's expectations and her child's future alcohol use is down to accurate maternal expectations and 48% is down to self-fulfilling effects. There was a stronger relationship between a mother's expectations and the child's future alcohol use among high self-esteem children than low self-esteem children. Positive expectations that underestimated children's future alcohol use had a stronger self-fulfilling effect on children's future alcohol use than did negative expectations that overestimated future alcohol use.

Conclusions

Children with high self-esteem were more susceptible to self-fulfilling prophecies than those with low self-esteem, and self-fulfilling prophecies tended to be helpful rather than harmful. A mother's expectations were about half accurate and half self-fulfilling. There is no evidence of an effect from social class or family income.

Evaluation of the study

Strengths

- The mother's expectations are naturally occurring to an extent and this is a naturalistic study, so it is more valid that previous laboratory or field experiments.
- A longitudinal design helps to show that the DV does not cause the IV. In a correlation it could be claimed that there are no conclusions that can be drawn about cause and effect between two variables. However, in a longitudinal study like this, the mother's expectations were measured first and the child's future alcohol use cannot have caused the mother's expectations, so there is some cause-and-effect understanding.
- The reliability of the child's self-report data about his or her alcohol use was checked, so the study has reliability to that extent.
- A large amount of data were gathered so that many different factors could be considered, and the researchers looked at many explanations in addition to a self-fulfilling prophecy, so they accounted for the complexity of issues.

Weaknesses

- Natural studies like this do not show cause-and-effect conclusions the way that experiments do, so it is hard to be sure about a self-fulfilling prophecy, which is about cause and effect. The self-fulfilling prophecy is said to be the cause of the behaviour or characteristic.

- There might be a third variable that was not looked at that caused both a mother's expectations and her child's future alcohol use. This could have been an uncontrolled predictor variable (although the study did measure many of those).
- In general, mothers had low expectations with regard to their children's alcohol use — they did not think they would drink much. The children reported little alcohol use even at the end of the study, so the effect of expectations should be generalised taking this into account.
- There were some differences in the questionnaires that the mothers and children completed. Children were asked if they *ever* drank but their mothers were asked if the children would *regularly* drink. These are two different levels of drinking, so comparing the replies might not have been fair.

Jahoda's study of names related to behaviour (1954)

An interesting study that is useful when considering whether behaviour can arise from a label gives strong evidence of the power of labelling. Gustav Jahoda (1954) studied the Ashanti (a Ghanaian ethnic group) and he noted that boys were named according to the day on which they were born. For example, Monday children were labelled according to the soul for that day (the kra), which would mean the child was quiet and peaceful. The kra for Wednesday, however, would lead to aggressive and quick-tempered characteristics in the child. If there was a SFP at work, then children born on Monday would be quiet and peaceful and children born on Wednesday would be more aggressive. Jahoda discovered from court records that children born on a Wednesday were more likely to be convicted for crimes against the person. There were noticeably fewer Monday children on record as having been convicted.

Table 1.8 *Evaluation of Jahoda's study*

Strengths	Weaknesses
• Data were valid and came from court records, so this was a naturalistic study where variables were not manipulated	• The study has not been replicated and so it is not certain that data are reliable
• The difference in name is clear and it is hard to see what other factors could have led to the findings, although other details about the tribe and their practices are not clear; on the face of it the findings are powerful	• Factors other than the Wednesday name might have led to the convictions (though it is hard to see what they would be, other than the child being treated differently according to expectations)

Evaluation of the SFP leading to crime

Strengths of the explanation

- Stephanie Madon (among other researchers), who studied the SFP in education, has looked at other areas where there can be false beliefs and has found some suggestion that it works in these areas too.
- Madon suggests that people with high self-esteem are more likely to be affected by their parents' predictions and she suggests that social class is not a factor in whether a parent–child relationship leads to a SFP.

- Studies do not appear to suggest that those with high self-esteem are more affected by a label in education, so it seems that the actual relationship affects the course of the prophecy — whether teacher–child or parent–child, for example, or peer-to-peer.
- This would further suggest that expectations about former criminals, such as labels applied to them in the local community, will lead to a SFP in some cases at least, depending on the relationship between those giving the label and the person being labelled.
- Jahoda's study gives strong evidence for the effect of labelling.
- Sociological theories link crime, labelling and the SFP but they consider wider issues, rather than labelling at an individual level.

Weaknesses of the explanation

- Much of the research into the SFP has been in education, the teacher–child relationship being a special one where expectations might be fulfilled. However, other relationships might not have this effect.
- The problem with studying the effects of labelling at an individual level is finding a false belief, as Madon has explained. This is probably why there are few psychological studies of labelling and the SFP.

Studies into eyewitness testimony

The methodology section of this chapter has looked in depth at eyewitness testimony, explaining what it is and how it is studied in psychology. This section asks you to define and evaluate three studies into eyewitness testimony: one laboratory experiment, one field study, and one other. You will study a laboratory experiment in detail in the section that follows — Loftus and Palmer (1974) — so use that study for this section as well. You will also cover a field study in detail in the following section — Yuille and Cutshall (1986). Therefore, only one more study is needed for this section, and a field experiment has been chosen. Yarmey (2004) was outlined in the methodology section of this chapter, so you can use the greater detail provided here to support your learning of methodology.

> **Study hint** Use your understanding of Loftus and Palmer (1974) and Yuille and Cutshall (1986), which are chosen in this textbook as the studies in detail that you need to know, to help your understanding of the methodology and content sections of your course. Refer to Yarmey (2004) as well, because it is an example of a field experiment, so it will help your discussion of field experiments as a research method.

Yarmey (2004): eyewitness recall and photo identification

There are concerns about generalising from laboratory study findings and their associated lack of realism and validity. Field experiments help to raise both the generalisability and ecological validity of studies. Such concerns are of particular importance in the field of eyewitness memory because of the need to apply findings about eyewitness testimony to actual court procedures.

Yarmey explained that, in general, research has found that objects and people more relevant and central to situations are better remembered by witnesses, and that witnesses tend to remember what fits best with their expectations. Haber and Haber (2001) analysed 48 studies on eyewitness identification in a line-up, where the person to be identified (the target) was present. They found that in 51% of the cases the target was correctly identified by the witness. In 27% of the cases a target was wrongly identified. In other studies, where the target was not included in the line-up, there was a 57% chance of incorrect identification.

Research has found that eyes are a main feature used in identification, so it was thought that covering the eyes would affect identification. Masking a hairline by use of a hat also reduces identification, according to previous studies.

The cognitive interview technique suggests that going over the event before recall and being asked questions helps witness recall. This is called giving **enhanced retrieval instructions**.

Aims

Daniel Yarmey's aim was to look at the effects on both males and females of being part of a field experiment related to eyewitness recall and photo identification. Another aim was to see how far a disguise (sunglasses and a baseball cap) affected retrieval. One issue was whether instructions given just before recall, to review an incident, would affect the identification. The study also used a 4-hour time gap and investigated the effect of this gap on eyewitness recall. Yarmey went on to compare what students believed about the success rate of photo identification before the study with the actual findings of the study.

Procedure

Participants

There were 215 male and 375 female participants, ranging in age from 18 to 70. Only white participants were used to avoid any race bias. Participants were randomly assigned to one of many different conditions listed below.

Conditions

The different conditions were:

- being prepared (told that they were going to be an eyewitness) or not
- a disguise present (sunglasses and baseball cap) or not
- retrieval instructions enhanced or not
- tested immediately or delayed by 4 hours
- the gender of witness (male or female)
- whether the target was present or not in a line-up

Two white women were the targets (to be identified).

Actual procedure

Participants were approached by a target in a public place and asked to help look for lost jewellery or asked for directions. After 2 minutes a female researcher went up to the participant and asked him or her to take part in the study. The researcher either asked then and there about the identification of the target or 4 hours later. Witnesses were given a questionnaire with 16 items, eight about the physical characteristics of the target and eight about her clothing. They rated their confidence about their answers on a 7-point scale. After completing the questionnaire witnesses were given a set of six photos. In half the cases the target was present in the photos, and in half the target was absent. Participants were asked to identify the target female (they were told she might not be in the photos, and they were shown each photo only once). At the end of the study there was a debriefing.

Another part of the study was to give the whole scenario in written form to students. The students were asked to comment on what they thought would happen and what would affect eyewitness recall.

Results

As there were so many conditions, the results and analyses were complex. In many cases significant differences were found between the various conditions. When the target was present in the photo line-up, about 49% of participants correctly identified the target, and 62% correctly said that the target was not there in the 'target absent' condition.

It is interesting to compare the findings about correct identification in the photo line-up with the student predictions. For example, it was found that where 62% of the participants correctly said the target was not in the photos in the 'target absent' condition, students thought this would happen for only 47% of the participants. Where 49% of the participants correctly identified the target when her photo was included in the photo line-up, 63% of the students thought that in that condition the target would be correctly identified. This is a significant overestimate.

Another finding was that the participants who were prepared for the test were better at recall but were not better at photo identification. With regard to physical characteristics, this study found that age estimates were reasonably accurate — more so than height or weight estimates. The study did not find that using enhanced imagery techniques helped recall, so it does not support the idea of the cognitive interview (although it only tested one small part of the cognitive interview technique).

Conclusions

This study found that about 50% of the time a witness makes a correct identification in a line-up when the target is present, which corresponds closely with the findings of Haber and Haber's meta-analysis (2001). Yarmey's study also has practical applications, as it casts doubt on the assumption that jurors should accept eyewitness accounts because the eyewitness was there, so it must be accurate. Students judging what would happen were not accurate, and jurors are likely to have similar assumptions to the students.

Evaluation of the study

Strengths

- The photo line-up findings support Haber and Haber's findings (2001), which suggests that there is some reliability in this study. Both studies found that witnesses tend to be about 50% accurate in line-up identification when the target is present.
- The study was carried out in the natural environment of the participants and so has ecological validity. The target female simply approached the first person available when she was ready and the participants were going about their normal business.
- The control over the conditions means that the study could be replicated and is likely to be found to be reliable, especially given the support of findings from other studies.
- The range of ages of the participants and the focus on gender to ensure a balance means that there is likely to be good generalisability of the findings.

Weaknesses

- While this study found that age was better identified than other physical characteristics such as height and weight, Yuille and Cutshall's study found more or less the opposite, so not all findings of studies into eyewitness recall support one another.
- The photo line-up is not the same as a real life line-up — a photo of a face is not the same as the actual person being there. There would have to be more focus on facial characteristics, such as hair and eyes, rather than build, stance and other forms of body language, which would also have been present. This means that the task lacks validity, even though the study has ecological validity.
- The witness recall focused on a situation where the participant had met and spoken to the target. This is not always the case for an eyewitness to an event, so the findings should only be applied to similar situations.

Methods of treating offenders

You are required to study the token economy programme and you must also choose one other means of treating offenders. In this textbook, the second treatment is anger management, but you can choose something different. Social skills training and punishment are two other ways of treating offenders that are suggested for your course, and these are explained in the online resources.

> **Token economy programmes (TEPs)** are a way of treating offenders in institutions to reward desired behaviour.
>
> **Behaviour modification** relies on learning principles to change behaviour, not focusing on cognitive elements (thinking), but on the behaviour that can be changed by reinforcement and punishment.

Token economy programmes

Token economy programmes (TEPs) are used to obtain desirable behaviour in closed institutions such as prisons, and they are used for juvenile and adult offenders. They are a form of **behaviour modification**. The programmes started to be applied to institutions in the 1960s and there was hope that they would be extremely successful, given the success of the use of learning theories in changing behaviour. Because the programmes were carried out in institutions, which are closed places, this was useful for the selecting of specific behaviours to reinforce and aim for.

Generalisation, which is part of learning theory principles, was also thought to occur. This means that desired behaviour, once reinforced and established in an institution, would be generalised to outside the institution, so appropriate behaviour would be established. Generalisation in learning theory is when a behaviour learned in one situation is transferred to another, or when learning of one behaviour is transferred to a similar behaviour.

TEPs are based on the principles of operant conditioning, and rewards and punishments. Operant conditioning principles were covered briefly earlier in this section when examining social learning theory as an explanation for criminal behaviour, because social learning theory uses such principles to explain why some behaviours are imitated more than others.

> **AS link** Review your learning of token economy programmes, if you used them as your example of a treatment using learning principles in your AS studies (pp. 337–39).

A token economy programme involves a system of rewards being set up for desired behaviour, sometimes with punishments to discourage behaviour that is not required. Rewards are usually tokens (hence the term 'token economy') or points, which can be exchanged periodically for something the individual would like (the 'economy' part of the programme). This is an important part of the programme, as the reward(s) must genuinely reward that person, and tokens in themselves are not rewarding.

> **AS link** Review your study of operant conditioning as part of the learning approach for the AS part of the course. Remind yourself about positive and negative reinforcement as well as punishment, primary and secondary reinforcements (pp. 327–32).

In the USA in the 1960s, Teodoro Ayllon set up a year-long programme to reward adolescents for required behaviour, and it was this programme that started the use of TEPs. Ayllon did not use the tokens as reinforcers; rather, it was what the tokens bought for the individual that was reinforcing.

Some token economies are more complex than simple positive reinforcement using tokens. Negative reinforcement can be used as well, so that behaviour is performed to avoid something unpleasant or something disliked. In many programmes the tokens have to be 'spent' quickly at first but, when the programme has been followed for a while, tokens can be collected for longer before exchanging for a reward. This means that, at first at least, the reward is quick. Such programmes are also used in institutions other than prisons, including hospitals and schools.

Procedure of a TEP

It is important that there are clear definitions of:
- what is desired behaviour

- what is a token
- how tokens are allocated
- what is a reward
- how there will be gradual changing of the giving of tokens to shape the behaviour
- how many tokens there are for each reward
- how the reward will be removed once the behaviour is achieved

The TEP rules must be obeyed by everyone in the same way. TEPs have been used for some time in prisons, with inmates saying that they like clear rules so that they know what behaviour is rewarded.

Evaluation of TEPs

In the 1970s when TEPs were evaluated to see if they worked, it was concluded that they did not. One early programme in the USA was SMART, which relied on negative reinforcement and was unsuccessful in its aims. Ayllon and Milan (1979) reviewed programmes and found they worked for clear behaviour such as the general keeping of rules and control over interpersonal aggression. It is recognised that there is a problem with the programme in that behaviour is rewarded in a specific situation but the learning may not be transferred successfully into the environment once the prisoner is released, or an inmate in a hospital is rehabilitated.

Reasons why TEPs might not work

- Staff are not committed to the programme, so they do not focus on it sufficiently.
- Inconsistent rewards are given for the same behaviour.
- There is a failure to plan for transferring to the home environment or any environment outside the institution.

Advantages of TEPs

- There needs to be no delay between the desired behaviour and the reward.
- Anyone can give the tokens.
- Clear rules mean staff know when to award a token, so the programme is relatively easy to administer.

Studies evaluating TEPs

Milby (1975) found that programmes were successful in psychiatric hospitals in controlling behaviour but felt that there should be more investigation of how the programmes worked alongside drug treatments. The programmes seemed successful in preparing someone to leave hospital, but follow-up studies were needed to see how long the effects lasted. Studies tend to suggest that successful programmes are clearly planned and managed.

For schizophrenia, there are findings (e.g. **Dickerson et al. 2003**) that programmes were successful in obtaining required behaviour, but again studies are needed to see how such programmes work alongside medication. Because the programmes evaluated took place in the 1960s and 1970s, new studies are needed.

Many evaluations have taken place in psychiatric hospitals, but there has been one notable recent study **(Field et al. 2004)**, which looked at the treatment of young people with behavioural problems, involving group work and token economy systems. The researchers found that, although the programmes were effective on the whole, there were still a number of young people who did not respond. A special programme was put in place for these 'non-responsive' youths, where rewards were more immediate and more frequent, and it was found that these amendments were successful. This suggests that a programme has to be carefully designed so that the pattern of rewards suits the individual.

Table 1.9 *Strengths and weaknesses of TEPs*

Strengths	Weaknesses
• Can be administered by anyone (with training) and tokens and rewards are relatively cheap, so the programme is not expensive and there are more benefits than costs	• Learning might not transfer to the home environment, so there might be recidivism
• Has been found to be successful by many studies, even though there tends to be 10–20% of people who do not respond well to TEPs	• Programmes have to be carefully planned and controlled, and there are many areas where problems can occur (such as lack of consistency from staff)

Anger management programmes

Offenders can be treated using anger management programmes, which focus on people with aggressive behaviour that needs to be controlled. There is a British Association for Anger Management, which suggests that anger is a large problem.

Anger management in general uses strategies such as identifying what triggers anger and learning to control those triggers. Proper eating regimes are suggested, as well as relaxation techniques. Learning to cope with different opinions from others is also important in the programme. **Cognitive–behavioural therapy** can be useful to help someone to control angry outbursts. This section focuses on anger management programmes in institutions — these can be one-to-one but more often involve group work.

> **Cognitive–behavioural therapy** is a form of psychotherapy based on the idea that problems are caused by thinking patterns.

Anger is considered a normal healthy response, but if it develops into rage that takes a person over, it is not healthy and puts strain on the body. Anger can trigger aggressive 'outbursts', which may lead to criminal behaviour such as harming someone else. Some offenders are put on anger management programmes as part of their treatment, because of the nature of the offence or because of personal characteristics. This theory of anger as an outburst links to Freud's ideas of 'negative' emotions being locked away in the unconscious, only to burst out. Freud believed sport and other energetic activities could release such emotions. Currently, however, there is more focus on what triggers the outburst of anger or aggression and how that trigger (which is often centred on learned thought patterns) can be changed. Such anger is thought of more as inappropriate thinking patterns and reactions than as 'outbursts'.

When someone seems to show 'uncontrollable' anger at name calling, for example, this is not in fact uncontrollable but is perceived by that person as a necessary response, because name calling is a huge insult in their culture. In order to help individuals to manage their anger it is necessary to understand their frame of reference — to know what is triggering the anger. Instead of being seen as 'uncontrollable', it is viewed rather as an understandable response to someone's provocative behaviour. This focuses on individuals' thinking patterns and reactions, as does the idea that anger is an 'outburst'.

An example of an anger management programme

A programme could take the form of a twice-weekly group meeting. A trained practitioner is likely to run the group, which in a prison might be a forensic or prison psychologist. There are also programmes set up to train prison officers in running anger management sessions. First, they focus on helping the group to work together, concentrating on social skills, to make sure that everyone is listened to and that there are ground rules for letting each person contribute.

Group skills are used, such as having a **check-in** for each session, where each person briefly explains how they are feeling, describes their day or talks about their progress in the group. During the sessions different techniques are used to help the members talk about their feelings. Relaxation techniques are also used.

Gradually, group work can turn to discussions of what makes each person angry, and such sessions would end with positive thoughts about group members' progress, what they enjoy, or being positive about someone they dislike. Members may be asked to think about the last time they were angry and what their thoughts were at the time, or to reflect on the last time they were kind.

The sessions progress in this way, by introducing the idea of changing the thoughts that relate to an angry response and ending with something positive. It is suggested that the course of group sessions ends by lengthening the time between the sessions, so that the support framework is not removed immediately.

One such programme is CALM™ (Controlling Anger and Learning to Manage). CALM teaches participants to monitor and understand their emotions in order to prevent problematic behaviour. Participants learn the skills necessary to reduce the frequency, intensity and duration of anger to lessen the likelihood of aggression.

The CALM sessions are practical, highly structured, sequential, and designed for delivery to groups of adolescent and adult males at risk for inappropriate, violent behaviour, and in many cases, criminal recidivism. Personal assignments, modelling, role-play, teamwork and self and peer-evaluation are used to teach and promote lasting change of inappropriate and unproductive thought and behaviour patterns.

Evaluation of the success of anger management programmes

A criticism has been made that anger management programmes do not focus on the victim and the harm caused, and nor do they deal with issues of morality. Offenders can gain from victims a better understanding of why violence is unacceptable. This element could be added to anger management programmes but is not.

It has also been suggested that men convicted of domestic violence become less physically violent after attending an anger management programme but may be more verbally and emotionally abusive. The programmes perhaps show people other ways of hurting people, and this is backed up by evaluations of specific programmes.

Prisoners evaluate the success of programmes for them, but they might be positive because of the change of routine, or they might feel they should say they value the sessions to show they are improving. Some prisoners are asked to keep anger diaries, which can be a useful measure of the success of a programme.

Studies evaluating anger management programmes

Watt et al. (1999) in Western Australia evaluated cognitive–behavioural anger management programmes for violent offenders. Violent male adult offenders on an anger management programme were compared with offenders on a waiting list, who acted as a control. The two groups were measured in terms of anger knowledge, anger expression, observed aggressive behaviour and misconduct in prison. The study found no special gain for the offenders on the treatment programme when compared with the control group, so it was suggested that anger management programmes with violent offenders may not have value.

Towl and Dexter (1994) evaluated nine anger management programmes in England and Wales and used a self-report questionnaire, which they administered at the start of each programme and then again between 7 and 14 days after the end of the programme. Fifty prisoners completed the questionnaires and reported a drop in feelings of anger at the end of the programme. However, when considering the data in depth, it was clear that six prisoners had experienced an extreme drop in their anger, whereas the others tended to remain unchanged. The data from those six had been enough to produce a significant change overall. However, the prisoners did report a drop in their internal anger and some decrease in their anger turned towards others (external anger). Overall the results were fairly encouraging.

Law (1997) carried out a similar study to that of Towl and Dexter, looking at four anger management programmes. They found that prisoners were trying to control their anger to a greater extent after the programme.

Ireland (2000) looked at 50 young offenders and found a difference (reduction) in the anger they felt after the programme, according to self-report data.

> **AS link**
>
> Review your learning from your AS course about self-report data (p. 216).

Strengths of anger management programmes

- Studies show the success of anger management programmes from self-report data, which are likely to be valid as they come from the prisoners themselves.
- The programmes focus on learning about triggers for angry episodes and give people the tools to control their anger in the future, so they should have long-term benefits.

Weaknesses of anger management programmes

- The programmes do not include a discussion of morality or understanding from a victim's point of view, which has been said to limit their success.
- It has been claimed that they turn physical aggression into other ways of expressing aggression, such as verbal or emotional abuse.
- Studies claiming success of the programmes use self-report data, where prisoners might want to look good and say the groups were useful, or they might simply have enjoyed the sessions as a break from routine.
- Many studies do not look further into the future to predict recidivism rates.

Examination-style questions

1 Describe two explanations for criminal behaviour. *(8 marks)*

2 Evaluate the social learning theory explanation for criminal behaviour. *(4 marks)*

3 Describe one laboratory experiment that looks at eyewitness testimony. *(5 marks)*

4 Outline two ways of treating offender behaviour. *(6 marks)*

Extension questions

1 Compare two explanations for criminal behaviour in terms of the actual explanation, as well as using evaluations of both. *(12 marks)*

2 Discuss the claim that eyewitness testimony is unreliable, using evidence from studies. *(12 marks)*

Studies in detail

For this section you need to cover two studies in detail. Loftus and Palmer (1974) is one that you must study, and fits in well both with the methodology section of this chapter and the content section. It is described and evaluated in detail in this section. The other study from a choice of three that is chosen for this textbook is Yuille and Cutshall (1986) because it too is a useful study both for the methodology and the content sections of this chapter. The other two studies from which you could have chosen one instead of Yuille and Cutshall (1986) are Charlton et al. (2000) and Gesch et al. (2003). Charlton et al. (2000) is a useful study that adds to information about the effects of violence on television, so it would be beneficial to know about for that part of the content for this chapter. It is explained in Chapter 6 as an example of a naturalistic experiment (pp. 319–20).

Loftus and Palmer (1974)

Loftus and Palmer carried out two experiments within this one study and both are explained here, though you can pick out the first one as being the main experiment if you wish.

According to researchers such as Bird (1927), people are inaccurate at reporting numbers relating to time, speed and distance. This is particularly true of speed, and one study of air force personnel who knew they would be asked about speed found estimates varying between 10 and 50 mph (Marshall, 1969). There are likely to be variables that could influence estimates of speed, which is what Loftus and Palmer's study is about.

> **Explore** Remember that you have to know three studies that look at eyewitness testimony for your course, and Loftus and Palmer (1974) can be one of them.

Aims

The aim was to see if the phrasing of a question would affect estimates of speed, applying these findings to the idea of leading questions in court. A leading question is one that suggests to the witness what answer is desired or leads him or her to the desired answer.

Experiment 1

Procedure

Forty-five students were put into groups. Seven films were shown, each involving a traffic accident, with each film lasting between 5 and 30 seconds. After every film the participants had a questionnaire to fill in. First they were required to give an account of the accident, and then to answer specific questions. The critical question was the one asking about the speed of the vehicles. Nine participants were asked 'about how fast were the cars going when they hit each other?' and equal numbers of the rest were asked the same question, but with the word 'hit' being replaced by 'smashed', 'collided', 'bumped' or 'contacted'. The same procedure was followed for each film.

Results

Four of the seven films used staged crashes, so the speed of the cars was known. One was travelling at 20 mph, two were at 30 mph and one was at 40 mph. Table 1.10 shows the average speeds estimated, according to the words used in the question.

It can be seen from Table 1.10 that 'smashed' gave the highest mean estimate of speed and 'contacted' the lowest mean estimate. 'Collided',

 Table 1.10 *Estimated speeds, according to which word was used in the question*

Word used	Mean speed estimated (mph)
Smashed	40.8
Collided	39.3
Bumped	38.1
Hit	34.0
Contacted	31.8

'bumped' and 'hit' had speed estimates that were fairly well spaced and decreased according to the perceived severity of the verb.

Conclusion

It was concluded that the form of a question can affect a witness's answer. Perhaps the participant is uncertain in judging speeds between 30 and 40 mph, so he or she uses the word in the question to help. Or it is possible that the question changes the memory of the accident so the participant sees the accident as more severe if the word 'smashed' is used. If it was about changing memory, then other aspects of memory may be affected. Loftus and Palmer's second experiment was run to test that idea.

Experiment 2

Procedure

There were 150 participants involved in this experiment. A film with a multiple car accident was shown, followed by a questionnaire. The film lasted less than 1 minute, of which the accident took 4 seconds. The questionnaire at the end of the film asked participants to describe the accident in their own words and then to answer more questions. Some were asked about the speed using the word 'smashed' as part of the question (see the first experiment), some were asked the same question with the word 'hit' replacing 'smashed', and some were not asked about speed. One week later the participants came back but were not shown the film again. They were asked more questions, including 'Did you see any broken glass?'. There was no broken glass in the film, but it was thought that the word 'smashed' used in the question the week before would lead to more broken glass being 'remembered' by those participants.

Results

 Table 1.11 *'Yes'/'no' replies to the question 'Did you see broken glass?', according to the question asked the previous week*

Response	'Smashed'	'Hit'	Control (not asked about speed)	Total
Yes	16	7	6	29
No	34	43	44	121

The mean estimate of speed for the question including the word 'smashed' was 10.46 mph and for 'hit' it was 8 mph. These mean averages were statistically different at $p \leq 0.05$. A chi-squared test was carried out and the result was 7.76, which was significant at $p \leq 0.025$. The probability of saying yes in response to 'smashed' was 0.32 and in response to 'hit' was 0.14. 'Smashed' gave more 'yes' answers to a question about whether there was broken glass (Table 1.11) and a higher estimate of speed.

Conclusion

The way the question is asked can affect the answer given, and the word change in the question had consequences a week later. Memory is fed by the event and by external information provided afterwards. Over time these are integrated as we only have one memory. The film provides the internal memory, and the 'smashed' or 'hit' question adds external information. Integrate the two and the memory is of a crash that is more severe than it was (broken glass was seen to represent 'severe'). The findings link with studies on verbal labels, which have been shown to affect recall. Verbal labels cause a shift in memory to 'fit' the label better. In these experiments, for example, a car crash for some was labelled a 'smash'.

> **Study hint** You can remember this as one study, giving the experiment using 5 words as the main study and the follow-up question about broken glass as the second part. You should mention that other participants asked about 'broken glass' when there was none were more likely to say they saw some if they were asked the question including the word 'smashed'.

Evaluation

Strengths

- Loftus and Palmer (1974) carried out a laboratory experiment with clear controls, such as that all participants watched the same film and were asked identical questions, except for one word change. The controls and careful documenting of the procedure mean that the study is replicable — in fact, the researchers replicated it themselves and found again that the use of the word 'smashed' gave a higher estimate of speed. Therefore, the findings are reliable.
- By using estimates of speed, the researchers gathered quantitative data and so they did not have to interpret the data at all, which makes their study more objective.

Weaknesses

- The students who were participants might not have been under the same emotional strain as if they had been witness to a real car accident, so the findings might not have validity.
- When an experiment is carried out using students as participants, it is said that the findings might not be generalisable to the whole population. This is not because students are not allowed their opinions but because being students they may have different motivation when carrying out the study.
- There might have been demand characteristics in the study, in that the students were able to work out what was required so they answered accordingly. There were questions in addition to the key one, and it would not have been clear that other participants had a different word in the key question, but participants may have picked up that this was about the car accident and that the word 'smashed' was meant to be leading, for example.

> **Explore** Look up this study or others carried out by Loftus to see what else she found out about leading questions. For example, Loftus and Zanni (1975) discovered that if participants were asked about 'the' broken headlight as opposed to 'a' broken headlight they were more likely to 'remember' broken glass, when in fact there was no broken headlight.

Yuille and Cutshall (1986)

Yuille and Cutshall carried out a study interviewing real witnesses of a real crime, so their study is different from the laboratory studies of Loftus and others. It is a field study because it looks at what happened in a natural setting, and it is more of a case study than an interview because, although data were gathered by interview, the study looks in detail at a particular crime.

The researchers began their study by pointing out that research on eyewitness testimony has focused on situations in the criminal justice system, and studies (e.g. Woocher, 1970) suggest that judges and juries do not focus on errors in eyewitness testimony, accepting it as truth. Malpass and Devine (1981) suggested that there was a need to know that laboratory findings could be generalised to more realistic situations. One problem, for example, is that slide sequences and filmed events are not relevant to real world events. Even staged live events do not represent the seriousness or consequences of actual events. If observers are deceived into thinking that events are real this has ethical consequences. Another concern is that the participants in laboratory studies are not representative — of 41 research articles about eyewitness testimony from 1974 to 1982, for example, 92% (38 of them) tested only students. There are problems with generalising from this group to the general public. Therefore, field observations are required to help to generalise laboratory study findings.

> **Study hint** In the description of the background to this study are issues that you can use when discussing methodology in general. For example, the point about having only student participants, and the validity problems that laboratory experiments have. This helps to show why you are asked to do so much evaluation in your study of psychology.

In their 1986 study, Yuille and Cutshall used witnesses who had observed a gun-shooting incident that occurred on a spring afternoon in Vancouver, Canada with several witnesses present. A thief entered a gun shop, tied up the owner and stole some money and guns. The owner freed himself and picked up a revolver. He went outside to take the car registration number but the thief had not got into the car and he fired two shots at the store owner from a distance of about 6 feet. The owner, after a short pause, fired all 6 shots from his revolver. The thief was killed but the store owner recovered from serious injury. Witnesses viewed the scene from different locations — from passing cars, buildings or in the street.

The researchers chose this case because:
■ there were enough witnesses to compare their accounts
■ the thief was killed and the weapons and money recovered, so there was a lot of forensic evidence to verify the witness accounts
■ the death of the thief closed the file, so research would not interfere with a police case

- there were many visible elements to the scene (car, gun boxes, a blanket) so the eyewitness statements could be checked and compared
- witnesses could be asked about elements the police would not have focused on, so previous police questioning would not interfere with or affect the study results

Aims

- to record and evaluate witness accounts
- to examine issues raised by laboratory research
- to look at witness verbatim accounts — their accuracy and the kind of errors made

Research shows that loss and distortion of memory takes place over time. The idea of the study was to look at eyewitness interviews immediately after the event, which were conducted by a police officer, and to compare these with interviews carried out by research staff. Misleading questions were incorporated into the research interviews to see how an eyewitness might be affected by distortion.

Procedure

Participants

Twenty-one witnesses to the gun shooting were interviewed by police after the incident. Twenty out of the 21 were contacted by the research team and 13 agreed to the research interview — two had moved from the area and five did not wish to take part. The other witness was the victim, who did not want to relive the trauma.

Interview procedure

The police had interviewed the witnesses and recorded the interviews by hand. Each witness was asked to describe the event in their own terms and then the officer asked a series of questions to amplify what had been said. The reports were verbatim (word for word).

About 4 or 5 months later, 13 of the witnesses were interviewed by the researchers and the interviews were recorded on audiotape and transcribed. The same procedure was followed — their own account followed by questions. There were also two misleading questions: one involved a headlight in the thief's car. Half of the witnesses were asked if they had seen *a* busted headlight and the other half were asked if they had seen *the* busted headlight, using Loftus's procedure. There was no broken headlight. The second misleading question was about the colour of a quarter panel of the car. Half were asked about *the* yellow quarter panel and the other half about *a* yellow quarter panel. The off-colour quarter panel was in fact blue.

The interview also asked about the degree of stress each witness experienced at the time of the accident. This used a 7-point scale, with 1 being perfectly calm and 7 being extremely anxious. They were asked about their emotional state before the incident and any problems afterwards, like sleeplessness.

Scoring procedure

A careful scoring procedure was used, because details from the research interviews had to be compared with details from the police interviews, as well as needing the actual details of the incident. The researchers divided the incident up into action details and description details, and the description details were further divided into object and people descriptions. Various reconstructions were set up and evidence was carefully researched so that the actual details were revealed.

An example of how details were divided up is shown in the statement 'he turned around and shot the guy in the shoulder', which was divided up into three action details. There were some difficulties with the scoring — for example, 'he looked like he was in his early 20s' was scored as incorrect, even though he did look as if he was in his early 20s, because he was in fact 35.

Results

Table 1.12 *Total reported classifiable details from 13 witnesses*

	Police interview	Research interview
Action details	392 (60.35%)	551.5 (52.20%)
Person descriptions	180 (27.72%)	267 (25.27%)
Object descriptions	77.5 (11.93%)	238 (22.53%)
Total	649.5	1056.5

The percentage figures are the proportions of the details or descriptions that the researchers laid down

It can be seen that the researchers obtained more detail than the police. This was because they asked questions of no interest to the police, such as what the blanket was like that covered the thief's body. The police achieved more action details than object or person details and the researchers had half action and half description details.

There was variability in what the witnesses reported but this was because they had seen different amounts of the incident. Of the 13 participants, 7 were central witnesses and 6 peripheral witnesses. However, both groups were equally accurate. In the police interviews 84.56% of the central witnesses were accurate, compared with 79.31% of the peripheral group. The accuracy remained similar and high for most of the witnesses even after 4 or 5 months had passed and errors were relatively rare. There were different details recalled through the interviews of the researchers, which were not recalled for the police. The misleading information had little effect on answers — 10 said there was no broken headlight or no yellow quarter panel, or said they had not noticed the detail.

Conclusion

The researchers point out that this was the first investigation of eyewitness testimony that involved a real incident and real witnesses. As there were only 13 witnesses and this was a unique event it is not easy to generalise from the findings. They conclude, however, that their findings show that eyewitnesses are not incorrect in their accounts, as was suggested by laboratory studies. Most of the witnesses were extremely accurate and remained so up to 5 months after the incident. It is possible that this was because the incident was memorable and unusual.

The researchers suggest they may have been investigating **flashbulb memory**, which is when a specific and relevant event is recorded in memory in great detail. It was found that those directly involved in the event remembered more, so the researchers suggest that laboratory studies would not capture this involvement, which could explain why these findings are different from laboratory study findings. Yuille and Cutshall believed that their scoring procedures undermined the accuracy of the accounts as they used conservative rules, as explained earlier.

It is interesting that the effort to mislead the witnesses did not succeed, which goes against some laboratory study findings. There was some investigation of the effects of arousal on memory, although that detail is not given here in the results section, and in general it was found that stress did not affect memory negatively. The researchers found that witnesses at the time felt more adrenaline than stress and that stress came later, so these areas need more research. Judges sometimes reject a witness account because of some incorrect detail, but Yuille and Cutshall here show that although some detail may be wrong (such as the colour of the blanket) that does not make other details wrong, and that the witness testimony should not then be rejected.

Evaluation

Strengths

- This is a field study that looks at a real incident with real witnesses. It has validity that laboratory experiments do not have and it was carried out because of that validity.
- Great care was taken when counting details from the real incident to make sure that witness testimonies did not alter what 'really' happened. Such care enables the findings to be seen to be reliable.

Weaknesses

- There are problems in generalising from this specific and unique incident. The researchers themselves suggest that this could be a case of flashbulb memory, which is a specific type of memory different from what is studied in the laboratory, so generalising the findings to use them to criticise laboratory studies may be unfair.
- The scoring of the interviews was done conservatively, with some inaccuracies noted even when the response in fact made sense. However, as the accounts were found to be largely accurate, emphasising inaccuracies would not have affected the findings in this case. Scoring turns qualitative data into quantitative data and there is always the chance of interpretation and bias when doing this.

Examination-style questions

1 Describe the procedure of Loftus and Palmer's study (1974) about leading questions. *(4 marks)*

2 Describe the findings (results and conclusions) of one study from Yuille and Cutshall (1986), Charlton et al. (2000) and Gesch et al. (2003). *(4 marks)*

3 Discuss the research method used in two studies in criminological psychology, including Loftus and Palmer (1974) and one from Yuille and Cutshall (1986), Charlton et al. (2000) and Gesch et al. (2003). *(12 marks)*

4 Evaluate Loftus and Palmer's study (1974) about leading questions. *(4 marks)*

Extension questions

1 Explain the difference between a field study and a field experiment, using one example of each research method in your answer to illustrate the differences. *(12 marks)*

2 Discuss two studies looking at witness testimony. In your answer refer to validity, reliability and ethical issues, as well as other issues if you choose to. *(12 marks)*

Key issues

For your study of criminological psychology you need to prepare one **key issue** and carry out a practical relating to your chosen key issue.

You can choose to carry out a practical that requires primary data gathering (content analysis) or one that requires examination of secondary data (article analysis). In this chapter an analysis of articles is suggested. A similar article analysis (focused on eyewitness testimony) is summarised in the *Getting Started* booklet that comes with your course and that can be found on the Edexcel website (**www.edexcel.com**), so you could look at that as well for guidance.

Note that you are studying two applications from the four set out in your course. Within those two applications you must do one content analysis practical and one article analysis practical, so make sure you include one of each in your studies. In this textbook an article analysis is chosen for this chapter on criminological psychology and the chapter on health psychology, and a content analysis has been chosen for child psychology and sport psychology. You are required to study the key issue, find material relating to it, carry out an analysis on that material, and then link your analysis to concepts that relate to the key issue. You need also to be able to describe the key issue itself.

Three key issues are suggested for your course:
- the reliability of eyewitness testimony
- offender profiling
- are criminals born or made?

However, you may choose any key issue. The methodology, content and studies in detail sections for this chapter have explained and discussed the issue of eyewitness testimony. The other two issues are summarised in brief here and given in more depth in the online resources, in case you would like to explore them instead of the reliability of eyewitness testimony.

The reliability of eyewitness testimony

Eyewitness testimony is defined and explained in the section on methodology for this chapter. The reliability of eyewitness testimony is in doubt, because of the findings of studies looking into such issues as the weapons effect and the misinformation effect. The misinformation effect is explained and evaluated on p. 8. The weapons effect is the way in which a witness focuses on a weapon such as a gun, if present, to the detriment of other aspects of the situation. You need to be able to describe the issue (why eyewitness testimony is said to be unreliable), and in what circumstances it might be particularly unreliable. The concepts and studies will be needed as part of your analysis of the two articles for the practical you are required to carry out.

AS link You might have studied problems with eyewitness testimony as a key issue in your work within cognitive psychology, and you may have learned about reconstructive memory and the use of schemata. If you did, review that material now, because it has great relevance to this section of your studies. If you did not study these areas, do not worry — they have been reviewed in this chapter.

Offender profiling

There has been no mention of offender profiling so far in this chapter. It is included here as an issue because it is of great public interest. The idea that someone can draw clues from a criminal's patterns when a crime is committed is an interesting one, and something that appeals to the imagination.

Offender profiling is the creation of a description of a criminal drawn from clues available from a crime scene or from past crimes. It is usually used in multiple crimes such as murder or rape because, sadly, more than one crime is often needed for a pattern to be noted. The profiler considers the geography where the crime(s) took place, including road and rail links, barriers to travel such as rivers, and so on. He or she will consider if the criminal needed to be strong, or able to drive — the scene can give such information or allow a best guess. There is consideration of the type of crime, such as if it is a sex crime, and whether there is something about the crime that is odd, as a criminal will often leave signals. If a crime scene is left tidy, for example, it would indicate a fussy person. There are studies looking at the effectiveness of offender profiling and how far it works to find a criminal.

Explore Look up offender profiling and some famous cases to find out how it has been used. You should also investigate research studies into its effectiveness.

More about offender profiling is explained in the online resources, in case you would like to choose it as an issue for your key issue and practical.

Are criminals born or made?

There has been little mention in this chapter about whether criminals are born or made. This relates to the nature–nurture debate about how far criminal behaviour comes from genes or biology and how far it comes from environment and experiences. 'Nature' refers to biology and genes, and 'nurture' to the impact of the environment on behaviour.

Social learning theory was given in the content section as an explanation of criminal behaviour and it is an example of how criminals might be 'made', not 'born' (i.e. nurture not nature). The other explanation offered in this textbook was labelling and the self-fulfilling prophecy, also clearly on the side of nurture and suggesting that social interactions can lead to criminal behaviour.

One further explanation can be found in the online resources — the idea that there can be a criminal personality or at least a personality type that might lead someone into crime. This is the idea that criminals are born not made. Studies have also looked at genes to see if there is one or more gene present for being a criminal, but there is little evidence that this is the case. However, there is some evidence, based on twin studies, that stealing is genetic.

More about whether criminality is born or made (or some combination) is explained in the online resources, in case you would like to choose it as a topic for your key issue and practical.

Practical: carrying out an analysis of two articles

An article analysis for your course requires you to find two relevant articles. These can be taken from magazines, newspapers, the internet or from a television programme (if you can write a summary of what was said or find a synopsis).

You need to find two such articles and then summarise them in your own words. You should then draw conclusions about the findings by linking to concepts from criminological psychology. Consider the theories you have studied, or perhaps the methodology if that is relevant.

Study hint You will find this exercise carried out in the booklet that comes with the specification for your course, and it can be found on the Edexcel website (**www.edexcel.com**). It is also on the e-spec (the CD-ROM that comes with the specification). The mock practical considers two articles on eyewitness testimony. You would be expected to find two different articles, but this example practical will help you to structure your own work. An example article analysis can be found in the online resources that accompany this textbook.

Examination-style questions

1 Describe one key issue you have studied within criminological psychology. *(5 marks)*

2 With regard to the practical you carried out for criminological psychology, answer the following questions. When 'analysis' is referred to, you can answer focusing on an analysis of two articles or a content analysis.

   (a) Did your method of gathering information involve primary or secondary data? Explain how these data were used. *(4 marks)*

   (b) Give one example of qualitative or quantitative data from your practical in the criminological approach, and explain why your data fit that description. *(3 marks)*

   (c) Relate the information you found to the key issue, using concepts and ideas from criminological psychology. *(6 marks)*

Extension question

With reference to two articles or to a content analysis, discuss one key issue that you have studied within criminological psychology. *(6 marks)*

Answers to practice boxes

Practice 1.1 (p. 8)

1 The 'broken glass study' hypothesis: more participants will 'remember' broken glass if they are asked about a car **smashing** into another than if they are asked about a car **hitting** another. The 'stop/yield sign study' hypotheses: participants given the suggestion that there was a yield sign are more likely to 'remember' a yield sign than those not given that information. Those not given the 'yield sign' information are more likely to remember the stop sign than those given the yield sign information. The 'barn study' hypothesis: participants asked about a barn that was not there will 'remember' a barn more than those not asked about a barn. The time before recall study hypothesis: those participants given longer between seeing the film and being asked to recall it, when given misinformation, are more likely to be swayed by this than if they are not given as long before being asked to recall.

2 The 'broken glass study' IV is whether the participant was asked about the car being 'smashed' or 'hit', and the DV is whether he or she says there was broken glass or not. The 'stop/yield sign study' IV is whether the participant is given the 'yield' sign misinformation or not. The first DV is whether he or she recalls a yield sign or not and the second DV is whether he or she recalls a stop sign or not. The 'barn study' IV is whether or not the participant is asked about a barn that was not there and the DV is whether he or she 'remembers' a barn or not.

The 'time before recall study' IV is whether the participant is given more or less time after seeing the film and the DV is whether he or she is more or less swayed by the mis-information.

3 The experimental design for the 'stop/yield sign study' is independent groups, as half were told there was a yield sign and the other half were not, so the two groups contained different people.

Practice 1.2 (p. 15)

1 Participants did not know that they were being asked about a barn that was not there, so they may have been made to look silly, which might distress them. They were deceived, so therefore they did not give informed consent.

2 Participants did not know at first that the woman was not a member of the public, so they were deceived, and they did not know that the syringe was not real, so they could have been distressed.

3 Participants did not know that they were going to have to describe the woman, and they may have thought, when questioned, that they should have recalled more. This could have caused distress. They were not asked for consent to take part in the study until afterwards, which means they did not give informed consent.

Chapter

Child psychology

This chapter is about child psychology, which is an **application** in psychology. This means that theories and studies are applied to issues of concern to society and the individual. Child psychology can include theories about problems in child development and about children's usual developmental progression. You will look at what happens when very young children are not cared for, as well as the effects of being separated from a main caregiver; the issue of daycare is also explored. Such issues as autism will be investigated as to how they affect a child's development.

Summary of learning objectives

Definitions

You have to be able to define the terms:

- attachment
- evolution
- deprivation
- daycare
- privation
- separation anxiety

Methodology

- the observational research method (naturalistic and structured)
- the case study research method
- evaluation of both observational and case study research, including their use in child psychology and issues of validity, reliability and ethics
- cross-cultural and longitudinal ways of studying children in psychology

2

Content

You have to be able to describe and evaluate:

- Bowlby's theory of attachment and link to the psychodynamic approach and the biological approach (an evolutionary basis for attachment)
- the work of Ainsworth (and the strange situation method as well as cross-cultural issues and child-rearing styles)
- research into deprivation/separation, including the maternal deprivation hypothesis (Bowlby) and the reduction of negative effects
- research into privation, including whether effects are reversible
- research into daycare, including at least one study each about advantages and disadvantages of daycare

You also need to be able to:

- describe the characteristics of and two explanations for one of: severe learning difficulties, autism or ADHD, and explain two ways in which the chosen developmental issue might affect a child's development

Studies in detail

You have to be able to describe and evaluate in detail:

- the study of Genie by Curtiss (1977)
- one other study from Bowlby (1944), Belsky and Rovine (1988) and Rutter and the ERA study team (1998)

Key issues and practical

You have to carry out one practical that focuses on a key issue of your choice, which relates to child psychology. The practical can be a content analysis of articles, programmes or other material about the key issue, or a summary of two articles, from which you then draw conclusions about the key issue or about an area of the application that you have studied.

Table 2.1 *Checklist of what you need to know for child psychology and your progresss*

I need to know about	Done	More work	I need to know about	Done	More work
Defining: attachment, deprivation, privation			Privation and reversibility		
Defining: separation anxiety, daycare			Daycare: advantages, disadvantages		
Evolution and evolutionary aspects of attachments			Characteristics of one from severe learning difficulties, ADHD or autism		
Observations, case studies and evaluation			Bowlby, attachments, maternal deprivation hypothesis (and psychodynamic link)		
Use of methods in child psychology, validity, reliability, ethics			Ainsworth, child-rearing styles and cross-cultural studies		
Cross-sectional and longitudinal research and child psychology			Deprivation, separation, reducing negative effects		

I need to know about	Done	More work	I need to know about	Done	More work
Two explanations for one of: severe learning difficulties, ADHD or autism			One from Bowlby (1944), Belsky and Rovine (1988) and Rutter and the ERA team (1998)		
How one from severe learning difficulties, ADHD or autism might affect child development			One key issue and a practical relating to it		
Genie (Curtiss, 1977)					

Definitions

Attachment and **evolution** are two terms defined when looking at Bowlby's work in child psychology, in the content section of this chapter. **Deprivation**, **privation** and **separation anxiety** link with Bowlby's work too — and the work of others — and these terms are defined and explained in the content section. **Daycare** is a type of separation and deprivation, and it is covered in the content section as well as being a key issue.

An introduction to child psychology

Child psychology is part of developmental psychology, and focuses more on infants and young children, though 'child' also includes young people and adolescents. Child psychopathology is included as well — this looks at problems with child development.

Picture Partners/Alamy

A young child involved in a psychological test

2

Teachers, social workers, educational psychologists, clinical psychologists and other care workers are interested in child psychology. It could be said that one side of child psychology is research to gain understanding of children, and the other side is the application that helps with issues and problems faced by children. In general, there are academic researchers and practising psychologists and these two groups tend to be separate, although some practising psychologists also carry out research.

Child development from birth to adolescence

The main focus of child psychology is the development of a child from birth to adolescence. The United Nations Convention on the Rights of the Child (1989) defines childhood as being up to the age of 18. Cognitive developmental psychology focuses on how a child develops its thinking processes, but your course focuses more on emotional development and how having little or no care at a young age can affect the child. You will look at academic research in child psychology and at the work of practising psychologists who apply academic understanding.

How childhood affects later experiences

Another important feature of child psychology is the claim that what individuals experience in childhood (through early childhood, middle childhood and adolescence) affects their adult experiences. With this approach, child psychology is not just about children but also about adults. Your course touches on this area — for example, when showing how Bowlby thought that a difficult attachment pattern as a young child can lead an adult to have problems with relationships in adulthood.

Study hint As you learn about the child psychology content for your course, add detail to this summary of what this application is about and what its main focuses are.

Examination-style question
Define what is meant by child psychology. *(3 marks)*

Extension question
Explain what is meant by the claim that there are two types of people working within child psychology, academic psychologists and practising psychologists. *(6 marks)*

AS link Note that you might be asked to draw on AS material for both the Methodology and Content sections of this chapter.

Methodology

Methodology is about research methods used and design decisions taken when studying any area in psychology. Child psychology involves using many different research methods, but in this section only some areas of methodology are considered.

AS link Review from your AS textbook the observational research method (both naturalistic and structured observations) from the learning approach (pp. 309–16); the case study research method from the psychodynamic approach (pp. 165–77); and longitudinal research methods (pp. 183–85). You need to know how to describe these research methods and how to evaluate them.

Observations

You must be able to describe and evaluate naturalistic observations and structured observations as research methods. When evaluating them you should think about how they are used in child psychology, and also consider them in terms of validity, reliability and ethics.

Summary of the naturalistic observation research method

Observations are naturalistic if they take place in the participants' natural setting, without the situation being set up. They can be overt and open, covert and secret, participant observations with the observer taking a role, or non-participant observations with the observer not taking a role. They can gather qualitative data if a story of what is happening is recorded, or they can gather quantitative data by recording actions using tallying. Inter-observer reliability means that more than one observer uses the same categories and participants, so that results can be checked to make sure they correspond.

AS link You should already know the terminology for this topic from your AS studies. Observations are described and evaluated on pp. 309–16 of the AS textbook.

Naturalistic observations in child psychology

M. B. Parten (1932) carried out naturalistic observations when looking at play and found categories of types of play, according to a child's age. She observed free play sessions to gather her data. Many other features of child development, such as language development, are studied using naturalistic observations. This is because the child in his or her natural setting will show natural behaviour, which is what the researcher wants to study.

This is the 'research' side of child psychology, and its naturalistic observations are extremely useful to child psychologists in helping them to understand 'real' behaviour, and thus to help children develop appropriate behaviour. This is because

2

there is little interference with the child's usual behaviour, making data valid. Children who are having problems at school are observed in the classroom, for example, to see what triggers certain behaviour patterns. From this observation, **interventions** can be suggested to help the child in some way. Naturalistic observations may take place when children are with their peers, as well as in the home.

Because behaviour happens in an environment, it is important to have an understanding of that environment. Naturalistic observations can help to see how often abnormal or deviant behaviour occurs, and time sampling can be employed. In time sampling, chunks of time are allocated and the observer can record what behaviour occurs during each chunk, to help build a detailed picture of a child's behaviour. Patterson (1982) recorded detail about parent–child interactions in this way, in order to understand what led to a particular behaviour. Dodge (1983) used naturalistic observation to study friendships (or the lack of them) in what he called 'rejected' children.

> **Explore** Look up the studies of Dodge, Patterson or Parten to see how naturalistic observation has been used to study children.

Structured observations in child psychology

In the applied side of child psychology, structured observations are used to gather evidence about a child's deviant or inappropriate behaviour. The teacher, researcher, psychologist (or someone else depending on the aims) decides which situations will be observed. They may set up a situation. Then the observer records certain information about the child's behaviour in that structured situation — the antecedent, the behaviour and the consequence. This is called ABC (A: antecedent, B: behaviour, C: consequence). The purpose is to find out what sets off the behaviour (the antecedent), then to observe the actual behaviour, and then to see what happens to or for the child as a result of the behaviour (the consequence). Problems in behaviour may have arisen at any of these stages. For example, the child may have been rewarded for their inappropriate behaviour (the consequence) and a structured situation can reveal this.

> **Study hint** When describing a research method it is useful to explain an example, as this helps to show your understanding and to illustrate the research method. The example needs more than just a name — say something about the aim and/or what was found.

In the 1970s Mary Ainsworth, working on the academic side to develop theory, carried out a special kind of structured observation called the 'strange situation' task. This is explained in detail in the content section of this application. Use what you learn there to explain and evaluate structured observations.

Evaluating observations in child psychology

Strengths of naturalistic observations

Naturalistic observations are carried out in a natural setting, with the aim of observing children doing what they normally do and interacting with others as they usually would. So in this way they have validity — more so than experiments or surveys. If time sampling is used carefully, with tallying, prepared categories and more than one observer, the data can have reliability since inter-observer reliability can be checked.

Weaknesses of naturalistic observations

Children can be influenced by being observed and they may display different behaviour from normal, which means data will not be valid. Similarly, there can be **observer drift** — observers tend to move away from what they planned to observe, and bias can be introduced, again meaning that the observations lack validity. Reliability can be a problem, as an observation often cannot be repeated because it is a particular time, day, situation and set of children and observers. If those circumstances are not exactly repeated, then data cannot be tested for reliability.

AS link Refer to the strengths and weaknesses of naturalistic observations that you learned about in your AS course (p. 315–16), where similar issues are discussed along with other details.

Table 2.2 Summary of the strengths and weaknesses of naturalistic observations

Strengths	Weaknesses
• Valid because in natural setting, so natural behaviour observed	• Not valid in that there is an observer, so the behaviour might be affected
• Reliable because tallying, time sampling, prepared categories and more than one observer can give inter-observer reliability	• Not valid because of observer drift, where observers move away from the plan
	• Not reliable because observation is at one time, in one situation, with particular observers, and the same situation is not likely to recur

Strengths of structured observations

Structured situations are set up and documented in enough detail that they can be replicated and so be tested for reliability. The point of the structured observation is to provide evidence, for example for a child's deviant behaviour and what might trigger it. Therefore, the situation must be carefully noted and the antecedent, behaviour and consequence clearly visible and able to be recorded. This means that reliability is more likely than for naturalistic observations. Structured observations can be efficient, because the behaviour to be observed might either not occur again or not occur for a long time, making it difficult to observe in any other way. Structured observations are time and cost effective.

Weaknesses of structured observations

Structured observations are set-up situations that are not natural, so they can be said to lack validity. They may not have been correctly set up, so may not represent reality. There is the chance of demand characteristics occurring — that the subjects know that the situation has been structured (set up) and will behave as they think they should. This too will affect validity. (Adults may show demand characteristics but very young children are likely to be less aware so are less likely to.)

Table 2.3	Summary of the strengths and weaknesses of structured observations

Strengths	Weaknesses
• Reliable because structure means they can be set up again and repeated • Time and cost effective as the behaviour might not occur naturally for a long time	• Lacks validity because the situation is set up, so might not represent a real situation • Lacks validity because of demand characteristics — subjects might behave as they think they should, knowing the situation has been set up

The usefulness of observations in child psychology

Observations are extremely useful in all areas of psychology. Practising psychologists (such as educational psychologists, clinical psychologists and forensic psychologists) work in similar ways. They are called upon in a certain situation, usually when a change in behaviour is required. Their first aim is to study the situation, which they do by observing. Such observation has to be as natural as possible to have validity.

Having gathered evidence by observing, the psychologist then plans an intervention and, finally, evaluates the intervention. Evidence is also likely to be gathered by interview and perhaps by using **psychometric testing**. Observation is an important method, because it involves the individual directly, whereas interviewing others does not. Psychometric testing also tends to be artificial, even though it can be useful.

Evaluating observations in terms of ethical issues

Ethical issues when observations are used in research

An important point about naturalistic observations used in research is that, if the behaviour being observed takes place in a public place, where someone would expect to be observed, then it is not unethical to make such observations. This is as long as other relevant ethical guidelines are adhered to, such as confidentiality. Only if the observation takes place where someone would not expect to be observed do ethical questions start to arise.

AS link

Review the ethical guidelines for using humans in research that you covered for AS (pp. 24–29 and pp. 175–76).

Ethical issues in psychology include informed consent, deceit, debriefing, the right to withdraw, competence, privacy and confidentiality.

Observations can involve deceit if they are covert but not if they are overt. With covert observations, debriefing can help — for example, after a full debrief the participants can be given the right to withdraw their data, which helps make a study ethical. In some covert observations, however, there is no right to withdraw from the study, as the participant could not know about the study. This raises questions about the ethics of such observations.

Structured observations are less likely to involve informed consent because, if participants knew about them, they might perform differently. So in a structured observation there is likely to be deceit, lack of informed consent and no right to withdraw. Again, a full debrief would be needed. In the case of a very young child, consent would be obtained from parents or guardians, so it may be felt that deceit is not an issue. All these issues require competence on the part of the researcher, as there will be some breach of ethical guidelines in all cases.

Ethical issues when observations are used in a clinical setting

There are different ethical guidelines for practitioners. In your AS course you looked at guidelines for researchers. These guidelines still apply to practitioners, but there are additional guidelines under the headings of contracting, consent, confidentiality, keeping records, supervision and working with other professionals. The British Psychological Society (BPS) has a number of documents relating to ethical guidelines for practitioners and the titles of some of these indicate both the range of issues dealt with and the importance attached to practising in an ethical way.

Guidelines for practitioners from the BPS

- ADHD (attention-deficit hyperactivity disorder) guidelines (2000)
- Challenging behaviour: a unified approach (2007)
- Childhood ASD (autistic spectrum disorder) (2006)
- Child protection portfolio (2007)
- Generic professional practice guidelines (2008)
- Learning disabilities: definitions and contexts (2000)
- Psychologists as expert witnesses (2007)

If, in a clinical setting, ethical guidelines relating to that setting are not adhered to then a psychologist faces criticism from the BPS and his or her peers. Chartered psychologists must, as part of their continuing professional development, keep a log and submit it every year, and ethics is part of that log. Psychologists usually work for institutions such as the NHS or the prison service, and those institutions will also demand a high level of ethical conduct. Members of the public can complain to the BPS if they feel they have not been treated in an ethical manner by a psychologist, and complaints are followed up.

> **Explore** Look up one or two of the guidelines mentioned in the bullet list above and make a note of the special issues involved. You could focus on the guidelines for autistic spectrum disorder, as this is studied in more depth later in this chapter.

Special ethical issues that apply when studying children

An important point about studying children is that it is usual to ask parents or guardians for consent on the child's behalf and to explain to adults what will happen, rather than to ask the children. Children's rights are an issue of interest currently, and researchers are now encouraged to ask children for permission and to explain to a child what a study will entail, as well as offering the right to withdraw. However, guidelines suggest that it is acceptable for a parent or guardian to consent on the child's behalf. The same issues apply to case studies. There is a need to pay special attention to ethics where children are too young to give consent, such as in the strange situation (see pp. 77–78).

2

Evaluation of observations with regard to ethics

- Observations of people in a public place are considered ethical.
- Covert observations do not have informed consent, the right to withdraw, and they involve deceit — a debrief must put these issues right.
- Overt observations involve informed consent, the right to withdraw and no deceit — a debrief is still needed.
- In a clinical setting there are very clear BPS guidelines and sanctions if these guidelines are not adhered to.
- There is an issue with regard to children's rights and children's participation.

> **Explore** Research the arguments about children's righxts and children's participation in decision-making that concerns them.

Case studies

You must be able to describe and evaluate case studies as a research method. You should consider how case studies are used in child psychology and also their validity, reliability and the ethical issues.

Summary of the case study research method

> **AS link**
>
> Case studies are described and evaluated on pages 165–74 of the AS textbook.

Case studies are in-depth detailed studies of a unique individual or a small group. They usually involve a number of different research methods, such as interviewing, observing and case histories. Freud used case studies but employed special research methods within them, such as dream analysis and free association. This was because he wanted to uncover unconscious wishes and needed special methods to 'trick' the unconscious into revealing itself.

Case studies in child psychology

You will cover the study of Genie (not her real name) by Curtiss (1977) later in this chapter. Genie was a child discovered at the age of about 13, unable to walk properly or talk, and who had been badly treated. The case study is about what happened to Genie after that. Other similar case studies of feral (wild) children have also taken place, such as the wild boy of Aveyron, reported by Itard. You may also have covered Axline's study of 'Dibs', another child with problem behaviour, when you looked at the psychodynamic approach at AS. In the AS course you will also have studied the story of Little Hans, which Freud used as evidence for the Oedipus complex.

> **Study hint** Use evidence from Little Hans, Dibs (if you have covered that study) and Genie to illustrate the use of case studies in child psychology, and to evaluate them.

These four children — Genie, the wild boy, Dibs and Little Hans — have in common that they showed behaviour that needed to be changed or understood. Case studies in child psychology are often carried out for this purpose — this is the 'application' side of child psychology. Some case studies on the research side are undertaken in order to learn from them, such as following a small child's development to capture information about how language develops. One such case study is that of Czechoslovakian twins by Koluchová, and this study is explained in more detail in the Content section of this chapter.

Evaluating case studies in child psychology

Strengths

Case studies tend to use many different research methods, which means that data are found by different means. The data can be compared and, if the same results are found, this gives reliability. Case studies also tend to be valid, because they often take place in the participant's natural setting and data are usually gathered within a situation.

Weaknesses

Although different research methods can mean that data can be verified if the same findings appear more than once, it is still the case that a case study may not be able to be repeated because it is about a unique individual at a certain moment in time. This means that case studies cannot be repeated to test for reliability and it also means that they are not easily generalisable, as they are about a unique individual (or small group) who has unique issues and problems, and so the findings might not apply to anyone else.

Table 2.4 *Summary of the strengths and weaknesses of case studies*

Strengths	Weaknesses
• Reliability is found to an extent, because the same data can be found from different research methods	• Case studies are of a unique individual at one moment in time, so are hard to replicate to test for reliability
• Case studies tend to be valid because they often take place in the real-life setting of the individual or small group	• For the same reasons they are not generalisable

The usefulness of case studies in child psychology

Case studies are useful in child psychology when considering practising psychologists who will be dealing with unique children presenting with individual problems and issues. A detailed study of a child like Genie will provide the necessary depth of data that can help prepare an intervention. Case studies could usefully include interviews with the child, parents, teachers and others, as well as psychometric testing and observation. Because case studies are often longitudinal, they show development features successfully.

However, case studies are not perhaps as useful when considering research in psychology to formulate universal laws about behaviour and to develop scientific findings. This is because it is hard to generalise from case studies — their findings might not be reliable and they are hard to replicate. Observations can be replicated more easily, and experiments and clinical interviews can be repeated, so that results can be more certain.

2

Evaluating case studies in terms of ethical issues

Case studies involve informed consent. It is not difficult to offer the right to withdraw and there is no need for deceit, because the aim is to uncover detailed and in-depth information. However, it is important to keep the participant up to date with findings and to check back frequently that the study can continue and that all is well. All the different research methods used — which might include observation, dream analysis, experiment or survey — must be ethically put into practice. Compared with an experiment (where it is hard to get informed consent, and deceit is often needed because of the necessary control), case studies are considered ethical.

However, there is still an issue where children are concerned that parents or guardians give their permission rather than the child. The issue of children's rights and of children's participation in what happens to them must be considered. Confidentiality can also be hard to maintain over time, because the participants in a case study can be sought out for interest or to find out what has happened to them and, in the end, information from the study can be used to track them down.

Evaluation of case studies with regard to ethics

- Informed consent and the right to withdraw are not hard to achieve but need to be focused on.
- There is no need for deceit.
- The issue of children's rights must be taken into account when children are the subject of the study.
- Confidentiality can be hard to maintain over time.

Cross-cultural ways of studying children

Mary Ainsworth's work, which is explained in the Content section of this chapter, takes a cross-cultural approach to understanding child psychology. Her research procedures are used in different cultures to draw conclusions about varying cultural practices. Other researchers have used her method as well, and have continued to compare different cultures. **Cross-cultural** approaches refer to when something is carried out in different cultures and then comparisons are drawn.

Although your course requires you to study a set procedure for comparing different cultures (the 'strange situation'), some cross-cultural studies are ethnographic.

> **Explore** Research some ethnographic studies and read about practices in different cultures. If possible, find out about childcare practices so that you have an example of how cross-cultural studies are used. One example is the Mundurucú culture from South America and a study carried out by Yolanda and Robert Murphy.

Ethnography links with anthropology and means using different research methods, with researchers immersing themselves in a different culture to learn about it thoroughly. Comparisons can be made between such in-depth studies to look at similarities and differences between cultures.

Nature–nurture issues

There is a nature–nurture issue when drawing conclusions from cross-cultural studies. If the same procedures are used in different cultures and the same results are found, then this suggests that what is found is due to nature, is biological and is a universal law. If different results are found, then it seems that what is found is because of nurture and comes from different cultural practices.

For example, it could be claimed that children who do not form attachments at a young age find it hard to form adult relationships. If this is the case no matter what the culture, then it might be concluded that strong attachments at a young age are the building blocks of firm adult relationships, and that this is a universal law of behaviour. Bowlby considered issues like this, and his work is explained in the Content section in this chapter.

> **Study hint** The nature–nurture debate is an important part of Unit 4 when you look at issues and debates, and is also a useful area of discussion when evaluating studies and research methods.

Evaluating cross-cultural procedures

Strengths

In cross-cultural studies where the procedures are kept the same, any differences in behaviour should be because of the cultural differences (nurture) and any similarities in behaviour should be because of natural similarities (nature). There is likely to be reliability as well, because the procedures are carefully documented so that they can be repeated in the different cultures. For ethnographic cross-cultural studies, the strengths are the same as for case studies.

Weaknesses

There are problems when using the same procedures in different cultures, because the way a procedure is understood is part of the findings and it might differ between cultures. If the understanding of what is required in the study causes differences in findings, then this means that such differences are because of the study rather than because of either nature or nurture, and the validity of the findings is questioned. If standard procedures are set up to compare behaviour in different cultures, then they are not likely to be valid because, by being standardised and by behaviour being made measurable, it is likely that such behaviour is not then 'real life'. Ethnographic cross-cultural studies have the same weaknesses as case studies, in that they are hard to generalise from and difficult to repeat.

Table 2.5	Summary of the strengths and weaknesses of cross-cultural procedures	
	Strengths	**Weaknesses**
	<ul><li>Cross-cultural procedures are a main way of studying nature and nurture issues</li><li>There is likely to be reliability when procedures are carefully controlled, so they can be repeated</li><li>Ethnographic cross-cultural studies are valid and in depth</li></ul>	<ul><li>There is a lack of validity in transferring a procedure from one culture to another, as there are likely to be different understandings of what the procedure is and how to react to it</li><li>There is a lack of validity in setting up a procedure that is controlled enough to be repeated in different cultures</li><li>If case studies and ethnographic methods are used, they are likely to be more valid, but they might be hard to compare and to generalise from</li></ul>

Longitudinal ways of studying children

AS link Review your AS material and your understanding of longitudinal ways of carrying out research, which were covered in the psychodynamic approach (pp. 183–85). Consider both description and evaluation.

A study that looks at participants over a length of time, documenting changes over that period, is known as a **longitudinal study**. As with cross-cultural studies, longitudinal studies can involve using the same procedures but over time to measure changes, or they can involve a more ethnographic or case study approach to gather data.

There are quite a few well-known longitudinal studies of children, in which children born at a certain time were thoroughly researched over a long period to document changes. These include Growing up in Australia; a study in Bristol called the Avon Longitudinal Study of Children and Parents; and the Early Childhood Longitudinal Program in the USA. These are often government-funded programmes, and many studies then draw their data from these large programmes. The Longitudinal Studies Centre at Essex University was established in 1999. The Effective Provision of Pre-school Education (EPPE) project in the UK and the National Institute of Child Health and Human Development (NICHD) study in the USA are both longitudinal studies looking at daycare, and these are described in the Contents section of this chapter.

Explore Investigate the work of the Longitudinal Studies Centre at Essex University.

There are also individual psychological studies that are longitudinal. One such study is that of Genie, which lasted a number of years.

Evaluation of longitudinal ways of studying children

Strengths

Longitudinal studies compare the same people over a period of time, which means controlling participant variables such as gender, temperament and IQ. They are a good way of studying development because, if the procedures are controlled, only the age changes, so cause-and-effect conclusions can more easily be drawn than if different people are used.

Even though the same people are used in the study, there will be many factors affecting the individuals' development, making it hard to draw conclusions about one feature that might cause any changes. There is often quite a high drop-out rate as people move away or no longer wish to take part. Those who do not drop out may have something in common that makes them a biased sample, such as having the same sort of family or being more confident about taking part.

Table 2.6 *Summary of the strengths and weaknesses of longitudinal ways of studying children*

Strengths	Weaknesses
• Uses the same people, so there is good control over participant variables • Only age changes, so strong conclusions can be drawn about how people develop over time	• Many factors change over time as well as age, so picking out particular cause-and-effect conclusions is difficult • The likely high drop-out rate can lead to a biased sample

Practice 2.1

Decide whether the following studies are examples of a case study, a longitudinal study, a cross-cultural study, a structured observation, a naturalistic observation or an ethnographic study.

1 Children's behaviour in the playground was watched by two observers, tallying behaviour according to whether it was aggressive or not.

2 A culture in Africa was studied by someone who lived with them for a year and made detailed notes from many different activities and sources.

3 A child who had not had the chance of forming attachments until the age of 3 was studied in depth at the age of 8 to see what her patterns of friendships and relationships were like.

4 A task involving play materials was carried out in three different countries to see whether young children understood someone else's point of view, in order to discover if the findings were the same in each country.

5 Ten children from 6 months to 6 years were studied by observing them and interviewing their parents, to see how their language patterns developed.

(Answers are at the end of Chapter 2)

Examination-style questions

1 Explain what is meant by longitudinal research and include an example to illustrate your answer. *(4 marks)*

2 Outline two ethical issues that have to be addressed when studying children. *(4 marks)*

3 Describe naturalistic observation as a research method in psychology. *(4 marks)*

4 Evaluate case studies as a research method in psychology, in terms of validity and reliability. *(6 marks)*

5 Explain what is meant by cross-cultural research and outline one reason why such research may be carried out in child psychology. *(4 marks)*

Unit 3

2

Extension questions

1 Compare naturalistic and structured observations, including their strengths and weaknesses. *(12 marks)*

2 Using examples, explain how both case studies and observations have been carried out in child psychology. *(12 marks)*

Content

You need to know about both Bowlby's and Ainsworth's conclusions about attachments, including the maternal deprivation hypothesis and the effects of child-rearing styles. Research into privation is covered, as well as looking at one developmental disorder. Daycare is also studied.

AS link Note that you might be asked to draw on AS material for both the Methodology and Content sections of this chapter.

Bowlby's theory of attachment

John Bowlby (1907–90) was a psychoanalyst who followed the ideas of Freud. He thought that an infant was strongly affected by the first few years of his or her life. Bowlby's family was upper-middle class and he saw little of his own mother during the day, when he was looked after by a nanny. He was sent to boarding school at the age of 7. These experiences may have affected his views on the importance of attachments in early life. By **attachment**, Bowlby meant that an infant should have a warm, continuous loving relationship with one person. Attachment is a two-way process, as the mother will also attach to the child.

Psychodynamic roots

Bowlby studied medicine and then psychoanalysis and he worked with maladjusted and delinquent children. His interest in such children led to the formation of his theories on the importance of early attachment for later development. Where psychodynamic theory suggests that relationship problems can arise from fantasies about relationships with parents, Bowlby thought that real relationships with parents could be the cause of later problems, which meant that he moved away from his psychodynamic roots. However, he used psychodynamic ideas: for example, he thought that the child's mother or main caregiver acted both as ego and superego, before these could develop.

AS link Review what you know about the psychodynamic approach, including the first 5 years in the development of a child's personality and the role of the ego and superego.

Bowlby's work with deprived and disturbed children led to the World Health Organization asking him to write a report on the effect of homelessness on the mental health of children in Europe following the Second World War. Bowlby considered the evidence at the time and published *Maternal Care and Mental Health* in 1951, in which he stated that a strong attachment with the mother (or permanent mother figure) was necessary for the good mental health of the child. This led to changes in policy and practice in institutions. For example, there were alterations in visiting procedures in hospitals to allow parental visits.

However, Bowlby later stated that there was little evidence at the time and not much theory from which to draw conclusions, so from 1969 he worked again on his ideas about the importance of attachments and further developed his theory.

> 'Mother love in infancy and childhood is as important for mental health as are vitamins and proteins for physical health.' (Bowlby, 1953)

An evolutionary basis to attachment

Bowlby considered many other theories in addition to psychodynamic ideas, including the work of Konrad Lorenz (1952) and others, who were using ethological studies. **Ethology** is the study of animals in their natural setting. Lorenz had noticed that animals such as ducks and geese, when hatched, followed the first moving object they saw, which was usually the mother. By following their mother (called **imprinting**), such animals would be more likely to survive.

Bowlby thought that human infants might have a similar 'attachment' instinct that would ensure survival, so he put forward the idea of the evolutionary basis of attachment. **Evolution theory** holds that any behaviour or characteristic that aids survival will mean that an organism survives to reproduce its genes, so a behaviour or characteristic will be passed on through genes. Any behaviour that goes against survival means that an organism will not survive to reproduce its genes and that behaviour will die out. This is survival of the fittest.

Study hint You will have come across evolution theory in other areas of your studies, so draw on what you have learned to help your understanding of Bowlby's idea that there is an evolutionary basis to an infant's attachment to its mother or mother-figure.

Bowlby's theory agreed with evolution theory because he thought that babies came into the world with an innate tendency to attach and bond to a main carer that would enable their survival. He maintained that infants are biologically programmed to form attachments. Separation, insecurity or fear would trigger the instinct to turn to the attachment figure. Crying and smiling are instincts to keep a baby close to its mother and the mother too has an instinct to form an attachment with the baby.

The theory

Bowlby suggested that children deprived of their mother — their attachment figure — would have problems later in life. He acknowledged that the bond could be with a main attachment figure, not necessarily the natural mother. Bowlby referred to **monotropy**, which means a warm and loving relationship with one person.

2

He thought that this first main attachment was different from any other attachment. Bowlby thought that social, emotional and intellectual development would be adversely affected if the mother–child bond was broken early in life — this is the **maternal deprivation hypothesis**. Bowlby believed such problems in adulthood are permanent and irreversible, meaning that once there are problems, nothing can be done about them.

The main features of Bowlby's theory of attachment are:

■ A child has an innate need to form an attachment with one person. This special attaching to one person is called monotropy.

■ This strong relationship with one person should continue unbroken for the first 2 years of life if adverse effects are to be avoided.

■ The maternal deprivation hypothesis holds that a broken attachment (or lack of an attachment) leads to problems for the child with relationships on reaching adulthood.

■ Broken attachment leads to delinquency and affectionless psychopathy.

■ Attachment provides a safe haven for when the child is afraid and a secure base from which to explore the world.

■ Separation distress/anxiety serves to draw the attachment figure back to the infant and is a survival mechanism.

Maternal deprivation means having an attachment broken through separation, and the first 2 years of life are very important. By 'deprivation', Bowlby seems to have intended both not having formed an attachment in the first place and having an attachment broken through separation. He was criticised for not separating deprivation (having an attachment broken) from privation (not having formed an attachment at all). Issues about privation are dealt with later in this section of the chapter (pp. 83–86).

Attachment includes features such as providing a **safe haven** when the child is afraid. He or she can return to the attachment figure/caregiver for comfort. There is also a **secure base** provided by the attachment figure so that the infant can explore. By keeping the infant close, the attachment also protects the child. Another mechanism is that, when separated from the attachment figure, the child will seek them out for comfort and show distress and **separation anxiety**, which has the effect of drawing the attachment figure back to the infant — a useful survival mechanism.

Bowlby's focus on loss

Deprivation and separation from a main attachment figure is all about loss. The idea of loss in early childhood connecting to later emotional ill health links back to the psychodynamic approach, within which Bowlby was working. **Object relations theory** developed within the psychodynamic approach and focuses on the way infants learn from their own relationships about how such relationships work, and from which they develop **internal working models**. Their later relationships are based on these models.

Object relations theory, which is linked with theorists such as Melanie Klein, focuses on fantasy relationships as much as real relationships, but Bowlby talked specifically about real relationships. Bowlby believed that infants build internal working models for relationships from their experience of attachments. Their internal working model would be about loss if they experienced separation or lack of a warm, loving relationship that characterises a strong attachment. People use their internal working models when interacting with others in life.

There is evidence for early experience of loss affecting later experiences, and one study you might cover in Unit 4 considers this issue. Brown and Harris (1978) found that girls who had lost their mothers before the age of about 12 years were more likely to be depressed as adults.

Defining deprivation and separation

Deprivation refers to an infant having the attachment with its main caregiver broken, either for a short or a long time. **Separation** refers to when an infant is no longer with its main caregiver for some reason, again either short-term or long-term. Therefore, separation leads to deprivation. Divorce or the death of one or both parents leads to long-term separation. There is also short-term separation, for example when a parent goes into hospital or is away for some reason.

Evidence for the importance of attachments

Bowlby provided evidence for his theory by carrying out a study of 44 juvenile thieves. This study is explained in detail in the next section of this chapter. Bowlby found that young people who had experienced separation from their mothers were more likely to have problems later in life. Bowlby also drew on evidence from others, including Harlow.

Harlow's study of monkeys and attachments

Harlow and his colleagues studied rhesus monkeys. In one well-known study (Harlow and Zimmerman, 1959), infant monkeys who had been removed from their mothers were the focus of study. One set of infants was allowed access to a towel-covered wire 'monkey' as well as a food-giving wire 'monkey'. Other monkeys could access only the food-giving wire 'monkey'. Those monkeys who could get comfort from the towel-covered monkey did so, and at the end of the study they were better adjusted physically and mentally. Harlow concluded that such comfort was important for the developing monkey and that it is not food alone that connects mother and infant. His research linked to the idea that attachment was part of the mother–infant relationship for monkeys. Bowlby used this as evidence that this was true for human children as well.

Evaluation

Strengths

■ Harlow filmed the studies and it is clear that the monkeys rushed to the towelling 'mother' when they were frightened or startled. There is validity to the findings, as there is 'real life' in the situations set up — it is clear that the monkeys really were frightened.

■ Harlow used monkeys, which are close to humans in their genes (chimps share 98% or more of their genes with humans), so there can be generalisation from infant monkeys to human babies, to an extent.

- Schaffer and Emerson (1964) found that young children formed multiple attachments rather than one single attachment. A baby tended to form an attachment to the mother, father, brothers, sisters, grandparents and others. This is evidence that attachment is not just about who feeds the child, as was thought by some theorists. Harlow also found that monkeys 'attached' to a 'mother' who did not feed them, so Schaffer and Emerson's findings support Harlow's findings.

Weaknesses

- Animals are not the same as humans, so generalising behaviour of monkeys to say it is true of human babies as well might not be legitimate.
- Ethically, Harlow's work has been questioned, as the monkeys were often frightened. Other studies have looked at whether monkeys without an early attachment figure make good mothers themselves, and they do not. Animals should be distressed as little as possible, whereas Harlow's work affected quite a few monkeys (those in the initial study and their offspring, who were deprived of good mothering).

Robertson's naturalistic observations

In 1948 Bowlby employed James Robertson to make careful observations of children in hospital or institutions. Robertson had worked with Anna Freud, Sigmund Freud's daughter, in her residential children's home. People working at this home were told to make detailed notes about the children's behaviour, so Robertson was well trained in observation. He was much affected by the distress of the children he observed and made a film called *A Two-Year-Old Goes to Hospital* (1953). The film showed Laura, aged 2, who was in hospital for 8 days for an operation. Bowlby realised that this film was going to be important evidence that young children suffer enormously without their attachment figure near, so the sampling of the child was random and a clock showed the real time of the filming.

Robertson's film and observations showed that children deprived of their attachment figure went through three stages. First, there was protest, and the child cried. At this stage a child also showed anger and fear, and Bowlby thought that this might be a survival instinct — loud protest to attract the attention of the caregiver. Then there was despair, when crying became even more urgent. Finally there was detachment, where — on the face of it — the child adjusted, as he or she stopped protesting and gave up on crying.

This final stage links with Spitz's claim that the child was severely depressed, and this claim is explained below. (Bowlby noticed that widows and widowers showed the same three phases in the face of their loss — protest, despair and detachment — and he went on to write about this type of grieving.) There were controls when making the film, to give scientific value to this evidence. The film led to great changes in procedures in hospitals. Robertson's graphic visual evidence further convinced Bowlby and his team of the importance of early attachments. Mary Ainsworth was part of the team involved in this study, and they were joined later by Rudolf Schaffer. The work of Ainsworth and Schaffer is explained later in this section.

Table 2.7	London hospital visiting times when Robertson was carrying out his observations	
Hospital	**Visiting times**	
Guy's Hospital	Sundays 2–4 p.m.	
Westminster Hospital	Wednesdays and Sundays, 2–3 p.m.	
Charing Cross Hospital	Sundays 3–4 p.m.	
St Bartholomew's	Sundays 2–3.30 p.m.	
St Thomas's	No visits for the first month, but parents could see children asleep between 7 and 8 p.m.	

This mother and baby are communicating with each other and an attachment is formed.

TopFoto

Evaluating Robertson's research

Strengths

■ Naturalistic observations such as those of Robertson produce valid data, because they involve real situations, such as a real child who is separated from his or her attachment figure.

■ Robertson made other films of children and found similar responses (protest, despair, detachment), so there was a form of replication and similar data were found.

Weaknesses

■ Robertson used naturalistic observation, with its related problem of reliability: since the actual situation will not be repeated, the observation cannot be replicated.

■ It is hard to generalise from naturalistic observations, because the observation is of one unique individual. Laura, in the first film, is one child who will have had unique experiences with her attachment figure and family. Another child will have had different experiences and so might react differently.

Spitz's study of children in institutions

When Bowlby worked on the World Health Organization report he researched studies at the time in the area of attachments, including the work of René Spitz, who had studied institutionalised children (1946). A hospital, prison, orphanage or residential home is an **institution** and, when children live in such a place, they are called 'institutionalised'.

Spitz studied children in hospitals and he found that children deprived of their attachment figure became depressed. If an infant had formed an attachment with his or her mother for the first 6 months of life, development was good. However, if that attachment was broken (such as by a child going into hospital), then over a 3-month period of being deprived of the attachment figure the child became increasingly depressed. At first the depression was partial but after a short time it became severe, which he called **hospitalism**. Partial depression meant the child would cry and cling to observers, but after about 3 months, the child's condition would get worse and he or she would move into severe depression.

Children still in the partially depressed stage when reunited with their mothers would readjust after about 2 or 3 months. Children still in hospital when they were severely depressed experienced weight-loss, insomnia, illness and a lack of emotion displayed in their faces. These children would not make the attempt to move and refused to interact with their carers, who were caring for their physical but not their emotional needs. As the years went by it was discovered that if these children remained in an institution then some even died.

Spitz found that separation and being deprived of the main caregiver had extreme consequences for a child. He went further, however, by suggesting that the lack of stimulation in an institution, where children lay in cots with no stimulation around them, was also to blame for their decline. Bowlby drew on this evidence of depression for his maternal deprivation theory.

Evaluation of Spitz's studies

Strengths

- As with Robertson's work, Spitz studied real children in real institutions so the data were ecologically valid — the situation and setting were real.
- His work continued over a long period and he continued to find that deprived children had a lower IQ and problems with development. When he introduced more care for the children they had fewer problems, so the depth of his work adds to the validity of the findings.

Weaknesses

- Spitz did not carry out experiments with controls and careful sampling. He used observations, testing (e.g. Intelligence Quotient (IQ) and Development Quotient (DQ), see p.76) and interviewing, so his sampling and observations were possibly biased, as there were no controls. He may have noted situations where separation led to problems and low IQ, rather than all situations.

- Measurement of both DQ and IQ is difficult, as it means applying standardised measures that are criticised, for example, with regard to cultural differences. IQ in particular is based on Western ideas and cultural attitudes, so someone who was not aware of such ideas and attitudes might do less well on such tests.

Goldfarb's study of children in institutions

Goldfarb (1955) studied 15 children who had stayed in an institution up to the age of about 3 before being fostered. He compared them with a group of children who had been fostered from about 6 months of age. The aim was to see if later fostering would be successful. He found that those who were adopted later showed problems in adolescence more than those who were fostered early. Those who were fostered later were emotionally less secure, intellectually behind the other group and were less mature. Goldfarb concluded that babies should not be put into institutions and he thought early deprivation would lead to later problems. Bowlby used this as evidence for his maternal deprivation hypothesis.

Evaluation of Goldfarb's study
Strengths
- His work has validity because it concerns real children who were in the institution and fostered at certain periods.
- He managed to find a control group of children who were fostered early to use as a baseline measure for developmental achievements, against which he could measure his 'late fostered' group of children.

Weaknesses
- It is possible that the early fostered group had something in common, such as personality or physical looks, which made them more likely to be chosen for fostering, so the sample of later fostered children might have been biased.
- There are so many different aspects of fostering, with many different experiences for a fostered child, that it is hard to draw the conclusion that it was the early or late fostering that 'caused' any differences in development, particularly in a group of only 15 children.

Lorenz's findings about imprinting

Ethological studies like that of Lorenz (1952), which showed how animals use imprinting as a survival mechanism, suggested to Bowlby that the attachment process in humans had the same purpose and is important for an infant's development.

Evaluation of Lorenz's findings
Strengths
- Lorenz used ethology and studied animals in their natural surroundings, so his findings are likely to have ecological validity. These were not experiments in an unnatural situation like a laboratory.

- There were experiments carried out later that replicated Lorenz's findings. One study used a yellow rubber glove as the first moving object ducklings saw, and they duly imprinted onto the glove.

Weaknesses

- It is not easy to establish that findings from animals can be said to be true of humans, as there are differences between animals and humans, such as use of language and problem-solving abilities.
- Only certain animals show imprinting — precocial animals that can move as soon as they are born — so the findings might be specific to these sorts of animal, not to humans or other animals.

How negative effects of deprivation and separation can be reduced

From the evidence it is clear that the negative effects of deprivation can be reduced by avoiding separation from the main caregiver, though this is probably not a helpful suggestion because separation is not always a matter of choice. If avoiding separation is impossible then, according to both Spitz and Robertson, reducing the length of the separation can be useful. Again, this is not really a helpful solution in many cases. In cases of the death of the caregiver or unavoidable separation, it is not possible to pick the attachment back up again, so neither of these two actions would work.

Link to the key issues and practical

Note that you can use the issue of how negative effects of deprivation can be alleviated as the key issue that you are required to cover in your study of child psychology, and for the related practical.

Easing short-term separation with a replacement attachment figure

James Robertson and his wife Joyce, who was a social worker who also worked with Anna Freud, became involved with what Robertson had witnessed in hospitals. They followed and filmed four different children whose mothers were going into hospital. One child was John (just under 18 months old), who stayed in a residential nursery and tried to get comfort from those working at the nursery, but did not succeed as they had little time to give. John became increasingly distressed and his father could not comfort him. When his mother returned, John rejected her.

Jane was a child of the same age as John, but this time Joyce Robertson fostered the child while the mother was in hospital. The Robertsons met the mother and father with the child before the separation took place. The child was provided with items to remind her of home, as something familiar during the separation. Mealtime routines were kept the same and Jane's father visited. When reunited with her mother, Jane happily accepted her.

Two other children, Thomas and Lucy, also had foster care during the separation from their mother. They settled better, were less distressed, and accepted the mother when reunited with her. The Robertsons concluded that replacing the attachment bond could work. In fact, they observed that the children found it hard to part from the new attachment figure in their lives.

Providing more individual care and stimulation

Some studies in orphanages showed that improvements could be made if there was someone provided to support the children (Skodak and Skeels, 1945) or if there was more stimulation. Improvements in IQ were found if there was more stimulation or a lower child to carer ratio. We return to this idea when the effects of daycare are discussed later in this section. It also seems from the evidence that the earlier the intervention the better (e.g. Goldfarb). The effects of institutionalisation seem to be able to be overcome — they are reversible — but only if additional care and more stimulation are introduced. Success also depends on the age of the child and how long the deprivation lasts.

Coping with divorce and separation

The above ideas are used when advising parents on how to cope with separation through divorce and other similar situations. A young child is likely to go through the stages of protest, distress and despair, unless steps are taken to ensure an attachment figure is there for them and that routines and familiar situations are maintained as far as possible. Older children can understand more, so decisions can be discussed with and explained to them, to minimise anger and distress.

The 'fight or flight' response is a survival trait that prepares someone for action when needed, and such a response can be triggered in young children when they are faced with a threat such as the departure of someone they rely on. Bowlby thought that the attachment process had an evolutionary basis and, in times of fear and threat, a young child would turn to his/her attachment figure. If fear and threat are reduced by offering explanations and comfort, problems from separation can be reduced.

Explore Look up current advice given to parents with regard to preparing for separation, and note down how findings from research such as that of Bowlby and the Robertsons have informed such advice.

Evaluation of Bowlby's ideas

Bowlby's ideas, and the studies that he drew on, have been criticised.

Strengths of Bowlby's theory of attachment

Bowlby drew on a great deal of evidence, which was a strength of his theory. He read up on studies by such psychologists as Spitz and Goldfarb, as has been shown.

For his first report (the one to the World Health Organization), he admitted there was not that much evidence, but after that he continued to gather theory and evidence from a wide variety of studies.

He also drew on many different theoretical areas, such as ethology and evolution theory in his explanation of the maternal deprivation hypothesis. He explored his psychodynamic background and he brought in ideas from child development, such as conclusions about the effects of separation on DQ and IQ (through Spitz, Goldfarb and others). DQ is **Development Quotient**, which is a score that comes from observing physical and mental milestones in young children. IQ is **Intelligence Quotient**, which is a score that comes from written tests that children complete when they are old enough to be able to do so.

Bowlby also commissioned and supervised the work of others, such as James Robertson's observations of children in hospital. A strength of his theory is the amount of evidence he amassed from many different sources, including his own, using naturalistic observation, ethology and interviews.

Bowlby's work led to changes in hospital visiting policies as well as in institutional practices. Hospitals opened up to parents and institutions recognised the need for a replacement attachment figure, such as a named worker for a child. The need for stimulation was recognised, as was the need to plan for a period of separation.

Weaknesses of Bowlby's theory of attachment

The observational studies in institutions lacked careful procedures. Neither Spitz nor Goldfarb gave great detail about their research methods when gathering evidence, so their procedures could have been biased. For example, the group in Goldfarb's study who were fostered early might have been chosen for a reason, such as seeming more settled or placid. The 15 who were fostered after the age of 3 might have had something in common (unattractiveness?), which means the sample was biased. Spitz's observations did not involve a controlled sample either.

Animal studies may not be generalisable to humans. Harlow and his colleagues studied monkeys and found they ran to towelling-covered 'mothers' when they were stressed. From this he drew the conclusion that monkeys needed comfort as well as food, and Bowlby surmised that this was true of human babies as well. However, drawing conclusions from monkeys and saying they are true of humans might not be possible, because animals and humans have differences in brain structures as well as in other abilities such as problem-solving and use of language.

Bowlby's own study of 44 juvenile thieves can be criticised. (The study is explained in the section that follows.) For example, he used a control group as well as the thieves, but he himself said that it was a pity that this control group also consisted of children in an institution, when children in a 'normal' school may have been a better control group.

Table 2.8	Summary of the strengths and weaknesses of Bowlby's theory of attachment	
Strengths	**Weaknesses**
• Bowlby drew on many studies and their findings • He drew on many different theoretical perspectives • He used or drew on many different research methods • His theory had clear practical application and was acted upon	• He used evidence from animals, such as Harlow's and Lorenz's work, and it might not be legitimate to generalise from animals to humans • Some of the studies whose findings he used did not use well-documented or well-controlled studies • His own study of 44 juvenile thieves, for example, lacked a 'normal' control group

Ainsworth's work on attachments

Mary Ainsworth worked with John Bowlby, extending his ideas by looking at different types of attachment, as well as considering issues such as sensitive parenting. Ainsworth was Canadian but came to England with her husband. She had already been researching in the area of attachments before starting work with Bowlby.

Ugandan studies

Ainsworth left London in 1954 to live in Uganda where she studied mother–child interactions. She noticed that there was a relationship between the **responsiveness** of the mother and the reactions of the child. Some mother–child interactions were secure and comfortable but others were tense and full of conflict. She found that the type of interaction was related to how responsive the parent was to the child's needs. She also noted that infants used their mothers as a **safe/secure base** from which to explore.

The strange situation test

Following her observations in Uganda, Ainsworth developed her own research methodology to study types of attachment between mothers and their babies. This was much later, in 1978. She used a structured observation and set up a test using standard procedures, so that each mother and child had the same experiences and a child's responses could be carefully recorded for comparison. Her procedure is called the **strange situation**, because the significant period is after children are put into a situation that is strange for them, and when they are experiencing separation from their mother (or main caregiver). Observers carefully recorded the child's response to the mother when she returned.

As explained earlier in this section, Harlow found that a monkey put into a stressful and fearful situation would cling to a towelling 'monkey', seemingly to get comfort. Therefore, an attached child is expected, after the stressful and fearful situation of being alone with a stranger, to cling to the mother for comfort. These are the issues Ainsworth was researching.

2

One version of the strange situation has eight parts, as shown in Table 2.9. The reunions are the important times and the focus is on how the young baby responds to its mother when she returns. Steps 5 and 8 are the times when the baby's reaction to the mother is carefully noted and, from its reaction, the baby is classified into one of three attachment types. Each step ideally lasts for 3 minutes. However, the mother is in control and can shorten the step or stop the procedure at any time.

Attachment types

Ainsworth and her colleagues reported that three attachment types were found from the strange situation procedure (although later another one was added). The three original attachment types are securely attached, anxious avoidant and anxious resistant.

Securely attached

Ainsworth called **securely attached** the children who were distressed when their mother left and wanted comfort from her when she returned. Ainsworth thought that a securely attached child would use his or her mother as a safe base and would also show separation anxiety when the mother left. So she was expecting distress when the mother left and for the child to seek comfort on the mother's return. This type of attachment is linked to a responsive mother who attends to the child's needs. In Ainsworth's study in the USA in 1978 around 70% of infants were securely attached.

Anxious avoidant

Anxious avoidant was the label given to children who were not distressed when the mother left and tended to avoid her when she came back. Anxious avoidant can be called avoidant insecure. It could be that the mother is neglectful or abusive and that the child has learned not to depend on her, and so is equally happy with the stranger as with the mother. However, other studies have given different (less negative) interpretations, such as coming from different parental expectations. In Ainsworth's study in Baltimore (1978) around 15% of the sample of 26 families had babies who were anxious avoidant.

Anxious resistant

Children were called **anxious resistant** when they stayed close to their mother rather than exploring, and became extremely distressed when she left. They went

Table 2.9	*A version of the strange situation, involving eight steps*

1 The parent and baby enter the room, which is in a laboratory but set up with toys and chairs to be comfortable for the participants.

2 The parent does not interact with the baby, who is left to explore.

3 The stranger goes into the room, talks to the parent, then approaches the baby. At this stage the parent quietly leaves the room.

4 This is the first separation. The stranger tries to interact with the baby.

5 The parent comes in and comforts the baby, then leaves again. This is the first reunion followed by the second separation.

6 The stranger leaves the infant alone.

7 The stranger enters the room and begins to interact with the baby again. The mother is still out of the room. The second separation continues.

8 The parent comes in, greets and picks up the baby, while the stranger quietly leaves. This is the second reunion.

for comfort when she came back but then rejected her comforting. Anxious resistant can also be called ambivalent insecure. There were not many anxious resistant children found in the USA sample that Ainsworth tested — only around 15%. It is not a common attachment type in the USA. It is suggested that the mother of a child showing this attachment type is someone the child cannot rely on all the time, and so is not sure about her. There may be cultural or other reasons for differences in attachment type.

A fourth type after Ainsworth: disorganised and disorientated

In 1986 Main and Solomon suggested that there is a fourth attachment type — disorganised and disorientated. This type of attachment is characterised by the child both approaching the mother on her return and avoiding her.

Links between attachment types and mothering styles

Ainsworth, along with colleagues such as Ainsworth and Bell (1969), looked at the type of mothering that might produce a certain attachment type in a child. They observed the children they used in the strange situation before that procedure was carried out. The observation was for 3 months and they were able to draw conclusions about the responsiveness of the mothering. For example, a mother who was insensitive to her infant's responses during feeding and to the infant's physical needs, who showed little face-to-face interaction and was less attentive when the child was distressed did not have an infant who was securely attached in the strange situation procedure — the child was likely to be insecurely attached. Mothers who had responded to their infant's needs in the first 3 months of their life, and who were sensitive to their child's demands, had securely attached children.

Insecure avoidant (anxious avoidant) children in Ainsworth's study were called Group A and securely attached children were known as Group B. Insecure ambivalent (anxious resistant) children were called Group C — they seemed both to welcome the mother back at first and then to push her away. Children who were insecure in their attachment had mothers who tended to push them away more and who were less sensitive to their needs.

Using the strange situation in cross-cultural studies

Cross-cultural studies are those carried out in more than one culture in order to compare findings. Ainsworth, for example, used the strange situation in Uganda and another study used children from Baltimore in the USA; the findings were then compared.

Ainsworth's work in Uganda

In Uganda around 1963, Ainsworth studied 26 families and observed the interactions, watching mother–child relationships. She also interviewed the mothers and gathered data about the mother's sensitivity. She found that mothers who knew a lot about their babies when interviewed were sensitive to their infant's needs.

They tended to have children who were what Ainsworth called securely attached, in that they did not cry much and used their mother as a secure base from which to explore. In contrast, less sensitive mothers had children who cried more and did not explore as much.

Ainsworth's work on the Baltimore project

In Baltimore, also around 1963, 26 families were observed, following each family from birth of the child through the first year. Naturalistic observations were used, looking at such issues as face-to-face interaction, responsiveness to crying and physical needs, feeding and close bodily contact. The observations took place in the family home, but the final observation involved the mother and child going to a laboratory to take part in the strange situation procedure, which was devised for that purpose. The main focus of the study was the pattern of interactions in the home and conclusions about the sensitivity of the mother related to the attachment type of the child. Most of the focus, however, was on the results from the strange situation procedure, tending to overshadow the evidence about the mother's responsiveness.

Comparing Uganda and Baltimore

There were many similarities in the attachment types and types of mothering in the two cultures. The general conclusion was that securely attached infants used their mothers as a secure base from which to explore and had sensitive mothers, whereas insecurely attached infants cried more, explored less and had less sensitive mothers. If this was found in two different cultures, perhaps there was a biological basis for such attachment types when linked to parenting style and maybe this was true of all cultures. If there were differences in attachment types linked to parenting styles in different cultures, then the links may have came from nurture and the differences in environment.

Study hint Cross-cultural studies are ways of looking at the nature–nurture debate. This is a strength of such studies, so you can use this comment in evaluation. Unit 4 includes coverage of the nature–nurture debate in more detail.

Other cross-cultural studies of attachment types

In Germany, in a study by Grossman et al. in 1985 that used the strange situation, more avoidant attachment types were found than in the Baltimore study. In Japan and Israel (in the Kibbutzim) there are more ambivalent types. The Israeli study was carried out by Sagi et al. (1985) and the Japanese study by Miyake et al. (1985).

A newer cross-cultural study can be found on the internet, carried out by Jin Mi Kyoung in Korea in 2005. In this study, which is reported from the University of Texas, 87 Korean families and 113 USA families were studied using the strange situation to look for cultural differences in attachment types. There were a greater number of securely attached infants, which reinforces the idea that attachment types are found in similar proportions across cultures and countries. (This is generally reported to be the case, in spite of the differences found in Germany, Israel and Japan, as reported above.) When comparing the Eastern and Western cultures, there were some differences in the behaviours of the securely attached children. For example, the Korean infants stayed less close to their mothers and explored more. When the Korean mothers returned to their infants, they were more likely to get down on the floor and play with their infants straightaway, and to stay there.

Study hint Use these studies as examples of cross-cultural research when answering questions about this research method.

Evaluating the cross-cultural studies

It was at first thought that there were more avoidant children in Germany because of a lack of responsiveness on the part of the parents. However, it was then suggested that it might be because parents valued independence more, making it more a matter of cultural features of parenting style.

In Japan and in Israel in the Kibbutzim it was suggested that there was less emphasis on getting on with strangers, so children were less used to other people and therefore more ambivalent when tested using the strange situation. What was thought to be a matter of difference in sensitivity of mothering was later thought to be because of a different cultural emphasis. The strange situation was perhaps more suitable for testing certain cultures — those that emphasised sensitive mothering in the same way as in the UK and the USA.

However, further examination of the findings of the studies suggest that, in fact, similar responses by the mothers led to similar attachment types, so it is now thought that the findings from the different cultures support each other more than was at first thought. The issue of whether the strange situation is suitable for use across different cultures is still being debated.

Strengths of the cross-cultural studies using the strange situation task

- The same procedure was used in the different cultures so, in theory, conclusions from each study can be compared with one another fairly. This gives the findings reliability in that the same procedures were used.
- There did seem to be consistency in the patterns observed — for example, the three types were identified in each of the studies.
- In general the main attachment type is securely attached and, when a different attachment type is found to predominate, this tends to be explicable by looking at cultural preferences regarding acceptable behaviour, rather than by 'bad' mothering.

Weaknesses of the cross-cultural studies using the strange situation task

- By using a procedure developed in the USA in cultures as different as Germany, Japan and Israel, it might be that the task itself gives differences in findings as much as differences in sensitivity of the mothers. For example, Japanese children who are less used to strangers than American children might be more fearful and so respond differently, rather than have a different attachment type.
- Cultures have many differences, including family structure, parenting styles, what is expected, and how children are seen in a society. With so many different

factors involved it is hard, if not impossible, to draw conclusions about which feature causes which effect. Where there are such complex issues, measuring them equally and fairly to allow comparisons is difficult, if not impossible.

Evaluation of Ainsworth's ideas about attachments

Strengths

- Like Bowlby, Ainsworth worked in the field of attachment and the effects of separation for many years, so she was able to draw on a wealth of data for her conclusions. She carried out many studies, and others used her strange situation procedure and drew similar conclusions.
- Ainsworth devised a well-controlled procedure for measuring attachment types, which was carried out in a laboratory and observed by many people. Therefore, inter-observer reliability could be found, and the procedure does seem to be reliable, because the same attachment types are found in different studies.
- Ainsworth could be criticised for using a procedure that was controlled and laboratory-based, but she also used naturalistic observation and interviews to make her findings valid and true to life.

Weaknesses

- A problem with the strange situation is that it is a laboratory procedure using an unnatural environment, so it could be the unnatural environment that causes the reactions of the infant to the mother, rather than (or as well as) being left alone with a stranger. This means there is a problem with validity.
- It could be argued that, if a fourth attachment type had to be added, then Ainsworth's conclusions were not complete, which is a weakness.
- If attachment depends on responsiveness and possibly also on the child's temperament, then it is hard to measure such complex issues. Scientific conclusions require measurable concepts.
- Attachment types were cleverly measured using the strange situation technique and sensitivity of mothering was measured by using observations. However, the temperament of the child was not taken into account, which emphasises the complexity of the child's interactions.

Table 2.10 *Summary of the strengths and weaknesses of Ainsworth's theory about attachment*

Strengths	Weaknesses
• There is a great deal of evidence, including the work of Bowlby and Harlow	• The strange situation is laboratory-based and artificial, so it lacks validity
• The strange situation is laboratory-based and replicable, so it is reliable	• A fourth attachment type was later added, suggesting her theory was insufficient
• Ainsworth also used naturalistic observations that were valid	• Attachment and responsiveness are hard to measure, so it is hard to study reliably

Research into privation

Privation is different from deprivation in that a child will not have formed any attachment and will lack almost all types of socialisation. With deprivation there would have been an attachment that a child would then be deprived of.

One of the best-known studies looking at the effects of privation is of a young girl called Genie, who was discovered after nearly 13 years of neglect, having been locked away in a room by her parents. Genie's story is covered in more depth on pp. 96–99. One conclusion from the in-depth study of her development after she was found was that she did not develop normal language or **motor movements** (e.g. walking), so early privation was thought to lead to irreversible problems. However, nobody knows whether Genie would have developed normally without the privation. Perhaps her parents thought or knew that there were developmental problems in the first place, which is why they locked her away.

Study hint Be ready to compare the meaning of the terms privation and deprivation

Study hint When looking at a question in an exam, make sure you read all the words carefully. You might be asked whether the effects of privation are reversible, which is a question with a different focus from being asked to evaluate the effects of privation.

In this section you will look at a few studies of privated children to see what the effects of privation are and whether negative effects can be put right — if such problems are reversible. Use what you learn later about Genie to inform this debate.

Koluchová (1972): the Czech twins

The psychologist Jarmila Koluchová looked at the story of identical twin boys who were born in Czechoslovakia in 1960. At first their development was reasonably normal, though they lost their mother not long after they were born and were brought up in an institution for a year, then cared for by an aunt for another 6 months. The twins seemed to have followed a pattern of normal development in their first 18 months. The twins' father had remarried and, when they were about 18 months old, they went to live with their father, stepmother and her four children.

However, their father was not often at home and their stepmother locked them away in a room and beat them. This carried on for over 5 years until they were found and rescued. When they were discovered, aged 7, the twins had rickets (a bone disease caused by lack of Vitamin D), were small for their age, could not talk and could not recognise pictures, so an IQ test was not possible. They were frightened of the dark and of other people. Their stage of development was that of a 3-year old. It was predicted that they would not develop normally and would remain well behind in intellectual development.

The boys were placed in a school for children with severe learning difficulties, which also helped with their physical development. Then they were adopted by a woman who took great interest in them and gave them exceptional attention.

2

Over time they began to catch up with children of their own age and went to a normal school. By the time they were 11 their speech was normal. Eventually, by the age of 15, their IQ was normal for their age. They both continued through school and went on to train in electronics.

Koluchová reported on the twins again in 1991 and both were married with children and were said to be happy, stable and to have warm relationships with their families. One is a computer technician and the other a technical training instructor. The main point is that, after such severe privation, the boys gradually caught up and led normal, happy lives. Their story suggests that the effects of privation are reversible. Sometimes this study is reported as a study of deprivation but, as the twins hardly formed an attachment to an adult before they went back to live with their father, it is presented here as a study of privation.

Evaluation of the Koluchová study

Strengths of the study

- It is known that the twins were normal in their development when they left the care of their aunt at the age of about 18 months. Therefore, when they were later found to be severely behind in their development, this could be said to be because of the privation they experienced. There was a normal baseline against which to measure their lack of progress.
- This was a case study, and so a great deal of information was gathered using different methods, such as IQ testing, interviewing and observing. The depth and detail of the material suggests that the data are valid about the twins' real experiences.
- The study was longitudinal and so the development of the twins could be tracked over many years, which helps when drawing conclusions about whether privation is reversible. It is known, for example, that the twins married and had children, whereas a much shorter study would not have documented any later development.

Weaknesses of the study

- The boys had each other and so could attach to each other, which may have been why they were able to catch up, develop normally and shake off the effects of their privation.
- They would have formed an attachment with their aunt and perhaps others in the social agency, so perhaps they were deprived rather than privated.
- It can never be completely known what life is like for the boys now they are adults, and they may not be happy and well adjusted. There is no reason to say they are not, but information about underlying anxieties and problems might not have been uncovered even now that they are adults.

> **Study hint** Use this as an example of a case study and of a longitudinal study when answering questions about such research methods.

Freud and Dann: children in Terezín

Anna Freud and Sophie Dann (1951) studied six children who were kept in the ghetto of Terezín, arriving there before the age of 1. (Terezin was a garrison town in

Czechoslovakia, and it became a Jewish ghetto during the Second World War, from where people were sent to extermination camps such as Auschwitz.) The children were looked after by adults 'passing through' — before the adults were sent to gas chambers or a similar fate. These children did not have the chance to form an attachment and are considered to have suffered privation.

When the camps were liberated, the children were brought to Britain. Later they were fostered and followed up to see how well they recovered from their early privation. When they were found in Terezín, they could not speak much, but were strongly attached to one another, showing separation distress/anxiety when separated. The children developed normal intelligence, though one sought psychiatric help as an adult and another described feeling isolated and alone. It seems that the effects of privation can be reversed, though in some cases not without problems in adulthood.

Evaluation of the Freud and Dann study

Strengths of the study

- This was a longitudinal study that followed the children through to adulthood, so information about the long-term effects of the privation could be found, which means that conclusions could be drawn to say that the effects of privation could be reversible. A longitudinal study is a good way of finding out such relevant information. The same people are followed through the whole situation so conclusions can be drawn more firmly.
- This was a real study of real children who endured privation in a situation that, for ethical reasons, could not have been set up. This study offers valuable insights into such situations and is unique. This is the value of a case study — it is in depth, detailed, valid and more ethical than setting a situation up for study.

Weaknesses of the study

- Although the study is said to be about privation, it is suggested from the data that the children formed attachments with each other, so they may not have been as privated as is suggested. However, it is clear that they were privated of adult care that would provide a safe base, so to an extent this criticism is not well founded.
- The study is not replicable and there are so many complex factors to consider that it is hard to draw conclusions about the effects of early privation. For example, the children's temperaments may have affected their survival and subsequent recovery, or other factors about the specific situation.

Are the effects of privation reversible?

The conclusions from both the Koluchová and the Freud and Dann studies are that the effects of privation are reversible. The Czech twins grew up to get married, have children, achieve good jobs and maintain warm relationships. The six children studied by Freud and Dann did the same, though one or two had some problems.

However, the study of Genie, which is detailed in the next section, showed that she did not recover from her early privation. Genie developed some language use but it was far from normal. She did not relate normally to adults.

Differences between the studies

It could be that, because Genie was found at the age of 13 — which is much older than the age at which the twins and the Terezín children were rescued — she may have passed the critical age for learning language and normal development.

A further consideration is that, in the cases of the twins and the Terezín children, they had each other for support. Indeed, it was documented that the children had formed attachments with each other. Genie had nobody. Perhaps any individual, even another child, is better than nobody when it comes to socialisation.

Similarities between the studies

All three are case studies, so they use the same research methods, and all are longitudinal in that they follow the participant(s) through to adulthood. They have similar validity and a similar lack of reliability.

All three studies involved at least one person who, after the privation was revealed, took care to help the child or children:

- Genie was helped by some of the researchers
- the twins were fostered by a committed and caring woman
- the children from Terezín were eventually fostered and cared for

It could be that the effects of privation are reversible only if this good quality care is given afterwards.

Daycare: an introduction

Daycare could be considered a form of short-term deprivation and the discussion about deprivation, attachments and separation distress/anxiety applies to this section on daycare. Generally, findings from studies suggest that, for some children, good quality daycare can be beneficial because it offers them stimulation and experiences they would often not get in the home. However, poor quality daycare is not a good thing and there is a suggestion that, for children under 1 year old, too long in daycare (such as more than 20 hours per week) is detrimental. It is not only the quality of the care that is important but the length of time daycare lasts. These are the sorts of finding considered in this section.

> **Link to the key issues and practical**
>
> Note that you can use the issue of daycare as the key issue that you cover in your study of child psychology, and for the related practical.

Defining daycare

Daycare is a term used for any situation where a child is cared for by someone other than its parents for some part of the day. Daycare can take place for a short time, such as in a crèche, or every day of the week, such as in a full-time nursery; some daycare is privately run and some is government run. In the UK all types of daycare are now subject to government inspection as well as government curriculum rules. This has not always been the case, and research you will look at involves daycare before such rules were put into place. The rules, in fact, often arise out of the research findings. One study, Belsky and Rovine (1988), was influential in changing views of daycare, and Jan Belsky is a prominent figure in the area of daycare research. You will look at Belsky and Rovine briefly in the section that follows, and it will be covered in more depth in the online resources. You can choose to study it in more detail for your course.

Explore Look up the Foundation Stage Curriculum and documents on *Every Child Matters* to become familiar with the kinds of regulation to which daycare providers have to adhere.

Some rules for daycare provision

Rules for daycare include what washing facilities are required, how many staff there must be, and what other facilities are provided, including window space and floor space per child and how many children can be in a room depending on its size. There are health and safety rules as well, and other rules such as how long children must play outside each day. Issues such as staff-to-child ratios have been decided because research into daycare has shown that, where there are sufficient staff, children benefit more. As well as these practical details, daycare providers must also follow a curriculum and 'tick boxes' when a child achieves certain milestones. This is to ensure that all children in daycare are receiving the same stimulation and experiences, with a view to making sure all children have equal opportunities. A formal curriculum can also help to make sure that daycare is good quality, as research shows it must be to be successful for the child.

Research into daycare

Apart from Belsky and Rovine (1988), there are many other daycare studies, and only a few can be explained here. Belsky used data from the NICHD (National Institute of Child Health and Human Development) study of early childcare and youth development and from the EPPE (Effective Provision of Pre-school Education) project in the UK.

The NICHD study in the USA

The NICHD study was a longitudinal study following children from birth, and the aim was to find out the effect of childcare on children. In general this is a study that highlights the disadvantages of daycare. The study was funded by the Institute of Child Care, which meant that the study was commissioned privately.

Aim

The aim was to look at the effect of childcare on children.

Procedure

The study was longitudinal and involved gathering data by different means, including observation, interview and survey. The 1,200 children involved were followed from birth to when they started school.

Results and conclusions

Length of time in daycare

The NICHD study concluded that children who spent early continuous and intensive time in daycare were likely to have more behavioural problems (such as aggressiveness or disobedience) later than children who did not. The problems were as rated by parents and teachers. This means that length of time in daycare affects outcomes.

Type of daycare

Another issue is the type of daycare. It was found that nursery-type care (as opposed to care in someone's home) led to improvements in cognitive and language development but also increased behavioural problems such as aggression and disobedience.

Quality of daycare

A third finding was that the quality of the daycare was important. Low quality daycare was particularly bad for children with mothers who lacked sensitivity. Good quality daycare was a matter of the responsiveness of the staff, how attentive staff were and also how stimulating the environment was. High quality care tended to mean higher cognitive and language functioning in the children.

Evaluation of the NICHD study

Strengths

- This was a longitudinal study, which followed a large number of children from birth to when they went to school, so the coverage was thorough and researchers were able to bring in many different aspects of the child's experiences from which to draw conclusions. Longitudinal studies are a better way of studying development than cross-sectional studies because the same children are involved and results are more secure.
- There was more than one research method used, which means that data from different research methods can be compared to check for validity and reliability. Using a different method is a bit like repeating the study so that, if the same findings are made, then reliability can be claimed. If different methods find the same results then this suggests that findings are valid.

Weaknesses

- The area of childcare involves so many variables and child development is so complex that it is hard to draw any meaningful conclusions. Researchers have to look for issues such as social background and the quality of the daycare, but factors such as the temperament of the child, the quality of their attachments, and cultural issues can also be important. It is difficult to take account of all these factors.

- Any study of childcare that takes place in one culture should perhaps have its findings generalised only to that culture. Cross-cultural studies, for example, have found differences in attachment types in different cultures. This suggests that the findings of a study of childcare in the USA ought only to be generalised to the USA. In this section, this study is being compared to a UK study.

The EPPE project in the UK

A project in the UK similar to the NICHD study was the EPPE project (1997–2003). This study, which received government funding, followed children from the age of 3 up to 11, and there was a special project for preschool children. The EPPE project was another longitudinal study following children in order to learn about their development. In general this is a study that highlights the advantages of daycare.

Aims

The aims of the study were to look at the impact of preschool provision on a child's intellectual and social/behavioural development, as well as to find out if social inequalities could be reduced by attendance in preschool settings. The researchers (Sylva et al.) also wanted to see whether some types of setting were better than others.

Procedure

The study was of 3,000 children, consisting of observations, as well as interviews with parents and practitioners. The subjects were from many different social backgrounds in an attempt to provide a range in the sample, to look at issues such as social background. There were two main groups: children in some types of daycare centre and children who stayed at home. The 'home' children acted as a control group and 144 centres took part in the study.

Results and conclusions

A general finding was that high quality care improved social, intellectual and behavioural development. The study found that the earlier a child started in a daycare centre, the better the intellectual improvement. Children also had better sociability, independence and concentration the longer they had been in daycare. It was found that full-time attendance led to no better gains than part-time attendance. An important finding was that disadvantaged children were better off in good quality daycare, particularly if they experienced a mixture of social backgrounds in the daycare centre.

Evaluation of the EPPE study
Strengths
- The procedure was carefully planned to include children from different social backgrounds, including a control group of 'home' children. This means that conclusions could be drawn more securely.
- The same advantages apply, both of the longitudinal design and the many research methods used, as explained when looking at strengths of the NICHD study.

Weaknesses

- A possible weakness is that the study had government funding and there is a question of how far the findings reflected government policy. However, this is true of much research, and this weakness should not be exaggerated as the research team is well respected in the field, and it is more likely that the funding did not affect the findings.
- The complexity of the issues and the related problem of drawing conclusions, as already discussed for the weaknesses of the NICHD study.
- The research was based on English daycare provision and so generalising the findings to any other country might not be appropriate.

Comparing the NICHD and EPPE findings

The findings from the EPPE project were more positive with regard to use of daycare than the NICHD study. The EPPE finding that children did not benefit more from being in daycare for the full day compared with part-time attendance reinforces the NICHD conclusions. However, the NICHD researchers went further and suggested that too long in daycare was a bad thing for the child, which the EPPE team did not conclude.

The EPPE idea that children benefit the earlier they start attending a daycare centre goes against the general conclusion of other studies, including the NICHD research, that a very young child does not benefit from much daycare. One of Belsky's studies is explained in the online resources, and conclusions from that study can be used when discussing daycare provision. Belsky concluded that too much time in daycare before the age of 1 was bad for the child.

> **Explore** Look up the EPPE project to find more about the findings. The EPPE researchers compare their findings with those of the NICHD study, which is useful, and they say that in some areas they found similar results.

Belsky's conclusions

Belsky considered the findings of the NICHD and EPPE projects and suggested that the UK government should put in place measures such as changing tax policies and encouraging parental leave, in order to ensure that children did not spend too long in daycare. In 2006 Belsky concluded that good quality childcare, including childcare in daycare centres, can lead to better cognitive and language abilities. However, the more time spent in daycare, especially more time in centre-based care, tended to lead to more problem behaviour. The important features of daycare are quality, quantity and type of daycare.

Evaluation of research into daycare

Strengths

- Studies have taken into account as many factors that can affect a child's experience of daycare as possible, such as the social background of the family, how long the child is in daycare, how stimulating the environment is, and the quality of staff–child interactions. Studies have been carefully planned to try to draw strong conclusions.

■ Studies have used large and carefully chosen samples, again in order to avoid bias.

Weaknesses

■ As explained when evaluating the two studies given in this section, the issue of the effect of daycare on a child is complex. It would be hard, if not impossible, to take all the relevant factors into account, such as a child's temperament or position in the family (two features not often mentioned).

■ Studies are often carried out within one culture, or within one country. Cross-cultural studies in other areas suggest that differences in culture affect findings about child development, so it might not be legitimate to generalise findings from one culture to another.

Autism

You are required to consider one developmental issue that affects a child's development, from a choice of three: severe learning difficulties, ADHD and autism. In this section, autism is chosen as the issue to study in detail. Autism is chosen because you may already have studied it as a key issue in the biological approach in the AS course. In this part of your A2 studies you need to consider the characteristics of your chosen developmental issue, two explanations for it (here a biological and a cognitive explanation are offered) and two ways in which the developmental issue might affect a child's development (here the effects of not having a theory of mind and not tuning into people's emotions are considered).

AS link The idea that autism is possibly an extreme male brain condition was discussed as a key issue in the biological approach (pp. 293–94) and you might have studied that key issue for your course. If so, review this material, because the argument was that the extreme male brain gave a biological explanation for autism.

Link to the key issues and practical

Note that you can use the issue of the extent to which autism has a biological explanation as the key issue that you are required to cover in your study of child psychology, and for the related practical.

Characteristics of autism

Usually it is **autistic spectrum disorder** (ASD) that is discussed rather than autism as such, because it is recognised that a child can show behaviour and characteristics that fall at any point between mild autism and severe autism. Mildly autistic is diagnosed as having Asperger's Syndrome and the autistic spectrum runs from mild Asperger's to severely autistic. In this section we focus on autism.

Autism is a developmental issue or disorder that affects more boys than girls. For Asperger's Syndrome, which is at the mild end of the autistic disorder spectrum,

2

there is usually thought to be a ratio of 10 boys to 1 girl. For autism the ratio is nearer to 4 boys to 1 girl. There are about 6 people in every 1,000 with ASD, and about 2 people in every 1,000 with autism, which is 0.2% of the population.

There is not a complete set of symptoms of autism but a variety of characteristics — groups of these characteristics lead to a diagnosis of autism. People with autism find it hard, if not impossible, to read other people's emotions and so they are poor at empathising. They usually have problems with communication too, either in talking or reading, or both. However, some autistic children talk clearly, though there may be no understanding of the words, and some read well too, but again with little comprehension.

One main characteristic of autism is that people affected find it hard to form relationships. They are, however, good at systems, and up to 10% have high ability in one special area that is usually connected with systems, such as playing the piano, doing maths, or drawing what is in the environment in perfect detail. Autistic people with this special ability are called **autistic savants**. Affected children often repeat patterns over and over again, when other children would have grown tired of doing so.

A child is usually only identified as being autistic from the age of between 2 and 3. It is likely to become apparent by then that the child is not using normal eye contact, for example, or not anticipating the needs or intentions of others. There are usually problems in social interactions. This, along with repetitive behaviour, signals autism.

Two explanations

Autism is thought of as a problem with the brain's development, which is why a biological explanation and a cognitive explanation are offered in this section — both being about how the brain works. There is no social explanation of autism, as it is not thought that it is caused by social interactions, although those with autism do have problems with interacting. There is more than one biological explanation — for example, there seems to be a genetic link, and it could also come from problems with the birth — but this section considers the suggestion that those with autism have an extreme male brain. This explanation is chosen to fit with one of the key issues suggested in your course for child psychology and also with your AS studies. The second explanation chosen is that autistic children do not develop a theory of mind, which is a cognitive explanation. Both explanations come from Simon Baron-Cohen, a leading researcher in the area of autism and the autistic spectrum.

Theory of mind and autism: a cognitive explanation

Baron-Cohen (with Leslie Frith in 1985) carried out a study of autistic children. He used a task that other investigators had used, where a child watches a researcher manipulate two dolls (Anne and Sally) in a pretend situation. Sally has a basket and Anne has a box. Sally puts a marble in the basket and then 'leaves' the scene. Anne then moves the marble from the basket into the box. This all takes place with the child watching carefully. Sally then returns. The important question asked of the child is where Sally will look for the marble. Children 'pass' the theory of mind test if they say that Sally will look in the basket. They 'fail' if they say she will look in the box. The child knows the marble is in the box, but Sally would not know that and a child has a theory of mind if he or she understands that Sally does not know.

Baron-Cohen and Frith studied 21 autistic children, 11 Down's Syndrome children and 27 children without developmental difficulties. Only the autistic children did not have a theory of mind. They were in the main not able to understand that Sally did not know what the child knew. Children from the age of about 3 have a theory of mind, but much older autistic children did not. Down's Syndrome children also have a theory of mind.

Cognitive psychology considers how information is processed in the brain as well as how thinking processes develop. Therefore, the explanation for autism that there is no theory of mind is a cognitive explanation. To explain further the idea that autistic people have no theory of mind, researchers have looked at low empathising people and high systematising people. 'Low empathising' means not being good at understanding the emotions and feelings of others. 'High systematising' means having the ability to use internal rules to organise internal events. Someone good at systematising will be able to sort things into groups, plan and build structures, work out patterns and work things out in their heads (internally). Someone poor at empathising will find it hard to work out external events, which means it will be difficult to discern what other people are thinking.

Autistic people are high systematisers and low empathisers. A child who finds it hard to work out external events would not have a theory of mind because he or she would find it difficult to look at things from the point of view of someone else. In the Sally/Anne scenario the child would not be able to work out what Sally knew or did not know.

Autism and the extreme male brain: a biological explanation

The idea that autism is an extreme male brain condition follows from the evidence that autistic people tend to be low empathisers and high systematisers. Baron-Cohen links the two explanations, as he has been involved in them both. It is only recently that he has put forward the idea that autism is a feature of having an extreme male brain.

Males are supposed to be better at visuo-spatial tasks such as map reading and jigsaws, whereas females are often better at language tasks and they use both halves of the brain more (males tend to use mainly the right-hand half of the brain). This tends to reinforce the idea that girls are better at empathising and boys are better at systems, which, as there are more boys with autism than girls, suggests that autism is linked to male sex characteristics. Autistic people also seem to be low at empathising and high systematisers, so that too goes with having a 'male' brain.

As children, girls tend to be more verbal and boys more spatial in their play, again fitting the characteristics of autism, as autistic people often have difficulties with language but are good at spatial tasks. Girls tend to show verbal aggression and boys more physical aggression — and to show verbal aggression perhaps girls have to know more what their victim is feeling. So this too fits with the idea of low empathising being a male brain feature and a feature of autism.

There is other evidence, too: people with autism tend to show greater growth in the brain, and boys' brains tend to grow more quickly than girls' brains. Females tend to be better at working out body language than males, which suggests they might be better at understanding interpersonal communication, something autistic people find hard.

How autism might affect a child's development

There are many ways in which a child's development is affected by autism, including finding it hard to make friends (because of problems with empathising) and finding communication difficult (including talking, reading and writing, which are all basic skills for learning).

Difficulties in making friends

Someone who has difficulty in empathising and in understanding the thoughts and emotions of others will find it hard to make friends. Autistic children tend to live in their own world, and indeed this is part of the condition. Advice for parents states that friendships are important to autistic children, even if they seem to prefer to be by themselves, and so friendships should be encouraged early on. Friendships can help prevent bullying, which can be a problem for autistic children. Parents can also help by inviting other children home to play, and teachers can encourage play with other children at school. Autistic children often develop friendships through shared interests such as computers.

Bauminger and Shulman (2003), researchers in Israel, have studied friendships of high-functioning autistic children and compared them with children without autism. Both groups tended to have friendships with children of the same gender and age, so there were few differences there. But their friendship patterns differed with respect to the number of friends, how often they met, how long they were friends and the activities they did together.

Bauminger and Kasari (2000) reported that autistic children were lonelier than other children but also understood loneliness less. They studied high-functioning autistic children between the ages of 8 and 14. All the autistic children said they had at least one friend but the quality of their friendships was not as good, providing less companionship and security.

These studies suggest that autism affects a child's development in terms of not making friendships in the same way as children without autism. However, autistic children are able to make friends and share interests.

Problems with communication

Autistic children have problems with communication, including learning language, and with reading and writing. They tend to have difficulty with the meaning of words and sentences. Some autistic children cannot speak, whereas others can talk fluently, so it is hard to generalise. However, in general, autistic children have communication and learning difficulties.

It is in using language that autistic children tend to have greatest problems. Even children who use language tend not to use it with meaning: for example, they might continuously count without reference to objects, or repeat sentences they have heard when it is inappropriate to do so. Autistic children may be able to speak in depth and knowledgeably about a topic that interests them but they are unlikely to be able to engage in a conversation about the topic. As autistic children do not use appropriate eye contact and have problems with nonverbal communication, such as using gestures to converse, problems with communication are linked to problems with friendships. So language and other communication problems restrict their learning as well as restricting their social interactions and friendships.

Examination-style questions

1 Outline what is meant by the maternal deprivation hypothesis.   *(2 marks)*

2 Explain two ways in which negative effects of deprivation can be reduced.   *(4 marks)*

3 Describe Ainsworth's strange situation task as a research method.   *(4 marks)*

4 Describe one study that looks at privation.   *(6 marks)*

5 Outline two explanations for one developmental disorder that affects children.   *(6 marks)*

6 Evaluate research into privation.   *(6 marks)*

7 Outline one study that looks at disadvantages of daycare.   *(4 marks)*

Extension questions

1 Discuss, using evidence, whether or not daycare is good for young children.   *(12 marks)*

2 Discuss, using evidence, whether the effects of privation are reversible.   *(12 marks)*

Studies in detail

You are required to examine two studies in detail. One is Curtiss's study of Genie (1977), and you then have a choice of one from Bowlby's study of 44 juvenile thieves (1944), Belsky and Rovine's study of daycare (1988) and Rutter and others who, in 1998, studied how children from Romania developed after being adopted. In this section, Curtiss (1977) and Bowlby (1944) are explained in detail. Belsky and Rovine (1988) is explained in detail in the online resources.

2

Curtiss's study of Genie (1977)

Genie was discovered in California, USA at the age of about 13. She had been locked away by her parents and had very little socialisation. Curtiss was one of the researchers who studied and looked after Genie (not her real name), and who wrote up the case study.

Background

Genie's mother said that she had a stormy relationship with her husband, who threatened to beat her, and she lived in fear. Her husband did not want children and was violent towards Genie's mother. When their first daughter (not Genie) was born, she seemed healthy and normal but she cried a lot and her father, irritated by the crying, put her into the garage so he would not have to listen to her. This child died of pneumonia at the age of 2. A boy was born 3 years later and the mother tried to keep him quiet and good. The boy had development problems, being late to walk and talk. The husband's mother took the boy and he thrived, later to return to his parents.

Genie was born 3 years after that. Her birth weight was normal and she had good head control when checked at 4 months. She had a hip dislocation that required a pillow splint. At 5 months she was said to be alert — this is important later, as it suggests that Genie was a 'normal' baby. Genie's mother said that Genie was not very cuddly and resisted any solid food. It was also known that Genie's father disliked Genie and did not allow his wife to pay her much attention. At 14 months Genie had an illness and was feverish. She saw a paediatrician who said she showed signs of possible retardation, but it was hard to assess her development because of the fever. Genie's father used this diagnosis as an excuse for the later abuse Genie suffered.

Not long afterwards Genie's father's mother was killed by a truck. Genie's father became embittered, moving the family into his mother's home and cutting them off from the outside world. Genie's father soon isolated Genie completely, tying her to a 'potty chair' during the day and into a crib at night. The room Genie was in was isolated from the rest of the family and there was little for her to hear. She occasionally made a noise to attract attention but was then beaten, so she stopped. Genie's mother began to go blind and found it hard to go to speak to her, and her brother imitated his father and did not speak to her either.

Genie's father thought she would not live beyond the age of 12 so he promised that after that age, if Genie lived, her mother could get help for their daughter. However, he went back on his promise — but when Genie was 13 her mother had a violent argument with her husband and threatened to leave if he did not contact her own mother to get help. Genie's mother took Genie and left the home. When they went to get help from the welfare office a worker there saw Genie and realised that something was very wrong, and the police were called. Genie's parents were charged with child abuse, but on the day of the trial her father killed himself. Genie was admitted to hospital with severe malnutrition.

Genie at the start of the study

Susan Curtiss provides a great deal of evidence about Genie's progress (or lack of it) when taken in by psychologists to help her and study her. At first Genie could not chew food, stand upright or straighten her arms and legs. She made few sounds and was incontinent. She was, however, alert and curious.

The researchers were interested primarily in her language skills. They knew she did not speak but wanted to discover how much she understood, so they started by questioning the staff in the hospital she had been taken to. They said she seemed to understand a few words, focusing on single words rather than sentences, and that she could understand if pointing was used in addition to words. She had very little language use at all, but she did imitate some words that were spoken to her.

Aim

The aim of the study was primarily to help Genie, but also to see if a child of just over 13 could learn language.

Procedure

Much of the data were gathered by working with and observing Genie. There were also weekly interviews with Genie's mother, but it seemed that she would say what she thought social workers wanted to hear, so the detail was not reliable. Information about Genie's early life had to be gathered from Genie's own behaviour and the few comments she made. There were daily doctor's reports about Genie, and video-tapes and tape recordings were made and catalogued, becoming a rich source of data. Psychological testing was used, with observations and language tests.

Case study evidence

Early progress

From January 1971 Genie was in the hospital and she started to become more social, as well as to develop cognitively and intellectually. When tested she could achieve some things an 8- or 9-year-old could do (such as cleaning up and bathing herself), but for other activities she only reached the level of a 2-year-old (such as chewing food). She displayed some awareness — in one incident in a classroom a teacher asked a child with two balloons how many balloons the child had. The child said 'three' and Genie, looking startled, gave the child another balloon. This suggests an understanding of numbers.

In time, language began to emerge and she started asking for the names of things around her. Curtiss's account gives many examples of how Genie learned language. She moved to a rehabilitation centre and began to develop, but her development was not normal. For example, she had delayed responses — she could be asked to do something but would respond up to 10 minutes later. She also chose the path of least effort and seemed lazy. Her language, however, did develop and by 1972 she used language for the first time when thinking about a past event.

In 1974 Genie asked for a cracker. Curtiss asked 'how many do you want?' and Genie replied 'five'. Then Curtiss said 'how about fewer?' and Genie replied 'four'. When asked 'how about fewer than that?' she said 'three', and three crackers were given to her. It seemed that Genie was starting to understand and use English, with the help of sign language, although her understanding was incomplete.

Case study analysis

Genie's progress in language was analysed in relation to what was thought of as the **critical period** for language learning. A critical period means that something has to be learned by then or it is not learned at all. It was thought that the critical period for language development was from 2 years old to puberty. The critical age has to do with the brain's maturity — it is not mature enough before the age of 2 and is fully mature by puberty. Animal studies showed critical periods for development of processes such as attachment — although it is now thought that perhaps instead of critical periods, **sensitive periods** should be considered. A sensitive period is a time when it is best to learn a particular attribute or have a particular experience, but it can still occur outside that period.

At the time of Genie's study, critical periods were being investigated. A problem with studying humans and critical periods was that experiments c ould not be carried out — a human could not be deprived to see what the results of such deprivation would be. In Genie, though, and in other so-called **feral** children (feral meaning 'wild' — those who had had no socialisation from birth or near birth), there was a natural experiment. Genie had been deprived of stimulation until puberty. If she could still learn language, then this was evidence against there being a critical period.

The difficulty with this study was that, although Genie did learn a lot of language and other skills, it could not be said that her development had caught up or that her behaviour and language use was 'normal', so it could not be concluded that there was no critical period for language development. Another difficulty was that there had been perhaps some language stimulation in Genie's development, but how much and what that was is not known. One feature of the study is that it was claimed that the language that Genie did develop was that associated with the right hemisphere of the brain, and tests were done that supported the idea that Genie was a 'right hemisphere thinker'. She used the right hemisphere for language and her language was abnormal. It was concluded that her case supported the idea of there being a critical period for 'normal' language development.

What is now known about Genie

After the study, when the arrangements for Genie's care were cut short because of a loss of funding, Genie went to stay in a residential home. Her case was not further studied, partly because it was recognised that the psychologists involved in the case had tried to help her to develop, but had also used her as the 'subject' of a study — there was thought to have been excessive testing, given her situation.

> **Explore** Find out more about Genie. There are various films available that show Genie when she was being studied and looked after. You could also look up the stories of other feral children and consider how far you think lack of socialisation leads to abnormal development.

Evaluation

Strengths

- This case study had so much information gathered during its course that the data are rich, detailed and thorough. There are both qualitative and quantitative data gathered, using many different research methods, so the data are valid.
- The study 'gave' Genie a pseudonym so that she could not be recognised and the family could not be traced. Her privacy was able to be protected so that after the study she could live anonymously and not be bothered by journalists. From an ethical point of view, this is a strength.

Weaknesses

- A major problem with the study is that it could not be shown that Genie would have developed normally with good socialisation, because there was the suggestion that she may have had developmental problems in infancy. It could be that after being discovered she did not develop normally because of inherent problems rather than because of her experiences.
- There are ethical difficulties about the study because Genie, although cared for during the study and living in the homes of psychologists, was the 'subject' of a study and was subjected to a great deal of testing and questioning. This could be seen as taking advantage of her situation and not treating her properly. For example, there was little mention of informed consent, a right to withdraw or debriefing. It might have been hard to cover these sorts of ethical issues given the unusual circumstances, but even so the testing would not be something that rehabilitation would normally entail.

> **Study hint** Genie is an example of a privated child, so use this study when writing about privation and the importance of attachments.

Bowlby's study of 44 juvenile thieves (1944)

In 1944 John Bowlby carried out a study of young people who were thieves to find out about their background and to see if he could understand the reason for them becoming thieves.

2

Background

In 1938 nine crimes out of ten were thefts and half of these were committed by someone under the age of 21. Over one-sixth of the thefts were carried by children under 14. There was also recurrence of crimes — at the age of 16 one-third of those who appeared in court had been charged before. Bowlby realised that it would be useful to study youthful stealing and look at how early deliquency starts. 'Almost all recent work on the emotional and social development of children has laid emphasis upon the child's relation to his mother', Bowlby claimed. He had talked to mothers and found that love for their child might be only one aspect of the relationship: 'often an intense though perhaps un-admitted dislike and rejection of him (the child) also came to light'. A large proportion of juvenile delinquents had had long periods away from home, which might be a factor, as well as possible traumatic events in early childhood. These were the sorts of issues that Bowlby focused on in his study, working within the psychodynamic approach.

Procedure

The study was carried out at the London Child Guidance Clinic from 1936 to 1939. Bowlby gathered various kinds of data using interviews, case histories and psychological testing to try to look for patterns in the backgrounds of young people at his clinic, in an attempt to establish why some would become delinquents.

There were various ways in which a child was assessed when he or she first came into the clinic. A psychologist carried out mental tests to assess intelligence, as well as undertaking an assessment of the child's emotional attitudes towards the tests. A social worker then noted preliminary psychiatric history. This testing and case history lasted about an hour. The social worker and psychologist gave reports to the psychiatrist (Bowlby), who then interviewed first the child and then the mother — this took another hour. A case conference followed and a tentative diagnosis was formed. Often more interviews followed, along with psychotherapy and the mother talking further to the social worker, so more in-depth data were gathered.

Only a few cases were studied because of the depth required — such as finding out about the emotional influences within the home, which affect the development of the child's object relationships. Bowlby admitted that more such studies were needed to substantiate the findings of his study.

Results

Bowlby gathered a lot of clinical material, which formed the results of his study:
- 44 cases of children stealing were studied — 22 were referred to the clinic by a school, 2 by a school at the parents' request, 8 were referred by parents directly, 3 were referred at a court's request and 9 were referred by probation officers.
- There was also a control group — this consisted of 44 children who were not thieves but who also attended the London Child Guidance Clinic. Their age and intelligence were similar to the 44 thieves — this was to compare the thieves with

other maladjusted children. Bowlby said he would have preferred some 'ordinary' schoolchildren as well, as another control group.

- 15 of the thieves were under 9 years old and half were under 11. Only one child under 11 had been charged.
- There were 31 boys and 13 girls in the main group and 34 boys and 10 girls in the control group. The clinic usually had 60% boys and 40% girls, so the groups were not representative of the usual intake.
- The average intelligence of both the thieves and the control group was quite high (using standardised tests). About one-third of each group was of above average intelligence.
- In 22 cases there was chronic and serious stealing, mainly over a long period. In 7 cases the stealing had lasted for more than 3 years. However, 8 of the thieves had been involved in only a few thefts and 4 had only been involved in one.

Characters of the thieves

Bowlby wanted to define juvenile delinquency and thought there might be three different types: some children had been unstable for years, some had received a sudden shock (such as bereavement) and some had an exceptional moral lapse. Bowlby then looked through all the data and sorted the thieves into six groups:

A normal   D hyperthermic
B depressed   E affectionless*
C circular   F schizoid

*The main category for the study was 'affectionless', which Bowlby defined as having a lack of normal affection, shame or sense of responsibility.

Two of the 44 thieves were normal in character but 42 had abnormal characters. The diagnosis rested on careful examination, but the problem was that psychiatric examination was not useful because the children were on their best behaviour and hid things. For this reason, Bowlby drew his conclusions about character based on his discussions with the mother and the school. Group E, the affectionless character, is the one of interest in this study, so only two of the other groups are briefly outlined here to give an idea of other categories.

Group A: normal

One child had been stealing since the age of 14, but only from his mother. However, his mother was taking a lot of his earnings. Another child was reasonably normal too — he was 8 and was only stealing a few pennies.

Group B: depressed

Five children suffered with mild depression, two of them having a very low IQ. Some children were severely depressed and often this arose from a specific event.

Group E: affectionless

Fourteen of the children had what Bowlby called an affectionless character — a lack of affection or warmth of feeling for anyone. They had been undemonstrative and

2

unresponsive from infancy. Two of the children sometimes showed affection but matched the personality type in other ways. They lied, stole and had no sense of loyalty, emotional ties or friendships. Bowlby thought that the affectionless character was depressive at an earlier stage in life and had suffered complete emotional loss of mother or foster mother during infancy and early childhood. He thought that misery lay below the mask.

Comparison with controls

There were no affectionless characters among the control group, but there were more depressed characters. Eight of the control group were of a type not found in the thieves (an over-conscientious child type referred to as 'priggish').

Table 2.11 shows that Group E, the affectionless characters, clearly stand out as being thieves and Bowlby focused on this differentiation between the thieves and the control group.

Table 2.11	Distribution of thieves and controls by character type

Character	Thieves	Controls
A: normal	2	3
B: (i) depressed	9	13
(ii) priggish	0	8
C: circular	2	1
D: hyperthermic	13	10
E: affectionless	14	0
F: schizoid/schizophrenic	4	9
Total	**44**	**44**

Conclusion

Table 2.12 shows that 93% of the affectionless thieves (13 out of 14 of them) are level IV with regard to stealing — the highest level, which is defined as stealing in a persistent and serious way. Thirteen out of the 23 persistent thieves (level IV) are affectionless too (56%). Bowlby linked the affectionless character with a lack of attachment and having some strong emotional loss in infancy.

Table 2.11	Distribution of thieves by character type and degree of stealing

Character	Degree of stealing (IV = highest)				
	I	II	III	IV	Total
Normal	0	2	0	0	2
Depressed	1	4	3	1	9
Circular	0	0	2	0	2
Hyperthermic	2	2	2	7	13
Affectionless	0	0	1	13	14
Schizoid/schizophrenic	0	0	2	2	4
Total	**3**	**8**	**10**	**23**	**44**

Evaluation

Strengths

■ There are a lot of in-depth and detailed data gathered from a number of different sources, including both qualitative and quantitative data and different research methods, so data are likely to be valid. This study has the strength of being a case study.

■ There was a matched control group of similar children (in that they attended the same clinic) who were not thieves, so the findings about the thieves could be compared with these controls. This gave Bowlby the ability to show that 14 of the thieves were affectionless characters whereas none of the controls was, so he could draw a conclusion that it looked as if the affectionless character would link with stealing. Without the control group he would not have been able to draw such a strong conclusion.

Weaknesses

■ Bowlby himself said he would have liked to have had another control group, this time children from a 'normal' school and not the clinic, as the control group he used also had problems.

■ Bowlby covered many areas such as emotional state, IQ, age and experiences with the mother. However, in a child's development there are many other areas of interest as well, such as the relationship with the father and other relatives, and experiences at school. He focused on loss in early childhood, but there may have been other variables of importance that he did not focus on. Perhaps, for example, the lack of affection in infancy was genetic.

Examination-style questions

1 Describe Curtiss's study of Genie (1977). *(5 marks)*

2 You have studied one study from Bowlby (1944), Belsky and Rovine (1988) and Rutter et al. (1998). With regard to one of these, evaluate the study in terms of methodology. *(4 marks)*

Extension question

You have studied Curtiss's study of Genie (1977) and one study from Bowlby (1944), Belsky and Rovine (1988) and Rutter et al. (1998). Compare Curtiss's study with one of the others in terms of methodology. *(12 marks)*

Key issues

For your study of child psychology you must prepare one key issue and carry out a practical relating to this. The practical can involve content analysis (primary data) or focusing on two magazine articles or other similar sources, where you should summarise the articles and draw conclusions from them (secondary data). See p. 105 for information about how the key issue practical works.

Three key issues are suggested for your course, but you may choose any key issue:
- daycare and its effects on child development
- how the negative effects of deprivation can be alleviated
- to what extent autism has a biological basis

The content section of this chapter has explained and discussed all three issues in some depth, so the issues are not repeated in detail here but just summarised.

Daycare and its effects on child development

Daycare is any form of care for a child where the parents or family of the child are not involved, but which is daily rather than overnight. It is a form of deprivation because the child is separated from its attachment figure, so detrimental effects might be expected. Some studies point to advantages of daycare, such as improving intellectual development as well as social/behavioural development (e.g. the EPPE project). Other studies point to disadvantages, such as if a child is there too long, or if the quality of the daycare is inadequate (e.g. the NICHD study).

How the negative effects of deprivation can be alleviated

Deprivation is the term used when a child has been separated from its caregiver. It has been shown that deprivation in early infancy can lead to mental health problems in adulthood as well as other problem behaviour. Negative effects can be reduced by explaining the need for the separation to the child if he/she is old enough, or by preparing the child for the separation.

To what extent autism has a biological basis

If there is one cause for autism it is not completely known, though a biological basis has been put forward. Autism could be linked to characteristics of an extreme male brain, and there could be cognitive deficits — and these two explanations are often seen as being related.

Practical: carrying out a content analysis

Content analysis involves examining information in the media to produce a summary of certain issues, comments or views. It involves drawing up categories and then tallying to count how many references there are to such categories. Actual terms can be counted as well, such as negative or positive terms, as they too can provide a picture. The content analysis must be about a key issue within the relevant application, in this case child psychology.

AS link Review tallying, which was explained in the learning approach for your AS studies (p. 315).

- Find material on the subject of daycare, deprivation or autism. Use the internet, newspapers, magazines or any other media source, including television programmes.
- Read the material or watch the programmes carefully. Make notes.
- Consider various themes from the concepts you have learned about in this chapter.
- Count the number of times each theme is mentioned, using tallying.
- Draw up a table of the results.
- Write up the findings and draw conclusions, linking to the concepts you have learned about in this chapter.

Examination-style questions

1 Describe a key issue in child psychology. *(4 marks)*

2 For the following questions, refer to what you did for your practical in child psychology, focusing on a key issue:

   (a) Explain two difficulties you encountered when collecting data, either for your content analysis or your article analysis. *(4 marks)*

   (b) Explain how your analysis shed light on your key issue. *(4 marks)*

Extension question

Discuss one key issue in child psychology, including using your own findings from your practical in this application. *(12 marks)*

Answers to practice 2.1 on p. 65

1 Naturalistic observation

2 Ethnographic study

3 Case study

4 Cross-cultural study

5 Longitudinal study

Chapter

Health psychology: substance misuse

Health psychology is an **application** in psychology, which means that theories and studies are applied to issues of concern to society and the individual. It includes views on health from different approaches and in your course you will look at biological and learning factors involved in substance misuse. Health psychology is also about promoting good health, and the specification requires you to consider two ways of treating substance abuse as well as an 'anti-drug' campaign. You will also look in depth at two drugs, one of which will be heroin, including their effects and how they work.

You are required to know two studies in detail as well as one key issue in the area you are studying, and you will also carry out a practical based on the key issue. The methodology section of this chapter considers how animals and humans are used to study the effects of drugs, and asks you to evaluate such research methods. Health psychology is a large field and can include such topics as stress, sleep, beliefs about health and attitudes to health, but your course looks only at the topic of substance misuse.

Summary of learning objectives

Definitions
You have to be able to define the terms:

- substance misuse
- synapse
- tolerance
- physical dependence
- psychological dependence
- withdrawal

Methodology

- using animals in laboratories to study drugs
- two research methods using humans, to study the effects of drugs
- evaluation of animal research, including looking at both practical and ethical issues
- evaluation of research methods using humans, including issues of reliability and validity

Content

You have to be able to:

- describe a biological explanation of substance misuse
- describe an explanation from the learning approach
- compare learning and biological explanations, including describing and comparing their strengths and weaknesses
- describe mode of action, short-term effects, tolerance, physical and psychological dependencies, and withdrawal, with regard to heroin and one other drug
- describe and evaluate two ways of treating substance misuse, including drug treatment in heroin dependence and one other way
- describe and evaluate one campaign that has encouraged people not to use recreational drugs

Studies in detail

You have to be able to describe and evaluate in detail:

- Blattler et al. (2002), a study looking at heroin
- one other study relating to one drug from alcohol, cocaine, ecstasy, marijuana or nicotine (smoking)

Key issues and practical

You have to carry out one practical that focuses on a key issue, which you choose, that relates to health psychology and substance abuse. The practical can be a content analysis of articles, programmes or other material about the key issue or a summary of two articles from which you then draw conclusions about the key issue.

Table 3.1 *Checklist of what you need to know for health psychology and your progress*

I need to know about	Done	More work	I need to know about	Done	More work
Defining: substance misuse, physical dependence and psychological dependence			Evaluation (including strengths and weaknesses, both practical and ethical) of research methods using animals		
Defining: withdrawal, synapse and tolerance			Evaluate research methods using humans, including issues of validity and reliability		
Animal laboratory studies when looking at drugs (describe and evaluate)			A biological explanation of substance misuse		
Two research methods using humans to study drugs (describe and evaluate)			A learning theory explanation of substance misuse		

I need to know about	Done	More work	I need to know about	Done	More work
Describe strengths and weaknesses of biological and learning explanations			Describe and evaluate one other way of treating substance misuse (other than drug treatment in heroin dependence)		
Compare biological and learning explanations			Describe and evaluate one anti-drug campaign		
Describe the mode of action, effects, tolerance, physical and/or psychological dependence and withdrawal with regard to heroin			Describe and evaluate Blättler et al. (2002)		
Describe the mode of action, effects, tolerance, physical and/or psychological dependence and withdrawal, with regard to a drug other than heroin			Describe and evaluate one study on one drug from alcohol, cocaine, ecstasy, marijuana or nicotine		
Describe and evaluate drug treatment in heroin dependence			One key issue and a practical relating to it		

Definitions

Substance misuse, **synapse**, **tolerance**, **physical dependence**, **psychological dependence** and **withdrawal** are all defined in the content section of this chapter.

An introduction to health psychology

Health psychology is concerned with any area where health is connected with mental processes, including sleep, stress and drug abuse, as well as health itself and ill health. Actual illnesses are studied in health psychology, such as how to deal with a terminal illness, HIV/AIDS, or dealing with caring for others. However, health psychology is as much concerned with prevention of ill health and promotion of good health as with understanding those with illnesses. Health psychology also looks at areas of people's lives that may put strain on a person and so might lead to ill health, such as bereavement and coping strategies in challenging situations.

The biopsychosocial model

Health psychology has a biological basis, in that it has arisen from the medical profession. There are different types of health psychologist, such as occupational, community and clinical health psychologists. Historically in the UK, health professionals worked within a medical model of health — a model that considered ill health to be caused mainly by biological factors. However, this has now moved

Health psychologists are interested in factors that achieve good health — not only physical aspects but also having social support, a healthy lifestyle and interests

to a biopsychosocial model of health, meaning that as well as there being biological causes for ill health, it is accepted that social and behavioural factors affect health too.

Illness is seen as a combination of biological factors, such as genes, and social factors, such as family relationships and social support. Cognitive and behavioural factors like stress and beliefs are also investigated. Cognitive–behavioural therapy, for example, focuses on negative automatic thoughts and helping someone to change these to more helpful thinking patterns. Depression and anxiety in particular are linked to what could be called faulty thinking patterns. This means that they are faulty for that individual, because certain thought patterns can lead to negative emotions.

Study hint   Questions about health psychology require you to have a good overview of what this area covers, including the importance of different factors when considering health, such as biological, social, cognitive and behavioural areas. Be ready to explain how each of these impact on health and ill health. A good way of doing this is to prepare an example for each factor.

The work of the health psychologist

Health psychologists work with health professionals such as doctors, dentists, nurses, occupational therapists and dieticians. They may carry out clinical work themselves, such as therapy or counselling, or they may undertake research. They are often involved in health promotion campaigns and their role is as much about prevention as cure. When carrying out research, health psychologists use research methods such as experiments, longitudinal studies, cross-sectional studies and case studies. They research any issue that might impact upon how health issues affect an individual.

It is important to note that work in the area of substance misuse is only one part of what a health psychologist might be involved in — they may also look at social support, emotional state, living conditions and diseases such as heart problems, perhaps considering genetic factors. They are interested in factors that lead to certain health problems and in how such factors can be reduced. One example would be to see how more social support could be put in place for a particular section of the population, such as the elderly. This demonstrates evidence for the biopsychosocial model in that, when considering help for an individual, the health psychologist will consider genetic background and medical features. They might also evaluate behavioural features such as whether someone smokes, and social factors such as social class or whether there is social support available.

Promoting good health

Health promotion is of great interest because not only is it good for someone to be healthy, but it is also cost-effective for a society to promote good health. It is cheaper to prevent health problems than to treat them. For example, health psychologists are involved in anti-smoking campaigns and promoting good diets. They also help to promote good health by working with individuals on behaviour change. Some are involved with giving advice to a wider audience, such as institutions and workplaces.

Promoting good health requires clear communication and education. Health psychologists work with doctors and other health professionals to help them to communicate clearly with their patients and clients, and to ensure that there is understanding of what is needed to achieve and maintain good health. For example, it has been found that a patient in a doctor's consulting room will not remember much of what is said, so it is important for a doctor to ensure that there is good understanding, for example by repeating the main points and questioning the patient. Promotional campaigns are also about education and communication.

Explore Look up a promotional health campaign and consider its main features, such as how the message is presented and what educational aspects there are.

Examination-style question

What is meant by health psychology? *(3 marks)*

Extension question

With reference to at least two areas, discuss the work of a health psychologist. *(12 marks)*

Methodology

AS link Note that you might be asked to draw on AS material for both the Methodology and Content sections of this chapter.

In this section you are required to cover the use of animals in laboratory studies as well as two research methods using humans to study the effects of drugs.

You will then evaluate the use of animals, considering both practical and ethical issues, as well as evaluating the use of humans, including looking at validity and reliability issues.

Animal laboratory studies into drugs

AS link Review what you have learned about animal laboratory studies when looking at the biological approach in the AS course (pp. 255–62).

In this section, animal laboratory studies — including those looking at drugs — are outlined as a research method.

Features of animal laboratory studies

Study hint You are asked to look at the use of animals in laboratory studies when researching into drugs, so you will need to know about animal laboratory studies and how they are used, especially when researching into drugs.

Laboratory studies using animals are laboratory *experiments*. Ethology is the research method where animals in their own environment are observed and studied but, in the study of drugs, experiments are used to test the effects of different drugs, so ethology is not suitable. Animal experiments involve observing an animal's behaviour, but there will have been manipulation of an independent variable, and it is the experimental method that is being discussed here, not the observational research method.

An animal experiment will have an independent variable (IV) that is manipulated to see the effect on a dependent variable (DV). There are strong controls, such as the environment, duration of the study, biochemical factors, gender, age, type of animal and whatever variables are important for a particular study. The aim is to control all variables except the independent variable, so that it can be shown that a change in the IV has caused any change in the DV. This means laboratory experiments can show a cause-and-effect relationship.

Table 3.2 *Summary of the features of animal laboratory experiments*

- Strong controls such as environment, care, type of animal, and state of animal (such as hunger and thirst)
- Manipulation of one feature, which is the independent variable (IV)
- Measurement of change in another variable (the dependent variable), as a result of manipulation of the IV
- Cause-and-effect conclusions are able to be drawn (to a large extent)
- Scientific procedures are often used, requiring scientific equipment

Using animals instead of humans has some effect on how a laboratory experiment is run because animals have to be fed, housed, looked after and handled in ways that humans do not. Such issues have to be incorporated into the study. Studies cannot last too long and they must be suitable for the species — animals are only able to act and react in certain ways. The animal also has to have the right features, such as biochemistry or brain structure, depending on what knowledge is sought. Part of a description of animal laboratory experiments, therefore, needs to include features such as preparing appropriate housing, feeding and care routines, planning the necessary controls and how they will be put into place.

On the whole, there can be more control with animals in laboratory experiments than with humans. The study would be scientific in drawing a hypothesis from a theory, controlling all variables except the IV, and often using scientific equipment to measure the DV.

Numbers and types of animal used

Figures for animals used in laboratory experiments in psychology are hard to find because the data tend to show overall animal testing numbers, not just use of animals in psychology studies. Home Office figures in the UK in 2004 showed nearly 3 million animals used, and figures had been rising up to then, so the number may be greater than that now.

Explore Find out about animal experiments to get an idea of which animals are used a lot and whether particular animals are preferred for particular studies.

AS link Review what you learned about the numbers and types of animals used in laboratory studies when you studied the biological approach for the AS course (pp. 255–62).

Explore Look up some of the many other animal laboratory experiments that are used to study the effects of drugs. The ones chosen here focus on nicotine, heroin and cocaine, but you could look at studies that consider other recreational drugs.

Different animals are chosen for different purposes. Insects, for example, do not have a brain structure at all similar to that of humans, whereas mice and humans share many characteristics. The size of mice is useful, they are low cost and they have fast reproduction rates. Genetically modified mice can be bred to suit whatever purpose is required. Other types of animal are used in experiments, such as rhesus monkeys, as explained in one example later in this section.

Animal experiments for research into drugs

In this section three examples of animal laboratory experiments are given, two using monkeys and one using mice.

The link between cocaine/heroin use and renal disease

Experiments have used animals to help to understand the prevalence of renal disease in heroin and cocaine users. Renal disease occurs when the kidneys fail to function properly. In the laboratory experiments, mice are given either heroin or cocaine in various doses and then their renal function is tested. Animal studies have shown that renal disease is linked more to cocaine use than to heroin, which could point to the drug itself being implicated in renal disease (rather than taking any drug).

Studies other than animal experiments have also investigated the link between heroin/cocaine and renal disease. For example, it was concluded with regard to heroin (Jaffe and Kimmel, 2006) that economic conditions, behavioural practices and culture were factors more likely to relate to renal disease than heroin use itself, partly because renal disease in heroin users is not as common as it once was. If heroin caused the renal disease then there would still be the same level of link, and there is not. Their findings support the animal experiments that found more of a link between cocaine and renal disease than heroin and renal disease. Animal studies can be used in this way to back up studies of humans.

> **Study hint** Link Jaffe and Kimmel's findings (2006) with the biopsychosocial model of health. They considered biological factors (use of heroin), social factors (socioeconomic conditions and culture) and behavioural factors (lifestyle), and drew the conclusion that the use of heroin was not the prime cause of renal disease in heroin users.

Evaluation

Strengths

- The human study cited reinforces the conclusions from the animal studies, which tend to give reliability to the conclusion that it is likely that cocaine affects renal function more than heroin does. Animal studies can be used to back up human studies.
- The animal studies are evidence for a biological explanation — that taking drugs into the body affects physical aspects of the body. This is possibly the case for some drugs more than others. Controls regarding biological aspects make animal studies useful in this way.
- An advantage of using mice is that such studies would not be possible with humans because you could not inject humans with cocaine or heroin and then test their renal function in such controlled conditions.

Weaknesses

- There are differences in brain structure between mice and humans, so conclusions about the effects of drugs on the brain and behaviour might not be generalisable.
- The human study shows how important it is to look at factors other than the drug-taking, because it seems that although taking heroin correlated with renal disease, there were other factors. Psychosocial factors are not studied using animals.
- The human study is evidence for the biopsychosocial model, which suggests that with complex human behaviour there are complex causes affecting such behaviour.

Looking at drugs as reinforcers

Meisch (2001) considered animal laboratory experiments into oral self-administration of drugs (taking it themselves by mouth). For example, rhesus monkeys were given the opportunity to take drugs so that researchers could see whether drugs are reinforcing. Here 'reinforcing' refers to the drug being taken as a reward, which would link to factors like addiction. Drugs used included barbiturates, opioids,

3

stimulants and ethanol. Animal laboratory experiments showed that drugs of this kind become reinforcers if they are taken by mouth, which means that the animal will choose to take the drug as a reward, so it will get pleasure from taking the drug.

AS link One study on the use of animals in laboratory experiments to look at cocaine as a reinforcer was Pickens and Thompson (1968), which was a study suggested in your AS course. Review this as an example of an animal experiment that looks at the effect of drugs (p. 361 and the AS textbook CD).

There are problems in animal experiments like this because the study has to take the taste into account (which the animal may not like). The delay before the drug starts to work also has to be considered, as it has to be clear that it is the effect of the drug that is the reinforcer rather than anything else. Animal studies have shown that monkeys will choose to take in more drug solution than water, which is taken to show that they choose the drug as a reward.

Evaluation

Strengths

- Monkeys share many of the genes of humans, so generalising from monkeys may be a reasonable thing to do.
- Humans can become addicted to certain drugs, which appear to be taken for their reward value, so the findings of the study of monkeys fits with known human behaviour, which gives them reliability.

Weaknesses

- Rhesus monkeys are not human, so generalising from what acts as a reinforcer for monkeys to humans might not be reasonable.
- Ethical issues about using animals might be raised, though if the guidelines for using animals are adhered to, then such experiments are generally allowed.

Testing the properties of amphetamines in reducing cocaine addiction

The researchers Czoty et al. at Wake Forest University School of Medicine in California have found that amphetamines can reduce in monkeys, for up to a month, the behaviour of obtaining cocaine for reward. According to an article written by the researchers in 2008, amphetamine seems to mimic cocaine, but without leading to drug abuse. This means that cocaine addiction could be treated in the same way as nicotine and heroin addiction — by prescribing a replacement drug.

The monkey was taught to press levers to get food or an injection of cocaine as a reward. The number of times the monkey had to press the lever to receive cocaine was increased until it was too much for the monkey to keep pressing. At this stage the cocaine was removed and the monkey was treated by injection (intravenously) with an amphetamine for 24 hours a day. A week later the monkey was offered the possibility of getting cocaine again and the researchers found a large decrease in the number of times the monkey responded. They tried different doses of amphetamine and found a moderate dose was the most effective. Cocaine use over the month was reduced by about 60%.

Evaluation

You can make the same points for the study on cocaine as the reinforcer study above:

- Monkeys are not humans so it is hard to generalise, but they do share many genes with humans, so perhaps some generalisation is possible.
- Human behaviour shows that cocaine is reinforcing, which suggests the study findings can be generalised.
- There are ethical issues you could discuss, such as asking how many monkeys were used (the researchers should use a restricted number) and how the animals were cared for (a licence is required, and caging should be suitable).

Evaluation of animal laboratory experiments

You are required to evaluate animal laboratory experiments, both as a research method and in terms of how useful experiments are in learning about the effects of drugs. In this section experiments are evaluated with regard to practical and ethical issues, as well as how useful they are in learning about drugs.

Evaluation focusing on practical issues

Strengths

- Animals are relatively small and usually easy to handle, which means some procedures are more feasible.
- Some animals have short gestation periods and reproductive cycles so generations and genes can be studied more easily than with humans.
- Some animals, such as mice, have a similar brain structure to humans so there is value in studying animals and relating results to humans.
- Some procedures are not suitable for humans but they can be done on animals (ethical guidelines allowing).
- There can be stronger control over the environment than for humans, which means that findings of studies are more likely to be objective.

Weaknesses

- The brains of animals are not exactly the same as those of humans, so relating the results from animals to humans may not be accurate. Furthermore, animals' genetic structure is not the same as that of humans, again making generalisation difficult.
- Human behaviour is complex, so isolating variables — especially in animals — will not address that complexity.
- There is a lack of credibility when using animals and concluding about humans because of differences in genes and brain functioning.

Evaluation focusing on ethical issues

Strengths

- Procedures can be carried out on animals that cannot be done on humans — there are ethical reasons for using animals rather than humans.

> **Study hint** Remember to make each point very clearly when discussing strengths and weaknesses.

- **Pro-speciesism** puts forward the view that we must do all we can to protect our own species, so using animals is one way of discovery that does not harm humans and which also benefits them.
- The knowledge found can sometimes benefit animals as well, which makes a study more ethical.
- There are strong guidelines that have to be followed when using animals in laboratory experiments, so there are safeguards that make such studies ethical, to an extent at least.

Weaknesses

- Many animals feel pain and become distressed during experiments, although there are guidelines to avoid unwanted discomfort.
- Some people believe that animals should not be treated as objects. They argue that humans are animals and there is an obligation to treat non-human animals well. This is the opposite view to pro-speciesism

Evaluation of experiments when researching drugs

You can evaluate animal laboratory experiments used to research drugs in the same way as you would evaluate them in general, by looking at practical and ethical issues as well as issues of generalisability, credibility, validity and reliability.

Validity

The validity of using findings from animal studies to apply to humans can be argued either way. Validity can be claimed or not. If an animal experiment is being used to test the effects of a drug, this is not a valid study because the effects of a drug on an animal will not necessarily be the same as the effects on a human being. However, neuronal transmission takes place in the same way in the brain of mammals as in humans, so it may be possible to generalise from the brains of animals to the brains of humans.

Explore Find out about the various organisations that are against using animals in experiments at all. There are a relatively large number of people in the UK who would like to liberate all animals from being used in this way.

AS link Review the process of neuronal or synaptic transmission from your AS learning of the biological approach. The recreational drugs you will be studying for this chapter work by neuronal transmission, so it is useful to remind yourself about the process (pp. 264–65).

Generalisability

Animals are different from humans, so to claim that findings from animals are true of humans may not be safe. One example is the drug thalidomide, which was tested on rabbits and found to be safe but was far from safe when given to pregnant humans. This suggests that any drug, including recreational drugs, might have a different effect on humans than on animals. Amphetamines have been shown to have a different effect on humans than on rats.

Reliability

Animal studies tend to be reliable because of the strong controls in the experimental situation, where more can be controlled than with a study using humans. Variables that might be controlled are the type of animal, size, age, gender, environment, what the animal has eaten, how thirsty it is, its body weight, and whether it is in a crowded situation. With such control and a well-documented procedure, it is possible to repeat the study and to show that the findings are reliable. Usually a study is repeated as a matter of course and findings are not published from just one study on one animal.

Using humans to look at the effects of drugs

You need to know two research methods, using humans, which look at the effects of drugs. This section considers three research methods related to **recreational drugs**. You are required to study only two such methods, but three are given here to help your choice and to assist with reviewing methodology from the AS course.

> **Recreational drugs** are drugs taken for pleasure rather than for medical reasons. Cannabis, heroin, cocaine, nicotine, ecstasy and alcohol are examples of recreational drugs.

The first research method chosen here is interviewing (as used by Blättler et al., 2002), the second is questionnaires (Ennett et al., 1994) and the third is PET scanning.

> **AS link** The research methods chosen here are the three that you studied in your AS course — interviews and questionnaires in the social approach (pp. 9–23) and PET scanning in the biological approach (pp. 240–42). You could be asked about your AS material, so you need to review it.

Interviewing

One research method that uses human participants to study drug behaviour and the effects of drug usage is interviewing. Interviews can be structured, semi-structured or unstructured. They usually involve gathering qualitative rather than quantitative data, although some interviews gather both sorts. Qualitative data involve attitudes, opinions and comment, and quantitative data are numbers such as scores, percentages and the number of 'yes' or 'no' answers.

Table 3.3 *Evaluation of interviewing as a research method*

Strengths	Weaknesses
• Interviewing can be in-depth, so data are likely to be valid because different issues can be explored (depending on the type of interview).	• Interviewers may influence responses by the way they dress, or their age or gender. This would affect reliability, as another interviewer might get different results.
• Interviewing can gain valid data because participants can use their own wording and are not as restricted as with questionnaires.	• The data have to be analysed, which can be subjective as there may be a lot of qualitative data to be put into themes, and these can come from the researcher's preconceived ideas rather than from the data. If analysis is subjective another researcher might analyse the results differently, so there would not be reliability.

Questionnaires

Questionnaires are used to study the effects of drugs and to look at substance misuse. Participants are asked questions, for example about their smoking habits, their family and friendships. Questionnaires tend to involve both open and closed questions: open questions gather qualitative data and closed questions gather quantitative data. Questionnaires can be administered to groups or individuals, and they can be posted or issued face to face. They often involve Likert-type questions that involve ranked data — such as whether someone strongly agrees, agrees, disagrees or strongly disagrees with certain statements. Other question types are also chosen, such as yes/no questions or circling factors that apply to the individual. With a questionnaire a pilot study is often carried out to check that the questions are appropriate and that it measures what it is supposed to.

Table 3.4 *Evaluation of questionnaires as a research method*

Strengths	Weaknesses
• They can be reliable because the same clear questions are set for everyone, with the same instructions.	• The fixed questions can limit validity because people must answer what is asked and may miss important areas of enquiry.
• There should be no bias, such as response set, because of careful planning and the use of a pilot study. With no bias, if the study were to be carried out again, the same results would be found, making the results reliable.	• There can be social desirability if people answer how they think they are supposed to answer. Therefore, answers would not be valid because they are not 'real life' answers about genuine beliefs and behaviour.

PET scanning

PET (positron emission tomography) scanning has been used to study drug use and the effects of drugs. Because drugs affect the brain, scanning can be useful to get a picture of what happens in the brain when drugs are taken. PET scanning involves a radioactive tracer that is taken into the body by adding it to a solution such as glucose, sometimes by injection. Glucose is taken up by the body and the tracer goes along with it. By looking at the progress of the tracer, which provides small positively charged positrons, a PET scanner can pick up 'hot spots' and follow blood flow to see which parts of the brain are active.

Table 3.5 *Evaluation of PET scanning as a research method*

Strengths: reliability and ethics	Weaknesses: validity and ethics
• PET is a relatively non-invasive way of studying brain activity, so it is reasonably ethical given the choices of ways of studying the brain (such as **lesioning**).	• Even though they are reasonably ethical, having to have an injection of a radioactive tracer can still be distressing.
• There tends to be reliability because the scans do not require analysis as such: they are pictures and can be repeated exactly. If carried out again, you would expect the same results.	• Although brain activity can be seen relatively clearly, it is difficult to pinpoint an exact area of the brain, so the findings can be limited. To an extent they are valid because they are 'real' pictures from a 'real' working brain, but the area covered is large, whereas the brain area affected may well be tiny.

Lesioning involves damaging a part of the brain to see the effect on behaviour. This is often done using animals but can be carried out with humans, though as part of a surgical procedure to help someone rather than as an experiment.

Study hint You are asked to evaluate research methods using humans, including issues of reliability and validity, so those issues have been focused on in this textbook. However, you can draw in evaluations of the research methods from your AS studies. Remember that you need to focus on reliability and validity.

Human studies into the effects of drugs

Here are three studies that employ the research methods explained with regard to using humans to study the effects of drugs. All three research methods are ones you have learned in depth at AS — interviews, questionnaires and PET scanning. Two of the studies below — Blättler et al. (2002) and Ennett et al. (1994) — are explained in detail in a later section in this chapter, so they are described only briefly here.

Blättler et al. (2002)

Blättler et al. (2002) used interviews to look at over 900 participants who were part of a project to study the effect of prescribed heroin as a treatment for heroin abuse, and to see how the treatment also affected the participants' use of cocaine (participants were users of both heroin and cocaine). The study was straightforward in taking a baseline measure at the start of the programme, some measures throughout and, at the end of 18 months, drawing conclusions about reduction in cocaine use. The researchers used urine testing as well as interviewing.

Ennett et al. (1994)

Ennett et al. (1994) carried out a study that worked out friendship groups, called cliques, from questionnaire data that, among much other detail, gave information about each participant's three closest friends. From this information the researchers could work out cliques in schools (they knew which schools the participants attended). They also asked whether or not the participant smoked. They found a link between whether the individual smoked and whether the friendship clique was a smoking clique or not, and discovered that cliques worked to stop smoking, not to encourage it.

Study hint You must be prepared to answer a question about one or two research methods that use humans to study the effects of drugs, so be careful when using studies such as Ennett et al., because they look more at what affects the use of drugs. Their study is relevant because you could say that the drugs have an effect on friendship cliques, but notice how your use of example must match the question.

Scott et al. (2004)

A study (Scott et al., 2004) using PET scanning on humans showed that smoking cigarettes stimulates the brain to produce **opioids**, which act in the brain to increase positive emotions and relieve pain symptoms. Morphine and heroin also affect the brain in the same way. The researchers studied the opioid system in the brain — PET scans are able to show opioid receptor activity. The researchers managed to find a way for human participants to smoke while in a PET scanner. Six healthy male participants stopped smoking for at least 10 hours before the study began and, during the scan, they each smoked first a cigarette with practically no nicotine and then a 'normal' cigarette. The researchers also asked the men how they were feeling at certain times during the study.

The scan picked up significant differences in opioid flow when the participant smoked the low-nicotine cigarette compared to the normal one. There was increased opioid activity when the men smoked the normal cigarette. The scans also showed that, after the normal cigarette, the men had fewer cravings and it was noted from the scan that the brain regions for memory, emotion and pleasure were less active. The men reported feeling more relaxed and less alert, which matches the scan findings. The same activity was not found in the low-nicotine cigarettes. The findings suggest that nicotine binds to the opioid receptors just as morphine and heroin do.

Table 3.6 *Evaluation of Scott et al. (2004)*

Strengths	Weaknesses
• This study uses PET scanning, which has validity because it shows a live brain actively processing.	• The study took place in unfamiliar surroundings, which may have affected the validity of the findings.
• The same participants were those who smoked low-nicotine and normal nicotine cigarettes, which would control for participant variables.	• The task was unnatural as, presumably, the smokers usually smoked a particular brand and type of cigarette, whereas in this study the choice of cigarette was prescribed, so the task itself lacked validity.

Examination-style questions

1 Describe one way in which animals have been used in the laboratory to research drugs. *(4 marks)*

2 Outline one practical strength and one practical weakness when using animals in psychology. *(4 marks)*

3 With reference to one research method using humans to study the effects of drugs, evaluate the method in terms of reliability. *(4 marks)*

4 Outline one example of animals being used in the laboratory to research into drugs. *(3 marks)*

Extension questions

1 Compare two research methods using humans to study the effects of drugs, including considering issues of validity and reliability. *(12 marks)*

2 Discuss practical and ethical issues with regard to using animals in laboratory studies when researching into drugs. *(12 marks)*

Content

This section is about substance misuse. It looks at two explanations of substance misuse, two drugs in more detail (heroin and nicotine), two ways of treating drugs (drug treatment and the token economy) and one anti-drug campaign. Before looking at the content in detail it is useful to define some of the terms.

AS link Note that you might be asked to draw on AS material for both the Methodology and Content sections of this chapter.

Substance abuse/misuse is when a **drug** — defined as a mind-altering substance — is used in such a way that the individual's physical and mental health are affected. The use of the drug is called 'misuse' or 'abuse' when it interferes with a person's social situation and responsibilities.

Taking a drug is not the same as misusing or abusing a drug. Alcohol is a drug, but not everyone who drinks alcohol is thought of as a drug abuser — at least not in most societies. It is when someone is addicted to a substance that it becomes substance misuse — when the individual does not necessarily want to take the drug but feels he/she must. Addiction/dependence is defined later in this section when particular drugs are discussed.

Substance misuse has a social and economic cost, because individuals who abuse drugs need to be treated, which costs money. A society will want to reduce the number of people addicted to drugs, so it will put together campaigns to minimise such behaviour and to improve health, and such campaigns are expensive. 'Drugs' in these contexts usually refer to **recreational drugs** but may also include prescribed drugs such as tranquillisers and sleeping pills, as people can become addicted to these.

'Misused' drugs include alcohol, heroin, cocaine, cannabis as well as glue and aerosols. Smoking cigarettes or drinking a lot of coffee can also come under the heading of substance abuse, as can the eating disorder bulimia nervosa, because it involves the misuse of food. In your course you are required to focus on two drugs, one of which must be heroin, and in this textbook heroin and nicotine are chosen.

You are asked to look at two explanations of substance misuse. One explanation has to be a biological one, and the other from the learning approach. You have a choice of explanations, but in this section the biological explanation chosen is how heroin works at the brain's receptors, and the chosen learning explanation is social learning theory and the role of models. A few other theories are briefly explained for your interest.

The biological approach

People are not likely to start taking a recreational drug for a reason other than some form of pleasure — they start using the drug and like the resultant feelings.

3

They might use the drug because of a reaction from friends or others, so the reason for starting to take a drug is not likely to be biological. A biological explanation, however, might reveal why someone keeps taking the drug, even if at some level they wish to stop. The brain seems to have an agenda of its own when someone who has started taking an addictive drug wants to stop, and this is the biological agenda. For example, cocaine is an addictive drug. The euphoric effect individuals receive from it influences them to try it again, and also changes the structure and function of the brain. The brain continues to change as the drug is taken in terms of biochemical structure, memory processes and in control over motor skills, until the person is addicted.

Drugs and neuronal transmission: a biochemical explanation

Drugs are chemicals and they work in the brain to provide a pleasure reaction and, for some drugs, an addiction reaction. Prescribed drugs such as tranquillisers and anti-schizophrenic drugs work in the same basic way. The drug acts like other neuro-transmitters (which are chemicals) — when released by an electrical impulse, the neurotransmitter crosses a synaptic gap to fit with receptors of another neurone. Recreational drugs, like other drugs, work at the receptor of a neurone. Drugs can also prevent re-uptake of a neurotransmitter, which means the neural transmission is blocked.

For example, heroin works in the brain like morphine and acts on opioid receptors. In some mice it acts on mu-opioid receptors and, in others, on delta-opioid receptors. This activity is able to cause changes at the receptors. It is the mu-opioid gene that is thought to be responsible for addiction, though other genes could also be implicated. A genetic explanation for substance misuse is another biological explanation.

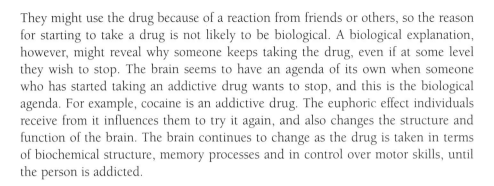

AS link Review your learning about neuronal transmission from the biological approach, including how synaptic trans-mission works in the synaptic cleft (pp. 263–65).

Study hint Note that there were slightly different findings from two studies using mice. Use such evidence when evaluating animal laboratory studies and whether findings from them can apply to humans. If there are differences in different types of mice, there could easily be differences between mice and humans.

Different drugs work in different ways, but both the dopamine and serotonin systems in the brain are involved in drug misuse and addiction — these neurotransmitters are linked to pleasure and positive emotions. Cocaine, for example, directly stimu-lates the dopamine receptors and this would give pleasurable feelings by increasing the availability of dopamine messages. However, opioids (e.g. heroin) slow down all brain activity, including the re-uptake of neurotransmitters, so dopamine messages stay active for longer. This means that it is as rewarding as increasing dopamine activity, but in a different way.

Some people do not become addicted and others do. This might be because of the individual's particular dopamine system, which could link with a genetic explanation. Some people might be more prone to addiction than others. There is currently research looking for an 'addictive gene'.

It is possible that the deficient dopamine system leads the person to seek more pleasure and to be susceptible to substance misuse in order to seek pleasure (Blum et al., 1996). This is known as the reward deficiency syndrome. In a different explanation, it is argued that it is the serotonin system that might lead a person to want more of a drug after starting to use it. Some addictive drugs increase activity in the serotonin system, which leads the person to want more. Some people might have a deficiency in the serotonin system, again linking to a genetic explanation. This is known as the serotonin deficiency hypothesis. A further theory looks at endorphin deficiency, because drugs also stimulate endorphin receptors, endorphin being the brain's own pleasure and pain-reducing neurotransmitter. Both heroin and alcohol increase endorphin arousal so perhaps people with endorphin deficiency are more likely to become addicted. These three explanations all link to the idea of drugs working at the synapse.

Other biological explanations

A pleasure centre in the brain?

Research by Olds and Milner (1954) suggested that there are pleasure centres in the brain, linked to motivation areas. The researchers experimented on rats and found that they would press a lever to get an electrical stimulation to the septal areas of the brain rather than press for food or drink. Rats would even cross a grid where they received painful shocks in order to reach the reward of stimulating these pleasure areas. The electrode the rats activated was attached to the rat's hypothalamus, so the pleasure area is thought to be in that area of the brain.

Genes and substance abuse

Another biological reason for addiction to a substance or substances might be that it is genetic. In 2002 reports from a team in Florida (Schinka et al.) stated that a gene had been found for addiction. This is the mu-opioid gene (which fits with the study using mice explained when looking at the neuronal transmission biological theory for substance misuse). This gene seems to give an increased risk of abusing drugs, including alcohol and nicotine. This is possibly a gene implicated in drug use in general, not just one particular drug. There may be other genes too, with which the mu-opioid gene might work.

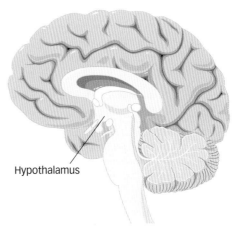

Hypothalamus

Family and twin studies also suggest that there is a genetic basis for the risk of drug dependency. There might be specific genes for the risk of specific drugs — such as alcohol or cocaine. Laboratory studies have reinforced this work, and mice without the

Figure 3.1 *Diagram of the human brain, showing that the hypothalamus is in the centre, near the area for emotions and where a pleasure centre is likely to be*

mu-opioid receptor did not drink alcohol even after they had been trained to drink it in other circumstances. Schinka et al. (2002) found that alcoholics lacked a form of the mu-opioid gene, when compared with the non-alcoholics in the study. It was because some of the alcoholics also used other substances that the researchers could not conclude that this gene was implicated in alcohol misuse only.

AS link

Review your learning about genes in the biological approach (pp. 266–67).

Evaluation

You are not asked to evaluate the biological explanation so much as to compare biological and learning explanations, considering their strengths and weaknesses. This comparison and evaluation is carried out after the learning explanations of substance misuse have been explained.

The learning approach

Another way to explain substance misuse is to say that it is a learned behaviour. You are required to know one explanation from the learning approach, and the main one focused on here is social learning theory and the role of models. This is because it links well to the second study in detail in this textbook, which is Ennett et al. (1994). You may choose a different learning explanation for substance abuse and some others are explained briefly in this section, to help your learning.

Social learning and the role of models

Social learning theory explains that learning takes place by observing role models, particularly those with whom a person identifies and who are similar to them, or who are admired, and then imitating their behaviour.

AS link Review your learning about social learning theory in the learning approach (pp. 339–42).

Social learning theory puts forward the idea of modelling, which is where behaviour is observed when watching a model, and then remembered and imitated. Features of modelling include observing the behaviour, paying attention to it, being able to perform it and being motivated to perform it. There are internal cognitive processes at play as well as learning processes, such as motivation and emotional responses and memory. Identification with the role model is also a feature of social learning theory. Therefore, if substance misuse is learned through social learning, then the role model is likely to be someone similar to the individual and with whom they identify, so that there is motivation to carry out the behaviour, and the observed behaviour is attended to and remembered.

It is said that parents and peers affect someone's drug misuse, which fits well with social learning theory, as both parents and peers are likely to be role models with whom a person would identify (Baer et al., 1987). Family studies show that drug misuse, such as alcohol and smoking, links to the family, which suggests not only a genetic component but also the likelihood of modelling. People who mix with peers who misuse a drug may also get positive reinforcement from misusing the drug, and positive reinforcement is another part of social learning theory, the idea being that there is a reward such as being part of a group. Akers (1992) has pointed out that television may have a role in promoting substance abuse by providing role models for children. High status people exert a stronger influence on behaviour than low status people (Winett et al., 1989) so it is important that those with high status act responsibly — depending on what is considered 'responsible' in a particular culture.

It is suggested that the social learning of substance misuse depends on the amount of exposure to peers who abuse drugs compared with exposure to peers who do not. It is also affected by the preference of the community towards the particular drug. The frequency of drug use among the peers is important, as well as the age of the individual. Younger adolescents are more susceptible than older adolescents.

An important feature of social learning theory is vicarious learning. At first, smoking seems to be an unpleasant experience. Social learning theory can explain why people continue with it — it is suggested that seeing family and friends enjoying smoking would mean getting a reward vicariously and would lead a person to continue to smoke. Vicarious reinforcement suggests that people persist in a behaviour they see rewarded because they expect reward in the future.

Classical conditioning and substance misuse

Another explanation of substance misuse from the learning approach is the process of classical conditioning. Classical conditioning suggests that feelings can come from stimuli that are paired. So, if substance misuse gives pleasure, which will be an automatic response because it is biological, then anything associated with the substance misuse will also give pleasure. For example, drug equipment such as syringes or even the place associated by the individual with substance misuse can trigger the pleasure response (Childress et al., 1994). This conditioning makes a relapse after successful treatment a possibility because, when individuals are exposed to objects or people that were linked to the substance misuse, they might experience the pleasure feelings again and trigger a desire to abuse the drug once more.

AS link Review what you learned about classical conditioning in the learning approach (pp. 325–27).

Negative reinforcement: the avoidance of withdrawal

Operant conditioning holds that behaviour is repeated if there is a reward and stopped if there is punishment. A reward can be positive (positive reinforcement), such as gaining pleasure, or negative (negative reinforcement), such as removing pain or a problem. Substance misuse can be explained using operant conditioning principles. Drugs can be taken for the reward of pleasurable feelings, which tends to be the case at the start, and drugs can be taken to remove the unpleasant feelings of withdrawal. (**Withdrawal** is explained in more detail later in this section and refers to the symptoms experienced when someone stops taking a drug after having become dependent on it.)

After the drug has been taken for a while, it is more likely that negative reinforcement causes the abuse to be continued, because taking the drug removes withdrawal symptoms. There are negative issues about continuing with substance abuse, such as financial and family problems, but the concern about the issues is not as immediate as the reward from taking the drug or from the removal of withdrawal symptoms.

> **AS link** Review what you learned about operant conditioning in the learning approach (pp. 327–30).

Considering strengths and weaknesses of the biological and learning approaches

Strengths of the biochemical explanation

- A biological explanation has value because the evidence is visible, in the sense that scans show activity under certain circumstances, such as PET scans, where it has been shown that neuronal activity when smoking a 'normal' cigarette was different from when smoking a low-nicotine one. This means that biological explanations have validity — they seem to measure real activity.
- Animal studies have shown how different drugs affect receptors in different ways, and because animal studies can be controlled and repeated, findings can be tested for reliability.
- Gene research has suggested the involvement of the mu-opioid gene, which matches the finding about mu-opioid receptors, so research in one area in biology can be used to reinforce findings from a different area.

Weaknesses of the biochemical explanation

- Animal studies show differences, such as those in mice when looking at different opioid receptors, and it is likely that humans will react differently again, so generalising from animal studies can be difficult.
- Although the findings of PET and other scans are valid in the sense that they are measuring real behaviour, the behaviour is nonetheless in an artificial environment in artificial conditions, so validity can still be questioned.
- The brain is obviously extremely complex in the way neurotransmitters work, and evidence cannot yet pinpoint that degree of complexity.

Strengths of the social learning theory explanation

- Social learning theory has been developed by Bandura (1977) and also in sociology (e.g. Akers) and has much evidence in many areas of social life. For example, Bandura and others have shown the influence of television and the media on behaviour. Social learning theory has been used to explain many areas of behaviour and has evidence to support it. This adds weight to its use in explaining substance misuse — the amount of evidence in other areas is large, which adds to the reliability of the explanation.

■ Social learning has been demonstrated in animals where, for example, monkeys have learned to fear objects that they would not normally fear, just by observing other monkeys showing fear. Therefore it seems justified to claim that such principles operate in humans too.

■ Social learning theory builds on operant conditioning, as it takes reinforcement into account and also incorporates cognitive elements, so it is a theory that has a reasonably complete explanation compared to, for example, classical conditioning.

A girl is likely to imitate her mother's behaviour through principles of social learning — her mother may be a role model, and will smile and give attention, thus reinforcing the behaviour

Weaknesses of the social learning theory explanation

■ The study by Ennett et al. (1994), which is explained in detail in the next section of this chapter, is useful when considering weaknesses. This is because the study found no link between friendship cliques and starting or continuing smoking — only that friendship cliques tended to go against smoking and lead to more 'non-smoking'. There is evidence to suggest, therefore, that peer groups do not lead to substance misuse, but have the opposite effect.

■ It is hard to show a definite link between observation and learning because there are often many factors involved. For example, it could be argued that family members act as role models because alcohol abuse tends to run in families, but genes are also handed down through families.

Comparing the biochemical and social learning theory explanations

Note that it is not the case that biological explanations are right *or* that behavioural explanations are right, as if they cannot both be true. Behavioural reasons may have started the taking of the drug, for example, but biological changes occurred to maintain the drug use (misuse). Those biological changes drive the behaviour to continue substance misuse. Behaviour changes are also needed to overcome the addiction. Both explanations, therefore, are important.

Comparing in terms of validity

Biological explanations are hard to test in terms of validity because of the difficulty in isolating variables for testing. What happens in the brain is hard to study in real terms. Social learning explanations are easier to test in real situations but are also difficult to test for validity because of the many factors involved in behaviour. Both biological and social learning explanations tend to be studied using experiments because of the need to isolate variables to study, and this emphasises the problems with validity. Scanning is valid to an extent but is done in artificial surroundings using artificial behaviour. It is difficult to pick out behaviour that is modelled and then reproduced without considering other explanations as well (such as classical conditioning, genetic propensity and the personality of the individual).

Comparing in terms of reliability

Animal studies and scanning have consistently indicated the role of neurotransmitters and receptors in drug use and misuse, so biological explanations appear to have reliability. Research into social learning theory, such as that by Bandura and others, has consistently shown that what is observed is imitated by children. There have also been animal laboratory experiments that have reinforced these findings. For social learning theory there are consistent findings that are reliable.

> **Study hint** Social learning theory is explored in greater detail in Chapter 5 when looking at clinical psychology, and it is there that animal studies are considered. The topic will be returned to when considering issues and debates in psychology, at the end of your course. Be sure that you can describe and evaluate social learning theory, including using examples from whichever part of the course you are discussing.

Comparing in terms of nature–nurture

It is worth noting that the biological explanations are firmly on the side of a nature explanation, because it is held that receptors react in specific ways according to brain functioning and this applies to all humans. Humans are born with brains that have specific brain functioning.

Social learning theory, however, is firmly in the 'nurture' camp. The theory claims that behaviour such as substance misuse comes from learning from the environment and from experiences, such as that experienced in a family or with friends. Therefore, in the nature–nurture debate, the two explanations are on opposing sides.

Study hint Comparing theories (and studies) is quite a difficult skill. One way of doing it is to run through issues such as validity and reliability and to comment on how each theory (or study) fares with regard to these issues.

Two drugs in detail

In this section two drugs are considered in detail. The specification requires you to consider heroin and one other drug from alcohol, cocaine, ecstasy, marijuana and nicotine. We focus in this textbook on heroin and nicotine, which were also the focus of the examples given in the Methodology section. You may choose to study one of the other drugs, however, in place of nicotine. Alcohol is explained in the online resources.

Heroin

Issues about heroin have been explained previously in this chapter (e g in the Methodology section when looking at animal studies and the study of Blattler et al.). This section reiterates how heroin works at the synapse (the **mode of action**), considers the effects of heroin, and explains tolerance, dependence and withdrawal.

Mode of action refers to how drugs work and focuses on biological and biochemical explanations.

Heroin is an opiate, which acts as a depressant and analgesic (painkiller) in the central nervous system. It is produced from morphine, which comes from the opium or Asian poppy (*Papaver somniferum*). It is in powder form, often white, and is usually injected — although recently with fears about the safety of needles it is sometimes smoked or snorted.

Mode of action

Heroin acts at the opioid receptor sites in the brain. It changes the action of dopamine in the reward pathway of the brain, releasing more dopamine than usual. Heroin is converted into morphine in the brain, and it is the morphine that works at the opioid receptors at the synapse. The morphine binds (fits) to receptors to reduce the inhibitory (preventing) effect of GABA (gamma-aminobutyric acid) on dopaminergic neurones. **Dopaminergic neurones** are those that release dopamine. The result is more dopamine activity and the release of dopamine into the synaptic cleft. If the dopaminergic reward pathway continues to be stimulated, this leads to feelings of euphoria and the high that is reported by heroin users.

Study hint

Use this explanation of how heroin works when describing the biological explanation for substance misuse.

Effects

Short-term effects include pleasure feelings as well as a reduction of pain, which occur because of neurotransmitter functioning at the opioid receptor sites. There is a 'rush', which includes a dry mouth, heavy limbs, flushing of the skin and possibly feelings of sickness and severe itching. In addition, there is a sense of relaxation and drowsiness, as well as a slowing of mental functions, breathing and heart rate. The rush happens at around 7 seconds after injection or within a few minutes if heroin is snorted or smoked.

Long-term effects come after chronic (persistent) use. There will be **psychological** and **physical dependence**, as well as **tolerance**. Cravings for the effects of heroin develop and, if it is not used regularly, there will be **withdrawal** symptoms.

> **Study hint** Note that substance misuse, synapse, tolerance, physical dependence, psychological dependence and withdrawal are the key terms for this chapter. All are defined in this section. Be sure you can define each term and be able to give an example to help your explanation.

There may also be overdose symptoms if heroin is taken in large doses, because heroin acts as a depressant. Overdose becomes more likely the more someone is addicted to heroin, the longer they have taken it and the more they use other drugs such as alcohol. There can be long-term effects from the repeated use of needles, such as infections or collapsed veins. Contaminants from the drug may affect the body, clogging blood vessels, for example. Other effects are difficulties with breathing or with fighting infection. There are problems for a foetus if the user is pregnant, and an increased risk of miscarriage. Psychological effects include difficulty in concentrating, lack of attention and memory problems.

Tolerance

Tolerance means that, as a drug is taken increasingly over a period of time, more of it will be needed to obtain the feelings that were produced at first. The same dose of drug will not produce the same feeling of euphoria. This is the case with many drugs, including heroin. Tolerance goes with being physically dependent on heroin because, when people need increasing amounts to get the same high, they are likely to become physically dependent on the drug. A stage may be reached where tolerance works to the extent that no amount of the drug will achieve the resulting high, and at this point the individual will continue taking the drug simply to delay withdrawal symptoms. Tolerance is linked to addiction, which is physical dependence because, when a plateau is reached and more of the drug does not change its effects, then the person is addicted and needs the drug for normal functioning.

Physical and psychological dependence

People can be physically or psychologically dependent on heroin, or both. Physical dependence means that the body becomes used to functioning with the drug in its system and so 'needs' it for what is then normal functioning. This is addiction — when the body needs the drug for normal physical and/or psychological functioning. One aspect of physical dependence is that the brains of heroin users tend to produce less endorphin and so addicted people will rely on heroin for their pleasure and reduction of pain experiences more than someone who does not use heroin. Physical dependence means that, when the drug is stopped, there will be withdrawal symptoms, which are also physical. Heroin rapidly develops tolerance, therefore someone can quickly become physically dependent on it.

Psychological dependence means heroin takes on a great importance in someone's life in a way that makes the cravings hard to resist. The drug is important not just physically but also for the person's mental state. Heroin is often taken by people with living difficulties, no social support, problems with employment and with low self-esteem, so psychological dependence is likely to occur because the feelings of pleasure and dulling of the senses are something such people might seek.

Withdrawal

Even if heroin is taken (in a sustained way) for only 3 days, withdrawal symptoms can occur when it is stopped. These tend to start about 6 hours after last using the drug, although this depends on how much tolerance there is and the quantity of the last dose. Withdrawal symptoms include sweating, anxiety, depression, sensitivity in the genital area, a feeling of heaviness, cramps in the limbs, tears, insomnia, chills and muscle aching. There might also be vomiting and diarrhoea. People might also have what can be called 'itchy blood', which leads to compulsive scratching. Withdrawal symptoms quickly disappear when heroin is taken again, which can lead to a cycle of taking the drug, trying to stop, then taking it again to reduce the physical symptoms of withdrawal. At this stage feelings of euphoria have disappeared because of tolerance.

Nicotine

This section focuses on nicotine, taken in to the body through smoking. The same areas are covered as for heroin: the mode of action, its effects, tolerance, physical and psychological dependence and symptoms of withdrawal.

Nicotine comes from the dried leaves and stems of tobacco plants. Cigarette tobacco contains varying amounts of nicotine, from 15 to 25 mg per cigarette, so smoking does not give nicotine poisoning in its fullest form, though nicotine is a toxin and extremely poisonous. Nicotine is also an insecticide, and is a very harmful drug.

Mode of action

Nicotine is a powerfully addictive drug that affects both the central nervous system and the peripheral nervous system. The central nervous system is the brain and spinal cord, and the peripheral nervous system includes other areas such as those where messages about the alarm reaction and fight or flight messages are located. The peripheral nervous system has two types of neurones: those for sensory information and those for movement.

When smoked, nicotine enters the lungs and is quickly absorbed through the lungs and then passed across cell membranes. Chewing tobacco or gum allows absorption by means of a different route, through mucous membranes. After being absorbed, nicotine enters the blood. If nicotine is injected it is absorbed and reaches the brain in about 1 minute. Because smoking takes nicotine directly to the lungs, however, it can enter the blood almost as quickly as by injection and might even get to the brain more quickly than if injected. Nicotine affects other areas as well as the brain, but this takes longer and the brain 'feels' the effect first. As the effects reach other areas of the body after a longer time, it is possible for someone to still feel the effects of nicotine after 24 hours.

Nicotine works at nicotinic receptors in the central nervous system and also in the peripheral nervous system. It inhibits the function of specific acetylcholine receptors, known as nicotinic acetylcholine receptors because they interact with nicotine. Acetylcholine is a neurotransmitter, and nicotine stimulates the acetylcholine receptor then blocks it. This has the effect of getting in the way of signalling ability. Acetylcholine levels rise because nicotine has disabled the receptors, and so acetylcholine is in the synaptic gap, not being picked up, and levels of the neurotransmitter norepinephrine (noradrenaline) also rise, which leads to better memory ability. Anxiety is reduced because of higher levels of endorphins.

Effects

The effects of nicotine poisoning are a burning feeling in the mouth, salivation, sickness, stomach pains and diarrhoea. The individual can feel agitated, have a headache, and feel dizzy, confused and weak. There can be a lack of coordination and an increase in blood pressure. The heart may be affected and there can be convulsions. Nicotine is a toxin (it is poisonous), and there is no antidote.

However, cigarette smoking does not include enough nicotine for there to be direct poisoning. A low dose of nicotine, such as from cigarette smoking, can help with relaxation and can cause mild euphoria. It can also help to improve attention and problem-solving skills. Dopamine levels increase with nicotine, which causes the same changes as those associated with using heroin, such as increased pleasure. Increased levels of norepinephrine improve memory ability and raised levels of endorphins decrease anxiety.

Nicotine also seems to affect how other recreational drugs affect the brain and body. In addition, cigarettes themselves cause harm: from inhaling burning plant and from the insufficient burning of some of the constituents of the cigarette and plant, some of which are carcinogenic (can lead to cancer). The lungs become coated in tar, which reduces lung efficiency.

Tolerance

Nicotine use quickly leads to tolerance. The body produces more acetylcholine receptors if nicotine is used over a long period, and this gives tolerance even only a few days after exposure to the drug. It is not the case that more and more nicotine is needed to give the effect so much as a plateau is reached quickly and the reaction to the nicotine is fixed. Therefore, at first smokers will need more and more nicotine to get the effects — relaxation, lowering of anxiety, higher levels of concentration and mild euphoria. This means smokers usually start to increase their use of cigarettes in a short time. They rise to a high level of consumption and then have to keep to that to get the results they want. This means that nicotine is addictive.

Physical and psychological dependence

The increased production of acetylcholine causes rapid physiological dependence, just as tolerance is reached quickly. Nicotine is addictive and the brain (and the peripheral nervous system) changes to the extent that nicotine is needed for normal physical functioning. There is psychological dependence as well, in that the individual will become used to the oral stimulation and without it would need to substitute something else, such as eating more (though that could be linked to physical issues as well). Nicotine involves a stimulant that leads to craving for the drug — which is as much a psychological element as a physical one. If smoking gives a reward, such as feeling calmer, then the behaviour is likely to be repeated to repeat the reward. If the effect after a puff of cigarette smoke is quick, this is believed to act as a strong reinforcer for taking the drug again. This links to operant conditioning and the power of reward as a reinforcer of behaviour.

Withdrawal

Withdrawal symptoms of nicotine include a desire for oral gratification (such as eating), anxiety, poor concentration and memory problems. There may also be depression and sleeping problems as well as an increased appetite. Withdrawal can give headaches as well and is almost the reverse of the effects of nicotine. For example, while nicotine relaxes a user, a withdrawal symptom is anxiety.

Two ways of treating substance misuse

This section considers two ways of treating substance misuse, the first of which is drug treatment in heroin dependence. The other chosen method is token economy for drug use, because you are likely to have studied token economy already. The specification suggests two other ways of treating substance misuse: aversion therapy and the AA (Alcoholics Anonymous) approach. These two are explained in the online resources. Alternatively you may choose another treatment altogether. The two methods explained must be described and evaluated.

Drug treatment of heroin dependence

Drug treatment is a major way of treating heroin dependence. Blättler et al.'s study (2002, explained in depth on pp. 138–142) is about whether drug treatment for heroin also affects cocaine use in those who are being treated for heroin. The conclusion is that drug treatment *does* help to reduce cocaine use, which is evidence of the success of such an approach.

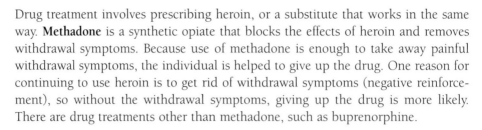

Drug treatment involves prescribing heroin, or a substitute that works in the same way. **Methadone** is a synthetic opiate that blocks the effects of heroin and removes withdrawal symptoms. Because use of methadone is enough to take away painful withdrawal symptoms, the individual is helped to give up the drug. One reason for continuing to use heroin is to get rid of withdrawal symptoms (negative reinforcement), so without the withdrawal symptoms, giving up the drug is more likely. There are drug treatments other than methadone, such as buprenorphine.

Methadone programmes

Methadone has been used as a treatment since 1964 and is prescribed officially. It is a maintenance programme, which means that it is a way of controlling heroin addiction. Methadone does not affect normal functioning and those taking it are not 'drugged'. It is taken orally and prevents withdrawal symptoms for about 24 hours. Methadone also removes cravings for heroin. Someone taking methadone who then takes a normal dose of heroin will not get a feeling of euphoria, so they will be less likely to want to take heroin as well as methadone.

People on the programme have to take methadone once a day and attend a clinic, usually daily, for their prescription. Dosages must be carefully monitored, especially for those who are taking medication for other problems such as HIV infection. People taking methadone may have problems when coming off the treatment, such as withdrawal symptoms, and methadone use can also create overdose problems.

Buprenorphine

Buprenorphine is a treatment being put forward as an alternative to methadone. It gives weaker opiate levels than methadone and is less likely to lead to overdose problems. There is also a lower level of physical dependence than with methadone.

Evaluation of drug treatment for heroin dependence

Strengths

■ Evidence suggests that drug treatment programmes work, as seen in the study of Blättler et al. (2002).
■ Wodak (2005) reported on the success of drug treatment for heroin addiction — methadone and buprenorphine — and reviewed studies to find that, when using such drug treatments, individuals tended to stay on the treatment more than if they were on other treatment programmes.
■ The National Institute of Health (1997) found that methadone maintenance treatment is effective in reducing heroin drug use and also helps in a social sense, by reducing crime as well as helping to prevent the spread of HIV/AIDS.
■ Studies from Australia, Europe, Asia and the USA have mainly found strong associations between methadone treatment and the reduction in frequency of opioid use, as well as advantages related to HIV.

Weaknesses

■ Many patients need treatment for at least 2 years, and studies suggest that 85% stay on methadone for 12 months. A long treatment has cost implications.

- Randomly assigning or not assigning people to the treatment (or to potentially less effective treatments) is not ethical. Therefore, it is difficult to evaluate the success of methadone maintenance treatment programmes.
- There is both philosophical and political opposition to drug treatment programmes for heroin addiction. Some people object to heroin users being given drugs as treatment, partly because of the withdrawal symptoms when the individual comes off the treatment.
- Politically, a cost–benefit analysis has to be carried out to ensure that the cost of methadone maintenance, or other drug treatment programmes, is worthwhile. In the USA there is said to be a treatment gap (those for whom the treatment is not available) of between 75% and 80% of all addicts (National Institute on Drug Abuse, 2006). The financial cost to the individual, family and society of untreated opiate dependence is extremely high.
- The programmes, even when government-approved, are highly regulated, which makes running them difficult.

Drug maintenance programmes, such as using methadone, almost always focus on psychosocial factors as well, such as social support and encouraging the avoidance of people and places linked with the addiction.

Token economy for drug use

Token economy programmes (TEPs) are used for treating drug use. TEPs work on the principle that behaviour is repeated for a reward. Rewards can take the form of positive or negative reinforcement.

Elements needed for a token economy programme

- Clear identification of what will be used as tokens: points, counters, stickers and so on. Tokens have to be given immediately and must 'buy' something desirable.
- Clear identification of the behaviour or behaviours to be rewarded.
- Clear identification of what the tokens can buy: outings, food, television, privileges etc.
- An agreed and clear time and place for exchanging the rewards.
- A system for recording behaviour.
- Consistent application of the programme by staff.
- A system for changing the rewards to shape behaviour, so that rewards are gradually given less frequently or for different behaviours, all of which must be clear to staff and those on the programme.

> **Explore** Find out about a token economy programme. For example, the Salvation Army hostels sometimes use these to promote required behaviour. They may take points away for undesired behaviour as well as rewarding required behaviour.

Contingency management therapy

One type of token economy programme in current use is contingency management therapy. This uses a voucher system where participants earn points if they test negative for drugs. They may exchange their points for items that encourage healthy living. The idea is to reinforce positively not using drugs with rewards that encourage healthy behaviour. One reason for this is that rehabilitation programmes for drug users aim to stop substance misuse but also to help to lower criminal activity and the associated issues with HIV/AIDS infection. A healthier lifestyle and not misusing drugs help to achieve these aims.

Evaluation of token economy programmes

Advantages

- A token economy programme suits everyone and focuses on praise. There is no strong punishment involved, so it is ethical in that regard.
- There is evidence that contingency management programmes (rewards) work to reduce substance misuse. Peirce et al. (2006) carried out a study in the USA involving six community-based settings with a methadone maintenance programme for heroin users. A control group underwent the usual treatment and another group had the chance to win prizes in a draw for 12 weeks. They were entered into the draw if they submitted negative samples (heroin- and alcohol-free) and, the more they abstained from using the drugs, the more draws they were entered into. It was found that continuous abstinence was twice as likely for the group with the chance to win prizes than for the control group. The conclusion was that such prize-based programmes worked in reducing substance misuse, alongside a methadone maintenance programme.

Disadvantages

- It can be costly to provide the rewards, train staff and manage the programme.
- Some staff find such a programme impractical, time-consuming and difficult to carry out effectively.
- Staff can neglect the rights of the individual by withholding essentials such as food and comfort.
- Staff who are not trained properly might inadvertently reward inappropriate behaviour, thus encouraging negative behaviour.

Campaigns against the use of recreational drugs

In this section you are required to look at one campaign that has encouraged people not to use recreational drugs. As nicotine has been chosen in this textbook as one of the substances to cover, an anti-smoking campaign is chosen here, but you may choose a different drugs campaign.

Anti-smoking legislation and policies

Laws against smoking have been established in many countries in recent times, such as the law passed in 2007 in England banning smoking in any public place, including pubs and clubs. Previous laws included banning cigarette advertising and placing strong health warnings on cigarette packets. There are also government policies and funding to discourage smoking. For example, funding has been given to encourage women to give up smoking in pregnancy.

A specific anti-smoking campaign

In 2008 the British Heart Foundation instigated an anti-smoking campaign that included what they call a 'hard-hitting' campaign, showing the harm that smoking can do by using strong images intended to shock people into quitting. The British Heart Foundation claims that 'stopping smoking is the single most important thing a person can do to avoid a heart attack.'

Explore Look at the website of the British Heart Foundation, where you will find information about its anti-smoking campaign. Investigate some of the information, such as the relationship between smoking and heart attacks.

The campaign gives information on how to stop smoking. There is information on using support groups and replacement therapy (such as using nicotine patches). Smokers can use the website to find their nearest support group, as well as information on what happens in the groups. They can share their experiences with others by using the site, and they can find out information about smoking and its effects. The site stresses that smoking cigarettes builds up fat on the artery walls and a clot can then block the artery, causing a heart attack. There is also a positive message about the benefits of stopping: reducing likely heart problems, feeling better, having healthier skin and getting back a sense of taste.

Evaluation of anti-drug campaigns

Strengths

- The British Heart Foundation website is a good source of information, along with posters and other forms of advertising aimed at reaching as many people as possible. As part of their campaign there was even a short television programme about smoking and heart disease, to catch people's imagination. Many different media were used, which is a strength, as more people are likely to be reached that way than by using just one medium.
- It is claimed that anti-smoking campaigns are generally effective. For example, in the USA, it has been said that smoking has fallen by half because of anti-smoking campaigns (Mechanic et al., 2005). A public health document (2000) commenting on an anti-smoking campaign in Scotland concluded that the campaign was cost-effective, although the conclusion added that this assumed that the figures for cessation were accurate and that the reduction in smoking was as a result of Smokeline (the campaign at the time).
- Hafsted et al. (1997) report an evaluation study of Norwegian media campaigns against smoking, and it was found using a questionnaire that smokers reacted more emotionally to the campaigns than non-smokers, and that women reacted more strongly than men. Those who reacted positively to the campaign were those more likely to give up smoking.
- These conclusions suggest that the BHF campaign would work.

Weaknesses

- The website gives a great deal of information, including helpline numbers, advice and even e-mails that someone can send to a friend to encourage them to stop smoking. However, this suits only someone who has already accessed the website and who is, therefore, probably already on their way towards giving up.
- A campaign may not be successful if there is advertising or another campaign working against it. For example, banning the advertising of cigarettes might work alongside a particular anti-smoking campaign, so it is unlikely to be just that campaign that is succeeding in stopping smoking.
- The problem with evaluating the success of a campaign like the BHF is that other events are happening at the same time, such as banning smoking in public and a general campaign about smoking being unsocial. However, if these factors lead to stopping smoking, the end result is the same.

Examination-style questions

1 Describe an explanation of substance misuse from the biological approach. *(4 marks)*

2 Outline two ways of treating substance misuse. *(6 marks)*

3 Outline two weaknesses of the learning approach when explaining substance misuse. *(4 marks)*

4 Outline the mode of action and withdrawal symptoms of heroin. *(6 marks)*

Extension questions

1 Compare the strengths and weaknesses of explanations of substance misuse from the biological and the learning approaches. *(12 marks)*

2 Compare two drugs with reference to some of or all the following: mode of action, effects, tolerance, physical and psychological dependence, withdrawal. *(12 marks)*

Studies in detail

For this section you are required to cover two studies in detail, one of which must be Blättler et al. (2002). The other study must focus on alcohol, cocaine, ecstasy, marijuana or smoking nicotine. As this chapter has already focused on smoking nicotine, the study that looks at nicotine (Ennett et al. 1994) is chosen here.

Blättler et al. (2002)

Blättler et al. carried out the study *Decreasing intravenous cocaine use in opiate users treated with prescribed heroin* within the Swiss Heroin Project, which was set up to study the effects of maintenance programmes for users of heroin.

Background

The idea behind the study is that, for heroin users who also use cocaine, a maintenance programme might not be successful because of continued contact with the drug scene and because of other criminal-related activities such as injection hazards.

In 1982, 900 patients in Switzerland were treated with oral methadone and by 1994 this number had increased to 14,000, from an estimated total of 30,000 users. Although the uptake of the treatment had increased significantly, it was still the case that many heroin users did not benefit from the treatment, so the Swiss government launched a research project on heroin maintenance therapy for opiate users. This project gave rise to a number of studies, but no research on heroin together with cocaine use. There was some earlier research that seemed to suggest that methadone had an effect on cocaine use (Verthein et al., 1996) but also some research to suggest it had no effect (Avants et al., 1994).

Aim

The aim was to look at maintenance treatment for heroin users who also used cocaine (poly-drug use), in order to see the effect of the heroin maintenance programme on their cocaine use. The study examined drop-out rates from treatment to see if it was higher when the heroin users used cocaine as well. It also looked at how cocaine use changed among those who stayed for treatment.

Specific questions the researchers asked were:
- Was there a reduction in cocaine use among those who remained in treatment for over 18 months?
- Which factors are associated with continued cocaine use?
- Was cocaine use before treatment a possible factor with regard to dropping out of the programme?

Procedures

The study used the Medical Prescription of Narcotics Programme (PROVE), which involved prescribing heroin for heroin users. The researchers chose a group of heroin users on the PROVE programme and compared baseline measures with follow-up data. The study took place in a naturalistic setting — the participants were on the programme in any case. This is called a cohort study, because one group or cohort of people is followed over the course of a programme. It is also a longitudinal study using the same participants. As well as following the main group, there was a series of clinical trials on a smaller subsample of the main group. Ethical approval was given and there was a safety assurance group that monitored the ongoing medical therapy.

Participants

From 1994 to 1995, 995 patients were selected. They had been admitted to a heroin-assisted maintenance treatment programme. At the end of the 18 months of follow-up, the interviews stopped. Of the original 995 patients, 486 did not have 18 months of follow-up, so were excluded from the study. The participants had to be at least 20 years old, addicted to heroin for at least 2 years, with at least two previous attempts to be treated without success, and they had to give informed consent. People on the treatment were expelled for drug dealing at the treatment centre, smuggling substances, using violent behaviour, or for non-compliance with the treatment or research guidelines. The confirmed use of illicit substances did not cause them to be expelled.

Assessments

- Trained independent interviewers questioned the participants at intake and every 6 months, using a standardised questionnaire.
- Urine tests (urinalysis) were carried out at intake and randomly with notice twice a month.
- Medical examinations for HIV and hepatitis were carried out at intake and every 6 months.
- There was a questionnaire for those leaving treatment, to discover their reason for doing so.
- Data were recorded about dosages, the time of administering the treatment, and any other medication being used.

Treatment

The treatment was a prescription of narcotics — a daily injection of heroin. There was also psychosocial and medical care, and counselling was mandatory.

Analysis

Chi-squared tests were carried out to look at differences between the groups. A Spearman's correlation coefficient was carried out to look at relations between age and frequency of drug use. A probability error of $p \leq 0.05$ (5%) was considered to be statistically significant.

Study hint Use this study when considering methodological issues such as ethical considerations, longitudinal studies, using qualitative and quantitative data, and considerations about correlations and self-report data.

Results

Results at baseline, when the participants started the treatment

There were 266 participants involved in giving baseline measures: 98 were female (37%) and 168 male. Their mean age was 30 and their mean duration of using heroin was 10 years, with the mean duration of regular use of cocaine being 7 years. The heroin maintenance programme took place in six clinics in Zürich, Bern, Oltel, Thun and Basel. Among the participants:

- 75% preferred to inject both heroin and cocaine
- 33% drank alcohol (30 g or more each day)

- 23% used no cannabis
- 31% were considered daily cocaine users
- 54% were occasional cocaine users
- 16% were non-cocaine users at intake

These measures included self-report data.

Results after 18 months

After 18 months, 247 participants were followed up. Self-report data and urinalysis were used.

Table 3.7 Negative or positive self-report use of cocaine, compared with negative or positive urinalysis

	Urine cocaine negative	One or more urine cocaine positive
Self-report negative (no use of cocaine)	51% (127)	2% (6)
Self-report positive (some use of cocaine)	24% (59)	22% (55)
Total	**75%**	**25%**

After 18 months of treatment with prescribed heroin the cocaine use decreased from 84% to 48%. For daily users this was a fall from 30% to 6%. The change in the number of non-users went up from 16% to 52%.

Conclusions

Non-users of cocaine went up from 16% to 52%, which is a large rise and would be considered successful. The number of daily users of cocaine fell from 30% to 6%, which is a large fall. Table 3.7 also shows that 75% of participants had urine tests that were negative for cocaine, even though some of them still claimed they used cocaine. Clearly the treatment did not mean that cocaine users had stopped using altogether, but there were many who did stop. It was reported that most of those who continued to use cocaine reduced their use from frequent use to occasional. Overall, 84% used cocaine at the start and 48% at the end, which is a successful difference.

It was found that behaviour corresponded to the results. For example, those who used to inject both cocaine and heroin, as discovered from the intake interview, were more likely to continue to use cocaine. Cocaine use at the 18-month follow-up was also linked to prostitution, illicit heroin use, illegal income and contact with the drug scene. However, these features decreased over the 18 months of treatment, so there was some effect on behaviour as well as on drug use.

Study hint You are asked to study the use of maintenance programmes for heroin addiction as a treatment, so you can use this study of how maintenance programmes for heroin are successful, at least to a certain extent, in reducing a heroin addict's use of cocaine.

Evaluation

Strengths

- There was good attention to ethical issues, including getting clear informed consent at the start and having the treatment and study monitored throughout.
- Using interviewing, questionnaires and urinalysis means there are qualitative and quantitative measures, which adds detail and validity to the results. For example, self-report about not using cocaine can be checked against urinalysis.
- This is a naturalistic study and there is no manipulation of variables, so the results should have ecological validity.
- The researchers checked as many variables as they could, including the price of cocaine between 1994 and 1996, which remained relatively low, so they do not think factors like that affected the findings. Reduction in cocaine use did seem to come from the treatment.

Weaknesses

- The drop-out rate from the treatment was 11%. Some participants left for alternative treatments. There may have been a pattern in drop out, and those left on the treatment may have been different in some way, causing a bias in the findings. However, the researchers checked for a pattern in drop out related to cocaine use and did not find one, so they were thorough in the sampling.
- It is possible that being on the study, and being interviewed, tested and observed affected the findings, because the attention may have altered the behaviour of the participants. Therefore, the findings might not be valid.
- The researchers have emphasised possible problems with generalisation. They point out that generalisation should be only to heavily dependent, long-term poly-drug users with multiple health and psychiatric problems. Generalisation should be in the light of the Swiss situation and the Heroin Project.
- The researchers also point out that the study relies on self-report data, which may not be 100% reliable.

Table 3.8 *Summary of the strengths and weakness of Blättler et al. (2002)*

Strengths	Weaknesses
• Sampling was careful, including checking drop-out rate and other factors	• Being on the study, and the additional attention, may have caused the change
• There was careful attention to ethics	
• Both qualitative and quantitative data were gathered, so validity could be checked	• Generalisation is limited to Switzerland and those types of participant
• The study was naturalistic, so had ecological validity	• Self-report data may not be reliable
• Many factors were checked for change over time, such as the price of cocaine, to try to ensure the treatment alone was responsible for any change	

Ennett et al. (1994)

Susan Ennett et al. carried out the study *Variability in cigarette smoking within and between adolescent friendship cliques*, which took place in the USA, using school friendship groups to see if smoking was linked with friendships.

Background

It has been claimed that peer groups link with adolescent smoking. For example, studies have found a correlation between an adolescent smoking and his/her peer group smoking (e.g. van Roosmalen and McDaniel, 1989). Most studies of adolescent smoking focus on the individual and conclude, from the individual's description of friends, that there is peer-group smoking. 'Peer group' in this sense is a group of people of the same age and possibly the same attitudes and opinions. A friendship clique, according to the researchers, is 'small interaction-based clusters of adolescents who spend time together and share similar attitudes and behaviours' (Ennet *et al.*, 1994, p. 296). With friendship cliques there should be **intragroup homogeneity** (similarity within the group) and **intergroup heterogeneity** (differences between different groups).

The study used formal social network analysis to identify adolescent cliques. Social network analysis gathers information about friends — in this case, by asking participants to name their three best friends — and links them up to show groups of friends. The study then asked about smoking behaviour, so that the researchers could relate smoking behaviour to friendships. **Clique connectedness** refers to how many links there are between clique members; a more connected clique should show more similarity regarding smoking. More friendship links give greater opportunity for communication, interaction and reinforcement of behaviours between members.

Aim

The aim was to look at adolescent smoking in relation to the smoking habits of friends and in relation to adolescent peer groups. The study looked for friendship cliques by analysing questionnaires that gave information about three best friends. The cliques were drawn up from the questionnaires. Data about smoking were also gathered so that members of the cliques could be compared with regard to their smoking habits.

Procedures

Students in the ninth grade in one area of the USA were the participants in 1980. The study reports that smoking rates have not declined since the data were collected, so the researchers claim that findings should generalise to present-day adolescents. The data were collected in the adolescents' homes from August to

December 1980 and were collected using a self-administered questionnaire. Data were also gathered from mothers to find out their own level of education, which was one of the variables considered.

Participants

The study used 1,092 ninth-graders (aged 14–15) across five schools and discovered 87 friendship cliques — 81% of all ninth-graders in the school system in that area. Initially eight schools took part in the study, but adolescents from only five of the eight schools were included in the analysis — three schools had interrupted cliques because of changes in the schools over the time, so were excluded. These three schools were similar demographically to the five used, so it was not thought that excluding them would affect the findings.

Clique identification

The cliques comprised three or more adolescents who link to most of the other members of their group with regard to their friendship (more than 50%) and who are all connected by a path of friendship links that lie entirely within the group. These data were arrived at by network analyses conducted at each school. As 95% of friendships were between people at the same school, the researchers looked only at cliques that were within a school. Links with adolescents not surveyed were ignored. A link from person A to person B was also assumed to be a link from person B to person A — to have ignored non-reciprocated links would have excluded quite a lot of the data. However, there was greater weight placed on reciprocated links: when scoring, 2 points were given to a reciprocated link and 1 to a non-reciprocated link.

Adolescents not in cliques were called isolates or clique liaisons. Liaisons were friends with other adolescents but not members of the cliques. In the study, 42.2% were clique members, 29.2% were clique liaisons and 28.6% were isolates.

How Ennett et al. (1994) built friendship cliques

- Person A declares person B as a friend, but person B does not mention person A: a 1-point link is made for this non-reciprocated link.
- Person A declares person B as a friend and person B declares person A as a friend: a 2-point link is made for this reciprocated link.
- Both person A and person B mention person C as a friend, and person C just mentions person A and not person B, so A/C is a reciprocated link and B/C is a non-reciprocated link.

Analysis

The analysis was carried out school by school. The number of clique smokers as a proportion of the number in the clique was calculated. The researchers also looked to see if cliques with greater connectedness (friendship links to and from one another) showed greater smoking homogeneity (similarity). To calculate this, a Spearman rank correlation coefficient was used. The researchers chose a level of significance of $p \leq 0.05$. However, as there were a small number of cliques at each school and because there was so little research of the type, they also used a significance level of $p \leq 0.10$.

You may recall from your AS course that it was said that $p \leq 0.05$ is the most generous level of significance used and that $p \leq 0.10$ would not be accepted, in that results that did not reach at least a 5% or less probability of being due to chance would not be accepted. This study is an exception and the researchers explain why, but results accepted at $p \leq 0.10$ would be treated with caution. This would be a useful evaluation point and it shows the importance of learning about statistics including issues such as levels of significance.

Results

Among the 1,092 participants in the five schools covered, 87 cliques were found, comprised of 461 adolescents (42% of the adolescents). There were between 10 and 24 cliques for each school and 93% of the cliques had between 3 and 10 members; the average clique size was 5 members. Cliques were largely homogeneous (similar) with regard to gender and race. Cliques with both boys and girls and cliques with both black and white members were excluded from the study, because there were so few.

The results showed that 89.8% of all clique members were non-smokers. The smoking rate among clique members varied from 3.9% to 15.5% across the schools; 68% of the cliques were comprised completely of non-smokers and 2% (two cliques) had entirely smokers. The smoking rate in the cliques (11.1%) was less than the overall smoking rate in the schools (15.2%).

Cliques were more internally homogeneous (similar within them) and more externally heterogeneous (different between them) than would be expected by chance. This was true for all-female cliques, all-white cliques and cliques with a lower level of education of the mother. However, it was less true for all-male cliques, all-black cliques and cliques with mother's education being relatively high. The homogeneous (similar) cliques were either all smokers or all non-smokers and the heterogeneous (different) cliques included both smokers and non-smokers. Both types of clique were equally well connected.

Conclusions

Adolescent clique members who smoke tend to associate with one another. Few cliques were smoking cliques — most of the adolescents were non-smokers. Perhaps peer groups contribute more to non-smoking than they do to smoking. This is the opposite of the idea that peer groups and peer pressure lead to smoking, though still backs the idea of social learning and imitating friends. Adolescents identified as isolates had the highest rate of smoking. There is similarity within cliques and variability between cliques with regard to smoking — smoking behaviour seems salient (relevant) to specific cliques. However, cliques contribute more to the maintenance of non-smoking.

It is possible that non-smokers may become cliques rather than accepting the opinion that cliques contribute to non-smoking. Perhaps smoking has a greater

3

social significance for girls than boys, as more all-girl cliques smoked than all-boy cliques. There was also the consideration that more mothers with lower education smoke than mothers with higher education levels.

Prevention activities focus on social skills development, assertiveness training and developing refusal skills to say 'no', but this study finds cliques tend to support non-smoking, which suggests that prevention focus is not useful.

> **Study hint** If you focus on a campaign to reduce smoking, use this study to evaluate such a campaign. Perhaps encouraging group support to help members not to smoke is more beneficial than assuming that social learning leads to smoking.

Evaluation

Strengths

- This study uses evidence about forming friendship groups to find out about smoking and other issues, rather than taking what individuals say about their friends. The friends provide their own data, which should be more valid, and the friendship cliques are worked out carefully, again giving more validity than previous studies in this area.
- Five schools were used and large numbers of adolescents contributed data, so the data should be generalisable, at least to that age group in the USA. As many as possible of the young people enrolled in the five schools were surveyed, so there was no restrictive sampling.

Weaknesses

- Adolescents were limited to listing their three best friends and no more, which may have affected the findings, meaning that the findings are not valid and would have underestimated the clique connectedness.
- The way of calculating friendship and taking non-reciprocated links as being reciprocated may have made the data not valid. It assumed that a person claiming someone else as a friend meant that the other person agreed, which may not have been the case.
- Self-report data can be unreliable — at another time and in another place (other than their homes, perhaps), adolescents might give different friendships or different comments about their smoking.

Table 3.9 Summary of the strengths and weaknesses of Ennett et al. (1994)

Strengths	Weaknesses
• Cliques are found from analysing the data and then members of cliques themselves say whether they smoke — valid data. • Thorough sampling (trying to get all ninth-graders) using five schools, so generalisation is possible up to a point.	• Only three best friends were asked about, which might limit the data's validity. • Non-reciprocated friendships were accepted as reciprocated, whereas the friendship might not have been 'real'. • There may have been social desirability in the responses about not smoking. • Self-report data can be unreliable.

Examination-style questions

1 Outline the procedures of two studies in detail from health psychology. *(6 marks)*

2 Describe the findings (results and/or conclusions) of Blättler et al. (2002). *(4 marks)*

3 Describe one study of substance misuse other than Blättler et al. (2002). *(6 marks)*

4 Evaluate Blättler et al. (2002). *(6 marks)*

Extension question

Discuss two studies that look at substance misuse, including Blättler et al. (2002). In your discussion, and alongside your description of the two studies, include at least one comparison point, as well as strengths and weaknesses of the studies. *(12 marks)*

Key issues

For your study of health psychology you must prepare one key issue and carry out a practical relating to this. The practical can involve content analysis (primary data) or focusing on two magazine articles or other similar sources, where you should summarise the articles and draw conclusions from them (secondary data). See pp. 48–49 and p. 105 for information about how the key issue practical works.

You can choose to carry out a practical that requires primary data gathering (content analysis) or one that requires examination of secondary data (article analysis). In this chapter an analysis of articles is suggested. A similar article analysis (focused on eyewitness testimony) is summarised in the *Getting Started* booklet that comes with your course and that can be found on the Edexcel website (**www.edexcel.com**), so you could look at that as well for guidance.

Note that you are studying two applications from the four set out in your course. Within those two applications you must do one content analysis practical and one article analysis practical, so make sure you include one of each in your studies. In this textbook an article analysis is chosen for this chapter on health psychology and the chapter on criminological psychology, and a content analysis has been chosen for child psychology and sport psychology. You are required to study the key issue, find material relating to it, carry out an analysis on that material, and then link your analysis to concepts that relate to the key issue. You need also to be able to describe the key issue itself. For the article analysis you can focus your practical on any area of the content of the application, not only the key issue.

Three issues are suggested for your course: how drug abuse can be treated; how to prevent drug abuse; and cultural differences in drug taking. Two ways in which drug abuse can be treated have been explained in the Content section of this chapter, and heroin maintenance programmes are further explained when looking at the Blättler et al. (2002) study. Some information on how to prevent drug abuse, such as one anti-smoking campaign and some conclusions from Ennett et al.'s study (1994), has been given in this chapter, so those two issues are summarised here. The issue of cross-cultural differences in drug taking is briefly mentioned here but you will need more material if you would like to explore these instead.

How drug abuse can be treated

This chapter has explained how token economy programmes can treat drug abuse by using a system of tokens as rewards, and the treatment was evaluated. Use that material to explain how drug abuse can be treated. Heroin misuse in particular is treated using maintenance programmes, such as using methadone. Smoking is treated using nicotine patches, which is a similar principle. Use what you have learned about this second way of treating drug abuse when discussing this key issue. You could also look for other methods of treatment. Two others are found in the online resources — aversion therapy and the AA approach, which are both for alcohol abuse.

How to prevent drug abuse

One anti-smoking campaign has been explained in this textbook (p. 137): the British Heart Foundation links heart problems and heart attacks to smoking and has funded an intensive anti-smoking campaign in order to improve people's health. There are many other campaigns about not taking drugs, and you could explore at least one of these as part of your study of this key issue. Evaluate the programmes and consider problems with preventing drug abuse.

The Blättler et al. (2002) study shows that it is not just physical addiction that has to be considered but also behavioural issues such as prostitution, criminal activities and being on the drug scene. There is also the issue of dealing with social learning, although Ennett et al. (1994), in the USA, suggest that adolescent friendship cliques work towards stopping smoking rather than starting it. You could include a nature–nurture discussion, as prevention of something often needs to consider what is thought to be the cause. If drug abuse is seen as biologically caused then biological treatment might be preferred, but if drug abuse is thought to be caused by the environment then treatment to change the environment or to change learning might be adopted.

Cross-cultural differences in drug taking

Blättler et al.'s study (2002) emphasises that the researchers felt their findings would not generalise well to other cultures, because the study was in Switzerland, which has maintenance programmes including social support. They discuss cross-cultural differences in drug taking. If substance abuse comes from physical and psychological dependence, it might be thought that drug taking would be the same whatever the culture. However, if the 'drug scene' is a large influence and if social learning theory is followed, then there might be different behaviour in different cultures.

Practical: carrying out an analysis of two articles

An article analysis for your course requires you to find two relevant articles. These can be from magazines, newspapers, the internet, or from a television programme if you can write a summary of what was said or find a synopsis. Once you have found two such articles you should summarise them in your own words, then draw conclusions about the findings by linking to concepts from health psychology. Consider the theories you have studied, or perhaps the methodology if that is relevant.

An example article analysis can be found in the online materials.

Examination-style questions

1 Describe one key issue that arises within the area of substance misuse in health psychology. *(4 marks)*

2 With regard to the practical you carried out in health psychology and focusing on one key issue, answer the following questions:

(a) Summarise one of the articles/programmes or material that you used to study your key issue. *(3 marks)*

(b) Using two ideas (concepts, theories, studies, findings etc.) from health psychology, explain your key issue. *(6 marks)*

(c) Explain one way in which the material you used explained your key issue. *(4 marks)*

Extension question

With reference to the practical you carried out within health psychology, and focused on a key issue, draw conclusions about the findings of the articles or reference material that you used, using concepts, theories and/or research as appropriate. *(12 marks)*

Chapter

Sport psychology

This chapter is about sport psychology, which is an **application** in psychology. This means that theories and studies are applied to issues of concern to society and the individual. Sport psychology includes reasons for choice of sport, the effects of arousal, anxiety and audience, why individuals perform differently in sports, and what can be done to improve performance. In the A2 applications you have to know two studies in detail as well as one key issue in the area you are studying. You will also carry out a practical based on the key issue. The methodology section considers how questionnaires and correlational designs are used to study sport psychology, and asks you to evaluate such research methods. There is also focus on qualitative and quantitative data, with their relative strengths and weaknesses. The key issues suggested include gender and sport, what makes a winner, and what makes a good coach. Sport psychology is a wide field and you will only touch upon some of the issues in this section of your course.

> **study hint** If you are taking sports studies/physical education at A-level you will come across similar issues, such as achievement motivation theory and the effects of arousal. It is useful to use what you learn in one course to inform another. However, you should be aware that courses probably have a different focus.

Summary of learning objectives

Definitions
You have to be able to define the terms:

- participation
- excellence
- intrinsic motivation
- extrinsic motivation

- arousal
- anxiety
- audience effects

- qualitative data
- quantitative data

Methodology
- using questionnaires to study sport psychology
- using correlations in the study of sport psychology
- evaluation of the use of questionnaires and correlations in sport psychology
- evaluation of questionnaires and correlations, including issues of reliability, validity and ethics
- considering qualitative and quantitative data, their strengths and weaknesses and comparing the two types of data

Content
You have to be able to describe and evaluate:
- the effect of personality traits (the biological approach) on individual differences in sporting participation and performance
- one other explanation for individual differences in sporting participation and performance, which must be chosen from the effect of socialisation, the effect of attribution and the effect of reinforcements
- the achievement motivation theory
- one other theory of motivation within sport psychology
- the inverted U hypothesis
- one other theory of arousal, anxiety or audience effects
- two psychological techniques for improving performance in sport

Studies in detail
You have to be able to describe and evaluate in detail:
- Boyd and Munroe (2003) on imagery and climbing
- One other study from Cottrell et al. (1968), Koivula (1995), and Craft et al. (2003)

Key issues and practical
You have to carry out one practical that focuses on a key issue relating to sport psychology. The practical can be a content analysis of articles, programmes or other material about the key issue or a summary of two articles that you then draw conclusions from about the key issue.

Definitions

Definitions explaining what **qualitative data** and **quantitative data** mean are to be found in the methodology section of this chapter, although they were explained in detail in the AS part of the course. **Intrinsic** and **extrinsic motivation, participation** and **excellence** are defined in this introduction. **Arousal, anxiety** and **audience effects** are terms defined in the content section in this chapter.

4

Table 4.1

Checklist of what you need to know for sport psychology and your progress

I need to know about	Done	More work	I need to know about	Done	More work
Defining: participation and excellence			Achievement motivation theory (and evaluation)		
Defining: intrinsic and extrinsic motivation			One other theory and evaluation (e.g. self-efficacy or cognitive evaluation theory)		
Defining: arousal, anxiety and audience effects			The inverted U hypothesis (and evaluation)		
Questionnaires, how they are used in sport psychology, and evaluate in terms of validity, reliability and ethics			One other theory of arousal, anxiety and audience effects and evaluation (inverted U and other theory must cover all three aspects)		
Correlations, how they are used in sport psychology, and evaluate in terms of validity, reliability and ethics			Two psychological techniques for improving performance (and evaluation)		
Qualitative and quantitative data, and compare strengths and weaknesses			Describe and evaluate Boyd and Munroe (2003)		
Personality traits as explanations of individual differences in participation and performance in sport (including evaluation)			Describe and evaluate one study from Cottrell et al. (1968), Koivula (1995) and Craft et al. (2003)		
One from socialisation, attribution or reinforcement as explanations of individual differences in participation and performance in sport (including evaluation)			One key issue and a practical relating to it		

An introduction to sport psychology

Sport psychology focuses on all aspects of sport: the choice of sport and what affects it, what affects individual performance, how motivation to win can be improved, team aspects of sporting performance, and factors leading to excellence in performance. The aspects of sport psychology covered in your course are just some of those covered by sport psychology but they will give you a flavour of the topic.

Performance means both taking part in a sporting event and how well someone does — sport psychology is often about helping someone to improve their performance. The word 'performance' also implies preparation and practice.

Sport psychology is the study of people's behaviour when undertaking sport, both its biological and social aspects. The amount of biological arousal felt, for instance, has a significant effect on sporting success or failure. **Arousal** is a biological term and is a physical state of readiness for action — the 'fight or flight' reaction. Arousal is explained in more detail in the content section of this chapter. In social terms, the psychology of sport is used to help individuals and teams of people succeed in sport. **Team cohesion** is about how well a team works together to succeed.

Self-confidence, self-esteem and **motivation** are features affecting success in sport. There are two aspects of motivation. **Intrinsic motivation** is something inside someone that gives them the willpower to get something done. **Extrinsic motivation** is something external to the person that gives them that willpower to achieve an aim. Pride, for instance, is intrinsic motivation while the promise of money is extrinsic motivation.

For some people sport is big business with large sums of money at stake, and sport psychologists are employed to aid success in such instances. Sport psychology focuses on goal setting, concentration, motivation, **attributional training** and having the right level of arousal. Attributions are the reasons given for something happening; attributional training is about helping people to identify the right attributions. An example of an attribution is **situational**, which means thinking of the situation as causing something. Another attribution is **dispositional**, which means thinking of oneself as causing something.

The history of sport psychology

Norman Triplett, born in 1861, is often credited with initiating the study of sport psychology, when he found that cyclists went faster in groups than they did on their own. This chapter looks at the effects of an audience on sporting achievement, which was one of the first areas studied. By 1920 sports laboratories were being set up in various countries and by the 1970s, sport psychology was often on the curriculum in universities in the USA. Initial interest was focused on factors enhancing performance, while later the focus changed to looking at how exercise improves health. More recently there has been interest in helping individuals to improve their performance, as well as how physical exercise can help people even if they may not participate in sport. Athletes often employ sport psychologists to improve their motivation and performance, to help them recover from injury and to overcome problems in competition.

Preference, participation and performance

The three areas of interest to sport psychologists focused on in your course are preference, participation and performance.

Preference is about choice of sport, which can be affected by gender — for example, in respect of 'girl' sports and 'boy' sports.

Participation, linked to preference, is about taking part in sport. This can be affected by socialisation and early experiences, personality or other factors.

4

Performance is about how good someone is at sport, which can be affected by whether there is an audience or not, how anxious someone is, or how motivated they are to succeed. Performance can also be affected by coaching and encouragement. A performance involves practising and becoming as competent as possible, and some 'elite' athletes aim for excellence. **Excellence** is about excelling (doing something extremely well). Excellence is a value, particularly among athletes, and its pursuit involves intrinsic motivation because it is a goal in itself with no other reward. Excellence comes from practice, goal setting and achieving what is possible. Aristotle said that excellence was a habit not an action.

> **Explore** Find a situation where a sport psychologist has helped an athlete or a team to perform better. Look at summaries of the articles in each edition of the journal *The Sport Psychologist* to see what topics are covered.

Applying sport psychology

Sport psychologists have studied what goalkeepers do when facing penalty kicks to try to give advice to improve their performance. Azar et al. (2005) analysed 286 penalty kicks that were taken in elite matches and found goalkeepers saved more goals if they stayed in the centre of the goal rather than jumping to the left or the right. However, in practice goalkeepers tend to jump to the left or the right. Goalkeepers saved 33.3% of penalties when staying in the centre, 12.6% when they jumped right and 14.2% when they jumped left. This is possibly because the goalkeeper feels better if he/she jumps, because he/she is making an active decision. In a survey 15 goalkeepers said they would feel bad about letting in a penalty if they did the 'wrong' thing and 11 of them said they would feel worse if they stayed in the centre. Sport psychologists can use such information when advising goalkeepers on how to improve their performance. They might not advise them always to stay in the centre (which could be picked up by those taking the penalty kicks, presumably) but would work with them on their feelings when they do not save a penalty kick. Goalkeepers have to deal with the fact that they tend only to get noticed when they make mistakes.

> **Explore** Locate Azar et al.'s study (2005) on the internet and read about it in detail.

Examination-style questions

1 What is meant by both intrinsic and extrinsic motivation? *(4 marks)*

2 What is meant by excellence in sport? Include an example in your answer. *(3 marks)*

3 Explain two areas of study that are involved in sport psychology. *(6 marks)*

Methodology

This section focuses on questionnaires and correlations, as well as qualitative and quantitative data. It looks at how these research methods and methodological issues are used to study sport. Issues of reliability, validity and ethics are discussed and evaluation is given.

AS link Note that you might be asked to draw on AS material for both the Methodology and Content sections of this chapter.

Questionnaires

Questionnaires are structured sets of questions, where all **respondents** usually answer all the questions and have the same set of **standardised instructions** as a **control**. In most questionnaires there are closed and open questions.

Closed questions

Closed questions involve forced choice answers, such as yes/no answers or a structured ratings scale like a **Likert-type scale**, where respondents rate a statement as 'strongly agree', 'agree', 'don't know', 'disagree' or 'strongly disagree'. An example of a closed question is 'on a scale of 1 to 5, rate how good you feel when you win a tournament'.

Closed questions generate **quantitative data** — numerical data where numbers are generated, such as the number of 'yes' answers compared with the number of 'no' answers. Percentages can be calculated from quantitative data.

Open questions

Open questions involve questions asking about attitudes or opinions, where the respondents can write in their own words and are not restricted in their answers. An example of an open question is 'how do you feel when you win a tournament?'

Open questions generate **qualitative data** — data that are in story form and in the participant's own words. Examples of questions that gather qualitative data are 'why do you participate in sport?' and 'what makes you want to win?'

Study hint When you come to look at the two detailed studies for this part of the course, you will find that more than one of them uses a 7-point Likert scale. You can use such studies as an example of a questionnaire using closed questioning.

If you have studied health psychology you may have looked at questionnaires as a research method. Review that material now (see p. 118).

4

AS link Review what you
learned about questionnaires
and qualitative and quantitative
data in your study of the social
approach for AS (pp. 9–18).

Study hint Note how a
research method has a basic
description and basic evaluation
points. You can use those
descriptive and evaluation
points for any question asking
about that research method,
whether it is an AS question, a
question about the A2 applications or a question about issues
and debates at the end of the
course. You will find research
method material is often
repeated, because it is central
to the study of psychology as a
science.

Tetra Images/Alamy

*Questionnaires can help to capture data about what an athlete
feels when winning and about their anxiety and self-confidence*

Test–retest and split-half reliability

Test–retest is where a structured set of questions is used to test a group of respondents and then repeated with the same respondents some time later. Data can then
be tested to see if they are reliable. If the first set of scores agrees with the second
set of scores, then the results are reliable. To find out if the first and second sets
of scores agree with one another, a correlation can be done, as explained in the
following section. One problem with test–retest is the practice effect — participants
may remember their answers from the first time.

Another way to test a questionnaire for reliability is to use **split-half reliability**.
This means that the items in the questionnaire are split into two halves by randomly
splitting items that measure the same construct into two groups. One person's
answers on the whole questionnaire can be looked at in these two groups and
scored accordingly, so that that person has two scores. Then a correlation can be
carried out to see if the two 'half scores' for each person correspond. If they do, then
the questionnaire is reliable.

Use of questionnaires in sport psychology

Questionnaires are used a lot in sport psychology. Three of the studies suggested for
your course are examples of questionnaires; two of them are summarised here to
give you some examples.

Boyd and Munroe (2003): using imagery in climbing

Jean Boyd and Krista J. Munroe's study (which is Canadian) is explained in detail on pp. 198–203 and must be covered for your A2 course. Its main aim was to look at the use of **imagery** and to see if beginner climbers differed from advanced climbers in their use of it. Imagery means using the senses to create an experience (image) in the mind. Another aim was to compare climbers' use of imagery with imagery used by track and field athletes.

The study involved 38 track and field athletes and 48 climbers. All the participants completed questionnaires. The questionnaire for the track and field athletes was the sport imagery questionnaire (SIQ) developed by Hall et al. (1998), while climbers used the climbing imagery questionnaire (CIQ), which is the SIQ adapted for climbers — for example, in some items the word 'climbing' was used instead of 'competing'.

The SIQ has 30 items and each statement is rated on a 7-point Likert-type scale asking respondents to say how often they use the five functions of imagery in their sport (the five functions of imagery are explained on p. 199). The scale runs from 1 for 'rarely' to 7 for 'very often'. Forty-eight questionnaires were given to climbers, with a 100% response rate, and 42 were given to track and field athletes, with a 91% response rate.

The conclusion was that the climbers and track and field athletes differed to an extent with regard to their use of imagery and the type of imagery they used. However, there was little difference in the use of imagery between beginner and advanced climbers.

Evaluation

Use the evaluation points from the study when it is explained in more detail below. Consider the issue of the reliability of rating scales. Someone might not rate themselves in the same way a second time, for example, but at least questionnaires are replicable so they can be tested for reliability. Consider the issue of validity — rating the use of imagery on a scale of 1 to 7 may not be a valid way of measuring it. One person's idea of the scale may be different from another's view.

> **Study hint** Boyd and Munroe's study (2003) uses a questionnaire and a modified version. Use an example like this to illustrate the use of questionnaires in sport psychology, so that your answers always link to the application.

Koivula (1995): gender and sport

Nathalie Koivula's study (1995) is one that is offered as a choice for your course and is explained in more detail later in this chapter. In Sweden, Koivula studied the effects of using gender **schemata** on what people think about different sports.

> **Schemata** are ideas and preconceptions that come from upbringing and experience.

Participants were asked to complete a questionnaire about themselves with regard to personality traits. From what they chose about personality and attitudes they were then put into categories according to how sex-typed they were. **Sex-typed** means 'typically male' or 'typically female'; a third category is **androgynous**, which means having both masculine and feminine qualities. The general idea of the study was that androgynous people would be less likely to categorise a sport as appropriate primarily for males or females than sex-typed people. The questionnaire used was the Bem sex role inventory (BSRI).

The participants also completed another questionnaire, rating sports according to how appropriate they were for males or females. Both questionnaires used a 7-point Likert-type scale. The question about appropriateness of sport ranged from 'very appropriate for men and not at all for women', through 'equally appropriate for men and women', to 'very appropriate for women and not at all for men'.

Participants then completed a third questionnaire asking for personal details, such as age, gender and ethnicity. Participants were allocated to one of eight groups using the BSRI scores. The participants were allocated a group depending on how 'gendered' (or 'sex-typed') their thoughts were likely to be. The sports were allocated a mean score. Sports rated as, for example, very appropriate for men and not at all for women (male sports) had a score of 1 to 3.5 on the 7-point scale. Sports rated neutral (equally appropriate for men or women) had a score of 3.5 to 4.5. Sports rated feminine (e.g. very appropriate for women and not at all for men) had a score of 4.5 to 7.

Koivula compared the results from the first two questionnaires — the 'gendered' categories from the BSRI and the mean scores given by each participant for each sport. She could then see, for example, whether sex-typed people were more likely to differentiate sports as male or female than androgynous people. In general it was found that sex-typed men are more likely to stereotype sports as masculine or feminine, whereas androgynous types did not use gender-based schematic information processing.

AS link Review what you learned about information processing when looking at the cognitive approach (pp. 91–92). You may also have studied the use of schemata if you looked at reconstruction theory as a memory theory (pp. 115–18). Gender-based schematic information processing means processing information using previous experience of gender information which has built schemata in the mind.

Explore Look up one of the questionnaires mentioned in the two studies described above, for instance the BSRI or the SIQ. Find out more about the types of questions asked and identify some evaluation points.

Evaluation

Use the evaluation points from the study when it is explained in more detail. You should also refer to the evaluation points for questionnaires and self-rating data given below.

Study hint Use the two studies briefly outlined here (and explained in more detail later) to evaluate the use of questionnaires. Use what you have learned about questionnaires to evaluate the studies (such as their validity and reliability).

Evaluation of questionnaires

In this section, evaluation points focus on reliability, validity and ethical issues. There is also consideration of questionnaires and their usefulness or weakness when used in sport psychology.

Reliability

Strengths

- The reliability of data from questionnaires can be checked using either test–retest or split-half reliability, although the practice effect is a potential problem with test–retest. Participants may remember their answers from the first time.
- Pilot studies are often carried out, to check the wording of questions in questionnaires for clarity, and to make sure that the answers match the questions that the researchers want to ask. With such testing it is likely that a questionnaire will get the same results if repeated, which means it is reliable.

Weaknesses

- It is possible that respondents would give different responses on another day because they are in a different mood or in another place, triggering different ideas. If different responses could be given by the same person, this means the results would lack reliability.
- Another reason for the results of a questionnaire not being reliable would be if there were **demand characteristics**, perhaps from the researcher's dress, manner or the questions themselves. If respondents picked up from the researcher what they thought was wanted in the way of answers, and a different researcher carried out the study another time, then results might vary and the survey would not be reliable.

Validity

Strengths

- Questionnaires are thought of as valid when qualitative data are collected through asking open questions. The respondent can answer freely, meaning that their replies represent the 'truth', rather than the choice of response dictated by closed questions.
- Validity can be checked by using different questions to measure the same constructs and then checking that the answers correspond.

Weaknesses

- Even open questions may provide limited information. There are usually only a few lines for the respondent to write down their answer, or the questions ask for set answers rather than allowing for any exploration. To that extent, questionnaires are not valid.
- Social desirability: when a respondent answers what they think they ought to in order to fit in with what society thinks. For example, if someone is asked whether they are racist, they are not likely to say that they are.
- There might be demand characteristics: a respondent guesses what the purpose of the questionnaire is and replies accordingly, either to help the researcher or to

go against what they think is wanted. Either way, their answers are biased, not truthful and, therefore, not valid.

Ethics

Strengths

■ Researchers can show participants exactly what they will be doing and can inform them, to a large extent, of the purpose of the study.

■ As questionnaires are presented in written form, every copy can carry a promise of confidentiality and anonymity.

■ The right to withdraw can be given through standardised instructions on the questionnaire and also at the end, if the questionnaire is completed face-to-face. Postal questionnaires give the right to withdraw, as they do not have to be returned.

Weaknesses

■ Although the respondent can see exactly what is being asked, they cannot be told what is important, otherwise there might be demand characteristics. This could be said to constitute some form of deceit.

■ With postal questionnaires it is hard to give any debrief because the respondent cannot usually be re-contacted, although a debrief can be offered via a web link.

AS link Review the five ethical guidelines that the course focuses on (covered in the social approach, pp. 24–29), as well as ethical issues with regard to privacy and confidentiality (the psychodynamic approach, pp. 175–76).

Evaluation of the use of questionnaires in sport psychology

Questionnaires are often used in sport psychology, possibly because a lot of sport psychology is about individuals and their motivation, attitudes, personality and decisions. Questionnaires are a good way of finding out about attitudes.

Standard questionnaires are developed by one set of researchers and then, because researchers often want to build on the studies of others, used again by another set. Use of the same questionnaire renders studies more comparable. Boyd and Munroe used the SIQ from Hall et al. (1998), for example. Koivula used Bem's questionnaire, the BSRI. Craft et al. (2003) — a study found in the online resources supporting this textbook — used the CSAI-2 (competitive state anxiety inventory: second version). This questionnaire has been extensively used to measure state anxiety.

Craft et al. (2003) carried out a meta-analysis to look at a number of studies using the CSAI-2. As they had used the same measure these studies were comparable. A **meta-analysis** is a study that looks at results from many other studies rather than gathering data themselves. From the four studies suggested for your course, three use questionnaires, which shows the popularity of this research method in sport psychology.

Strengths

- Much of sport psychology is about performance, participation, motivation and excellence — all of which include people's attitudes, personality and other internal factors. Questionnaires are a good way of measuring such internal factors.
- The same questionnaires are used in different studies. The findings can be compared because the data were gathered in the same way.

Weaknesses

- There have been suggestions that the standard questionnaires used, such as the CSAI-2 and BSRI, are not valid, in that they might not measure what they claim to measure. The CSAI-2, for example, measures cognitive anxiety, somatic anxiety and self-confidence as three separate measures, whereas it appears that they rely on one another and are not separate.
- Questionnaires have limitations (e.g. social desirability or demand characteristics), and this might be true when they are used in sport psychology too. For example, when climbers are asked about their hardest climb they may want to exaggerate, particularly if they are new to climbing.

Correlations

Correlations are a technique for analysing data, rather than a research method. Questionnaires and other research methods, such as experiments, can involve correlations. Indeed, many questionnaires involve correlations, including that of Koivula (1995).

> **AS link**
>
> Review your learning about correlations, which were explained in the psychodynamic approach (pp. 177–182).

Describing correlational technique

Wherever there are two sets of scores, usually generated by the same people, a correlational test can be carried out to see if the variable that generated one set of scores is related to the variable that gave the other set of scores. For example, if age goes with the 'gender' ratings of sport, then either the higher the age the more sports are 'gendered' by someone, or the higher the age the less sports are 'gendered'.

To find a correlation, scores are set out and then each set is ranked. A made-up example is given here to illustrate and explain. Score 1 in the list represents a person's score on half of a questionnaire (out of 50) and score 2 represents a person's score on the other half of the questionnaire (out of 50), using matching items for each half. If the questionnaire is reliable then the same person's score on one half will be at the same rank on the second half. This is a **split-half reliability** test. If someone scores the highest on femininity on one half of the questionnaire, for example, you would expect them to score highest on femininity on the other half, if the questionnaire is reliable. Equally, the lowest scoring person would be expected to score lowest on both halves. If there was a perfect match between each person's two scores this would be a very reliable survey.

| Table 4.2 | Made-up scores where score 1 (out of 50) is from half the items on a questionnaire and score 2 is from the second half (out of 50) — a perfect positive correlation |

Participant	Score 1	Score 2	Rank of score 1	Rank of score 2
1	45	39	4	4
2	32	29	3	3
3	15	23	1	1
4	48	42	5	5
5	27	25	2	2

The ranks match exactly which, if tested, would give a perfect positive correlation (+1).

| Table 4.3 | Made-up scores where score 1 (out of 50) is from half the items on a questionnaire and score 2 is from the second half (out of 50) – a perfect negative correlation |

Participant	Score 1	Score 2	Rank of score 1	Rank of score 2
1	45	25	4	2
2	32	29	3	3
3	15	42	1	5
4	48	23	5	1
5	27	39	2	4

The ranks are completely opposite which, if tested, would give a perfect negative correlation (–1).

Correlational techniques can also be used to test for reliability using a test–retest situation. The participant's scores on the first questionnaire can be ranked against their scores in the repeat version to see if they are in the same position. If they scored highly in the first and in the second, or had low scores in both, then the questionnaire would appear to be reliable.

Positive and negative correlation

When a test such as Spearman's is carried out, the result is from –1 to +1, for example –0.45 or +0.68. The nearer a correlation is to +1 or –1 the more the correlation is likely to be significant and the scores relate. The nearer a correlation is to 0 (equally distant between –1 and +1) the less there is a correlation and the scores do not relate. However, significance links to the chosen significance level and number of scores, as well as to how near to –1 or +1 the result of the test is. +1 is a perfect **positive correlation** and –1 is a perfect **negative correlation**. 0 is no correlation at all. One other issue about correlations is the strength of the correlation. The closer the result of a test is to +1 or –1 the stronger the correlation — for example, +0.68 is a stronger correlation than +0.45. A correlation can be weak (e.g. 0.35) and yet significant (for example, because of the chosen significance level).

Correlations in sport psychology

Two studies using correlations are referred to here, both of them suggested studies in your course. The first, Koivula (1995), has already been summarised and is explained fully on pp. 204–08. The second, Craft et al. (2003), is explained in detail in the online resources supporting this textbook. Its use of correlations is summarised here.

Use this study as an example of the use of correlational techniques in sport psychology. Koivula (1995) carried out two correlations: (1) whether age related to the gender classification given by the BSRI, and (2) whether age related to 'gendering' the sports. Neither test found a relationship.

Craft et al. (2003)

This is a meta-analysis of 29 studies that looked at the relationship between anxiety and sports performance, and used CSAI-2 (competitive state anxiety inventory-2), which gives scores for cognitive anxiety, somatic anxiety and self-confidence. **Cognitive anxiety** is the psychological side of anxiety and **somatic anxiety** is the physical side.

Since all of the studies involved in Craft et al.'s study used CSAI-2, correlational tests (such as Spearman's) could be applied to the resulting data. There were many findings, but the overall finding was that it is mainly self-confidence that relates to performance. Another was that the different types of anxiety did relate to one another. Table 4.4 shows this relationship and the results of the correlational tests, to illustrate the use of correlational techniques in sport psychology.

Table 4.4 *The relationship strength between the three different types of anxiety — cognitive anxiety, somatic anxiety and self-confidence*

Type of anxiety as measured by CSAI-2	Result of correlational test
Cognitive anxiety related to somatic anxiety	$r = 0.52$
Cognitive anxiety related to self-confidence	$r = -0.47$
Somatic anxiety related to self-confidence	$r = -0.54$

All three results are strong enough to be significant. Note that the first one is a positive correlation, which means as cognitive anxiety rises so does somatic anxiety. The last two are negative correlations — as self-confidence rises cognitive anxiety falls, as does somatic anxiety. These results are what would be expected, given our understanding of what anxiety and self-confidence are. Self-confidence can be seen as the opposite of anxiety.

Evaluation of Craft et al. (2003)

A more detailed description of the Craft et al. study is given in the online resources. A full evaluation of this study is given below.

Strengths
- Only those studies that used the same questionnaire, the CSAI-2, were summarised so that the data gathered were similar, the same questions were asked and the same constructs measured, allowing comparison.
- As just under 30 studies were looked at, with many participants in each, it is likely that the findings can be generalised to other populations. If studies use different sampling techniques and different types of participant and there are comparable findings, then such a large and wide sample might mean the findings are generalisable.

■ A meta-analysis does not use participants directly, so it might be seen as more ethical than carrying out a study gathering primary data. Primary data are data gathered first-hand.

AS link   Review your learning about sampling techniques in the social approach (pp. 30–35).

Weaknesses

■ The CSAI-2 may not be a reliable instrument. Craft et al. (2003) pointed out that they did not find a straightforward relationship between cognitive anxiety and performance (it was not the case that as cognitive anxiety grew, performance deteriorated). However, it seemed that when other variables were taken into account there might be a relationship. If those other variables were different each time, then different results from the questionnaire might be found each time — for example, using different sports, or individual instead of team sports.

■ Use of a questionnaire that measures three constructs might not be enough to produce valid data. In fact, with the addition of **moderator variables**, such as type of sport, type of athlete, and time before performance that the questionnaire was carried out, Craft et al. found that as cognitive anxiety rose so did performance. Thus a questionnaire can only measure part of a situation and its findings might not, therefore, be valid.

■ The studies used in the meta-analysis are bound to include different sports, different types of athlete, different timings for the questionnaire administration and other differences. It is therefore hard to compare these studies.

Evaluation of correlations

Correlational techniques are evaluated here in terms of their reliability, validity, ethics and use in sport psychology. It is not so much a correlation that is reliable, valid or ethical (or not) so much as how the data that the correlation uses are gathered. If gathered by questionnaire, then the same strengths and weaknesses apply as for questionnaires. If gathered by interview or other test, then the strengths and weaknesses of those other research methods apply.

Reliability

Strengths

■ Correlations can be done over and over again, so are replicable and to that extent reliable. It has to be clear how data are gathered so they can be gathered again. Questionnaires can easily be repeated with different participants.

■ Correlational data can come from standardised questionnaires that have been used many times. Reliability of these questionnaires will have been tested by test–retest, split-half reliability or some other measure, so the questions should be clear and capable of being answered in the same way if a participant is asked to repeat the test.

Weaknesses

■ Correlations may not be reliable because the data are often gathered by survey, and attitudes can change from day to day. For example, an attitude to someone's sports performance might change after a win and after a loss.

- Demand characteristics from the researchers — such as the way they dress or the way they ask the questions — can affect the data and make them unreliable.

Validity

Strengths

- Correlations are demonstrably valid if they are about real-life variables, such as chronological age or number of wins.
- Correlations do not claim to be about cause-and-effect relationships. As they do not claim to represent anything other than 'some relationship', they do not falsely represent real-life situations.

Weaknesses

- Correlations tend not to be valid when they come from variables that are quite hard to measure and so might not represent real-life situations or experiences. For example, the CSAI-2 measures three types of anxiety as if those three types exist separately, whereas they could be constructs developed in order to make 'anxiety' measurable.
- Social desirability is a problem in answers, for instance an athlete might not want to admit (perhaps even to themselves) that they are not going to succeed in competition. They may answer as they think they are supposed to, because their coach has said they must always think positively.

Ethics

Strengths

- Correlations are simply techniques to look for relationships and are unlikely to cause distress. The issue of ethics usually arises in relation to the choice of research method.
- Confidentiality can be adhered to because there is rarely a need to publish names when doing a study using a correlational technique. As long as care is taken where individuals could be identified, confidentiality and privacy can be promised.

Weaknesses

- Findings might be detrimental to participants or society, or cost could outweigh benefit. It is relatively easy to carry out correlational techniques; they should not be used because they are easy to apply but because of the potential usefulness of findings.
- The research method used to gather the analysed data might not be ethical (e.g. lack of informed consent). Questionnaires are reasonably ethical but there might be problems with confidentiality or competence, for example.

Evaluation of correlations as used in sport psychology

Strengths

- It is possible to build a body of knowledge because the same tools (the tried and tested questionnaires discussed above) are used in different studies to make findings comparable.
- Using a correlation technique can show the results of such questionnaires clearly (for example 0.68 can be easily and statistically compared with 0.23).

4

■ Sport psychology focuses on personal issues, most of which can be tested by questionnaire or interview and a score generated. Personal issues lend themselves well to correlational analysis.

Weaknesses

■ Correlations do not show a cause-and-effect relationship. They only show that two variables change together.
■ There might be other related variables that have not been found.

Qualitative and quantitative data

For this section you need to be able to outline what is meant by qualitative and quantitative data and to compare the two types of data in terms of strengths and weaknesses.

Qualitative data are gathered by **open questions** in questionnaires and can also be gathered by other research methods, such as a case study, diary method or interview. They are data that involve stories and detail, opinions and attitudes. For example, a sportsperson explains why they enjoy climbing.

Quantitative data are gathered by **closed questions** in a questionnaire and can also be gathered by other research methods such as experiments, content analysis or observations. They are data that involve numbers, such as the percentage of people that strongly agree that winners need at least some anxiety to motivate them to win.

Comparing qualitative and quantitative data

Strengths of qualitative data/weaknesses of quantitative data

■ Qualitative data involve stories, detail and depth, whereas quantitative data do not give depth, being percentages and numbers. Depth gives richness and greater validity to data.
■ Qualitative data are useful when an area has not been widely studied so initial hypotheses are needed and information on which to base such hypotheses is sought.

Strengths of quantitative data/weaknesses of qualitative data

Study hint Questionnaires and correlations are often used in sport psychology but other research methods are used as well. Cottrell et al. (1968) used the laboratory experimental method — read about it in the online resources that support this textbook.

■ Quantitative data are easier to analyse as there are definite numbers to use with descriptive and inferential statistics, and calculations can be checked. Qualitative data have to be sorted into categories, which takes longer and is harder, and does not allow statistical analysis.
■ Quantitative data are analysed more objectively because tests are used which, if analysed by different people, would still give the same result. Qualitative data, needing themes to be generated, might be analysed more subjectively.

Examination-style questions

1 What is meant by 'positive correlation'? *(2 marks)*

2 Describe, using one example, how questionnaires are used in sport psychology to gather data. *(6 marks)*

3 What is meant by 'qualitative' and 'quantitative' data? *(4 marks)*

4 Evaluate questionnaires in terms of two ethical issues. *(4 marks)*

5 With regard to questionnaires, why are both qualitative and quantitative data often gathered? *(4 marks)*

6 Outline one strength and one weakness of correlations as used in sport psychology. *(4 marks)*

Extension questions

1 Describe the use of questionnaires in sport psychology and evaluate them in terms of reliability and validity. *(12 marks)*

2 Using at least one example, discuss the use of correlations in sport psychology. *(12 marks)*

Content

For this section, certain areas within sport psychology are studied. Two explanations for individual differences in participation and performance are covered, as well as two theories of motivation. The inverted U hypothesis and one other theory looking at arousal, anxiety and the audience effect are discussed, as are two psychological techniques for improving performance in sport.

For this part of the course you are required to study the effect of personality traits on performance and participation, and this includes a biological explanation. You also have to study one other explanation from three — the effect of sociali-sation, attribution or reinforcements. In this textbook socialisation is explored. Attribution is covered in the online resources supporting this textbook.

The biological explanation for individual differences in sporting performance and participation

Personality traits have been said to explain both sporting participation and sporting performance, and personality traits are biological features of personality.

Traits are enduring characteristics of a person that affect their behaviour, including whether they participate in sport and how well they do. Biological theories are **dispositional** ones, which means they focus on the disposition or character of the individual as opposed to **situational** theories, which focus on the influence of the situation on behaviour. A trait is relatively stable. For example, if aggression is a trait, then someone who is aggressive in one situation is likely to be aggressive in another. Trait theories suggest that people are made individual by their set of traits and are different from one another. With regard to sport, trait theories consider individual differences such as why one person likes team sports and another likes individual sports. Personality traits might also help or hinder an individual with regard to sporting success.

Cattell developed a trait theory of personality, as did Allport before him, but it is Eysenck's theory that links most clearly to a biological approach. All three are explained briefly here, before looking at evidence that traits affect sporting participation and performance.

Allport (1936) considered terms in the English language that describe personality, such as 'good humoured', 'kind' and 'thoughtful', and categorised the words into three levels. According to him, **cardinal traits** are major, dominating characteristics of a person; other people often know an individual by their cardinal traits. **Central traits** are more general ones forming the basic personality and, like cardinal traits, are often used to describe an individual but they do not influence how they are seen as strongly (for example intelligent, honest, anxious). The third category Allport called **secondary traits**. These might only appear in an individual in certain situations rather than all the time, such as being impatient when waiting but not impatient in other circumstances.

Eysenck's personality theory (1947)

Hans Eysenck drew up a theory of personality that has been referred to as a type theory as well as a trait theory. Usually in a type theory, if someone is one type they cannot be the opposite type. So, for example, in Eysenck's terms if someone is introvert they cannot be extrovert. However, Eysenck did accept that people could be somewhere between introvert and extrovert, so his is not directly a type theory. He focused on three dimensions of personality, into which other traits fitted.

Other researchers, like Allport, talk about a trait **continuum** with two 'ends', such as happy–sad, and individuals can be placed somewhere along that continuum. In Eysenck's theory, the personality terms fit into his three dimensions or types, which are introversion/extroversion, neuroticism/emotional stability, and psychoticism (a dimension he added later).

Introversion/extroversion

Introversion means focusing internally rather than on other people, and means not requiring stimulation from outside events. **Extroversion** means focusing outward and looking for stimulation. Someone highly introverted might be quiet, reserved and controlled, whereas someone highly extrovert might be outgoing, sociable and keen on excitement.

Neuroticism/emotional stability

Neuroticism is a kind of moodiness, where someone tends to become emotional and upset. **Stability** is the opposite and refers to someone who remains constant in their emotions.

Psychoticism

Psychoticism is a mental health dimension and refers to people who find it hard to deal with reality. They may be antisocial and manipulative.

Eysenck's theory came from information gathered from 700 soldiers who had not had a mental or physical illness. He used 39 items and analysed them, finding that two factors in particular did not go together in the individuals he tested. These two factors were introversion/extroversion (E) and neuroticism/stability (N). He suggested that people were not both introvert and extrovert or both neurotic and stable. Someone could be a stable introvert, a stable extrovert, a neurotic introvert or a neurotic extrovert, but people were not both stable and neurotic or both introvert and extrovert — these were separate dimensions. In 1986 Eysenck added another dimension, psychoticism (P). He used questionnaires that used 'yes' or 'no' answers to find out which personality traits applied to the respondent.

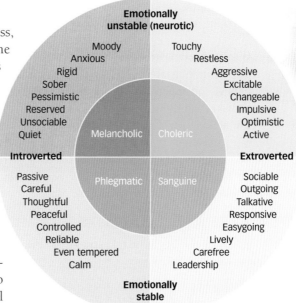

Figure 4.1 *Eysenck's model of personality, showing the two dimensions of introvert/extrovert and neurotic/stable; he added the psychoticism dimension later*

Source: H. J. Eysenck and M. W. Eysenck (1958) *Personality and Individual Differences,* Plenum Publishing

Eysenck suggested that criminals are more likely to be neurotic extroverts, because an extrovert is harder to condition and would have a weaker conscience because of this.

A biological explanation (E)

Eysenck thought that personality traits are inherited and go with biological make-up. He thought that introversion/extroversion (E) was about having a balance between excitement and inhibition. The **ascending reticular activating system (ARAS)**, which is found in the brain stem at the base of the brain, functions to dampen down (inhibit) incoming sense data or to enhance (excite) it to maintain an individual's emotional balance. Extroverts have a strong nervous system and their ARAS tends to inhibit it, which makes an extrovert under-aroused, so they seek excitement.

An introvert has a weaker nervous system that the ARAS excites more, so the introvert tends not to seek further stimulation.

A biological explanation (N)

The neurotic/stable (N) dimension relates to the **autonomic nervous system (ANS)** and differences in the limbic system. The **sympathetic branch** of the ANS activates the **fight or flight response**, or alarm reaction, and prepares the organism for action. This alarm reaction leads to raised heart rate, increased breathing rate, sweating, higher blood pressure and the production of adrenaline (see also pp. 187–88, where arousal is defined). A person who is high on the N scale (high on neuroticism) has an ANS that reacts with alarm to stressful situations. A more stable person reacts more slowly.

A biological explanation (P)

Psychoticism might be related to male hormones such as testosterone, but this is not proven by any means.

> **Explore** Use the internet to find a test (such as the 'Know your own mind' test) that allows you to see where you fit in Eysenck's theory of personality. Remember that there are criticisms of his ideas and some think that 'personality' might not even exist, though most agree that we are born with a temperament.

Evaluation of Eysenck's biological theory

Strengths

- There is evidence that extroverts tire more easily (Eysenck, 1967) and this follows the theory, because if extroverts have an inhibited system, they work harder to excite it and so would become tired more easily.
- Similarly, there is evidence that introverts do better on tasks where they can concentrate for long periods, which again supports Eysenck's theory about the ARAS.

Weaknesses

- Eysenck relied on questionnaire data requiring 'yes' or 'no' answers. These closed questions leave no room for individual differences, because answers have to be simplistic and might not be valid.
- Most testing is of those who fall on either side of the dimensions. Not much is done to test or find out about those in the middle of the scales.

Cattell's trait theory of personality (1965)

In 1965 Raymond Cattell put forward a now well-known trait theory of personality, which suggested that people show surface traits, with source traits beneath. These source traits are the fundamental dimensions of personality. Surface traits are used to describe someone, but underlying source traits need to be uncovered to understand someone's personality. Cattell thought that personality would change over time as the individual changed; he did not think that personality was biologically given. This theory is explained here as a contrast to Eysenck's biological theory.

An important feature of Cattell's theory is the methodology needed to uncover source traits. Cattell suggested using three sources of data: L-data (life data), Q-data (questionnaire data) and T-data (data from tests).

L-data

L-data come from observations of people. Cattell listed all the words he could find describing personality and then took out all words repeating a meaning, coming up with 171 traits. He trained observers to study a small sample of students for 6 months and to rate the students on all the traits that he had listed. He then used factor analysis (a method to find out which traits go with one another) to identify source traits and found 15 of them. Table 4.5 lists some of Cattell's traits.

Table 4.5 *Four of Cattell's 16 personality traits (16PF)*

	1 2 3 4 5 6 7 8 9 10	
A	Reserved, detached, critical, aloof	. . . .	Outgoing, warm-hearted, easy-going, participating
B	Less intelligent, concrete thinking	. . . .	More intelligent, abstract thinking, bright
L	Trusting, adaptable, free of jealousy, easy to get along with	. . . .	Suspicious, self-opinionated, hard to fool
O	Self-assured, confident, serene	. . . .	Apprehensive, self-reproaching, worrying, troubled

Each trait is circled on one of 10 scores from 1 to 10

Q-data

Q-data come from the results of personality questionnaires and are self-report data. Questions were based on the 15 source traits found from L-data. Factor analysis of the self-report data took place and 16 source traits were found. Twelve of these were the same as the original 15, but four were new. These 16 traits were then tested using the 16PF (personality factors) questionnaire, which asked people to rate themselves on the traits by saying they applied to them (yes), they did not (no) or sometimes they did (occasionally).

T-data

T-data used objective tests (such as **galvanic skin response**), which measure skin features such as sweating, and reaction time. These tests are objective because the individual cannot control the answers. Factor analysis of this type of data gave 21 traits.

Study hint Cattell used observations, questionnaires giving self-report data, and objective (scientific) tests such as galvanic skin response tests. Use Cattell as an example when discussing these areas of methodology.

Unit 3

Evaluation of Cattell's trait theory

Strengths

- Cattell found two surface traits: exvia/invia (closely related to extroversion and introversion), and anxiety. These seemed to correspond to Eysenck's E and N, which gives the two theories some validity.
- Cattell was able to generate scores from quantitative data and could, therefore, use an analysis with scientific standing like factor analysis (objective and replicable).

Weaknesses

- Cattell's theory used a questionnaire to gather data. The forced choice answers could mean that individuals were unable to vary their responses from what was being asked. Such limited answers could make findings less valid.
- Cattell could measure personality perhaps but not show where personality comes from. The nature–nurture issue remains to be considered (does personality arise from genes and biology or from upbringing and environment, or an interaction of both?)

The five-factor theory of personality

Cattell focused on many traits and Eysenck on very few. A different theory then arose from their work, giving five core traits that interact. These five factors are extroversion, agreeableness, conscientiousness, neuroticism and openness.

The biological approach to personality linked to sporting participation/performance

Evidence that personality affects performance (success in sport)

Eysenck's theory suggests that introverts need less stimulation and should be better at sports that need more concentration and precision. Extroverts seek arousal because of an inhibiting ARAS and so can cope better with an audience or when under pressure. International athletes are found to be more competitive and more outgoing than non-athletes (Cooper, 1969), which would support Eysenck's ideas about extroverts and introverts. Extroverts seek stimulation, which could mean they are more competitive. Terry (2000) found that athletes who performed well had more positive mental states and were less anxious, more vigorous, less confused and more extroverted.

Williams and Parkin (1980) looked to see if the international players in a particular sport differed in personality from its club players. Using the 16PF it was found that international male hockey players differed significantly in personality from club players, which suggests that those who excel in a sport do so because of personality (at least in hockey). Williams (1985), using the 16PF, found that national-level competitors are higher in emotional stability, more self-assured and mentally tougher than other players.

Aidman (2000) carried out a longitudinal study in Australia of 32 elite young football players. The participants completed the 16PF in their best junior year when they won the National Championship. There was a follow-up 7 years later to see how they had done. Thirteen had made it through to senior high level and 19 had not. These two groups were compared, but no significant differences were found in their personality profiles using 16PF. However, when their coach's predictions at junior level about their physical ability were taken into account together with the 16PF results, a difference could be seen. It seems that personality can be a factor predicting success in sport, but perhaps alongside other factors such as physical ability.

Evidence that personality affects participation (choice of sport)

Kroll and Crenshaw (1970) used the 16PF and found that footballers and wrestlers had similar personalities, whereas gymnasts and those doing karate were different both from one another and from the footballers and wrestlers. It does seem that personality influences which sport is chosen, rather than personality making someone good at sport in general.

Skirkan (2000) compared college athletes with college non-athletes to look at the effects of stress and coping with daily life. The study considered the effects of gender, sense of coherence and hardiness on coping with stress, as well as whether a person was an athlete or not an athlete. The study looked at 135 athletes and 135 non-athletes, all at college at New York University. They completed four questionnaires to measure their hardiness, sense of coherence, daily hassles and mood states. Correlations were carried out and a significant positive correlation was found between perceived stress and psychological symptoms both for athletes and non-athletes. Athletes scored higher on hardiness and a little higher on sense of coherence than did non-athletes. Gender did not give differences.

There was a significant negative correlation between hardiness and perceived stress and psychological symptoms, and between sense of coherence and perceived stress and symptoms. This means that the greater the hardiness, the lower the perceived stress and symptoms; and the greater the sense of coherence, the lower the perceived stress and symptoms. This was true for both groups, athletes and non-athletes. The findings suggest that personality (sense of coherence and hardiness) affects perceived stress and psychological symptoms, and athletes perhaps showed these personality traits a little more than non-athletes.

Research has focused on the relationship between personality and exercise. It could be that exercise affects personality (Mikel, 1986) or that personality affects whether someone takes part in exercise (Courneya and Hellsten, 1998). Personality might also affect how people feel during or after exercise (Lochbaum and Lutz, 2005). Studies have looked to see if personality correlates with participation in exercise and fitness programmes (e.g. Courneya et al., 2002).

Studies mainly show that extroversion links to exercise behaviour, which is what Eysenck's theory would predict (extroverts seek stimulation because the ARAS inhibits). Conscientiousness and openness to new experiences also positively relate to exercise behaviour (e.g. Courneya et al., 2002). Neuroticism tends to mean less exercise behaviour and there is a negative relationship. However, the studies only show weak links between personality and exercise behaviour — personality accounts only to some extent for sports behaviour, and there are other factors involved.

Personality testing suggests that footballers and gymnasts have different personalities

Study hint   Note how the studies cited here use questionnaires and correlations. You can use these studies to help explain these research methods with reference to sport psychology. You can also use the strengths and weaknesses of such methodology when evaluating the studies themselves.

Evaluation of personality theories in explaining sporting performance and participation

Strengths

- The 16PF gives a quantitative measure of personality, which is otherwise hard to measure. Quantitative data allow factor analysis (a statistical test to see which traits go together) as well as comparisons of data.
- It is argued that reducing the many ways of describing personality to a manageable number of personality factors is viable and useful. This allows, for example, the generation of quantitative data and comparisons, such as comparing personality between sports.

Weaknesses

- Using questionnaires is thought to limit the data gathered, as respondents are forced into certain choices, which may make the data less valid with regard to explaining sporting performance.
- Self-report data may not be valid because people may not answer honestly. There

might be demand characteristics if the respondent guesses what the purpose of the study is, or social desirability if respondents want to portray themselves in a particular way.

- It is recognised (including by Cattell) that the 16PF may be answered differently on a different day and in different circumstances, which means it may not be a reliable measure of someone's personality, which would affect conclusions about sporting performance.
- A lot of research has focused on college students, so findings might not be generalisable to all those who participate in sport.
- There is evidence that it may not be personality guiding sporting success so much as sporting success influencing personality. By interviewing 63 international athletes, Hemery (1986) found that 89% said they were shy and introverted when they began competing. This suggests that competing gives confidence rather than that confident people choose to compete. It may be that personality features such as confidence are not biologically given but learned; this goes against Eysenck's biological explanation.

Socialisation as an explanation for individual differences in sporting performance and participation

Socialisation has been said to explain both sporting participation and sporting performance. If personality is biologically given, it comes from someone's nature, but socialisation comes from their **nurture**. Study of the effect of socialisation on sporting performance and participation involves looking at how upbringing and environment might not only lead to someone choosing and participating in a certain sport, but also influence how successful they might be.

Defining socialisation

Socialisation refers to the way an individual learns about their culture and society. It includes learning social norms and rules about gender, age, class and race, what is accepted and what is not, as well as how others in society are viewed. Such socialisation processes allow someone to live within a culture and to be an active member of a society. Socialising influences include family, school, peers, media, religion and friends. Socialisation can be summarised as being the transmission of culture.

In sociology, socialisation is divided up into primary socialisation processes, which involve the family, and secondary socialisation, which involves school, friends, media and other influences. Socialisation has recently been defined as a two-way process, in that an individual does not have 'socialisation' done to them but is active in the process. For example, how a child responds to praise and reward is specific, and their response could influence later reinforcement patterns.

Social learning

The way people are socialised is influenced by their interactions with other people. One way in which socialisation takes place is through observing others, particularly role models and significant others. Social learning theory suggests that learning comes from paying attention to some behaviour shown by a role model, remembering the behaviour and being motivated to repeat it. Vicarious learning — learning from observing the behaviour of others being reinforced or punished — can also take place.

Operant conditioning

Another way someone might learn social norms is through operant conditioning, where they are positively reinforced for relevant behaviour and either negatively reinforced or punished for inappropriate behaviour, from society's viewpoint. Operant conditioning can also be used to shape behaviour, by gradually rewarding what is required. Gender behaviour, for example, is learned when parents and others in society reward, often using attention or praise, what is seen as appropriate gender behaviour.

> **AS link** Review your learning about social learning theory (pp. 339–42) and operant conditioning (pp. 327–30) from the learning approach.

Socialisation and sporting participation

Socialisation takes place from birth, through family values and later social influences such as school. Studies have suggested that socialisation in the family sets up schemata in the individual — ways of looking at the world. Gender-based schemata seem to be used when judging the appropriateness of certain sports for males or females. Koivula (1995) studied this area (see pp. 204–08). Schools encourage certain types of sports participation and it has been found that this encouragement, which is socialisation, influences adult behaviour. So two factors affecting sporting participation are socialisation within a family (setting up gender schemata) and socialisation within a school (setting up ideas about appropriate sport participation). The media are a socialising influence and media influences are also found to be factors in sporting participation.

> **Explore** Carry out a content analysis of media coverage of sport. Note down how much time is given to coverage of 'male' sport compared with 'female' sport.

Predicting sport participation

Scheerder et al. (2006) carried out a longitudinal study following on from the general idea that active participation in sport by adolescents would affect their level of participation in sport when adult. A sample of 257 female adults, who had been involved in a much larger-scale questionnaire study 20 years previously, were sinterviewed. It was found by comparing the new data with the old that there was a correlation between taking part in sport as an adolescent and taking part as an adult. Sport participation when young only partly explains adult sport participation, but it is a factor. The study concluded that late adolescent sport experience and the programme of sport in school play an important part in whether that person is involved in sport as an adult. Youth sport programmes seem to pave the way for continued sport participation, which supports the idea that adolescent participation predicts adult participation.

Study hint Scheerder et al. (2006) used questionnaires and interviews to gather data, then they used correlational analysis to check comments about sport participation by young individuals with their comments as adults. This is a longitudinal study because the same people were tested 20 years apart. Use this as an example when answering questions about methodology.

Participation and 'gendering'

Hardin and Greer (2007) studied gender and sporting behaviour. The study looked at how sport is 'gendered' in the USA and how this affects sport participation. There were 340 college students in the study and it was found that most sports were rated as masculine. Socialisation factors such as gender role and media influences seem to be the most influential in sex-typing sports. Watching a lot of television (including watching sport on television) and attitudes towards women were the factors that affected sports being said to be masculine.

Koivula (1995) found that sports are 'gendered' and some people are more likely to perceive sports as masculine or feminine than others. Koivula used the Bem questionnaire, finding that gender-based schematic processing seemed to guide at least some people when judging participation in a particular sport.

Study hint If you choose Koivula's study (1995) as one of your studies in detail, then you can use its detail to explain the effect of socialisation on sporting participation. Evaluation of the study can be used to evaluate the role of socialisation as well.

Sport used as a socialising agent

Children can be socialised through sport as well as being introduced to sport through their socialisation. When playing in a team, for example, children learn about leaders and followers and about cooperating in a team, as well as learning from members of the team. When competing, children learn about losing, fair play and social norms such as turn-taking.

Factors affecting sporting performance

It is sometimes said that parental influence is the key factor when it comes to nurturing talent, which is what leads to sporting success. Hellstedt (1998) suggested that medium parental involvement led to the best likelihood of success. A range of methods of involvement can be seen, from paying the cost of training and transport to competitions to providing a role model for imitation. Parental involvement is clearly important if a child is to excel. Coaches are also important, though this is perhaps less about socialisation and more about motivational factors.

4

There are factors other than cultural norms that lead to sporting success. These factors include personality and cognitive factors such as appropriate thinking patterns. Motivation is a key feature of sporting performance, as is the level of arousal or whether there is an audience. These features are explained in more detail below.

Evaluation of the effect of socialisation on sporting participation and performance

Strengths

■ Studies like Koivula (1995) have shown by using questionnaire data that people consistently allocate sports 'masculine' or 'feminine' labels and that such allocations match cultural norms arising from media and society influences. Evidence suggests that cultural norms are followed and it seems sensible to say that this is because of socialisation influences such as media, family and school.

■ Questionnaires are used repeatedly (such as the Bem sex role inventory used by Koivula) and get similar results. Data are therefore thought to be reliable in such studies.

Weaknesses

■ Socialisation (that children learn from those around them what cultural norms are) is a broad concept that is hard to prove. Features of the nature of an individual, such as personality and genes, could affect sporting performance and participation. It is hard to separate nature and nurture for the purposes of study.

■ Much of the data come from questionnaire and correlational analysis, such as Scheerder et al. (2006). Correlational analysis can help to show relationships between variables. However, such analysis does not show that one variable causes another. Adolescent sporting behaviour may appear to predict adult sporting behaviour as a result of socialisation, but nature factors could also lead an adolescent to take part in sport and to continue to take part in adulthood.

Table 4.6 *Strengths and weaknesses of the idea that socialisation affects sporting participation and performance*

Strengths	Weaknesses
● Evidence suggests that 'gendering' sport is consistent within a culture, which is evidence for the importance of socialisation	● Socialisation is about nurture and it is hard to separate this from nature, which may have a role to play either instead of nurture or in combination with it
● Questionnaire data appear to be reliable	● Correlational data cannot show cause and effect

Theories of motivation

This section of the course requires two theories of motivation to be studied. One theory must be the achievement motivation theory. In this textbook, the second theory chosen is Bandura's self-efficacy theory, because it links with social learning theory and socialisation (explained earlier). A third theory suggested is the cognitive evaluation theory.

Defining motivation

Motivation refers to reasons why someone behaves in a particular way. It might be an innate need to minimise pain and maximise pleasure, or a need to eat or sleep. Motivation might be about needs such as achieving a particular goal or ideal. These needs may come from nurture or nature.

Theories often refer to two different types of motivation. The first, **intrinsic motivation,** describes reasons for behaviour originating from within a person, such as personality or inner drive, wishes or desires. In sport, enjoying taking part would be intrinsic motivation. The second type, **extrinsic motivation**, describes external reasons for behaviour, such as money or career progression. In sport, being cheered on would be extrinsic motivation because it is something external to the individual.

Positive and negative motivation

All of McClelland's needs (see below) are positive ones, in the sense that the need is *for* something rather than to *avoid* something. An example of a more negative type of motivation is the need to avoid failure.

Studies tend to find that the positive form of motivation — to succeed — is a stronger motivator than the negative form of motivation — not to fail. Halvari and Thomassen (1997) reported on a Norwegian study of 150 high school athletes. They found that success related to a strong motivation to succeed rather than a wish to avoid failure.

Atkinson (1964)

Achievement motivation in sport was studied by Atkinson (1964) and refers to how far an athlete will go in order to succeed — that is, how he or she approaches or avoids a competitive situation. An achievement situation is one in which an athlete expects his or her performance to be evaluated. Atkinson later looked further at motivation and developed a model called the McClelland–Atkinson model. This looks more at sporting achievement, so is outlined here after McClelland's theory, which tends to use examples from business.

Maslow's hierarchy of needs

Achievement motivation is often linked to **Maslow's hierarchy of needs**. Abraham Maslow suggested that primary needs such as food and warmth are basic, and people seek to satisfy those needs first. Then come other needs such as interacting with others, loving and being loved. The top of the hierarchy of needs is **self-actualisation** — a person's desire to fulfil their potential. An athlete with high achievement motivation is likely to train hard and try hard because of internal motivation to fulfil such needs.

4

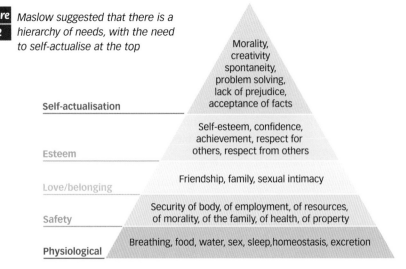

Figure 4.2 *Maslow suggested that there is a hierarchy of needs, with the need to self-actualise at the top*

Veroff (1969)

Joseph Veroff suggested three stages of achievement motivation:

- Stage 1: the **autonomous competence** stage, where children up to the age of about 5 focus on achieving mastery of skills and not on what others can do.
- Stage 2: the **social comparison** stage, when a child is about 5 or 6. This stage is about comparisons with others and understanding external standards. Children who do well at this stage might go on to compete, but others are not likely to. Those who compete and get good feedback about their performance are more likely to continue.
- Stage 3: the **integrated** stage, when a child has both mastered skills (autonomous competence) and is able to compare him or herself with others and with external standards. Such children can swap between these two focuses when there is a need to. For example, a sport can be practised and mastery can continue, but the child also competes regularly.

McClelland's achievement motivation theory

David McClelland developed achievement motivation theory (e.g. 1961), putting forward the idea that an individual has three needs, including a need for achievement, but may not have these needs in equal amounts. The three needs are the need for affiliation, the need for power and the need for achievement. McClelland was researching in the field of work and thinking about motivation at work, but his theory can be applied to sport.

People have differing levels of these three needs, which motivate someone to work hard, become a leader, or excel at sport, for example. McClelland suggests that someone can be taught to promote these different needs in themselves. He also thought that while every individual has all three needs, one can be stronger than the others. For example, in some people the need for affiliation predominates, whereas in others it is the need for achievement.

Knowing a person's balance of needs can help to show how they might behave in certain circumstances. Someone with a higher need for affiliation than for achievement, for instance, is likely to play well in a team sport and to be focused on helping the team to win, rather than showing their individual abilities. The same person may not, however, excel at individual sports. Someone with a high need for power might be better competing in an individual sport. A high need for achievement, with its focus on intrinsic motivation, should benefit all athletes. If someone is motivated extrinsically, they would perhaps do better at a sport where there is an external reward such as prize money.

> **Study hint** The terms 'intrinsic' and 'extrinsic' motivation were defined earlier in this chapter. These two types of motivation are key terms for this application. Be sure you can define them both, with an example.

McClelland's three needs

Need for achievement (N-Ach)

The need for achievement (N-Ach) refers to how a person desires to accomplish certain things and to master skills. It is about having high standards and control. N-Ach is related to how hard a task a person chooses. Those with low N-Ach would choose easy tasks so that they do not fail and very difficult tasks so that if they failed nobody would think badly of them. Those with high N-Ach would choose reasonably difficult tasks, so that they are challenging but possible to achieve. Those with high N-Ach will look for challenges and independence and their reward is that their achievements are recognised. High N-Ach comes from internal strength, praise for success and parents who encouraged independent behaviour.

McClelland used the **thematic apperception test (TAT)** to find out people's views about success and competing. This test involves showing people a particular picture and asking them to write the story they think the picture tells. What they write can be used to reveal their thinking.

In one study, McClelland aroused the concern of one group of participants about their achievement in the test, while another group were not aroused in this way. He found that whether people were aroused or not made no difference — there were people who were concerned and unconcerned about their performance in both groups. He drew the conclusion that some people were more concerned about their achievement (had a higher N-Ach) than others. Other studies have shown that people in demanding jobs such as managers and entrepreneurs have a high N-Ach. Someone with a high need for achievement is likely to do well in sport because they care about what they are doing and want to do well.

In another study McClelland asked people to throw rings over a peg. He found that those with high N-Ach chose to stand at a distance away from the peg that would make the task not too hard and not too easy. This would help them to achieve mastery over the task. Those with lower N-Ach just threw from any distance at random — sometimes too near and sometimes too far away. Importantly, McClelland seems to have thought that people can be taught to have a high N-Ach, suggesting that even if it is an innate need in some people it is one that can also be learned.

4

Need for affiliation (N-Affil)

The need for affiliation (N-Affil), according to McClelland, is the need for a sense of belonging. People with a high affiliation need to look for warm personal relationships and like having people around them. Such people are likely to make good team players but not such good leaders. People do not necessarily have a high need for affiliation all the time. Depending on the situation and the person, there can be a greater need for affiliation in stressful situations and teams are likely to pull together when there are problems. It is suggested that the need for affiliation depends on whether it is useful or not. When having others around is useful, such as to diffuse stress, then someone's N-Affil will be high. When having other people around is not useful, their N-Affil will be lower.

Need for power (N-Pow)

McClelland also considered that people have a need for power (N-Pow), and that this explained why people often feel the need to be in charge. People with high N-Pow like to see things moving in the direction they feel is important. The need for social power, for instance, is demonstrated by people wanting to sway others to a point of view (e.g. political power) and the need for personal power is demonstrated by those wanting to be in control within a company. An aspect of social power is the possession of charismatic power (e.g. Martin Luther King).

The McClelland–Atkinson model

The McClelland–Atkinson model suggests that achievement motivation is to do with someone's motivations to achieve success as well as their fear of failure. The theory says that:

$$achievement\ motivation = intrinsic\ motivation/fear\ of\ failure$$

The model additionally needs to include extrinsic motivation, and Atkinson later added this. It was also recognised that in some cases women seem less motivated to succeed than men, and it was suggested that 'fear of success' needed to be added to the model. However, it is more likely that women seem less motivated to achieve because of the masculinity of sport. This shows the strength of socialisation on the development of individuals' motivation tendencies. Bem's sex role inventory has been used to study gender differences in achievement motivation. It was found that those who were more **androgynous** had higher achievement motivation. Therefore, people whose characteristics were moving away from the 'feminine' had higher achievement motivation. This adds to the evidence suggesting that females have lower achievement motivation.

> The word **androgynous** as used in sport psychology means women with views and opinions showing both male and female characteristics.

Evaluation of achievement motivation theories

Strengths

- Achievement motivation theory links well with other theories, such as the role of socialisation in behaviour. For example, encouragement and praise are said to improve achievement motivation, which links with the role of operant conditioning in socialisation.

■ McClelland used TAT rather than other tests because he wanted to look at an actual situation that someone cared about, rather than measure personality traits in isolation. He felt that it was the situation that would show such things as need for achievement, and that this was not a static personality trait.

■ Studies in achievement motivation have tended to focus on the West and have been said to represent Western values. Individual achievements are praised in the West, where culture tends to be individualist. In other countries, such as China, where the culture is more collectivist, it has been found that social achievement is valued more (e.g. Bond, 1986). Thus it can be seen that cultural norms affect type of motivation. This underlines the power of socialisation in issues such as motivation to succeed. China, Russia and other collectivist cultures might be expected to succeed particularly in team sports, which in fact tends to be the case. Their athletes' need for affiliation is as high as their need for achievement and the two relate, whereas in the West the need for affiliation and the need for achievement are not related. This suggests that achievement motivation comes from nurture not nature, and links to the discussion about the influence of socialisation on sport participation and sporting performance.

Weaknesses

■ Participants reporting their attitudes by using attitude scales is a problem, as self-report data is not considered to be reliable.

■ The validity of self-report data can be challenged because these data relate to attitudes and might not reflect behaviour.

■ The model was unable to predict behaviour because the constructs (intrinsic motivation, fear of failure, need to achieve and so on) are not measurable and the relationship between achievement motivation and performance was not clearly outlined. If a model does not have the power to predict behaviour then its usefulness is limited.

Table 4.7 *Strengths and weaknesses of achievement motivation theory*

Strengths	Weaknesses
• Uses the idea of socialisation so two theories reinforce one another	• Self-report data may not be reliable
• TAT includes the whole situation and not just personality trait testing in isolation	• Self-report data about attitudes may not reflect behaviour
• Findings tend to be about the Western world and individualistic cultures rather than more collectivist cultures such as China	• The model may not predict behaviour and so has limited application

Bandura and the self-efficacy theory of motivation

The idea of self-confidence has been studied more than the idea of achievement motivation, partly because it is more likely to predict performance. It was realised that those with a high need for achievement had higher self-confidence than those

4

with a low need for achievement, so self-confidence became the focus of study. Bandura (1977) suggested a theory that would explain why athletes who think they will do well generally go on to do well. This is a theory of self-efficacy.

What is self-efficacy?

Self-efficacy is the belief a person has that he or she can do well and is competent at a task. Efficacy is the power to bring about an effect (i.e. competence). Self-efficacy emphasises that an individual believes they have that power, even if they do not. If someone has high self-efficacy he or she will take a task on; if self-efficacy is low, then that person might avoid a task. Self-efficacy includes self-confidence but refers in particular to confidence shown in specific areas of life. Someone can have self-efficacy in one type of sport or situation, for example, but not in another.

There is a difference between self-efficacy and self-esteem. Self-esteem is about someone's self-worth; self-efficacy if about their perception of their ability to achieve a goal. Self-esteem is general but self-efficacy can focus on a particular task. Someone can have high self-efficacy for one task and low self-efficacy for another task, whereas self-esteem tends to affect the who le person. If someone has low self-efficacy for a particular task, this may not affect their self-esteem as they might not invest their self-esteem in that task. For example, they may not think they are good at playing snooker but they may not worry about it with regard to their self-esteem.

Factors affecting self-efficacy

Self-efficacy is part of Bandura's **social cognitive theory**, which examines the relationship between someone's behaviour, environment and cognitive factors. Bandura thought that people do not learn behaviour without taking into account their environment (including other people around them). Cognitive factors — which refer to their thinking and how they think about themselves — are also important. Individuals with high self-efficacy are likely to view difficult tasks as something to master, whereas those with low self-efficacy might avoid difficult tasks.

According to the theory there are four factors affecting someone's level of self-efficacy:
- **Performance accomplishments** — past performance and how successful it has been. Success raises self-efficacy and failure lowers it.
- **Vicarious experience** — if someone watches someone else do a task well they are more likely to think that they themselves will do well at that task, particularly if the model is someone who is looked up to, which matches Bandura's social learning theory.
- **Social persuasion** — encouragement from others. Positive persuasions (encouragement) increase self-efficacy; negative persuasions (discouragement) lower self-efficacy. It is usually easier to lower self-efficacy than it is to improve it.
- **Physiological and emotional state** — how the individual interprets his/her feelings of arousal. In stressful situations, people show signs of distress such as aches and pains, fear and nausea. How someone perceives these responses can affect their self-efficacy. For example, someone with low self-efficacy might

interpret pre-match nerves as their lack of ability, whereas someone with high self-efficacy might see such signs as normal.

Bandura suggested that those with high self-efficacy think their destiny is in their own hands whereas those with low self-efficacy feel that they have less control over their own lives.

Study hint Note that vicarious experience links with social learning theory and encouragement from others links with operant conditioning, so link to your AS studies of these areas and use evaluations of those areas to evaluate here.

The main feature is performance. If someone is successful their level of self-efficacy will be raised, and if they are not this will lower it. The odd failure will not affect a person's self-efficacy. One way to achieve a high level of self-efficacy is for a model to perform the task successfully (perhaps a number of times) and then help the person to perform the task themselves. Jourden et al. (1991) found that if someone did a task well but thought it was due to their innate abilities, they were not very enthusiastic about the task. If, however, they attributed their success to their own efforts, then this raised their self-efficacy.

Comparing people with high and low self-efficacy

People with high self-efficacy are likely to attempt tasks that they cannot achieve; those with self-efficacy that is lower than necessary (because they do have the ability and resources to do the task in question) are likely to be low in achievement. The optimum level of self-efficacy is just above ability, since this will encourage individuals to try tasks that are challenging and this will give them experience and is likely to raise their self-efficacy.

People with high self-efficacy are likely to persist more in a task, so in terms of sporting performance they might practise more. However, having low self-efficacy might lead to more research being carried out, such as about how to carry out a task, and those with high self-efficacy might not prepare enough and/or might not practise enough. If someone with low self-efficacy does not plan a task well because they think it is hard, then this can lead to stress. Those with low self-efficacy are, therefore, likely to suffer more stress.

Individuals with high self-efficacy will attribute failure to external reasons but those with low self-efficacy are more likely to blame themselves. Conner and Norman (2005) suggested that health behaviours such as not smoking, or dieting and exercising, tend to depend on perceived self-efficacy. Self-efficacy affects how much effort someone will put into maintaining health behaviours and how long they will persevere. The same applies to sporting behaviour.

Evaluation of the theory
Strengths

- The theory is useful because it can be applied. In order to succeed at a task someone can be helped to increase their self-efficacy. This can be done by encouraging them, helping them to achieve success using small steps forward, and letting them watch someone else succeed.

- Experiments have shown that self-efficacy helps in the learning of maths and language skills (e.g. Schunk, 1989). Specific attainable goals help this process, alongside three other procedures: modelling useful learning strategies, encouraging performance and providing positive feedback. This means the theory has predictive power — if you follow the ideas then they work.

Weaknesses

- The theory was developed in relation to social learning, not skills learning such as in sport. It might be that social learning and learning motor and physical skills are not the same process, so findings from studies that look at one may not be applicable to the other.
- Self-report data (for example, about self-confidence and confidence in ability) tend to be used in research. These can lack both reliability (if someone is in a different mood or a different situation) and validity (if someone is talking about what they might do rather than what they would do, for example).

Table 4.8 *Strengths and weaknesses of the self-efficacy theory*

Strengths	Weaknesses
• The theory has useful applications for helping performance	• The theory was tested on social learning and not on the learning of motor skills
• Experiments have used the ideas in an educational environment for the learning of skills and have shown that the ideas work; the theory has predictive power	• Self-report data can lack both reliability and validity

Ways to develop motivation

Studies looking at motivation suggest that a sports coach would be well advised to:
- encourage self-talk
- encourage drilling and practice
- provide a role model by carrying out the task successfully themselves
- give a lot of praise and positive reinforcement
- allow children to experience repeated success (competition at the outset might not be a good thing); success is not about winning but about doing better and developing skills

Ways to encourage self-confidence are to:
- set goals when training so success can be shown
- use imagery to build self-confidence
- use positive self-talk and not focus on errors

Theories about arousal, anxiety and the effects of an audience

For this section the course requires you to study two theories that between them cover arousal, anxiety and the effects of the audience. One theory must be the inverted U hypothesis (arousal and anxiety). In this textbook the second theory chosen is evaluation apprehension theory, because it is clearly about the effect of an audience on performance.

The catastrophe theory and the optimal level of arousal theory are explained in the online resources supporting this textbook.

The inverted U hypothesis

The inverted U hypothesis is a theory that is covered in different areas in psychology, including counselling and health psychology. This is because it refers to levels of biological arousal, which affects many areas of human experience. The hypothesis suggests that some arousal is a good thing as performance is improved, whereas too much arousal causes performance to suffer.

What is arousal?

Arousal is both a physiological (biological) and a psychological state involving areas of the brain as well as the autonomic nervous system. Arousal can mean a state of being awake, referring to consciousness involving areas of the brain such as the reticular activating system (RAS). Arousal also involves motivations and the **fight or flight response** (also called the emergency reaction).

The brain and spinal cord form the **central nervous system**. The rest of the nervous system is known as the **peripheral nervous system**. The control of breathing, heart rate, digestive functions and other regulatory systems is carried out by the **autonomic nervous system**, a part of the peripheral nervous system.

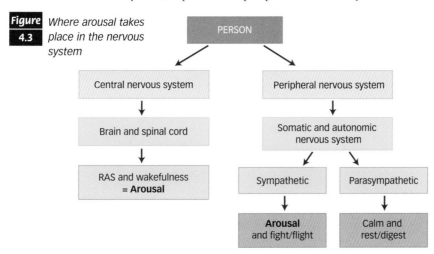

Figure 4.3 *Where arousal takes place in the nervous system*

There are two parts to the autonomic nervous system, the **sympathetic** part, which puts into motion what the body needs for action ('fight or flight'), and the **parasympathetic** part, which acts to calm down the system and get back to a resting state ('rest and digest'). Arousal involves the sympathetic part of the autonomic nervous system which prepares the body for action: increased heart rate and breathing rate, raised blood pressure, dryness of mouth and raised blood sugar levels take place, as well as other changes. If arousal continues unchecked by the calming action of the parasympathetic part of the autonomic nervous system, then too much energy is used up, leaving the body's immune system under threat.

The state of arousal is neither good nor bad for a person. When aroused, someone is in an energised state, which can be useful.

The Yerkes–Dodson Law (1908)

Yerkes and Dodson looked at levels of arousal and came up with the idea of the inverted U shape. In general the Yerkes–Dodson law says that performance rises with arousal but that optimum arousal for performance is reached at some point. After that point is reached then performance will gradually deteriorate as arousal continues to rise. The Yerkes–Dodson law goes further and suggests that sports requiring fine motor skills and precision (e.g. golf) need low arousal for optimum performance, whereas sports that need less skill and more strength (e.g. wrestling) need high arousal for optimum performance. It was also found that complex tasks were completed better with low arousal but simple tasks could be performed better with high arousal. The type of task is therefore also important when deciding whether sporting performance will be positively or negatively affected by arousal.

There is an optimum level of arousal for each person depending on the task and the individual. When preparation for a performance is right, the right decisions have been made and the level of arousal is appropriate then performance can be excellent. But if any of these factors go wrong then performance can be adversely affected.

Figure 4.4 *The inverted U hypothesis suggests that performance rises as arousal rises up to a certain point, after which continued arousal will cause performance to deteriorate*

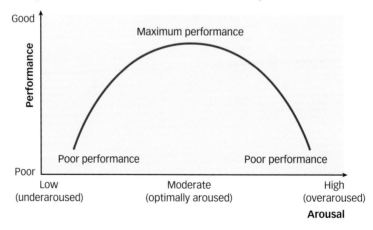

Beginners usually do better with low arousal, perhaps because for them the task, whatever it is, will seem complex. Attention is easier to focus if arousal is low and a beginner experiences **perceptual narrowing** (having to focus carefully on a task) and **cue utilisation** (the need to use relevant cues). Experienced performers do not need to attend to the task as much as inexperienced ones, so might do better with higher levels of arousal.

The inverted U hypothesis is about arousal but as arousal is related to anxiety, the theory also includes anxiety. As anxiety rises, arousal levels are likely to rise and, after an optimal level of arousal/anxiety, performance will start to deteriorate. If someone has to focus very intently they can narrow their focus so much that they experience blind panic.

What is anxiety?

Anxiety is both a physiological and psychological phenomenon, as is arousal. The two go together because the physical aspect of anxiety is arousal.

Anxiety is related to emotions such as fear, negative thoughts such as not being able to cope and other behavioural aspects. The biological aspects of anxiety — sweating, not sleeping, feeling tense, headaches, raised blood pressure and problems with eating/digestive functions — are also features of arousal. Anxiety seems to stem from the amygdala and other brain functions, rather than from the autonomic nervous system. With regard to sport, anxiety is about the biological, cognitive, behavioural and emotional aspects of performance.

State anxiety and trait anxiety

State anxiety is short-term anxiety. It is the state of emotional arousal following a perceived threat or other particular reason or circumstance and links to the fight–flight reaction. **Trait anxiety** is long-term anxiety and means that the individual has anxiety as a personality trait. This trait refers to individual differences in responding to a situation with state anxiety, which means producing an arousal response. For example, people with higher trait anxiety are more likely to be aroused in certain situations than others.

The state of 'worry' refers to a cognitive element in anxiety and includes whether a person perceives that they have sufficient resources to cope with a situation. 'Emotionality' refers to the amount of physiological response to anxiety, such as headaches and sweating.

The multi-dimensional anxiety theory

The multi-dimensional anxiety theory splits anxiety into cognitive anxiety and somatic anxiety. **Somatic anxiety** refers to the physical features of anxiety (arousal). The multi-dimensional theory also uses the inverted U explanation for somatic anxiety, in suggesting that as it rises, performance rises, but if there is too much somatic anxiety, performance deteriorates.

Cognitive anxiety refers to anxious thoughts. These can continue for an athlete even after performance has started. The multi-dimensional anxiety theory with regard to cognitive anxiety suggests that cognitive anxiety consistently affects sporting performance negatively with no initial benefit, as with somatic anxiety.

Evaluation of the inverted U hypothesis

Strengths

- The inverted U hypothesis can explain the real-life observation that performance may in fact decrease if arousal is high. This goes against the drive theory (which suggests that performance consistently increases as arousal increases, with no decline in performance at high levels of arousal).

■ Study of somatic anxiety through the multi-dimensional anxiety theory and study of arousal through the inverted U hypothesis both show that too much anxiety/arousal will affect performance negatively, so the two theories support one another.

Weaknesses

■ The main hypothesis does not consider the effects of the type of task or whether the performer was a beginner or not, so the basic idea of performance at first rising and then falling as arousal increases needs some modification.

■ Somatic anxiety and arousal could be regarded as more or less the same thing. There are many different theories that look at anxiety and arousal without it being clear how the two relate to one another. Anxiety includes trait, state, somatic and cognitive anxiety as well as competitive anxiety, whereas arousal is defined as the physiological response. These areas of anxiety and arousal perhaps need to be more clearly linked to one another.

Table 4.9 *Strengths and weaknesses of the inverted U hypothesis*

Strengths	Weaknesses
● The inverted U goes further than drive theory and explains real-life observational data	● The main hypothesis needs extending to take account of the type of task and the experience of the performer
● The multi-dimensional anxiety theory also uses the idea of an inverted U, which gives support to the hypothesis	● It is difficult to separate anxiety and arousal; theories talk about them separately so it is hard to link findings from both to form an explanation

Evaluation apprehension theory

Evaluation apprehension theory looks at the effects of arousal on performance, as does the inverted U hypothesis, but it focuses on the effect on a performer of having an audience or the effect of expecting to be watched.

Sporting performance often takes place in front of an audience. The effect of having an audience on sporting performance is called the **audience effect**. The audience is made up of **primary spectators** who are present at an event and also possibly **secondary spectators** who are not present but watching in some other way, such as on the television. **Passive spectators** are on nobody's side while **supportive spectators** are on the side of a particular athlete or group of athletes. Issues about what type of spectator is being referred to can affect the analysis of the effect of an audience on performance.

When the effect of the presence of others improves performance this is known as **social facilitation**. As well as the audience effect and social facilitation, there can also be a **coactor effect**, which is the effect on the sportsperson of the other people performing alongside them.

Cottrell's evaluation apprehension theory

Cottrell (1968) considered the effect of an audience on performance, focusing on the type of audience rather than the type of task. He argued that whether a performance improved in front of others depended on whether they were seen as supportive or not. Cottrell found that sportspeople (and other performers) were apprehensive about being watched, and the quality of their performance depended on this apprehension about being evaluated by others. This is the evaluation apprehension theory. If a sportsperson thinks they are being evaluated their arousal levels are raised. The strength of the arousal depends on the power the sportsperson thinks that the watcher has to reward or punish them. Someone may not be worried about their performance in itself but may be anxious about how others will judge it.

Evidence for the audience effect

The level of difference an audience makes to a performance can depend on how good the performer is. This might be because a beginner is more apprehensive about being judged and so experiences more arousal, whereas an expert may not be so apprehensive. Michaels et al. (1982) showed social facilitation at work when they found that pool players of above average ability achieved 69% of their shots when playing alone, but managed 80% when a group of four people watched them. Below average pool players achieved about 36% of their shots alone and only 25% when watched by four people. When someone is good at a task the correct response is the **dominant response**; when they are not good at something the incorrect response is dominant. However, this study only shows that having an audience affects performance and that how good someone is at the task is also important. It does not show that being apprehensive about being watched and/or judged is important.

> **Study hint** The study by Michaels et al. (1982) does not demonstrate that it is the fear of being evaluated that affects performance, just that having an audience affects performance. When reading about studies always be ready to be critical of the study and/ or the findings in this way.

Evidence for evaluation apprehension

A study that tested evaluation apprehension theory was carried out by Bartis et al. (1988). Again the study looked at whether performance would be improved by the presence of an audience for a simple task but made worse for a complex task. The participants in the study were divided into two groups. One group were asked to think of uses for a knife and the other group were asked to think of creative uses for a knife. It was thought to be harder to think of creative uses than just to list uses for a knife. To test the evaluation apprehension theory rather than simply test the effect of having an audience, in both groups half of the participants were told they would be individually identified and half were told that their results would be anonymous. It was thought that knowing they could be identified would make the participants more fearful of being judged by the audience.

It was found that in the evaluation apprehension condition, which was where participants believed they would be identified, more uses for a knife for the simple task were suggested than in the group that did not think they would be identified.

In the group that thought they would not be identified there were more creative uses for a knife than in the evaluation apprehension condition. The conclusion was that evaluation apprehension makes someone do a simple task better than a complex one. Evaluation apprehension led to a worse performance on the complex task than if there was no evaluation apprehension.

The study was not a natural one (it was carried out in laboratory conditions), so the findings lack validity. The findings are not related to sport.

Aiello and Kolb (1995) looked at workers who were being evaluated electronically. The workers were stressed and worried about being evaluated. The performance of highly skilled workers improved when they were monitored, compared with when they were not. However, the performance of less skilled workers deteriorated when they were monitored. This is evidence for the evaluation apprehension theory. The findings can be applied to sporting performance and a conclusion could be that those who are good at the sport would do better when closely monitored than those who lack the skills for success at sport, who would do less well when an audience was monitoring their performance,

Schmitt et al. (1986) carried out a study in which participants did two tasks — a hard task or an easy one. Participants did the tasks either on their own (the individual condition), or in the presence of someone blindfolded (the mere presence of others condition), or being closely watched by someone (the evaluation apprehension condition). Schmitt et al. found that the easy task was performed faster and the difficult task was performed more slowly in the mere presence of others than in the individual condition. However, there were only small differences between the mere presence of others condition and the evaluation apprehension condition. This goes against the evaluation apprehension theory and suggests that the audience effect comes from the mere presence of others. With regard to sporting performance, this suggests that having an audience present would affect performance, which would be improved. However, whether the audience was paying attention to the performance or not would not make any difference to performance. This goes against the idea of evaluation apprehension.

Links to the inverted U hypothesis
It can be claimed that performing a dominant response that is an incorrect response gives more arousal than performing a dominant response that is correct. If fear of being evaluated by an audience also leads to arousal, then someone who is not good at a task who is also apprehensive about being evaluated would show a high level of arousal and low performance. Someone fearful of evaluation but performing a correct dominant response might not reach the levels of arousal that would cause performance to decline, so might do better. These findings can be explained by the inverted U hypothesis as well as by the theory of evaluation apprehension.

Evaluation of the evaluation apprehension theory
Strengths
- The theory finds that a correct dominant response is performed better with an

audience and an incorrect dominant response is performed less well, which agrees with the inverted U hypothesis, so the findings support one another.

- The strength of using experiments, both field and laboratory, is that because of the careful controls they can be repeated to find reliability.

Weaknesses

- Studies are often carried out in laboratory conditions, such as Bartis et al. (1988), and this means that findings might not be ecologically valid as the setting is not a real life one (although sportspeople expect an audience, so even in a laboratory such a situation may be valid).
- Laboratory studies are often not natural tasks (e.g. listing the uses of a knife), so the task might lack validity.
- The theory is hard to prove because of the complexity of the variables being tested. There is, for example, the level of arousal in each individual, the complexity of the task (which would differ for each individual), and the type of audience. It is hard to prove that task response differs because of fear of being evaluated by the audience when there are so many other factors to take into account. It is hard to operationalise the 'fear of being evaluated' to test it.

Table 4.10 *Strengths and weaknesses of the evaluation apprehension theory*

Strengths	Weaknesses
• Findings match the inverted U hypothesis findings about arousal • Experiments give reliable findings	• Laboratory studies like Bartis et al. (1988) lack ecological validity • Laboratory studies lack validity with regard to the task • It is hard to operationalise fear of being evaluated in order to test it

Psychological techniques for improving performance in sport

For this section you are required to cover two psychological techniques for improving sporting performance. Three techniques are suggested for your course. Imagery is chosen here because it links well to the Boyd and Munroe study which you have to cover. Goal-setting is the other technique chosen here, because it links well with theories of motivation. Attribution retraining is the third technique and is covered in the online resources supporting this textbook.

Using imagery to improve performance

The technique of using imagery means creating mental perceptions of all the aspects of an experience that would be present if the experience was real. Using imagery

Unit 3

4

often means using visualisation. However, in practice imagery can be auditory or kinaesthetic (which is about body position and physical touch) as well as visual. The sportsperson might imagine hearing the roar of a crowd or feeling their body position as they wait to compete.

The idea is to create a mental representation of what should happen or what the athlete wants to feel. Imagery can be used to visualise the outcome of a performance, such as winning the race or running a certain distance in a certain time, or to visualise the feeling of relaxation and rest. The aim is for the athlete to imagine a scenario and then to 'step into' that feeling when they need to.

Sportspeople use imagery to practice specific physical skills mentally, to improve confidence and positive thinking about outcomes, to control arousal and anxiety, to prepare for a performance and to review a performance. For example, visualising a shot in tennis just before playing it can be useful, as can visualising a whole performance before the match so that imagery can be used when performing. Boyd and Munroe (2003) looked at how climbers use imagery for such tasks as planning a route up a rock face. Their study explains five functions of imagery (these are explained on p. 199); you should use these functions when explaining how imagery can be used in sport.

Studies looking at the use of imagery in sport

Feltz and Landers (1983) carried out a meta-analysis of 60 studies where mental practice was used by half of the participants and the other half acted as a control. They found that in general mental practice influenced performance more than having no practice, but was less effective than physical practice.

Isaac (1992) carried out a field experiment that involved actual sport skills, where previous studies tended to look at participants learning new tasks. Isaac wondered if people who were good at imagery found it more useful. She tested 78 participants and grouped them into novice or experienced trampolinists. Half of each group were then divided into those who would use mental practice and those who would not (the control group). She also divided participants up into high or low imagers by using their initial skill level. All the participants then went into training as trampolinists. The experimental group used both physical and mental practice in their training, and the control group did the physical practice and a mental task not related to the sport (such as a maths problem). The study found a difference between the experimental and the control group: mental practice improved performance. It was also found that high imagery participants in general improved more than low imagery participants. It was concluded that imagery helped performance no matter what the initial skill level was and that those used to using imagery improved more than those who did not usually use imagery.

Martin and Hall (1995) looked at whether use of imagery could improve golf skills. Thirty-nine beginners were put into either an imagery group or a control group and were all taught how to hit golf balls. The imagery group also practised in an imagery training session on how to hit golf balls. It was found that the imagery group were more realistic in what they expected of themselves, stuck to their training more and set higher goals for themselves, which suggests that using imagery can affect motivation as well as performance.

Orlick et al. (1992) tested children to see if table tennis skills can be improved in 7–10-year-olds using mental imagery, and it was found that imagery was useful. It appears that use of mental imagery helps children as well as adults, though most studies involve adults.

Conclusions about the use of mental imagery in sport

Visual imagery seems to be more effective than no physical practice but is not as effective as physical practice. Studies suggest that a mixture of physical and mental practice can improve performance and also that visual imagery can improve motivation.

Evaluation of the use of imagery to improve performance

Strengths

- Studies have shown that mental practice works and a meta-analysis looking at many different findings drew the same conclusion.
- It is thought that different people use different learning styles (some are visualisers and others verbalisers, for instance), so it is likely that imagery helps learning, perhaps if it matches learning style. Two areas of study support one another.
- Studies have been experimental, using a control group, so they are replicable; careful controls suggest they are reliable in their findings.

Weaknesses

- Studies tend to be experiments and many of them involve novice skills rather than practised skills. This means that there is a lack of validity in the findings of at least some studies.
- Such studies do not include the pressure of the sporting situation or the influence of the audience, which has been shown to have an effect on performance.
- The experimental group in a study are asked to use mental imagery and they are often given more to do than the control group, such as in the study on practising golf shots. In that study the experimental group (who used the imagery) had more practice than the control group, in that they focused on the skill more. This may have given the improved results rather than the use of imagery, or the improvement might be the result of the experimental group receiving more attention.

Using goal-setting to improve performance

Goal-setting helps a sportsperson to focus on what they want to achieve and how to achieve it. This is a mental process, and so to an extent involves imagery. The idea is based on goal-setting theory, which has three main principles (e.g. Locke and Latham, 1990):

- Setting difficult goals leads to higher performance than easy ones. If something is too easy then people tend not to be motivated to do it again, but attempting something challenging promotes a sense of personal achievement, which means there is motivation to repeat the behaviour.

■ Specific goals lead to higher performance than general goals.

■ Feedback on performance is very important, so that the person knows how much they have achieved and how effective their achievements are.

Goals must always be clear and attainable, meaning that there must be a way of measuring what has been achieved. If a goal is too vague or general, or too difficult to achieve, then it should be broken down into manageable smaller goals. The individual has to accept the goal and participate in setting the goal so that he or she is committed to achieving it. Rewarding achievement is important, and extrinsic rewards are often found to be useful in addition to intrinsic ones.

Goal-setting is about increasing motivation and purpose and can lead to greater satisfaction as well as less anxiety. However, inappropriate goals can lead to stress and anxiety. Goals therefore need to be specific, measurable, adjustable, realistic and time limited (SMART). Goals that focus on self-improvement are thought to be more successful than goals such as 'beating an opponent'. Process goals are useful as steps to achieving the main goal and can include, for example, maintaining concentration, getting to the right level of physical fitness and having a game plan. The main goal is known as a performance goal.

Mellalieu et al. (2006): the effects of goal-setting on rugby performance

Mellalieu et al. (2006), researchers in Wales, assessed the performance of five male rugby players at national collegiate level aged between 21 and 24 over a whole competitive season. These players had set their own goals and targets. Findings of previous studies had suggested that specific, difficult and self-generated goals have more beneficial effects on performance than do easy goals. This study aimed to see if goals that were set by the players led to better performance.

There were measures of performance, such as the number of times a player moved forward with the ball in his hand or the number of tackles made. The researchers measured successful kicks and the number of turnovers won and carefully defined how exactly these and other rugby behaviours were measured. All matches were filmed and the frequency of each type of behaviour was calculated. A few matches were chosen at random and analysed separately to check for inter-observer reliability, which was found.

The study covered 20 games over one season. The first ten matches were studied to give a baseline measure and then the intervention was put in place in the break, before the last ten matches. The intervention was in three stages — deciding the goal, setting the goal and reviewing the goal. For deciding the goal each player chose something they would like to improve about their game (such as number of tackles made), and they chose this at the start of the season. Then the frequency of that behaviour was recorded for the first ten matches.

During the break between matches 10 and 11, goal-setting took place; these goals could arise from the first half of the season's performance. Each player chose a goal to achieve in the second half of the season, such as a specific number of tackles attempted. Each goal was reviewed with each participant 48 hours before every match, where the score for the target behaviour up to then was reviewed. Coaches were not aware of which players were taking part in the study. To find the results the change in behaviour of both the targeted and the non-targeted areas was considered from the first half of the season and the second half of the season. Two coaches also commented on the participants' changes in behaviour at the end of the study.

Results showed that, between the end of the first half of the season and the end of the season:

- participant 1 improved in ball carries per game by 77%
- participant 2 made 32% more tackles
- participant 3 decreased the number of tackles missed by 55%
- participant 4 improved successful kicks by 26%
- participant 5 improved turnovers won by 118%

For all participants the desired change in behaviour was found after the goal-setting intervention. There were some changes in non-targeted behaviour but these were usually smaller than the targeted behaviours. This study strongly suggests that goal-setting (under certain conditions) works to improve performance.

Evaluation of Mellalieu et al. (2006)

Strengths

- The study was carried out in the field and tested goal-setting within a real sporting (valid) environment, so to that extent it should provide valid findings.
- The baseline measure was carefully set and goals focused on clearly measurable behaviour, so comparisons before and after the intervention could be clear and tested for reliability.

Weaknesses

- The measures were precise (e.g. number of tackles made), whereas in each game there are other factors such as weather, the strength of the opposition and the number of opportunities to exhibit the behaviour. These need to be taken into account and would affect the targeted behaviour.
- There is the possibility that taking part in the study may have affected the players' behaviour, so there is a question about validity (although non-targeted behaviour did not show the same degree of change, so it is likely that it was the goal-setting that led to the changes in the targeted behaviour).
- Only five participants and one sport were involved — small numbers from which to generalise.

Evaluation of goal-setting to improve performance

Strengths

- Goal-setting uses measurable goals and targets, so studies such as Mellalieu et al. (2006) can give reliable findings.
- The individual is involved in the setting of the goals and reviewing their progress, which helps to improve their motivation and performance. The goals are not imposed on them by the coach.

Weaknesses

■ Much of the research, which tended to be applied to employment in its early days (in the 1970s), has focused on college students, so it might not be appropriate to generalise to the whole population.

■ Research tends to be laboratory based and not in 'real' situations, so there are doubts about the validity of findings, although Mellalieu et al. (2006) provides a field study.

■ Goal-setting is hard to separate from the use of imagery or other techniques, including simply concentrating more on performance without goal setting.

Examination-style questions

1 Outline two explanations for individual differences in sport ing participation. *(4 marks)*

2 Evaluate one explanation for individual differences in sporting performance. *(4 marks)*

3 Describe the achievement motivation theory of motivation. *(4 marks)*

4 Evaluate the inverted U hypothesis. *(4 marks)*

5 Explain, using examples, two psychological techniques for improving performance in sport. *(6 marks)*

Extension questions

1 Describe and evaluate one explanation for individual differences in sporting participation and/or performance, other than the effects of personality traits. *(12 marks)*

2 Describe and evaluate psychological research into the effects of the audience on a sportsperson. *(12 marks)*

Studies in detail

The course asks for two studies to be examined in detail for this section. One must be Boyd and Munroe (2003), which is discussed below. The other study needs to be chosen from Cottrell et al. (1968), Koivula (1995) and Craft et al. (2003). Koivula (1995) is chosen here partly because the study links to the key issue of gender and sport. The other two studies are also useful and are explained in the online resources supporting this textbook. Craft et al. (2003) is briefly summarised in the methodology section, as it is useful for considering the methodology used in sport psychology.

Boyd and Munroe (2003)

Boyd and Munroe (2003) looked at how using imagery, which can help with performance in different sports, links with the type of sport, and also whether experienced sportspeople use imagery more than beginners do.

Background

Many people are interested in risk and adventure, and climbing is one of the most popular risk and adventure sports. This has led researchers to look at the psychological and social aspects of climbing (e.g. Maynard et al., 1997). Research in imagery stems from Paivio (1985), who suggested that imagery serves a cognitive or motivational function. There have been studies more recently than Paivio and Maynard et al. into the use of imagery in climbing (e.g. Jones et al., 2002). Imagery is defined as 'using all the senses to create or recreate an experience in the mind' (Vealey and Walter, 1993, p. 201). Orlick and Partington (1988) found that 99% of Canadian Olympic athletes reported using imagery before the 1984 Olympics, and that it was effective in improving performance.

There are five functions of imagery:

- **Cognitive specific imagery (CS)** can be used to carry out specific skills and is said to improve sports skills; this is especially true if used with physical practice (Hall, 2001). An example is a tennis serve.
- **Cognitive general imagery (CG)** can be used for development of a strategy, such as for gymnasts to increase their memory span of performances or for dancers to remember complex routines.
- **Motivational general-mastery (MG-M)** refers to being mentally tough, confident and in control (Hall et al., 1998). For example, a football player could imagine themselves remaining in control if a referee makes what they think is a poor call. MG-M increases self-confidence and belief in ability. This also links to achieving a **flow state**, because elite athletes who have achieved a flow state report feeling 'out of body' or 'as if they are watching themselves', both of which are about imagery.
- **Motivational general-arousal (MG-A)** is about controlling anxiety and arousal when preparing for an event.
- **Motivational specific (MS)** refers to focusing on a goal such as winning the championship so that athletes, for example, can keep up preparation even without a specific reward.

Table 4.11 *The five functions of imagery*

Imagery function	Explanation	Example
Cognitive specific	Learn specific skill	Tennis serve
Cognitive general	Learn a strategy	Dance routine
Motivational general-mastery	Learn self-confidence, belief in ability	Control when referee makes a poor decision
Motivational general-arousal	Learn to control anxiety and arousal	Not being anxious when performing
Motivational specific	Learn to focus on goals such as a championship	Keep motivated when training, even if no immediate reward is in sight

Munroe et al. (1999) found imagery use to be different for different sports, although gender does not affect imagery use in sport. Individual experiences can affect the

4

use of imagery as well as the sporting situation. It is believed that more experienced athletes have better quality imagery sessions (e.g. Butler, 1996) and use imagery more often (Hall et al., 1998).

Climbers use imagery, but there is no difference between novice and experienced climbers in their imagery use

Climbers are used in this study. It is suggested that they do not feel as lonely away from home as some people do, and also that they might have lower stress levels and be less anxious than the general population. Climbers have been found to be imaginative and creative people (Mitchell, 1982), and they tend to report a sense of flow and positive mood changes when climbing — reducing tension and depression and increasing vigour. According to Mitchell (1982), experienced climbers seemed to be **intrinsically motivated** (motivated by the internal sense of achievement) and less experienced climbers seemed to be **extrinsically motivated** (such as climbing for recognition and as a social activity).

Aims

One aim of the study was to look at how far beginner and advanced climbers use the five functions of imagery. Another aim was to discover if climbers' use of imagery differs from track and field athletes' use of imagery. A further aim was to see how beginner and advanced climbers differ in their use of imagery.

Procedures

Hypotheses

There were two main hypotheses:

Climbers differ from track and field athletes in their five functions of imagery

- Climbers would use CG strategy for route finding (the way up a climbing wall).
- Climbers would use CG more often than track and field athletes.
- Climbers would use MG-A extensively to control feelings of anxiety and fear.
- Climbers would rate low on use of MS (which focuses on extrinsic motivation), compared with track and field athletes.

Beginner and experienced climbers will differ in their use of the five functions of imagery

- Beginners would use more MG-A because they might be more susceptible to fear and anxiety.
- Advanced climbers would use more CG because they are more experienced and climb more difficult routes.

Participants

Thirty-eight randomly selected track and field athletes (13 females and 25 males) were used from one university track and field team. Their mean age was 21.39 years. Forty-eight climbers (28 males and 20 females) were used from a climbing group in Toronto and one in Windsor. They were also randomly selected. The mean age of the climbers was 24.19 years. In the climbing group 18 were beginners and 30 were advanced climbers.

Materials

The sport imagery questionnaire (SIQ) was used, as well as a modified version for the climbers, known as the climbing imagery questionnaire (CIQ). The SIQ is a 30-item questionnaire designed to measure the frequency of imagery use on the five imagery subscales. A 7-point Likert scale was used to find out how often an athlete uses the five functions of imagery (1 = rarely and 7 = very often). The questionnaire is one that has been tested for internal consistency. It was modified for the climbers quite simply, for example by replacing 'competing' by 'climbing' in the questions. Questionnaires were given to track and field athletes, with a 91% return rate, and to climbers, with a 100% return rate.

Completing the questionnaires

The track and field athletes completed the SIQ as a group and the CIQ was completed independently by the climbers. Climbers were also asked about the hardest climb they had completed on top rope or lead. Top rope means the rope is anchored above you and leading means climbing with the rope, clipping as you go. Leading is more difficult. Climbs were rated from 5.0 to 5.15 with 5.0 being the equivalent of climbing a ladder and 5.15 being the hardest kind of rock climb attempted in the world. A rating of 5.9 or below was beginner level and over 5.9 was advanced.

Results

- There were no significant differences between males and females.
- Climbers and track and field athletes differed on the MS (focusing on winning) subscale, with track and field athletes having a higher mean score.
- There were significant differences between climbers and track and field athletes on the MG-M subscale (learning self-confidence), with climbers having a lower mean score.
- There were also significant differences on the MG-A subscale (learning to reduce arousal), with track and field athletes having a higher score.

- Both track and field athletes and climbers used MG-M (linked to self-confidence) most often and MS (linked to goal-focusing) least often.
- There was no significant difference between beginners and advanced level climbers on the five imagery subscales (see Table 4.12).

Table 4.12	The mean score of beginners and advanced climbers on the five subscales	
	Beginner climbers	**Advanced climbers**
CS	4.26	4.71
CG	4.31	4.90
MS	3.22	2.79
MG-M	4.47	4.73
MG-A	4.03	4.40

Conclusions

- There were significant differences between climbers and track and field athletes on three different imagery subscales — MS, MG-A and MG-M — with climbers being lower on all three. The hypothesis suggested that climbers would use CG a lot, MG-A a lot and MS less often, so there is some support for that hypothesis.
- MS was used less possibly because climbers were taking part for internally motivated reasons and so did not need to focus on winning. Images linked to being congratulated on a win are less useful in climbing.
- MG-M was high for track and field athletes, which is not surprising as they need high confidence levels. It is surprising, however, that climbers scored low on this, as they are reported to have a high level of self-confidence. This may be because although all university-level athletes in the study were advanced, some of the climbers were beginners. But MG-M was low for the experienced climbers too.
- MG-A differed but went against the hypothesis, because it was lower in climbers. The SIQ asked about competitions and the CIQ asked about climbing, so perhaps the track and field athletes answered focusing on a recent competition. If climbers have lower trait anxiety, then they may need MG-A less.
- The idea that climbers would use CG more than track and field athletes was not supported, perhaps because climbers were participating indoors when doing the study and climbs indoors tend to have more clearly marked routes. Climbers may use CG more in an outdoor setting. Beginners may not see the importance of route planning and so may use CG less.
- Perhaps beginners and advanced climbers were not so different in MG-A because advanced climbers had harder climbs and therefore a relatively similar use of MG-A due to a similar level of anxiety.

Evaluation of Boyd and Munroe (2003)

Boyd and Munroe made the point that they used a relatively small sample size not only as a whole but because when the 48 climbers were split into beginners and advanced, the sample size became quite small (18 and 30). This may affect the generalisability of the findings.

Strengths

- The questionnaire used (SIQ) is a standard one that had been used before so there was some testing available for its consistency, and findings could be compared with the findings of other studies using the same tool. This should mean that the questions have some reliability.
- The climbers and track and field athletes were given a similar questionnaire and the same procedures with just their sport differing, so the study was well controlled.

Weaknesses

- There was a relatively small sample, especially of beginner climbers against advanced climbers, so generalising might not be appropriate. The sample was taken from climbers climbing indoors, which might mean care should be taken when generalising to outdoor climbing. Features of the sampling mean that it is hard to generalise from the findings.
- The climbers and the track and field athletes used different questionnaires, although they were similar. The climbers were asked about climbing and the track and field athletes were asked about competing. This may have given a different emphasis on certain functions of imagery and may have affected the findings, which means they were not valid.
- If climbing a ladder is rated at 5.0 and extremely difficult climbing at 5.15, the rating of 5.9 for a beginner climb seems quite tough. There might be a problem with categorising climbers as beginners or advanced (such as 5.9 is beginner level but 5.10 is advanced level).
- The track and field athletes completed their questionnaires as a group and the climbers answered their questionnaires independently. Differences in the procedure may make the results invalid.

Table 4.13 *Strengths and weaknesses of the Boyd and Munroe (2003) study*

Strengths	Weaknesses
• Used a standardised questionnaire giving some consistency and reliability • Used the same procedures and questions in the main, so the study had good controls	• Small sample and only climbers climbing indoors were used, so bias in sampling may make generalising hard • The two questionnaires differed, so comparing them may not be valid • Assignment to beginner or advanced for each climber was by self-report, which may not be reliable, and the decision about where to cut the climb rating was sudden • One group did the survey together and the others completed it independently

4

Koivula (1995)

Nathalie Koivula was interested in how people's ideas about gender might affect their views on sport.

Background

Gender differentiation occurs from birth when an infant is immediately labelled as a boy or girl. In Western cultures, differentiation encourages 'passive submissive nurturing girls' and 'active, aggressive, autonomous boys' according to Bem (1974). In a study in 1981, Bem suggests that there are 'male' and 'female' activities in a society. According to Eccles et al. (1990) parents have gender stereotypes about their children's activities and this affects their child's self-perception.

Greendorfer (1977) suggests that the way in which gender-appropriate behaviour is viewed leads to different **socialisation** of boys and girls with regard to sports. For example, it might be thought that athletics is not compatible with a female role. Messner (1990) found that sports and physical activities tend to be seen as 'male'. Sports themselves are stereotyped as being for men, women or being neutral (e.g. Salminem, 1990) and this stereotyping leads to a person's choice of sport, as well as whether it is continued with (e.g. Engel, 1994).

Study hint If you look at issues of sport and gender as your key issue, use some of the following information to inform the debate.

Explore Carry out a survey asking people to rate how society sees particular sports — for example, as male, female or neutral. Then ask about the respondent's general views about sport. Would someone's own views about sport match the views of their society? If someone thinks society sees football as 'male', for instance, would they also see football as 'male'? This is what Koivula's study is about.

Koivula's point is that other research suggests that stereotyping in sport has come about as a result of '**gender-based schematic information processing**'. People are socialised to conform to gender behaviour and gender aspects of society and this is how their **schemata** are built.

AS link Review your learning of information processing, which you covered in the cognitive approach (p. 91). You may also have come across the idea of schemata, which are packets of learned information that guide our thinking and perceptions (p. 116).

Koivula suggests that people are comfortable when schemata and external activities agree, which means that if someone has a gender-based schema about a particular sport, then they are likely to go along with that view in their lives. They would, therefore, feel uncomfortable taking part in a sport that does not fit their schema and comfortable taking part in a sport that does. This participation might also help to reinforce their self-image.

Koivula also thought that some people use gender schemata more than others, possibly because of their upbringing and socialisation, and that some people are more sex-typed than others. **Sex-typed** means making strong use of society's gender ideas when processing information.

Aims

The main aim of the study was to look at gender-based schematic information processing and to see whether people who are strongly gender based in their processing (sex-typed) are more likely to stereotype sports as 'male' or 'female' than less sex-typed individuals. The more specific aim was to look at the effects of gender on the ratings of particular sports, depending on whether a participant rating the sports is male or female.

Procedures

Participants

The study used 104 females and 103 males and their mean age was 25.2 years. Of the total 207 participants, 146 were psychology students at Stockholm University and were taking part because of course requirements. Eighteen were volunteers and 43 took part during their first day of enrolling into the military. 96.6% were Caucasian, 2.9% were Arabic (half of them born in Sweden) and 0.5% were black.

Materials

Two questionnaires were used.

The Bem sex role inventory (BSRI)

This was used to classify the participants as sex-typed or not. The BSRI asks respondents to indicate on a 7-point scale the extent to which 60 personality traits describe them. The scale goes from 'never/almost never true' to 'always/almost always true'. There are 20 filler items so that not all the items are about masculinity or femininity. Twenty items reflect Western ideas of male traits and 20 items reflect ideas of feminine traits. From the BSRI each respondent can be given a masculinity/femininity score and the score can be used to classify respondents as sex-typed, cross sex-typed, androgynous or undifferentiated.

Sex-typed respondents show strong use of the 'right' gender traits to describe themselves. Cross sex-typed respondents show strong use of 'gender' traits to describe themselves, but in the opposite direction from expected (e.g. males rating themselves as having 'female' traits and females as having 'male' traits). Androgynous respondents fall in the middle of the two types, using both male and female traits to describe themselves. Undifferentiated means not being classified as 'normal' stereotyping, 'opposite' stereotyping, or 'no/both' stereotyping.

Seven-point scale questionnaire

A further questionnaire was used to ask about the appropriateness of males or females participating in particular sports. Different sports were rated for gender appropriateness. The ratings used a 7-point scale from 'very appropriate for men and not at all for women' to 'very appropriate for women and not at all for men'. A score of 4 meant 'equally appropriate for both men and women'. The respondents were asked to rate according to what they felt, not according to society's views or what they thought friends and family would think. They were also asked not to rate according to how many males or females participated in the sport.

When the total answers for all the sports were considered, averages were used to categorise the sports as 'male', 'female' or 'neutral' using the 7-point scale. The overall scores' mean was used to rate each sport. Sports that were rated 3.5 to 4.5 were called 'neutral'. A sport with an average score of 1 to 3.5 was rated 'male' and an average score of 4.5 to 7 was rated 'female'. This led to 34 'neutral' sports, 18 'masculine' sports and 7 'feminine' sports. 'Feminine' sports were aerobics, ballet, dance, figure skating, gymnastics, horse riding and synchronised swimming. 'Masculine' sports included baseball, boxing, football, motor sport, rugby, weight-lifting and wrestling.

Completing the questionnaires

Participants were told they were going to complete questionnaires about personality and personal attitudes to some issues and that this was an anonymous survey. They completed the BSRI and then the questionnaire about gender and sports. Finally they completed another questionnaire asking about their age, sex, and ethnicity. All questionnaires were completed individually.

Participants were then allocated by gender and BSRI score to one of the gender identity groups — sex-typed, cross sex-typed, androgynous and undifferentiated. The BSRI gave eight groups — four gender identity groups for males and four for females. Koivula then looked to see how the gender identity fitted with the scores for the sports. For example, a strongly sex-typed male would be expected to score 'male' sports as 'male', 'female' as 'female' and so on, whereas an androgynous male would be less likely to do this. To find this out the individual mean rating for each person on each of the groups of sports (male, female and neutral groups) was calculated and matched against their gender identity category.

Finally a correlational test was carried out to look for possible connections between age and BSRI results and age and sports ratings.

Results

- The BSRI found 'sex-typed' to be the largest group both for males and females (see Table 4.14)
- Most sports were rated as neutral, followed by masculine (there were 34 neutral sports and 18 masculine sports).
- The mean score for neutral sports was 3.83, for masculine sports 2.85 and for feminine sports 4.99.
- Gender appropriateness of sports — for almost all sports — was rated close to 'equally appropriate' for androgynous women, which is what was expected.
- The three sports rating groups were rated significantly differently, which is

evidence that there are 'social' views about sports being linked to certain genders. In general the participants agreed on rating the sports male, female or neutral.

- There was a significant difference in sports rated male compared with female ($p < 0.001$), and also between male or neutral sports and feminine or neutral sports (both at $p < 0.001$).
- The eight BSRI groups also differed significantly on their ratings of the three sports groups.
- Sex-typed men rated masculine sports as more masculine than did androgynous, cross sex-typed and undifferentiated women.
- Age did not correlate with BSRI scores or with sports ratings.

Table 4.14 *The BSRI categorisation of the eight groups taking part in Koivula's 1995 study*

	Women (%)	Men (%)	Total (%)
Sex-typed	43.3	47.6	45.4
Cross sex-typed	23.1	11.7	17.4
Androgynous	13.5	20.4	16.9
Undifferentiated	20.2	20.4	20.3

Conclusions

Sports are affected by gender labelling and people are fairly consistent in deciding which sport is appropriate for males or females (or neutral). In general people are sex-typed, which means that they use gender-based schematic information processing. The category someone is in according to how they rate personality traits (their BSRI score) seems, to an extent at least, to predict how they rate the 'gender' of a particular sport.

The study suggests that men use stereotyping more than women and that androgynous and undifferentiated types do not in general use gender-based schematic information processing. Androgynous and undifferentiated types may know about social norms but want to change them. Perhaps men stereotype sports more because sports are traditionally seen as a male domain, or maybe sex-typed people are more constrained by traditional views and norms. According to Koivula, sports and physical activities may serve to validate male domination in society. Boys model on fathers, who demonstrate gender appropriate characteristics. Gender schemata are learned by children from watching adult behaviour, and therefore masculinity and sport are likely to continue to be linked.

Evaluation of Koivula (1995)

Koivula offers some interesting evaluation points. She believed that being asked about gender triggers gender thinking and gender schemata and this is a confounding variable. She also suggested that participants may have found it hard to separate their own views from those of society when rating sports, so they provided society's views. For example, they might be driven by media coverage of sports, which tends to give less time to sportswomen (Cohen, 1993). Perhaps participants could not imagine females in a particular sport if they had not seen them linked to that sport. Their ratings of sports may not have been entirely their own decision.

Strengths

■ The participants themselves rate the sports as either male, female or neutral, rather than the researchers starting off with the sports already categorised. This gives some validity to the gender categorisation of the sports.

■ The BSRI is used, which has been used in other studies and to that extent has some reliability. There are, for example, 20 filler items to try to avoid demand characteristics in spotting the gender element of the personality traits.

Weaknesses

■ This study was carried out in Sweden, so although it might be expected that Swedish social views represent Western views, it might not be the case with regard to sport. Possibly the findings should only be generalised to people in Sweden, as views about gender are likely to be culture-specific.

■ The study uses self-ratings with regard to personality type, and self-ratings might not be reliable. On another day in a different situation or a different mood someone might rate themselves differently. This means there might be a problem with reliability of the data.

■ The process of asking about gender to study gender might cause the participant to guess the purpose of the study (demand characteristics) or use gender processing in a way they would not normally do. There might therefore be a problem with validity.

■ The study uses mostly students and mainly white participants. The sample is, therefore, possibly biased according to age (young), occupation (students) and race (mainly white). This could affect any generalising from the findings.

Table 4.15 *Strengths and weaknesses of Koivula's study*

Strengths	Weaknesses
• Participants decide if a sport is male, female or neutral, so there is some validity in the categorisation	• There might be a problem in generalising results from Swedish society and culture
• The BSRI has 20 filler items to avoid demand characteristics	• Self-ratings might lack reliability
	• Asking about gender to test gender might mean findings are biased by demand characteristics and not valid
	• The sample is restricted (mainly young white students) so generalising may be difficult

Examination-style questions

1 Describe the Boyd and Munroe (2003) study of the use of imagery in climbing. Include aims, procedures, results and conclusions. *(5 marks)*

2 Outline the procedure of one study from Cottrell et al. (1968), Koivula (1995) and Craft et al. (2003). *(4 marks)*

3 Describe the results and conclusions of one study from Cottrell et al. (1968), Koivula (1995) and Craft et al. (2003). *(6 marks)*

4 Evaluate two studies from Boyd and Munroe (2003), Cottrell et al. (1968), Koivula (1995) and Craft et al. (2003). *(8 marks)*

5 Compare the procedures of Boyd and Munroe (2003) and one other from Cottrell et al. (1968), Koivula (1995) and Craft et al. (2003). *(4 marks)*

Extension question

Describe and evaluate Boyd and Munroe's study (2003), with particular focus on the findings and their limitations. *(12 marks)*

Key issues

For your study of sport psychology you need to prepare one key issue and carry out a practical relating to your chosen key issue. The practical can involve content analysis, so that you are collecting primary data, or it can involve using secondary data, for instance a summary of two magazine articles or other similar sources from which you are asked to draw conclusions. In this chapter a content analysis is suggested. A similar content analysis (focused on daycare) is summarised in the *'Getting Started'* booklet that comes with your course. This can be found on the Edexcel website (**www.edexcel.com**) if you would like further guidance.

Note that you are studying two applications from the four set out in your course. Within those two you must do one content analysis practical and one article analysis practical, so make sure you include one of each in your studies. In this textbook article analysis is chosen for the chapters on criminological psychology and health psychology and content analysis for the chapters on child psychology and sport psychology.

You must study and describe the key issue, find material relating to it, carry out an analysis on that material, and then link your analysis to concepts that relate to the key issue.

Three key issues are suggested for your course, but you can choose any key issue. The suggested issues are 'gender differences in sport', 'what makes a winner', and 'what makes a good coach'. The content section for this chapter has explained and discussed all three of these issues in some detail. Summaries are given below.

Gender differences in sport

Koivula's (1995) study shows that there is a tendency to categorise sports as either feminine, masculine or neutral and that socialisation tends to mean that individuals use gender-based schematic information processing (they look at the world through 'gender' eyes). In general it seems that females do not suffer more stress or arousal than males. Gender was also focused on when considering socialisation and its effect on sporting choice and participation in sport. For example, it was said that in general girls choose 'female' sports to participate in and males choose 'male' sports.

What makes a winner

Someone who does well and wins in their chosen sport is more likely both to use imagery in some way and to improve their motivation by using goal-setting. The need for achievement seems to affect performance, with high need for achievement being linked to winning. Different arousal levels can also affect performance, with the inverted U hypothesis suggesting that too much arousal can stop someone from winning. However, although in some sports low arousal might promote winning, in others (such as wrestling) high arousal can do so. Personality traits might affect whether someone is a winner or not, with introverts doing better at individual sports such as archery and extroverts performing better in team sports. Overall it is possible that extroverts perform better.

What makes a good coach

A good coach uses both imagery and goal-setting in their coaching, as both have been found to improve performance. When looking at motivation, it has been suggested that a good coach should provide encouragement and act as a role model. When considering the role of self-efficacy it has been suggested that a coach can help to raise self-efficacy in a sportsperson. Operant conditioning principles work, so a coach can use rewards and reinforcement, including perhaps negative reinforcement. When setting goals a coach should ensure that the sportsperson is involved in the goals (as the study looking at rugby players discovered), and should encourage them to set achievable goals that are measurable.

Practical: carrying out a content analysis

Content analysis involves a detailed examination of information in the media to produce a summary of certain issues, comments or views. Categories are drawn up and then **tallied** to count how many references to such categories are present. Actual terms (negative or positive) can be counted as well, as they too can provide a picture.

An example content analysis can be found in the online resources supporting this textbook.

AS link

Recall or review tallying, which was explained in the learning approach for your AS studies (p. 315).

- Find material on the subject of gender and sport, winning or losing in sport, or coaching in sport. You can use the internet, newspapers, magazines or any other media source including television programmes.
- Read the material or watch the programmes carefully. Make notes if you need to.
- Consider various themes. Themes about gender participation, sporting performance and success, and achieving high motivation, together with issues around arousal, anxiety and the audience, can come from the concepts you learned about in this chapter.
- Count the number of times each theme is mentioned, using tallying.
- Draw up a table of the results.
- Write up the findings and draw conclusions linking to the concepts you have learned about in this chapter.

Examination-style questions

1 Describe a key issue in sport psychology. *(4 marks)*

2 For the following questions use what you did for your practical in sport psychology, focusing on a key issue:

(a) Outline how you gathered the data for your practical. *(3 marks)*

(b) Explain one problem you had with gathering the data. *(2 marks)*

(c) Describe two ethical issues that you had to take into account. *(4 marks)*

(d) Explain whether your data were valid. *(4 marks)*

(e) Explain whether your data were reliable. *(4 marks)*

Extension question

Discuss one key issue in sport psychology including using the findings from your practical in this application. *(12 marks)*

Unit 4
How Psychology Works

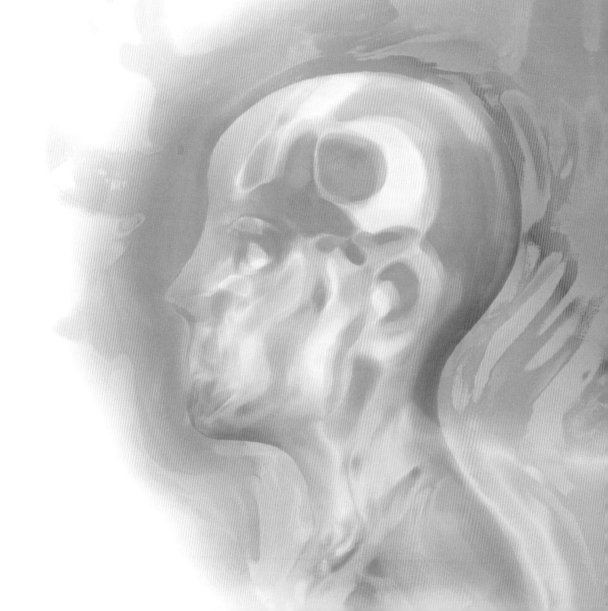

Chapter

5

Clinical psychology

This chapter is about clinical psychology, which is an application in psychology. This means that theories and studies are applied to issues of concern to society and the individual. Clinical psychology includes many areas, focusing on describing, explaining and treating mental disorders. In your course you will just touch on some of these issues. You will look at some general issues around diagnosing mental illnesses and then focus on two disorders. As you are accustomed from your AS studies, in the A2 applications you have to know studies in detail. For clinical psychology you need to know *three* studies as well as one key issue in the area you are studying. You will also carry out a practical based on the key issue.

Summary of learning objectives

Definitions
You have to be able to define the following terms:
- statistical definition of abnormality
- social norms definition of abnormality
- schizophrenia
- reliability
- validity
- primary data
- secondary data

Methodology
- describe and evaluate the use of primary and secondary data in research
- explain how validity and reliability arise in clinical psychology
- describe and evaluate two research methods used in the study of schizophrenia, including one study for each of the two methods

Content

You have to be able to:

- describe and evaluate (in terms of their suitability) the statistical and social norms definitions of abnormality
- use studies to describe: the use of the DSM; issues of validity; issues of reliability; cultural issues in the diagnosis of disorders
- evaluate issues of reliability, validity and culture with regard to the diagnosis of disorders
- choose one disorder (from a list) as well as schizophrenia and describe the features and symptoms of both
- describe and evaluate a biological explanation for schizophrenia and one other explanation (from an AS approach other than the biological approach)
- for your other chosen disorder, describe and evaluate two explanations (from two different AS approaches)
- describe and evaluate two treatments (from two different AS approaches) for schizophrenia and for your other chosen disorder
- describe and evaluate one treatment or therapy from each of the five AS approaches

Studies in detail

You have to be able to describe and evaluate in detail:

- Rosenhan's (1973) study 'On being sane in insane places'
- two other studies, one of which must be about schizophrenia and one about your other chosen disorder

Key issues and practical

You have to carry out one practical that focuses on a key issue that you choose which relates to clinical psychology. For the practical you must prepare a leaflet using secondary data for a specified audience about your key issue. There should be a commentary about the leaflet explaining why decisions were made, who the audience was and what outcomes were intended.

Table 5.1 *Checklist of what you need to know for clinical psychology and your progress*

I need to know about	Done	More work	I need to know about	Done	More work
Defining: the statistical and social norm definitions of abnormality, and schizophrenia			Two research methods used to study schizophrenia and one study as an example for each (two studies)		
Defining: reliability, validity, primary data and secondary data			Describing and evaluating the two definitions of abnormality (statistical and social norm definitions)		
Using primary and secondary data in research			DSM and issues of validity, reliability and cultural issues regarding diagnosis of disorders		
Issues of reliability and validity in clinical psychology			Symptoms of schizophrenia and one other disorder from a list		

I need to know about	Done	More work	I need to know about	Done	More work
A biological explanation for schizophrenia and one other explanation (from an AS approach other than biological)			Rosenhan's (1973) study of 'being sane in insane places'		
For the other disorder I have chosen: two explanations from two different AS approaches			Two other studies, one about schizophrenia and one about my other chosen disorder		
Two treatments each for schizophrenia and another disorder (from two different AS approaches)			One key issue and a practical relating to it		
One treatment each from the five AS approaches					

Definitions

Clinical psychology is about the study of mental health and mental disorders. Your course focuses on certain aspects of clinical psychology and you need to be able to explain two definitions of abnormality. These are the **statistical** and the **social norm** definitions and they are described and evaluated early in the content section, so you will be able to define them once you have covered that section. You will look at the disorder of **schizophrenia** in detail, starting with how it is studied and continuing with its symptoms, explanations and treatments. The concepts of reliability, validity, primary and secondary data are covered in the methodology section, and the issues of reliability and validity with regard to diagnosis of mental disorders are covered in the content section.

An introduction to clinical psychology

Clinical psychology is about diagnosing, explaining and treating mental illness. Your course focuses on schizophrenia and one other disorder, chosen from unipolar depression, bipolar depression, phobias, obsessive–compulsive disorder, anorexia nervosa and bulimia nervosa. In this textbook the second disorder focused upon is unipolar depression; it was said to be so common in the UK in 2008 that it is called the 'common cold' of mental health issues. Anorexia nervosa is covered in the online resources supporting this textbook. Unipolar depression is generally referred to in this chapter simply as 'depression'; bipolar depression is a different disorder, sometimes called manic depression.

Defining mental disorder: what is meant by abnormality?

The content section of this chapter looks at two definitions of abnormality — the statistical definition and the social norm definition. There are other definitions, and the fact that there are many definitions shows that it is not an easy term to define. It depends, for example, on what is normal. It could be said that anything not normal is abnormal. However, it is not easy to define 'normal' — the concept 'normal' depends on culture, as what is normal in one culture might be abnormal in another.

Study hint Use the content, studies in detail and key issue sections of this chapter to extend your idea of what clinical psychology is, so that you can define what is meant by 'clinical psychology'.

Diagnosing and explaining mental disorder

The content section of this chapter looks in more detail at the reliability and validity of diagnosing mental disorder. Mental disorders are hard to diagnose. Often there is no physical evidence and diagnosis relies on a list of symptoms and features that have to be present. For example, to diagnose a phobia there needs to be an intense and irrational fear, not just a fear. A fear becomes a phobia when it stops someone living the life they need or want to live. People suffering from a phobia can usually point to an exact thing they fear — this distinguishes a phobia from generalised anxiety. Someone who does not quite fall within the list of 'requirements' for the disorder is not diagnosed with it, although they continue to live with the symptoms. Features of mental disorders may also be subjective, such as how long a person feels they have been suffering.

Explanations for mental disorders are not fixed or definite and there is often more than one explanation for a particular disorder. It could be argued that if there is more than one explanation, then this indicates more than one disorder. Perhaps there is a label attached to certain symptoms that are then thought of as one disorder, when in fact similar symptoms have different causes and relate to different disorders. For example, schizophrenia can be caused by a single bad experience — it is then called reactive schizophrenia. However, it could be genetic, as suggested by the fact that there can be many cases of schizophrenia in one family. Another explanation for schizophrenia is expressed in the dopamine hypothesis, which suggests that it is caused by the presence of excessive dopamine (a neurotransmitter).

Some people have claimed that dysfunctional families can cause mental disorder. Sociologists suggest, for example, that low socioeconomic status might be a cause for schizophrenia. Others have said that schizophrenia is just a state that some people are in, and not a 'disorder' or 'medical problem' at all (e.g. Szasz, 1960). These are the sorts of issues that surround explanations for mental disorder, and some of them are covered in detail in this chapter.

Treating mental disorder

There are variety of ways of treating mental disorders. Anti-schizophrenic drugs are one way to treat schizophrenia. Other medical treatments include ECT (electro-convulsive therapy). Psychotherapy can be used, perhaps particularly for depression, where cognitive–behavioural therapy (CBT) is currently a popular treatment. Specific treatments are used for specific mental disorders — systematic desensitisation can be used for phobias, for instance. The content section of this chapter covers some treatments and related issues.

Examination-style questions

1 Outline two mental disorders that are considered in clinical psychology. *(4 marks)*

2 Outline two treatments for mental disorders that are considered in clinical psychology. *(4 marks)*

3 Define what is meant by the term 'clinical psychology'. *(4 marks)*

Extension question

Describe and evaluate at least two difficulties within clinical psychology, such as problems in diagnosing specific mental disorders or problems with evaluating treatments for mental health issues. *(12 marks)*

Methodology

For the methodology section for clinical psychology you are required to cover primary and secondary data and how they are used, as well as to evaluate their use. You must also consider issues of validity and reliability.

This section discusses two different research methods used in the study of schizophrenia. This should help your understanding of the nature of clinical psychology, what is covered, and how research is carried out. One study for each of the two research methods is required as an example. As always, evaluation of the research methods is important.

AS link Note that you might be asked to draw on AS material for both the Methodology and Content sections of this chapter.

Primary and secondary data

Data can be qualitative or quantitative, primary or secondary.

Primary data are gathered first hand from source, directly by the researcher(s). For example, Milgram (1963) collected primary data when he studied obedience in a laboratory, and Bandura et al. (1961) collected primary data when they looked at children copying role models. Psychological studies usually gather primary data. Questionnaires, observations, content analyses and experiments are all ways to gather primary data.

Secondary data have already been gathered by someone and are used by someone else for further research. For example, government statistics from a census can inform researchers about the number of females living alone. A **meta-analysis**, in which researchers pool data on a particular topic, uses secondary data because the data studied are not gathered first hand.

Study hint Primary and secondary data are included in the key terms for this chapter, so make sure you can write a definition for each with an example from clinical psychology.

You will have gathered both primary and secondary data when studying two applications of psychology from criminological, child, health and sport psychology. Use what you learned then when explaining what primary and secondary data are and how they can be used.

Craft et al. (2003), which you may have studied in sport psychology, is a meta-analysis, as is Bachrach et al. (1991), a study that you might have covered in your AS course when looking at the psycho-dynamic approach.

Evaluating the use of primary and secondary data in research

Primary and secondary data can be compared in terms of cost (one is relatively more expensive than the other), validity (one is more valid, perhaps) and strength of the conclusions (one is more trust-worthy and credible). Primary data may be more recently gathered than secondary data.

Relative cost

Primary data are expensive to obtain because each researcher or research team has to start from the beginning of a study and follow the whole study through, finding participants, organising materials and running the study. Secondary data are cheaper because they already exist.

A lot of psychological research is carried out using other people's research and government statistics, which provide secondary data from which to draw conclusions

Validity

Primary data are gathered first hand, following careful operationalisation of variables and using carefully chosen procedures. Consideration is given to what is being gathered in terms of data so that they are about 'real life'. Operationalising the IV (the variable being manipulated) is done so that it represents what is to be measured. In general, therefore, primary data should be valid because the study is designed and carried out for the main purpose of the research.

Secondary data, on the other hand, are likely to have been gathered for some other purpose or for an unclear purpose. Often secondary data have already been analysed, which can bring in an element of subjectivity. If secondary data gathered for one purpose are used for another they may not be valid for that second purpose.

Credibility

Primary data might be considered to be more trustworthy, in that they have greater validity than secondary data. If they are collected objectively, with careful planning and sampling, controls in place and other features of methodology adhered to, then they are likely to be scientifically gathered for the stated aim of the study. This means they are more credible. If, however, data gathered for one purpose are used for a different purpose or aim, then this use of secondary data might lack credibility.

Time period

Primary data are likely to be gathered at the time of the study and conclusions will be drawn then. Secondary data, however, might have been gathered some time ago. Conclusions drawn from these data might not be valid, as cultures, for example, change over time, as do people.

Summary of evaluation

Table 5.2 *Strengths and weaknesses of primary and secondary data*

	Primary data	Secondary data
Strengths	• Operationalisation is done with the research aim in mind, so there is likely to be validity with regard to the aim • More credible than secondary data, because they are gathered for the purpose with chosen research method, design etc.	• Relatively cheap compared with primary data, as they are already collected • Can be in good quantity, so there might be detail • Can be from different sources, so there is a possibility of comparing data to check for reliability and validity
Weaknesses	• Expensive compared with secondary data because data gathered from the start • Limited to the time, place and number of participants etc., whereas secondary data can come from different sources to give more range and detail	• Likely to be gathered to suit some other aim, so may not be valid for the purpose of the study • When analysed to be presented as results, there may have been subjectivity • May have been gathered some time before, so not in the relevant time period

Examples of studies

One study that used both primary and secondary data is Gottesman and Shields (1966), who studied schizophrenia and related health issues in twins. This study is explained in more detail below. Hach et al. (2004), whose study compared interview data with medical records to see if diagnosis of mental health disorder was valid, also used primary and secondary data.

Hach et al. (2004)

Hach et al. (2004) looked at the prevalence (frequency) of mental disorders and the prescription of drugs for mental disorders in young women in Germany. A total of 1555 18–25-year-olds were involved in the study. The aim was to consider the patterns of drug use in young women in Germany in relation to how common mental disorders were.

A standardised interview was used to diagnose mental disorders using Axis I of the **Diagnostic and Statistical Manual of Mental Disorders** (DSM-IV). The interview also asked the women what medication they were being prescribed. The researchers gathered information about each woman's diagnosis from her doctor, using medical records, including the medicines prescribed. The interviews provided primary data and the doctors' diagnoses and prescriptions were secondary data from records.

> The **Diagnostic and Statistical Manual of Mental Disorders (DSM)** is a list of mental health disorders, with their symptoms and features intended to aid diagnosis.

For each person, the researchers compared the DSM diagnosis from the interview with the doctor's diagnosis. They also compared the medication the women said they were on with the medication that was being used according to the records. They found that mental disorders were frequent among the young women. There was not much agreement between the diagnosis from the interviews and the doctor's diagnosis. However, there was general agreement between what the women said they had been prescribed and what their medical records said about their prescriptions. The conclusion of the study was that the prescription of drugs by doctors for mental health issues should be checked, as the validity of the mental health diagnoses might be questioned. This study shows that using both primary and secondary data can help to show the usefulness of one or the other. In this case, it might have led to questioning the doctor's diagnosis.

Reliability and validity

Validity is found in studies where what is measured is what is claimed to be measured. For example, if someone is studying anxiety and draws conclusions about it, then finds that the people being studied are suffering from depression, then the conclusions would not be valid. **Reliability** is found when what was done in one study is repeated and the same results are found. For example, if someone links depression with loss in early childhood (such as loss of a parent) and then the study is repeated with different participants (or even with the same participants) and there is no such link found, then the results lack reliability. Such issues are important in clinical psychology, particularly with regard to diagnosing a mental disorder.

If one doctor gives someone a diagnosis of depression and another gives the diagnosis of anxiety — and perhaps a third doctor diagnoses schizophrenia — then that person would not think they had been reliably diagnosed. Reliability of diagnosis is important for the individual, as treatment depends on diagnosis. If someone is not being treated for the right disorder then they are not likely to improve. Such issues are explored in more detail in the content section that follows.

If the three doctors given in the example above are all using the same symptoms and the same manual to diagnose the same person with different mental disorders then the diagnosis is neither reliable nor valid. For a diagnosis to be valid it has to be measuring what it claims to measure. If a patient's set of symptoms can be interpreted to be different disorders, as in the example being used here, then the list of symptoms in the manual being used is not a valid measure. Such issues are explored in more detail in the content section that follows.

Two research methods in schizophrenia studies

Researchers looking into schizophrenia can use many different research methods. Gottesman and Shields (1966) used twin studies, looking at MZ (identical) and DZ (non-identical) twins to investigate the effects of nature and genes on schizophrenia. Goldstein (1988), one of the studies suggested for your course and explained in detail below, drew on secondary data and interviewing to gather data about gender and schizophrenia. Rosenhan (1973), the main study you have to know in detail, used a field study to find out if diagnosis of schizophrenia was valid. There are many other studies and research methods, including case studies and animal studies. However, twin studies and interviewing are the two methods considered here.

Twin studies

Twin studies involve comparing MZ and DZ twins to see what differences there are in the incidence of a certain characteristic. **MZ (monozygotic twins)** are identical in genetic make-up (sharing 100% of their genes), as they come from one egg. **DZ (dizygotic twins)** share 50% of their genes like any other brother/sister pair, as they come from two eggs. The idea in studying twins is that if a characteristic is completely genetically given (**nature**), MZ twins would both show the characteristic. If a characteristic is not genetically given but comes from environmental influences and factors (**nurture**), then MZ twins will not share that characteristic any more than DZ twins. In practice, it is not expected that a characteristic is totally shared between MZ twins, so a higher sharing of that characteristic for MZ twins than for DZ twins is thought to indicate a genetic component for that characteristic.

With regard to schizophrenia, if one twin has schizophrenia and the condition is inherited it would be expected that with MZ twins the other twin is more likely to have schizophrenia too, but with DZ twins this is less likely. Gottesman and Shields (1966) set out to study this.

> **AS link** Review the 'twin studies' research method that you covered for the biological approach (pp. 232–35). You may have looked at the study of Gottesman and Shields (1966) as well, in which case you should review it. Remember to focus as much on evaluation as on description.

Evaluation of the 'twin studies' research method

Table 5.3 Strengths and weaknesses of twin studies

Strengths	Weaknesses
• There is no other way to study genetic influences so clearly, because no other humans share 100% of their DNA • Although the amount they share their DNA differs, both MZ and DZ twins share their environments, so there is a natural control over environmental effects	• MZ twins share their DNA but even in the womb they may experience different environments, which may lead them to develop differently • MZ twins may be treated more alike than DZ twins because they are identical and share their gender too, so their environments may not be as controlled as might be thought

Study using twin studies: Gottesman and Shields (1966)

Aims

Gottesman and Shields (1966) wanted to look at how far schizophrenia was genetic and also to try to replicate other studies that had found a genetic link with schizophrenia.

Procedures

The researchers gathered secondary data from one hospital in the USA, about twins who had been diagnosed with schizophrenia. Starting in 1948, they accessed 16 consecutive years of records to obtain information. Out of 392 patients that seemed to fit their criteria, they found that 68 patients were one of twins and had some sort of diagnosis of schizophrenia or related psychosis. Three patients were discounted because they were from overseas and a further three discounted because it was not easy to tell if they were MZ or DZ twins, leaving 62 patients. Of these, five cases showed that both MZ twins had been diagnosed with schizophrenia, leaving 57 pairs where at least one had been diagnosed as having schizophrenia. Gottesman and Shields then tracked down the other twin in each case.

There were 31 males and 31 females in the group of patients (patients were the 'diagnosed' half of the pairs), born between 1893 and 1945 and with ages from 19 to 64. The average age was 37. They used blood and visual tests to check whether the twins were MZ or DZ. Data were collected in multiple ways: using hospital notes, case histories for the twins, tape recordings of 30-minute samples of verbal behaviour gathered by semi-structured interviews, personality testing, and a test to look at thought disorders.

The question was whether, when one twin had developed schizophrenia, the other was also diagnosed with schizophrenia, and whether they were MZ or DZ twins. In practice, the researchers also recorded disorders close to being schizophrenic but not indicating a full diagnosis.

Gottesman and Shields looked at the **concordance** rate within MZ twins to see in what percentage of cases when one twin was diagnosed with schizophrenia, the other one was too. They did the same with DZ twins, and found a high concordance rate for MZ twins and schizophrenia or a related disorder. They found a much lower concordance rate for DZ twins.

When one twin is found to have the same characteristic as the other twin this is known as **concordance** — agreement.

Results

The results were reported in terms of concordance looking at the following features:

- Pairs where both twins were diagnosed as having schizophrenia.
- Pairs where one diagnosis is a psychiatric one but not schizophrenia, and the other twin has schizophrenia.
- Pairs where there appears to be psychiatric abnormality from some of the researchers' own measures.
- Pairs within normal limits.

Table 5.4 *The number and percentages of twins in certain categories for Gottesman and Shields (1966) study*

Category of twins	MZ		DZ	
	Number	%	Number	%
1 — both diagnosed with schizophrenia	10	42	3	9
1+2 — both diagnosed with schizophrenia or close	13	54	6	18
1+2+3 — both somehow rated abnormal	19	79	15	45
Normal	5	21	18	55
Total	24	100	33	100

(Note: numbers are cumulative in the first three rows.)

Gottesman and Shields' study showed that in MZ twins there was a concordance rate for schizophrenia of between 35% and 58% and in DZ twins a concordance rate of between 9% and 26%. This means that, for MZ twins, around 42% of the time when one twin has schizophrenia the other has it too. For DZ twins the average figure is around 17%. If the most severe cases of schizophrenia were looked at, the concordance rate for MZ twins was between 75% and 91%. The study therefore strongly suggests that there is at least some genetic basis for schizophrenia.

Conclusions

The researchers thought that the diathesis–stress model was the one that best explained the results. The **diathesis–stress model** suggests that behaviour comes in part from genetic predisposition and in part from environmental triggers. Gottesman and Shields thought that particular genes predispose someone to schizophrenia by lowering the threshold for coping with stress. Even if it is suggested that there is a single gene for schizophrenia (Gottesman and Shields believe there is a set of genes responsible), their explanation still stands — that there is a genetic tendency to schizophrenia, which environmental factors can trigger.

Gottesman and Shields concluded that the 11 other studies they looked at did agree with one another, and although there were methodological criticisms such as the sampling, they felt that the results of the studies were compatible and that their study supported previous findings. They therefore felt that their findings — that there is a genetic element in schizophrenia — were reliable.

Overall, they concluded that, in Western societies at least, the identical twin of someone with schizophrenia is at least 42 times as likely to have schizophrenia as someone from the general population, and a fraternal (non-identical) twin of the same sex is at least nine times as likely. Therefore, genetic factors seem to be responsible for the specific nature of most schizophrenias. The genes are necessary for it to occur but environmental triggers may also be necessary.

Evaluation of Gottesman and Shields (1966)

Strengths

- The study replicates other studies and the results are backed up by them, which means they are likely to be reliable. For example, Inouye (1961) in Japan found a 74% concordance rate for people with progressive chronic schizophrenia and 39% where twins had mild transient schizophrenia. These figures are similar to those of Gottesman and Shields.
- It addresses criticisms of previous studies by detailing the sampling carefully so that it was understood which twins were included and why. There is great detail about the different diagnoses — for example, whether the diagnosis was schizophrenia, some other psychosis or some abnormality.

Weaknesses

- The researchers felt that a concordance rate simply notes whether if one twin has some abnormality, the other has it too. It would have been useful to have information about the degree of the abnormality, such as a scale showing 'schizophrenia' through 'other psychiatric diagnoses' to 'some abnormality' to 'normal'.
- The researchers suggest there might be different forms of schizophrenia. They also suggest that some of the disorders diagnosed might come from life experiences (such as being a prisoner of war) rather than genes, and the study did not easily distinguish between reasons for schizophrenia.

Interviewing

Interviewing can take the form of questionnaires, in which case the interviews are **structured** ones. The questionnaire will remain the same for all respondents, so each person is asked the same questions in the same format.

Another form of interviewing is the **semi-structured interview**, where there are set questions (as in a questionnaire) but there is also some freedom for the interviewer to explore issues in order to extend answers. When an interviewer is free to explore areas without any set questions, this is known as an **unstructured interview**. In spite of its unstructured format it will still have a schedule and areas for the interviewer to cover.

The interviewer will find out about the **personal data** required for the study, such as gender, age, marital status, employment status and other details of relevance. The interviewer will use some **standard instructions** at the start of the interview so that the respondent is aware of ethical issues such as **confidentiality** and the **right to withdraw**. The respondent will also be told something about the interview and what the purpose is.

> **AS link** Review what you learnt about interviews (pp. 19–23) and question-naires (pp. 9–12) from the work you covered in the social approach. Include revision of evaluation points as well.

Evaluation of the use of interviews

Strengths

- Unstructured interviews are useful for obtaining qualitative data because there can be exploration of the issues and the respondent is able to use their own words and ideas. The qualitative data offered by interviews give more depth and detail than quantitative data.
- Data tend to be more valid in interviews than questionnaires because the respondent can use their own words and issues can be explored.

Weaknesses

- The interviewer may affect the findings because of the way questions are asked, the way he or she is dressed or other characteristics. This is known as **interviewer bias**.
- There might be **subjectivity** involved in analysing interviews. When categories and themes have to be identified from in-depth and detailed data, probably involving a transcript, the researcher may allow personal judgements and experiences to affect the analysis. **Objectivity** is required to build a body of knowledge, so subjectivity is to be avoided where possible in research.

Study using interviewing: Goldstein (1988)

Goldstein's study (1988), which looks at differences in how males and females experience schizophrenia, used both secondary and primary data from interviews. Secondary data were used when looking at case histories of patients diagnosed with schizophrenia to see if the diagnosis was reliable. Goldstein used trained interviewers to gather data about the symptoms of the patients and she used questionnaires administered by an interviewer to gather information about their past histories, family structure and previous experiences. Her study is explained in detail later in this chapter so is only summarised here.

Aims

Goldstein's aim was to see if females with schizophrenia experience a less severe course of the illness than males. She also wanted to see if a diagnosis using DSM-III was different from a previous diagnosis that used DSM-II. Her aim was to look at other factors affecting the course of schizophrenia, including subtypes of the illness, **premorbid** history (past experiences and environments before the illness) and social functioning.

Procedures

Goldstein and others re-diagnosed 90 patients from a New York psychiatric hospital, to see if the schizophrenia diagnosis (and subtypes) remained the same. In general, she found some differences in diagnosis between the two DSM systems but it was interesting that she found reliability in diagnosis between herself and the others carrying out the diagnoses with her, even though the others were blind to her hypothesis. She used trained interviewers to go through symptoms to check them to aid the diagnosis, as well as the hospital's case histories.

Goldstein also wanted to know about past experiences and other data such as age, class, ethnicity, whether married or not, level of education, level of social functioning and gender, and she used questionnaires to obtain this data. Secondary data and records were used to find out two important features of the course of the illness for each patient: the number of re-hospitalisations and the lengths of each stay in hospital.

Results and analysis

The main part of the study was to look at gender differences. Goldstein looked at gender and the number of re-hospitalisations, gender and lengths of stay in hospital each time, and then at gender against these two features of the course of the illness (re-hospitalisation and lengths of stay) and other factors, such as premorbid factors and social functioning. She carried out complex analyses to separate these different features and to study their effects on one another.

Goldstein found that women with schizophrenia did have a less severe course for the illness than did men. Women had fewer re-hospitalisations and shorter lengths of stay. Premorbid factors affected the re-hospitalisations more than they affected the length of a stay. Social functioning affected lengths of stay more than the number of re-hospitalisations.

Conclusions

Goldstein concluded that her study reinforced the findings of many other studies — that women had a less severe experience of schizophrenia than men. She also concluded that DSM-III was a reliable tool for diagnosis, though between DSM-II and DSM-III there were some differences. She found that premorbid functioning and social functioning were both important features of the illness.

Evaluation of Goldstein (1988)

Strengths

- Goldstein used secondary data which were already available and factual (the number of re-hospitalisations and lengths of stay), so the data were objective and needed no interpretation.

- She asked two experts to check her own diagnoses using DSM-III and was, therefore, able to show that her diagnoses were reliable.
- She used interviewing to gather information about symptoms, so she was able to explore issues. This is necessary when studying patients with a mental health disorder, where issues such as symptoms may not be easy to describe or record.

Weaknesses

- Goldstein did not include patients over 45 and it has been shown that 9% of women who are diagnosed with schizophrenia are over 45, whereas this is not the case for men. Women over 45 have a more severe form of the illness.
- Her sample was relatively small and mainly white middle class American patients in a particular region (New York), all of which may have meant that the findings were hard to generalise.
- The interviewers may have affected the data by the way they asked questions about, for example, symptoms.

Examination-style questions

1 Give one example each of how issues of validity and of reliability arise in clinical psychology. *(4 marks)*

2 Define what is meant by primary and secondary data. *(4 marks)*

3 Compare primary and secondary data in terms of their usefulness. *(4 marks)*

4 Describe one research method used to study schizophrenia. *(6 marks)*

Extension question

With regard to two research methods used to study schizophrenia, describe and evaluate one study using each of the methods. *(12 marks)*

Content

For this section most of the focus is on two mental disorders: schizophrenia and one disorder from a choice of unipolar depression, bipolar depression, phobias, obsessive compulsive disorder, anorexia nervosa and bulimia nervosa. In this chapter, unipolar depression is the second disorder chosen; anorexia nervosa is covered in the online resources that support this textbook.

AS link Note that you might be asked to draw on AS material for both the Methodology and Content sections of this chapter.

You are required to know the symptoms of the two disorders, explanations for them and treatments of them. First, though, you need to consider two definitions of abnormality, a difficult concept. You must also consider the *Diagnostic and Statistical Manual* (DSM) and look at issues of validity, reliability and cultural issues with regard to diagnosis of mental health disorders. Then, depending on what treatments you have already covered, you need to make sure that you know about and can evaluate one treatment or therapy from each of the five AS approaches.

Two definitions of abnormality

It is far from clear what 'abnormality' means. It means different things in different cultures, and the definition may be understood in various ways by different people. On one level it could be defined as 'not normal', but the concept 'normal' is also hard to define. 'Not normal' could mean 'not done by most people' or 'against social norms'.

Two definitions of abnormality include the statistical definition and the 'social norms' definition, both of which are described and evaluated in this section. There are other definitions, but these are not needed for your course.

Explore Look up other definitions of abnormality, such as Jahoda's (1958) ideas of what is needed for mental health (anything else being abnormality), and Rosenhan and Seligman (1989), who give a list of seven features of those people likely to be abnormal compared with normal people.

The statistical definition of abnormality

The statistical definition of abnormality is about statistical infrequency. According to this definition, behaviour that is statistically rare is said to be abnormal. **IQ (intelligence quotient)** is often given as an example of the working of this definition, because IQ is normally distributed across the population and anyone outside the normal limits is said to be abnormal.

Measuring IQ

IQ is a measure that was originally devised for children, and using it as an example helps to explain the statistical infrequency definition of abnormality. When IQ tests were first set up they asked general questions that it was thought a certain age group of children should be able to answer, at that time. These might be questions on maths, language, general knowledge or problem solving. For example, a large number of 8-year-olds might sit a test and their average score on the test would then become the norm for that age group. Then any 8-year-old could be tested using that test and it would be known what score would be expected for a 'normal' child of that age. Other age groups were also tested to get scores across different age ranges. Whatever the group of children achieved on average was given a score of 100 and that was considered normal IQ for that age group. If someone scored well over 100 on a test, they were seen as bright, whereas someone achieving quite a bit less than 100 was seen as needing help — in educational terms they had special needs.

Normal distribution

To understand the idea that abnormality is anything that is statistically infrequent it helps to know about **normal distribution**. A characteristic of behaviour is seen as 'normally distributed' if the mean average, the median and the mode all fall at the same place — in the middle of the scores. This simply means that there are roughly the same number of scores each side of the average — the scores are normally distributed around the average. Some made-up scores are given here to illustrate what it means to say data are normally distributed (Table 5.5). Shoe size will not give a mean average because it is not a mathematical score but more of a rating, so only the median and mode are calculated to see if they are similar for this example.

Table 5.5	The frequency of the shoe size of a sample of 100 women in the UK

Shoe size for women	Frequency
1	0
2	0
3	0
4	10
5	22
6	35
7	25
8	8
9	0
Median	**6**
Mode	**6**

Figure 5.1	The frequency graph of the data from Table 5.5 shows that there is a pattern to the data that fits a normal curve

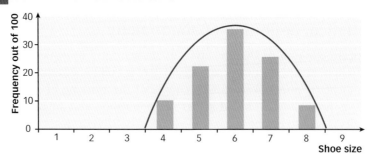

Knowing that data are normally distributed, as shoe size is, means that anyone a long way 'outside' the average could be regarded as abnormal. So, according to these data, anyone with a shoe size of 3 or 9 would be abnormal. This is what is meant by the statistically infrequent definition of abnormality. Obviously anyone with large or small feet is not 'abnormal' in the sense of being mentally ill, and this is a criticism of the definition, as explained later in this section.

Standard deviation

IQ is bound to be normally distributed because it is measured as being 100 if normal. The more over or under 100 someone is, the more they are abnormal, according to the 'statistically infrequent' definition. It is important to decide how far above or below someone has to be in order to be labelled 'abnormal'. This is done by using the **standard deviation** of the scores.

Standard deviation is calculated by working out how far each score is away from the average. It expresses the spread of scores around the mean. A high standard deviation means a large spread and a low standard deviation means a low spread of scores.

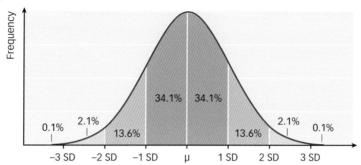

Figure 5.2 A set of normally distributed scores will have a set percentage at each standard deviation (SD) from the mean

zA normally distributed set of scores will have a set percentage of scores within each standard deviation from the mean. Looking at Figure 5.2, 34.1% of the scores lie within one standard deviation each side, which makes 68.2% of all the scores within the normal range. Then 13.6% of scores lie on either side within the next standard deviation, meaning that 47.7% lie within two standard deviations either side of the mean. This means 95.4% of scores lie within two standard deviations of the mean on either side, and this too is within normal limits. However, this is where 'normal limits' stop. On either side 2.2% are outside normal limits (the percentages don't quite add up because of rounding up).

> **Explore** It is useful to be able to visualise the curve and the percentages of Figure 5.2 — even if only rough percentages — so that you can explain the statistical infrequency definition clearly.

Standard deviation of IQ

IQ has a standard deviation of 15 and the mean is 100. Therefore, one standard deviation either side would be from 85 to 115. Two standard deviations either side is from 70 to 130. This is where 'normal' ends. So 130 and above is an abnormally high IQ score (only 2.2% are above 130). A score of 70 and below is an abnormally low IQ score (just 2.2% of the population have an IQ score of 70 and below). In practice, as the scores for IQ were set a long time ago it is said that the 'norm' has moved up about 10 points so the figures given here might be argued with. However, for the purposes of explaining the statistical infrequency definition of abnormality these figures are good enough.

The statistical infrequency definition summarised

An IQ of 70 and below, or 130 and above, is considered abnormal. Any measurable characteristic can be judged in this way. As long as the mean and the scores are known, the standard deviation can be calculated. Any score two standard deviations or more away from the mean denotes abnormality. This is applied not only to IQ but to other mental health criteria. The DASS (depression, anxiety and stress scale) uses a questionnaire to measure depression, anxiety and stress. A very high score would be considered abnormal and in need of treatment. DASS scores would be expected to fall around the middle, though in practice more people would have a low score than a high one and be functioning 'normally'.

Evaluation of the statistical definition of abnormality

Strengths

- It gives a quantitative measure that is objective. The advantage of an objective measurement is that it is more likely to be reliable and therefore suitable: someone else administering the same test is likely to get the same result and draw the same conclusion about abnormality.
- Some areas of functioning, such as IQ, highlight abnormality as lack of 'normal' functioning in some way. On a practical level this can be useful as evidence in support of requests for assistance and funding for those individuals identified. Having a 'number' is not only useful because it is seen as objective but also because it is accepted as more scientific.

Weaknesses

- 'Abnormal' in both a statistical and a mental health sense may not be 'undesirable'. An IQ score of 130+ is likely to be seen as desirable. What is statistically infrequent, like genius, is not necessarily considered 'bad'. 'Undesirability' is not a valid measure of what is thought of in society as abnormality.
- There are statistically frequent behaviours that are still considered abnormal. Depression is said to be frequent in current UK society. However, it is considered a mental health disorder and abnormal. Again, this shows the limitations of the definition.
- Abnormal behaviour is not rare. Most people are likely to show abnormal (atypical) behaviour at some time in their lives.

The social norms definition of abnormality

This definition states that behaviour which conforms to social norms is 'normal' and behaviour that does not is 'abnormal'. **Norms** are social rules that are not laws but customs, and people in a society abide by such rules in their behaviour. If someone's behaviour goes against a particular society's norms it is understandable that their behaviour would be called 'abnormal', which is what the **social norms definition of abnormality** says. There are aspects of society, though, to be taken into account when making a judgement about someone being 'abnormal'. These aspects include culture, the situation, age, gender and historical context.

The effect of culture

In one society there are likely to be different cultures and subcultures; any behaviour regarded as abnormal would tend to be seen as so in all cultures in that society. For example, hearing voices in one culture might be normal and interpreted as being connected to spirits, whereas in another culture it might be seen as abnormal. It is therefore difficult to define norms that have to be adhered to in a society to make behaviour 'normal'.

The effect of context/situation

The situation and context for the behaviour are both important. A behaviour might be normal in one context but abnormal in another. For example, if someone chose to go out in the street wearing a chicken suit, it might be considered normal if it is for a charity event, when going to a fancy dress party or for advertising a product. However, if that person chose to wear the chicken suit all the time, including going shopping or to church, then they might be classified as 'abnormal'.

The effect of age and gender

Age is another factor in making a judgement about abnormality. For example, a 3-year-old might take his clothes off in public and it would be considered within social norms; this would not be the case for a 40-year-old (given no special context). Equally, what is seen as normal behaviour for a male might be seen as abnormal for a female and vice versa. For example, given no special context, society would not expect a man to wear a dress and high heels, though such behaviour might now be more acceptable than it used to be.

Someone wearing a chicken suit would not be defined as abnormal except in certain circumstances — the situation affects whether or not a behaviour conforms with social norms

Jupiter Images/Creatas/Alamy

The effect of historical context

What was considered the norm many years ago might have changed more recently. For example, becoming pregnant outside marriage was considered evidence of a mental health problem 100 years ago. Women could be put into an institution for becoming pregnant. This is not the case in the twenty-first century.

Explore Look up mental disorders in the early 1900s and find a list of what society then considered reasons to label someone as mentally ill.

Evaluation of the social norms definition of abnormality

Strengths

■ The idea of abnormality as behaviour that goes against social norms matches what is expected in daily life when talking about abnormality. For example, it takes into account that someone who is highly intelligent is not considered abnormal in the sense of being mentally ill.

- This definition explains why different cultures have alternative ideas of what is abnormal/normal behaviour and takes into account that there is no universal rule about what is 'abnormal'.

Weaknesses

- If culture, age, situation, historical context and gender have to be considered then it is hard to have a reliable idea of what is abnormal. Therefore, diagnosis is difficult, as there are no set symptoms to rely on, which would make this definition unsuitable to help with diagnosis.
- Any definition of abnormality would lack validity except in one particular culture, at one time, with one gender and age group, and in a particular situation. Therefore, not only is it hard to diagnose abnormality reliably but the validity of any diagnosis is also in doubt. It is difficult to measure abnormality objectively and scientifically according to this definition, as there are so many issues to take into account, and a definition that does not allow objectivity might be seen as unsuitable.

The DSM

This section looks at the *Diagnostic and Statistical Manual of Mental Disorders* (DSM). The DSM is published by the American Psychiatric Association (APA) and provides criteria from which a mental disorder can be diagnosed. It is used around the world. It was first published in 1952 and since then there have been five revisions, from DSM-I to the current DSM-IV-TR (DSM four text revision). DSM-IV was published in 1994 and the text revision was published in 2000. DSM-V is due out in May 2012, with a draft version appearing in 2009.

The DSM system was developed in response to the need for a census of mental health disorders; the US army had developed a system to diagnose mental disorders using mainly descriptions and classifications, such as **neuroses** and **psychoses**. From such classifications and descriptions, lists of symptoms gradually developed and were refined, and the DSM evolved.

> **Neuroses** are mental health issues that fall just outside normal functioning, but the individual is still in touch with reality and knows they are ill. **Psychoses** are mental health issues where the individual has lost touch with reality and is not on a continuum with normal mental health.

The DSM is the most studied and utilised of the available diagnostic tools. Another popular diagnostic system is the **International Statistical Classification of Diseases and Related Health Problems (ICD)**, which is used more often than the DSM in some parts of the world. The same diagnostic codes are used and the two systems are developing together. The strengths and weaknesses of the DSM generally apply to other diagnostic systems.

> **Explore** Check to see if any version of DSM-V has been released as you study your course.

A multi-axial system

The DSM has five axes: each diagnosis of a disorder is split into five levels called axes that relate to different aspects of a disorder. A patient is put into a category using symptoms; the nearest prototype for a mental disorder suggested by these symptoms provides the diagnosis.

- Axis I considers clinical disorders, major mental disorders, developmental disorders and learning disorders. Some common disorders include schizophrenia, depression and phobias. Axis I also looks at other conditions that may be focused upon and these tend to be problems that need immediate attention from a clinician.
- Axis II looks at underlying personality conditions, including mental retardation. The axis has a rating scale to measure mental retardation. Some common personality conditions include paranoid personality disorder and antisocial personality disorder as well as obsessive–compulsive personality disorder. Problems in this area may not need immediate attention but should be taken into account as they can affect treatment.
- Axis III is about medical and physical conditions. Some common physical conditions include brain injuries and existing diseases. Axis III is about general medical conditions and these are important because even if the problem seems to be a mental one, such psychological disorders can come from illnesses such as diabetes or a heart problem.
- Axis IV focuses on psychosocial and environmental factors that affect the disorder. Factors include poverty and dysfunctional families. Any other factors in the person's environment that might affect their functioning are considered.
- Axis V is an assessment of global functioning. The question asked is how is the patient functioning? There is an overall rating of someone's ability to cope with normal life. The rating scale goes from low scores, which are about persistent danger of the client severely hurting themselves, to 100, which refers to a superior level of functioning with reference to a range of abilities.

This section looks at the reliability, validity and cultural issues of the DSM. It also focuses on important studies that investigate and produce evidence of such issues. Whether a diagnosis stands the test of time (reliability) and is correct so that treatment works (validity) is extremely important, as is whether someone is unfairly treated as a result of a doctor's misdiagnosis, arising from a failure to take their culture and beliefs into account.

Study hint When answering questions about the reliability and validity of diagnosis, including using the DSM, remember to include research evidence. You do not have to explain whole studies; use findings, together with the names of the people who did the study. In an examination question about applications in psychology, you could be asked to 'use psychological research'. This means that you must make use of the findings of studies. You could also use theories, as they will have been tested using studies. Always try to include some named evidence.

Changes in the DSM

There have been a number of revisions to the DSM, partly in response to criticisms such as that arising from Rosenhan's study (1973) of what it was like to be sane in insane places. This study is explained in detail in a later section of this chapter. Rosenhan found that eight 'normal' people (in the sense of having no psychiatric symptoms or behaviour) were accepted as mentally ill by mental health institutions, highlighting the lack of validity in diagnosis of mental illness at the time. As a result, the DSM was revised to take such criticisms into account.

Following the course of attitudes to homosexuality can reveal how the DSM has changed and how it responds to new research and changing cultural attitudes. During revision, the DSM is studied by many groups of people, who consult research as well as other data about diagnoses. Sometimes there is lobbying to get aspects changed. For example, in 1974 DSM-II no longer listed homosexuality as a category of disorder, both in response to research such as Kinsey's and to protests from gay activists. The category 'homosexuality' was replaced with 'sexual orientation disturbance'. In 1980 DSM-III replaced the category 'sexual orientation disturbance' with 'ego-dystonic homosexuality', but that was removed in 1987. DSM-IV-TR has the category 'sexual disorder not otherwise specified', which is characterised as 'persistent and marked distress about one's sexual orientation'.

Evaluation of the DSM

Strengths

- The DSM allows a common diagnosis. Through its many revisions, the DSM has stood the test of time. Even with the problems outlined above, it is perhaps the best attempt at diagnosis in existence, given the limited understanding of mental disorders. When more than two doctors use the DSM, they should come close to the same diagnosis.
- One study that tested the reliability of diagnosis between DSM-II and DSM-III is Goldstein (1988), which is explained in detail in a later section in this chapter. She found there was evidence of reliability within the DSM-III (but less so between DSM-II and DSM-III).

Weaknesses

- The DSM is seen as a confirmation of the medical state of mental disorder, as sufferers are 'patients' and 'treatment' is suggested. Mental health issues are 'disorders' and 'illnesses' and so 'cures' are looked for. However, it might be said that some mental disorders are simply ways of living, and who is to say whether they are 'illnesses' or not. Laing suggested that schizophrenia is another way of living where a person is trying to get back to their true self, and it is not therefore a medical illness.

Explore Look at Laing's ideas; you may find it useful to read his book *The Divided Self* (1960). He did not deny that people needed treatment as such, just that the medical model failed to recognise other ideas about functioning in society.

Reliability, diagnosis and the DSM

The DSM's reliability rests on the question of whether one person's set of symptoms would lead to a common diagnosis by different physicians. If different doctors give different diagnoses for the same set of symptoms (e.g. for the same person), then the diagnoses are not reliable and treatment may not work.

Studies looking at the reliability of the DSM

Goldstein (1988)

Goldstein tested DSM-III for reliability and found that there was reliability. Her study is explained in detail in this chapter. She looked at the effect of gender on the experience of schizophrenia, and she also re-diagnosed 199 patients using DSM-III when they had originally been diagnosed using DSM-II. There were some differences but, as DSM-III was a revised version of DSM-II, this was to be expected. What was of interest, however, is that Goldstein also asked other experts to carry out the re-diagnosis separately, using a **single blind technique**.

A **single blind technique** does not allow the hypothesis of a piece of research to be known, so that it cannot be a cause of bias in judgement.

Goldstein realised that she herself was aware of the hypothesis and so she asked two experts to re-diagnose a random sample of eight patients. The experts were given copies of case histories with any reference to the original diagnosis removed. She found a high level of agreement and **inter-rater reliability**. This suggests that DSM-III is a reliable tool. As later versions of the DSM have focused on improving validity and reliability, it is likely that DSM-IV-TR is also reliable.

Brown et al. (2001)

Brown et al. set out to test the reliability of the DSM-IV. They studied anxiety and mood disorders in 362 outpatients in Boston, USA. The patients underwent two independent interviews using the anxiety disorders interview schedule for DSM-IV, known as the lifetime version (ADIS-IV-L). For most of the DSM-IV categories there was good to excellent reliability, with inter-rater reliability. If there was disagreement it tended to focus not on what the symptoms were but whether there were enough of them, whether they were severe enough or whether they had lasted long enough.

The study also showed boundary problems for some disorders such as generalised anxiety disorder and major depressive disorder. Sometimes it was hard to diagnose disorders at the boundaries. The study highlighted some problems with the DSM, but overall it emerged as reliable.

Stinchfield (2003)

This study tested both reliability and validity. It looked at the diagnosis of **pathological** gambling (a gambling habit that is severe enough to cause someone to have problems in living and functioning).

Pathological behaviour means behaviour diagnosed as abnormal due to its extreme or excessive nature.

The study looked at 803 men and women from the general population of Minnesota and 259 men and women who were on a gambling treatment programme. A questionnaire using 19 items was used to measure the DSM-IV diagnostic criteria for pathological gambling. There were other validity measures as well. It was found that the DSM-IV diagnostic criteria were reliable and valid. The DSM criteria were used to sort out those who were linked with pathological gambling and those who were not.

Kirk and Kutchins (1992)

The above three studies have shown that in general, from DSM-III to DSM-IV, reliability is thought to have improved to the point where it is no longer an issue. Kirk and Kutchins, in their review paper (1992), argued that there are methodological problems with the studies used to test the reliability of the DSM up until 1992, and that these limit the generalisability of the findings. The studies outlined above used interviews and questionnaires to gather data; Kirk and Kutchins argued that training and supervision of interviewers was insufficient and that they lacked the commitment and skills to be accurate. They also pointed out that the studies they looked at tended to take place in specialised research settings, which means their findings might not relate to clinicians in normal clinical settings. As an unreliable diagnostic tool also lacks validity, Kirk and Kutchins suggested that the DSM could lack validity.

Assessment of Kirk and Kutchins' points

- Some of the points about interviewing — such as that different interviewers may affect the situation and lead to different data — might be important when considering generalising findings from studies. Goldstein (1988) did not, however, use interviewing to test reliability — she used re-diagnosis using secondary data, and also found reliability.
- The patients in the studies described above were not all from research settings. The 'gamblers' in Stinchfield's study were on a gambling treatment programme, not in a research institution. The patients in the study by Brown et al. were out-patients at a hospital.
- Kirk and Kutchins' study took place before Brown et al. and Stinchfield's studies showed that DSM-IV-TR could be regarded as reliable. It might be concluded that further work has been done since DSM-II and reliability has improved.
- Goldstein (1988), Brown et al. (2003) and Stinchfield (2003) all provide evidence that diagnosis is reliable.

Validity, diagnosis and the DSM

If the DSM were not reliable it would not be valid either. If a diagnosis was done again and the DSM provided a different one, then it would not be a valid diagnosis (it would not be measuring what it claimed to measure). Reliability and validity go together.

> **Study hint** It is wise to keep validity and reliability separate in answers, though you could make the point that if diagnosis is unreliable then it cannot be valid.

Operationalising mental disorders

If the DSM is to define mental disorders, then mental disorders need to be operationalised. Lists of symptoms and behaviour are the result of making a mental disorder measurable. It has been argued, however, that in operationalising a concept such as depression, something is lost from the understanding of the nature of the whole experience of depression, which means that the DSM is not a valid tool. There is a lack of **construct validity**, in that the constructs drawn up, for example to represent depression, might not be representative enough.

Another problem with validity is that although revised versions of the DSM have taken into account personal and social factors (Axis IV) as well as how the person is functioning (Axis V), this is taking such factors into account in relation to a mental disorder. Such factors might in fact be separate from the mental disorder. For example, if someone with depression is not functioning well in society, it might not be because of depression but for some other reason (such as unemployment, solitude or financial problems). So a diagnosis of depression would not be valid in that case.

Some people argue that a number of categories, such as those related to sexual issues like female hypoactive sexual desire disorder (having a low sexual drive), should not be in a list of mental disorders. Both epilepsy and circadian rhythm sleep disorder used to be listed as a mental disorder but now are not. These changes to what is considered a mental disorder suggest low validity.

Concurrent, predictive and convergent validity

Concurrent validity

Concurrent validity is when the result of a study or test matches a result from another study or set of data done at the same time. So if a diagnosis using the DSM comes up with the same mental disorder that another diagnosis has given at the same time, then the new diagnosis is likely to have concurrent validity. For results to have concurrent validity the second diagnosis has to match a first diagnosis or result that has been shown to be valid. There can be a different way of measuring in each case. If a test is simply done again and obtains the same result, this is reliability.

Predictive validity

Predictive validity is the same as concurrent validity, except that the result being compared was obtained at another time. So instead of two results being compared with one another at one time to see if one valid one backs up another result, two results are compared in different time periods. To find predictive validity, a test would be carried out and a result collected. Then another or different measure would be done some time later that would test the same feature. If the test matched the other measure then this shows validity. For example, DSM could be used to diagnose a mental disorder. Then another later measure for that mental disorder — perhaps a doctor's view, family comments, the person's own self-rating or observations by mental health personnel — could be taken to see if the diagnosis and the other measure agreed. If they do agree, then the diagnosis (and, therefore, the DSM) would be said to have predictive validity.

Convergent validity

Convergent validity is when a test result converges on (gets close to) another test result that measures the same thing. A correlational test would be carried out. If two scales measure the same construct, for example, then a person's score on one should converge with (correlate with) their score on the other. The difference between convergent validity and predictive/concurrent validity is that in convergent validity the two measures should be measuring exactly the same thing, whereas in the other two types of validity there can be a different way of measuring in each case.

Studies looking at the validity of the DSM

Kim-Cohen et al. (2005)

Kim-Cohen et al. studied the validity of DSM-IV with regard to conduct disorder in 5-year-olds. This was a longitudinal study. The study was to test the concurrent, convergent and predictive validity of DSM-IV with regard to conduct disorder. A longitudinal study that was already underway was following 2,232 children and these children were also used as the focus of this study. Researchers interviewed the mothers of the children and asked teachers to complete postal questionnaires — in both cases asking about conduct disorder symptoms over the last 6 months.

Children with three or more symptoms were diagnosed as having a conduct disorder, and if a child had five or more symptoms, they were diagnosed as having moderate to severe conduct disorder. The study found that 6.6% of children were diagnosed with conduct disorder and 2.5% with moderate to severe conduct disorder. The study also found that the children who were diagnosed with conduct disorders were significantly more likely than comparison children to say that they had antisocial behaviours (self-report). They were also more likely to behave disruptively during observational assessment and to have risk factors relating to conduct disorder. Five-year-olds diagnosed with conduct disorders were significantly more likely than comparison participants to have behavioural and educational difficulties at the age of 7.

The different measures in this study — mother's responses to an interview, teachers' responses to a questionnaire, comparisons with other children with regard to antisocial behaviours using self-report data, observational data, and data about behavioural and educational difficulties at the age of 7 — all led to a diagnosis of conduct disorder, so it was concluded that the diagnosis was valid. This is an example of using different data sources to check for validity.

Hoffmann (2002)

Hoffmann looked at the different diagnoses of alcohol abuse, alcohol dependence and cocaine dependence to see if such differences showed up using a structured interview that was computer-prompted, and to see if they corresponded to the DSM-IV-TR criteria. The study looked at prison inmates. It was found that the DSM diagnosis was valid and the interview data supported the idea that dependence was a more severe syndrome than abuse (both alcohol and cocaine abuse). The symptoms from the automated interview matched the DSM diagnosis.

Lee (2006)

The purpose of this study was to see if the DSM-IV-TR diagnosis of ADHD would be suitable for Korean children. The study also focused on gender differences in the features of ADHD recognised in the DSM. These features include inattention and hyperactivity/compulsivity. The DSM-IV-TR contains 18 ADHD criteria with regard to children's behaviour.

Lee's study used a questionnaire with 48 primary school teachers and asked them to rate the behaviour of the children. In total 1,663 children were rated — 904 boys and 759 girls. The idea was to compare the DSM-IV-TR criteria for diagnosing ADHD with criteria arising from the questionnaire data. If the two agree, then the DSM-IV-TR is said to be valid (concurrent validity). Another measure used the ADHDT (attention deficit, hyperactivity disorder test) to find out what behavioural and psychological characteristics are related to ADHD and to see if those characteristics match those used in the DSM-IV-TR diagnosis.

Previous studies showed that children with ADHD often had oppositional defiant disorder (ODD) as well, and had problems with peers and with discipline. If this study found those features as well, this is evidence for the validity of DSM-IV-TR (construct validity). The findings of Lee's study meant that correlations could check for reliability, as different measures were used. Teachers' opinions were associated with the ADHD diagnosis using the DSM-IV-TR, so it was concluded that the DSM has validity. The other measures also gave findings that fitted the DSM criteria (such as inattention, hyperactivity and impulsivity). The study's findings suggest that for girls the fit with DSM criteria was not as complete as for boys.

Evaluation of validity, diagnosis and the DSM

Strengths — validity of diagnosis

- The above studies show that the DSM — in particular the later versions — is valid in its diagnoses. Different mental health issues were chosen in the different studies cited here, which reinforces this conclusion. It is likely that symptoms for disorders such as alcohol abuse, dependence, cocaine abuse, pathological gambling and ADHD are well established, given that the DSM has had many revisions to date. Different research methods such as interviews and questionnaires yield data that, for those with mental health disorders, match the DSM criteria.
- The claim that the DSM is valid is supported by the claim that it is reliable, as reliability and validity go together. If the DSM is not reliable it will not be valid.
- Great efforts have been made to make the DSM-IV-TR more valid, such as adding culture-bound syndromes, which are looked at later in this section.

Weaknesses — validity of diagnosis

- It has been said that **co-morbidity** — the state of having more than one mental disorder — is hard to diagnose using the DSM, a system which relies on the user choosing the one closest match from lists of symptoms and features.

■ It could be claimed that splitting a mental disorder into symptoms and features is **reductionist** and that a holistic approach might be more valid. For example, in a counselling situation, symptoms are treated as aspects of the whole person and mental health is the focus, not mental disorder. In counselling a diagnosis is not as important as treating the individual.

■ It is possible that questionnaires and interviews produce the findings they are searching for. For instance, if it is well known that 'children with ADHD are impulsive and hyperactive', and teachers know which children have that label, they will then say that those children are impulsive and hyperactive. The diagnosis is self-fulfilling.

Cultural issues, diagnosis and the DSM

With regard to its list of symptoms and features, the studies outlined above have suggested that the DSM-IV-TR is both reliable and valid. However, one area where there has been a great deal of criticism of previous versions of the DSM is of its usefulness across different cultures.

Culture does not affect diagnosis — mental disorders are 'scientific'

The DSM was developed in the USA and is used widely in many other cultures. This is a valid use if mental disorders are clearly defined with specific features and symptoms; for instance, schizophrenia or depression present as the same illness all over the world, with particular symptoms and features. In other words, mental disorders are scientifically defined illnesses that are explained in a scientific way. It is interesting that one study cited above (Lee, 2006) was conducted in Korea deliberately to see if the DSM-IV-TR was valid in a non-Western culture, and it was found that it was (for ADHD).

Culture does affect diagnosis — a spiritual model

There are studies that have shown that culture can affect diagnosis. For example, symptoms that are seen in Western countries as characterising schizophrenia (such as hearing voices) are interpreted in other countries as showing possession by spirits, which renders someone special in a positive way, not a negative ('disorder') way. Depending on cultural interpretations of what is being measured, the DSM is not always valid. A clinician from one culture must be aware that a patient from anther culture is guided by their own frame of reference.

Cultural differences in symptoms of schizophrenia
More catatonia in other cultures — or different treatment regimes?

It does seem to be the case that there are actual cultural differences in mental disorders like schizophrenia. It has been reported that catatonic schizophrenia is on the decline and this could be because of health measures that prevent the development of this type of schizophrenia. Chandrasena (1986) reported more incidences of catatonia in Sri Lanka (21%, compared with 5% among British white people). However, it was found that in Sri Lanka it was less likely that patients had received early interventions with drug treatment; this was not therefore a cultural difference in the attitude to the mental disorder, but a difference in treatment availability.

More auditory hallucinations in Mexican-born people than white Americans

Auditory hallucinations were reported to doctors by patients more in Mexican-born Americans than in non-Mexican-born Americans. The study by Burnham et al. (1987) looked at this using self-reports and interviewing, and checked the evidence and found that there was a difference. No other explanation could be found, except that culture had led to the difference.

More grandiosity in white Americans

White Americans were reported (using patients' records) as showing more 'grandiosity' as a symptom compared with Americans of Mexican origin, again showing cultural differences. It is important to look at individual symptoms if looking for cultural differences in symptoms of mental disorders. The DSM looks at a set of symptoms; without specific studies such cultural differences would not be found.

Schizophrenia in all countries has more similarities than differences

Lin (1996) summarised schizophrenia in other cultures and noted that it is found in all cultures that have been studied, and the prevalence seems similar across all cultures. With regard to symptoms, similarities outweigh the differences. Good outcomes appear more likely in developed countries.

> **Study hint** Note that there is evidence of subcultural differences in the research discussed in this chapter. Goldstein (1988) suggested that females have a less severe course through schizophrenia than males. Use such evidence as evaluation of the claim that schizophrenia across cultures has mainly similarities but some differences.

Evaluation

Simply because the symptoms seem the same and symptoms under the heading 'schizophrenia' occur in all cultures as far as it is known, does not mean that 'schizophrenia' in all cultures is in fact the same thing, with the same cause and the same course through the illness, which is what the DSM tends to assume.

Ideas for overcoming cultural bias in diagnosis

Take emphasis off features that might be affected by culture

It is important for the DSM to note which features might be affected by culture so that a different emphasis can be placed on them to take account of cultural differences. In order to give greater reliability and validity, less emphasis must be placed on symptoms that show cultural differences and more emphasis on symptoms and features that seem to be universal. For example, something bizarre in one culture might not be bizarre in another culture (such as hearing voices), so 'bizarreness' might be a symptom that has less emphasis placed on it when making a diagnosis using the DSM. The review of DSM-IV to create DSM-IV-TR looked at removing 'bizarre' from the list of symptoms, but it was so central that it was not felt this could be done. Instead, a warning of the need to be mindful of the cultural differences the judgement 'bizarre' can entail was added.

Move away from emphasis on first-rank symptoms and interpretation

One problem is that with schizophrenia, first-rank symptoms tend to be weighted as more important when making a diagnosis. First-rank symptoms include hearing voices, delusions and other features of distortions in thinking. However, first-rank symptoms are also more open to interpretation, which means that there might be cultural issues with regard to interpretation. Flaum et al. (1991) found a lack of reliability when using the DSM with regard to first-rank symptoms and that was with a similar sample from one culture. Therefore, it is likely that such unreliability would be magnified if using first-rank symptoms across different cultures. Minimising first-rank symptoms and taking care with 'bizarre' features would mean less unreliability with regard to diagnosis across cultures.

Focus more on negative symptoms as they are more 'objectively' measured

Similarly, with regard to diagnosis there should be a greater emphasis on symptoms that are objectively measured. Flaum suggests that negative symptoms (for example poverty of speech) are more objectively assessed and measured than positive symptoms like hallucinations.

Explore In 1996 Juan Mezzich edited *Culture and Psychiatric Diagnosis: A DSM-IV Perspective*, containing a range of papers about culture and diagnosis. Use this or any other reference to familiarise yourself with more studies and research into the effect of culture on diagnosis.

Study hint Notice that studies and research findings are given in the sections about reliability, validity and cultural issues and diagnosis. This is because research findings are likely to form part of an examination question. Make sure you can give evidence as well as making general claims.

Culture-bound syndromes

Culture-bound syndromes are mental health problems (or other illnesses) with a set of symptoms found and recognised as an illness only in one culture. Many psychiatrists reject the idea of culture-bound syndromes. However, the most commonly recognised ones are listed in the DSM-IV.

Penis panics

In some cultures males may think that their penis will retract into their bodies — and women may think the same about their breasts. This is known as genital retraction syndrome (GRS). Such panics have been found around the world but mainly in Africa and Asia. The origin of the idea can be related to witchcraft.

Kuru

Kuru is an incurable brain disease found in Papua New Guinea. The symptoms are headaches, shaking and aching limbs; death can occur, in the worst cases, within about 18 months. It is related to Creutzfeldt-Jakob disease and is only found in one area in Papua New Guinea and nearby tribes, where there is intermarriage. It might be related to the funeral practice of eating the brain. Kuru is not a mental disorder, but its symptoms are similar to mental disorder.

Evaluation of cultural issues, diagnosis and the DSM

Strengths

- The DSM-IV-TR takes account of cultural issues in acknowledging culture-bound syndromes.
- There has been an attempt to remove focus from bizarre symptoms in schizophrenia, as it was acknowledged that such symptoms are open to interpretation and that there are cultural issues in such interpretations.

Weaknesses

- Other features of symptoms of schizophrenia that are listed in the DSM could lead to cultural bias. 'First-rank' symptoms (like 'bizarreness') should perhaps receive less emphasis.
- Negative symptoms of schizophrenia are more objectively measured and so should be given greater attention. In practice, the focus is on positive symptoms (including bizarreness, because this includes hallucinations).
- There might be some cultural differences in the symptoms of schizophrenia (such as grandiosity and auditory hallucinations) so these should be considered separately rather than as elements of a range of symptoms.

Symptoms and features of schizophrenia

This section of the chapter covers the **symptoms** and **features**, two explanations and two treatments for two mental disorders from a specific list including schizophrenia.

Schizophrenia is explained first. The second disorder chosen is unipolar depression. Bipolar depression, phobias, obsessive–compulsive disorder, anorexia nervosa or bulimia nervosa could be chosen instead. Anorexia nervosa is covered in the online resources supporting this textbook.

> **Features** of a mental health disorder usually involve statistics about the disorder, or aspects of it such as how the illness develops or how other factors such as gender and age link.
>
> **Symptoms** are what characterise the disorder with regard to how the person thinks, feels or behaves.

Symptoms and features

Schizophrenia is a mental illness that can affect the way someone thinks, speaks or feels to such a degree that they lose focus on reality. There are a number of ways of characterising schizophrenia, including giving first- and second-rank symptoms or positive and negative symptoms. First-rank symptoms include hearing voices and ideas about being guided by others. Second-rank symptoms include flattened emotions. Positive and negative symptoms are explained below.

As yet there is no physical way of diagnosing schizophrenia, although research looking at the possibility of using a blood test or eye tracking is currently underway. Only a psychiatrist can make a diagnosis of schizophrenia using symptoms and features.

5

Positive and negative symptoms of schizophrenia

Positive symptoms are additions to behaviour and actual symptoms that can be noted. They include first-rank symptoms. Negative symptoms are where normal functioning is not present. Diagnosis of schizophrenia according to the DSM requires 1 month of two or more positive symptoms.

Positive symptoms

Positive symptoms are about changes in thinking in the person. These include:

- **Hallucinations**, such as seeing or hearing things that are not there. Hearing voices in some cultures is not seen as a sign of mental disorder, but of a personal spiritual capability. In these cases the voices are often kind and positive, whereas with schizophrenia the voices are often harsh and critical. Critical voices provide a running commentary on what the person is doing. Controlling voices tell the person what to do — usually uncharacteristic acts.
- **Delusions** (false beliefs), such as someone thinking their movements are being controlled by someone else. A common form of delusion is the paranoid delusion; the sufferer believes that someone is trying to mislead, manipulate or even kill them. Someone suffers from delusions of grandeur when they think they are in a prominent position of power, such as a king, or that they possess special power, such as to cure cancer. Delusions can also take the form of the person thinking that unrelated things are in fact intended to relate to them; they may feel that a newspaper headline carries a secret message for them. Delusions can lead to strange behaviour, such as covering windows to shut out the sound of the voice of God.
- **Thought disorders**, which make someone's speech hard to follow. They might also lose concentration at work or complain of having muddled thinking. The person may become disorganised. Further developments of thought disorders are 'thought insertion' (a person thinks their own thoughts are put there by someone else) or 'thought broadcasting' (thinking others can hear their thoughts).

Evaluation

Positive symptoms tend to have greater weight when diagnosing schizophrenia but, as was explained earlier, they can be affected by cultural differences so perhaps should not be weighted as strongly as negative symptoms, which might be more objectively measured.

Negative symptoms

Negative symptoms often start before positive ones, sometimes years before schizophrenia is diagnosed. This is known as the **prodromal** period. They include:

- lack of energy and apathy — for example, no motivation to do daily chores
- social withdrawal — for example, avoiding family and friends, and not going out
- flatness of emotions, where the face becomes emotionless and the voice dull with no rise and fall
- not looking after appearance and self, and generally not adhering to expectations with regard to preserving a sense of self

Evaluation

Negative symptoms seem less affected by cultural factors and it has been suggested that they can be more objectively measured. Hearing voices, for example, is hard if not impossible to measure. Lack of energy, flatness of emotions or social withdrawal might be more easily monitored. Prodromal features have been found to be present in many adolescents and cannot be taken to indicate the onset of schizophrenia on their own.

Distinguishing features from symptoms

It is hard to separate features from symptoms. Symptoms are what the person presents with to the doctor. Features are wider, for instance that there are different types of schizophrenia or that schizophrenia is found in all countries where research has been carried out. According to Jablensky (2000), schizophrenia is found in any nation at a rate of about 1.4–4.6 per 1000 people. These are features of schizophrenia because they are not symptoms but 'facts' about the disorder. About a quarter of people who have had a schizophrenic episode recover and do not get another one. About a quarter of those who have schizophrenia have it continually without any breaks. That leaves 50% who have periods of recovery and periods of symptoms. The positive symptoms, such as hallucinations and delusions, can be overcome but the negative symptoms tend to remain.

Types of schizophrenia

It could be said to be a feature of schizophrenia that there are different types:

- **Paranoid schizophrenia** is characterised by someone being suspicious of others and having delusions of grandeur. There are often hallucinations as well.
- **Disorganised schizophrenia** is characterised by speech being disorganised and hard to follow, as well as the person having inappropriate moods for the situation. There are no hallucinations.
- **Catatonic schizophrenia** is when someone is very withdrawn and isolated and has little physical movement.
- **Residual schizophrenia** is where there are low level positive symptoms but psychotic symptoms are present.
- **Undifferentiated schizophrenia** is when the person does not fit the other types.

Unit 4

Two explanations for schizophrenia

One explanation that you learn must be a biological one, and in this section the dopamine hypothesis is covered. The other explanation has to come from one of the other AS approaches; social class has been chosen for coverage here.

The dopamine hypothesis

One biological explanation for schizophrenia is that it is related to neurotransmitter functioning.

> **AS link** Review your learning about synaptic transmission and the role of neurotransmitters in sending messages around the brain (pp. 263–65).

Research suggests that the presence of an excess number of dopamine receptors at the synapse contributes to schizophrenia. It is possible that an increase in dopamine in one site in the brain (the mesolimbic pathway) contributes to positive symptoms and in another site (the mesocortical pathway) contributes to negative symptoms of schizophrenia. There are many ways in which such sensitivity to dopamine can arise, from genetic inheritance to brain **lesioning**, so the conclusion seems to be that there are many ways to develop schizophrenia, or at least many ways in which such 'supersensitivity' to dopamine can occur. Much of the research to look at how excess dopamine receptors arise has been done on animals. Other research has been carried out using PET scanning and other scanning methods.

Explaining the dopamine differences

There is discussion of how dopamine receptors can be present in the brain in different numbers and it has been suggested that development of the receptors in one area might inhibit their development in another. For example, lack of activity in the prefrontal cortex and limbic system might lead to lack of inhibition of their production in the striatum. These areas of research are currently being studied. There is some evidence that people with schizophrenia have enlarged ventricles and smaller frontal lobes, and that they also have a higher incidence of head injury in childhood. Any of these features link with prefrontal cortex damage. The prefrontal cortex finishes developing in adolescence, which links with the (common) onset of schizophrenia at this age.

Evaluation of the dopamine hypothesis

Evidence for the dopamine hypothesis (strengths of the explanation)

1 **Amphetamines give similar symptoms to those of excess dopamine**
   Some evidence comes from the effects of drugs such as amphetamines. These can cause excess dopamine, resulting in symptoms of psychosis. This psychosis is called 'amphetamine psychosis' and the symptoms are similar to the positive symptoms of schizophrenia. However, excess dopamine also has a stimulant effect, such as overconfidence and high alertness, which are more symptoms of mania than schizophrenia, so the explanation does not fit exactly using this evidence.

2 **Phenothiazines block dopamine receptors and reduce schizophrenic symptoms**
Phenothiazines (a group of drugs including chlorpromazine, given to schizophrenics) alleviate the symptoms of schizophrenia and work by blocking dopamine receptors. If the receptors are blocked, then less dopamine will be taken up so that the effects of excess dopamine are avoided. This supports the conclusion that excess dopamine is a cause of schizophrenia.

3 **Schizophrenics are more sensitive to dopamine uptake**
Scanning shows that if those with schizophrenia are given amphetamines there is greater release of dopamine than if non-schizophrenics are given amphetamines. This suggests that those with schizophrenia are more sensitive to excess dopamine than other people — again, evidence that dopamine is involved in the disorder.

4 **Drugs to increase dopamine production in sufferers from Parkinson's disease give psychotic symptoms**
People given Levodopa (which adds to dopamine production) for Parkinson's disease can experience symptoms similar to schizophrenia. This is another piece of evidence that dopamine relates to schizophrenic symptoms.

5 **Some genes link with dopamine production and are found with greater frequency in those with schizophrenia**
Genes that are likely to increase sensitivity to dopamine are found in those who develop symptoms of schizophrenia, so it is likely that there is a genetic explanation for schizophrenia as well.

6 **Brain differences might link with dopamine sensitivity**
The brains of those with schizophrenia seem to be different (such as grey matter differences in the front and temporal lobes). Such brain changes, at an early age, link with sensitivity to dopamine.

Evidence against the dopamine hypothesis (weaknesses of the explanation)

1 **PET scans show that blocking dopamine receptors does not always remove the symptoms**
PET scans have suggested that drugs that block dopamine did not reduce the symptoms of schizophrenia in patients who had had schizophrenia for 10 years or more, even if the block was 90% effective. However, if antipsychotic drugs are administered early on in the disorder, then more than 90% of patients respond.

2 **Blocking dopamine receptors takes a few days to work**
It is also interesting that anti-schizophrenic drugs block the dopamine receptors almost immediately but any calming effect is not noticed for several days. This suggests that something other than excess dopamine is causing the psychotic symptoms. (This is the same criticism as is made against the neurotransmitter malfunctioning explanation for depression, explained on p. 259.)

3 **Amphetamines produce only positive symptoms**
Amphetamines only produce symptoms that are like the positive symptoms of schizophrenia, which suggests that the dopamine hypothesis is not a sufficient

explanation. There are symptoms of mania where amphetamines are used; these are not involved in schizophrenia.

4 **Different types of dopamine receptor in different brain areas give different results**
Research suggests that the striatum, limbic system and cortex are the three areas of the brain where there are excess dopamine receptors in everyone. When the striatum was examined in schizophrenic patients it was not found that there were more dopamine receptors than in non-schizophrenics. Also, there were fewer dopamine receptors in the prefrontal lobes. It has been suggested by research that the decreased level of dopamine receptors in the prefrontal lobes links with negative symptoms of schizophrenia. Although this still focuses on dopamine and psychotic symptoms, it is not just that there are excess dopamine receptors. When different types of dopamine receptors are considered (D1, D2, D3 and so on), there are different results from excess or reduced receptors.

5 **Glutamate might also be implicated**
Another neurotransmitter, glutamate, is also thought to cause psychotic symptoms if there is excess present. Again, this shows up in those who take recreational drugs (such as PCP — angel dust). So perhaps dopamine is not the only neurotransmitter involved. However, animal studies (such as Schwabe et al., 2004) have shown that if an animal is sensitised to PCP it is also sensitised to dopamine and there is an increase in the number of dopamine receptors in the brain. This suggests a relationship between PCP and dopamine, which might explain the psychotic symptoms, rather than glutamate.

6 **Social and environmental factors are also involved**
Social and environmental factors seem to trigger schizophrenia, so a biological explanation is not sufficient. Perhaps stressful events in life can trigger production of excess dopamine. The link between social class and schizophrenia is explained below.

Table 5.6 *Strengths and weaknesses of the methodology used to study the dopamine hypothesis*

Strengths	Weaknesses
• Many different sources of evidence point to dopamine receptors being involved in some way in schizophrenia, from animal studies to PET scanning. Evidence also comes from unrelated events, such as how medication affects those with Parkinson's disease or how using recreational drugs leads to psychotic symptoms.	• Animals are used to investigate dopamine pathways and the effects of drugs on them. Lesioning is also used with animals to explore the effects of dopamine on their functioning. It is possible that findings from animal studies cannot legitimately be generalised to humans, because there are obvious differences in animal brains and the functioning of their nervous systems.
• Dopamine receptors are implicated in many different studies, which tends to give the hypothesis reliability.	• Scanning is carried out, which is a reliable and objective measure. However, there is a lack of sophistication so that detail is hard to study, even though functioning of the brain can be looked at.
• 'Biological' research methods such as scanning and animal studies can have good controls and tend not to involve subjective interpretation of data, so such methods are scientific, which means the findings are credible.	• Something else to do with schizophrenia may have caused the differences in dopamine receptors, rather than dopamine receptor differences causing schizophrenia.

Social class — the 'environmental breeder' hypothesis

There is evidence that people in the lowest social classes, and groups such as immigrants, have a higher incidence of schizophrenia than others in the UK. It looks as if social class might either be a cause of schizophrenia or at least be involved in its development. In the UK an incidence of above 4 people per 1000 has been found, both in the lowest social class in the white population and in black immigrant groups. Studies regularly show that schizophrenia is found more in the lower classes and among the unemployed and those living in deprived city areas. Those in lower classes also experience a different course for the illness and receive different medical care.

Official statistics and census figures confirm such differences. Lower-class patients are more likely to be brought to get medical help by the police or social services, to become compulsorily admitted and to become long-term cases. In the 1960s it was thought that lower class was a causal factor in schizophrenia. This was known as the social causation hypothesis, also known as the environmental 'breeder' hypothesis.

The idea of social drift

It has been suggested that those with schizophrenia become lower class because of the difficulties that arise from having schizophrenia. One study that compared the social class of schizophrenic men with their father's social class, using official statistics, found that though the schizophrenic men were in the lower classes, their fathers generally were not. Those who developed schizophrenia did not achieve well in their education as children, had problems in adolescence and had difficulties with keeping a job.

The idea of social movement — the social drift hypothesis — with regard to schizophrenia is now widely accepted. However, recently studies have suggested that there may also be an environmental cause for schizophrenia. Social disadvantage and environmental factors are not likely to be the main cause for schizophrenia but might be a factor that increases the likelihood of schizophrenia developing.

The idea of social adversity

Schizophrenia is more associated with cities than rural communities, so it might be that something in city life leads to schizophrenia (Eaton et al., 2000). There are people in the lower classes in rural areas, so the social drift hypothesis does not explain the city/country split. Schizophrenia shows clustering in declining inner-city areas, so perhaps being brought up in such areas leads to schizophrenia (Harrison et al., 2001).

A study that took place in Sweden (Hjem et al., 2004) showed that 'social adversity' in childhood relates to the development of schizophrenia later. In the UK, census data have consistently shown a higher incidence of schizophrenia in the African-Caribbean and black immigrant population (e.g. the 1991 and 2001 censuses), again pointing to social situation as a possible causal factor. It is estimated that there are four times as many incidences of schizophrenia in these populations as in the white indigenous population, and some studies suggest a higher figure than that (e.g. Fearon et al., 2004). Black immigrants in lower classes cannot be said to have suffered from social drift.

It is not thought that there is a genetic reason for higher levels of schizophrenia in black immigrants. The evidence for this is as follows:

- The risk of schizophrenia is greater not only for African-Caribbean immigrants but also for African-born black immigrants and, to an extent, for Asian immigrants.
- In Caribbean countries the incidence of schizophrenia is similar to that for the indigenous UK population — lower than for immigrants in the UK.
- The rate for second generation African-Caribbean immigrants is higher than for the first generation immigrants.
- It is not thought that those who came into the UK as immigrants in the 1950s and 1960s had weaker mental health — in fact, it is thought that immigrants would have been 'upwardly striving' individuals.
- African-Caribbean people with schizophrenia are likely to be unemployed, living in poor inner-city areas and in a worse situation than other African-Caribbean people. They are likely to be living alone, and to have been separated from their parents when younger.
- The immigrant population tends to be disadvantaged with regard to educational attainment, social class, standard of housing and discrimination. They tend to live in over-crowded conditions.

Features in the environment that might affect the development of schizophrenia seem to be adversity in adult life, unemployment and poverty, social isolation, living in inner-city areas with poor housing and overcrowding, high levels of crime and drug use, and separation from parents as a child.

Evaluation of the environmental 'breeder' hypothesis

Strengths of the idea that environmental factors lead to schizophrenia

- Not everyone with certain environmental circumstances develops schizophrenia although there might be environmental triggers. Other causes are possible, such as genetic and neurotransmitter functioning (there is a lot of evidence for dopamine receptors being involved in schizophrenia). It is possible that both explanations are useful; one explanation does not have to push out the other.
- The idea helps to explain the fact that although there are more people with schizophrenia in the lower classes, they are concentrated in inner-city areas, and that black immigrants are more likely to be diagnosed with schizophrenia than white lower-class groups. The environmental 'breeder' hypothesis helps to explain these two pieces of evidence better than social drift.

Weaknesses of the idea that there are environmental causes for schizophrenia

- Those in lower socioeconomic groups, living alone, unemployed and living in poverty might be more likely to be diagnosed with schizophrenia, suggesting a diagnosis problem, not an environmental problem.
- It might be that poverty, unemployment and lack of social support are stressors and it is this stress that causes the schizophrenia, not the environment itself.
- It is hard to separate environmental factors to see if they *cause* schizophrenia, as they could be the *result* of schizophrenia, as the social drift hypothesis suggests.

The social drift and environmental 'breeder' hypotheses are social approach explanations for schizophrenia. You could look at an explanation from the psychodynamic approach, the cognitive approach or the learning approach, as you need to choose an explanation other than a biological one for your second explanation.

Two treatments for schizophrenia

Each of the two treatments you choose has to come from a different AS approach. The three treatments covered in this chapter are biological, social and cognitive.

Biological approach: drug treatment

Drug therapy was hailed as an important step forward in the 1950s, as up to then treatment for psychotic patients was rudimentary and did not allow patients to function normally. Drug treatment in many cases will allow some form of normal functioning.

It follows that if neurotransmitter functioning causes symptoms, drug treatments that affect such functioning can help to treat those symptoms. Drugs such as phenothiazines are used for this purpose, for example Chlorpromazine (first used in 1952), which acts by blocking dopamine receptors so that there is no excess dopamine.

The drugs used in the treatment of schizophrenia are called 'antipsychotic' drugs and they work to suppress hallucinations and delusions. Usually the first psychotic episode results in drug prescription. Antipsychotic drugs are known as 'typical' and 'atypical'. **Typical** ones are well-established and atypical ones are newer and less widely used. **Atypical antipsychotic drugs** tend to have fewer side-effects and act in different ways to typical antipsychotic drugs. Drug treatment can be called '**chemotherapy**', which is an overall term for therapy using chemicals.

Each patient is only put on one antipsychotic drug at a time. However, antidepressants can be used at the same time and anticonvulsants might also be prescribed. Some clinicians prefer certain drugs and some people respond differently to different drugs, so it is not that there is one drug for one mental disorder.

Effectiveness of drug treatment (Meltzer et al., 2004)

Meltzer et al. (2004) carried out studies to look at the effectiveness of drug treatment in schizophrenia. They chose 481 patients with schizophrenia and randomly assigned them into groups. The groups had a placebo, an investigational drug (there were four of them) or haloperidol (an established antipsychotic drug) for 6 weeks. The investigational drugs were four new antipsychotic drugs. The study gathered information about positive and negative symptoms, severity of the illness and a score from a psychiatric rating scale. The study found that haloperidol gave significant improvements in all aspects of functioning tested compared with the placebo group so the study appeared to have validity. Two of the new drugs also showed improvements in several of the measures (such as positive and negative symptoms) compared with the placebo. There were two groups of new drugs that did not show improvements, however. This study shows that haloperidol improves symptoms for the patient, and that some new drugs at least also show improvements over a placebo. This is evidence that drug treatment works, at least to an extent.

Side-effects of antipsychotic drugs

Chlorpromazine, thiorizadine, haloperidol and trifluoperazine are examples of typical antipsychotic drugs. Side-effects of these drugs can include:

- sleepiness and tiredness
- shaking and muscle spasms
- low blood pressure
- problems with sex drive
- weight gain

Risperidone, olanzapine and quetiapine are three atypical drugs. Common side-effects of atypical antipsychotic drugs are similar to those listed above for typical antipsychotic drugs.

Explore Look up these typical and atypical anti-psychotic drugs to read about and compare their effects and side-effects.

Study hint When you learn about Rosenhan's study, you will see that pseudopatients diagnosed as having schizophrenia in remission were prescribed different drugs for the same diagnosis. There are different preferences for treatment by different drugs; one is not necessarily 'better' than another at controlling symptoms.

Evaluation of drug treatment

Strengths of drug therapy for schizophrenia

- Drugs are thought to be better than former (pre-1950s) treatments as they are seen as more ethical and more effective
- Drug treatment rests on strong biological evidence about the causes of schizophrenia so is underpinned by theory, which helps in considering its effectiveness.

Weaknesses of drug therapy for schizophrenia

- Schizophrenic patients often do not continue to take the drugs that are prescribed for them. It is estimated that this is the case in about 50% of patients. It might be that problems with functioning mean that someone who has schizophrenia is not able to remember to take their medication regularly, or they may find the side-effects too uncomfortable.
- From an ethical point of view, drugs have been called a 'chemical strait-jacket', and some people think that such control by society is unacceptable.
- Drugs have side-effects that are unpleasant and can themselves require medication. Antipsychotic drugs are not a

Study hint Rosenhan found that patients in the institutions in his study preferred to hide their drugs rather than take them. This is evidence that people with schizophrenia do not take their medication.

'cure-all' treatment, as they seem to help most with positive symptoms of schizophrenia rather than negative ones.

■ Drugs do not take into account a patient's environmental or social problems, which might contribute to re-hospitalisation and relapses. Social treatments, such as assertive community programmes, address such issues.

A social approach: psychosocial treatment

Assertive community therapy (ACT) is used to help schizophrenic patients who have frequent relapses and bouts of hospitalisation. This therapy is used by community mental health services with clients who have difficulties meeting personal goals, getting on with people, making and keeping friends and living independently. Leonard Stein and Mary Ann Test were two of the developers of ACT, which was originally called the Madison Project because it developed in Madison, Wisconsin.

ACT links with the idea of deinstitutionalisation and care in the community. In the 1970s large numbers of patients were being discharged from hospitals and strong community support for these people was required.

Characteristics of assertive community therapy

■ A focus on those who need the most help from the community health service.
■ Helping with independence, rehabilitation and recovery, and to avoid homelessness and re-hospitalisation.
■ Treatment of the patient in real-life settings — visiting them and helping, rather than offering therapies, with enough staff to offer this support and related treatment.
■ Working with other professionals, such as psychiatrists, nurses, social workers and people with whom the treatment has worked, so that a whole team can focus on the individual in question.
■ A commitment to spend as much time with the person as necessary in order to rehabilitate and support them, offering a holistic treatment that looks at all of the individual's needs in a multidisciplinary approach.

The ACT approach has been adopted in many countries, including Australia, Canada and the UK, having been developed in the USA. There is some problem with replicating the programme in less populated areas and where people needing such support are widely spread. ACT tends to be used with other interventions as well, such as social skills training and family therapy.

There have been many outcome studies that have shown the success of a programme of assertive community training (PACT). This programme, which started with schizophrenics, has been extended to those with other mental illnesses.

> **Explore** Search for information about different treatments for schizophrenia and find out how effective these different treatments are. Consider the difficulties in evaluating the treatments and in assessing their effectiveness.

Evaluating ACT

Dixon (2000) points out that since the 1980s ACT has been seen as the model for mental health practice. Bond et al. (2001) summarised 25 controlled studies that looked at the effectiveness of ACT — called an evidence-based treatment, because there is evidence for its effectiveness. They concluded that, compared with standard community care, ACT was highly effective because it engaged clients, prevented re-hospitalisations, increased housing stability and improved the quality of life of the client.

ACT is used in severe mental health cases, not only schizophrenia. The more carefully implemented an ACT programme is, the more effective it is. Surveys tend to suggest clients appreciate ACT (e.g. Mueser et al., 1998) and studies looking at its effectiveness report no negative aspects of the programme. ACT seems to work with all age groups, both genders, and across different cultures.

However, there are critics. Gomory (2001), for example, suggests that ACT is paternalistic and coercive, in that the client does not have the choice of whether or not to undergo such treatment. It is suggested that about 11% of clients feel forced into the treatment. It seems that case managers are more active in setting limits for clients who have more symptoms, more arrests, many hospitalisations and more recent substance abuse, so there may be some coercion in such severe cases. Bond (2002), however, points out that by preventing hospitalisation the treatment increases a client's choice, and by helping them to live in the community, the treatment increases a client's freedom.

Strengths

- It is thought to be good for those who have many relapses, because it might be problems with living outside the hospital that lead to such episodes. Social skills training such as family therapy can help someone to improve their interactions with others. Treatments based on improving the individual to function in society have been shown to help and can be incorporated into an ACT programme.
- Bond (2002), in a review of evidence, found that ACT was extremely effective in most mental health disorders, across gender, age and culture, and suggests that it allows client choice. Only about 11% of clients in surveys say they find it restricting.

Weaknesses

- Although therapies such as ACT help to prevent relapses they do not seem to have an effect on actual functioning, such as reducing positive and negative symptoms of schizophrenia or helping with employment prospects. Supportive employment programmes would have to be provided, as well as ways to reduce the effect of schizophrenic symptoms.
- ACT works best in heavily populated areas where there is a high incidence of schizophrenics needing care in the community. This is because of the effort and intensive focus that is required as part of the treatment. Adequate staffing is required to undertake this hands-on therapy.
- Gomory (2001) pointed out that the client is offered little choice and surrenders all responsibility for making decisions and taking care of themselves.

Symptoms and features of unipolar depression

Symptoms and features, explanations and treatments of unipolar depression are presented in this section. Unipolar depression is also known as major depression, clinical depression or unipolar disorder. It is usually abbreviated to 'depression' and this short form is often used in the discussion that follows. Depression in the sense of a low mood is not a disorder, so the word unipolar is used to indicate a disorder with one aspect. Bipolar depression indicates depression with two aspects — mania and depression.

Study hint In an examination answer it would be time-consuming to write 'unipolar depression' repeatedly, so you could write at the beginning of your answer that you mean unipolar depression when you write 'depression', and then refer to depression after that.

Symptoms and features

Depression is called the 'common cold' of mental illnesses. It is a mood disorder that features sadness, disappointment, self-doubt, loneliness and hopelessness. The feelings can be intense and last a long time. The individual might cope with daily activities but such activities are difficult.

Symptoms of unipolar depression

The symptoms of depression include extreme lethargy, disturbed sleep (which can mean early waking, waking up tired or difficulty in getting to sleep), permanent anxiety and irritability, feelings of despair and hopelessness, lack of concentration, loss of interest or pleasure in usual activities, lack of sex drive, and irrational fears and suicidal thoughts. Headaches and digestive problems are also reported.

Chris Rout/Alamy

Depression is characterised by lethargy, feelings of despair and hopelessness and loss of interest in usual activities

There are other disorders with similar symptoms, such as sleep and anxiety disorders and obsessional behaviour. There is no test for depression; diagnosis relies on self-report data or information from family and friends.

Features of unipolar depression

Depression is twice as common in women as in men, although men are more likely to commit suicide. Depression usually occurs from the age of 30 to 40 and reaches

Unit 4

a peak at between 50 and 60. Some cases of depression only occur once, whereas other people suffer permanently, though with more or less severity, over the years. Depressed individuals tend to live a shorter life than non-depressed people, possibly because depression relates to heart disease and other illnesses. Depression tends to affect work and family life as well as functioning, such as sleeping and eating. According to the National Institute of Health in the USA, over 20 million people suffer from depression and this affects their everyday lives. Depression affects over 3.5 million people in the UK.

Two explanations for unipolar depression

Each of the two explanations you study for your course must come from a different AS approach. Depression can be triggered by a significant life event, hormone or neurotransmitter deficiency, or other areas of a person's life such as drug dependency and alcoholism.

In this section a biological explanation is considered — the monoamine hypothesis — along with a psychological explanation — aspects of faulty thinking.

Biological approach: the monoamine hypothesis

Monoamines are a group of neurotransmitters that include **serotonin**, **norepinephrine** (noradrenaline) and **dopamine**. One role of serotonin is to regulate other neurotransmitters; without regulation, erratic brain functioning and thinking patterns occur. Low levels of serotonin can produce low levels of another neurotransmitter, norepinephrine (which is required for someone to show alertness, energy, anxiety and attention to life). Some antidepressants can be used to increase levels of norepinephrine. Others are used to increase levels of another monoamine neurotransmitter, dopamine (dopamine is related to the ability to show attention and motivation, to feel pleasure and reward). The idea is that, for treatment, the drug is matched to the symptoms of depression. Whichever symptom of depression is presented, a drug would be chosen to increase the particular monoamine concerned.

Many antidepressants work by increasing the patient's levels of serotonin. It could be concluded then that lack of serotonin is a biological cause of unipolar depression, and this explanation is therefore known as the **monoamine hypothesis**. Lack of serotonin appears to be related to anxiety and compulsions. Symptoms of depression such as disruption of sleep patterns also seem to relate to deficiencies in monoamine neurotransmitters.

Genetic or environmental factors

The diathesis–stress model shows that a biological explanation may link to a stress trigger. It suggests that people with a pre-existing genetic or environmental vulnerability to depression (the diathesis) will have it triggered by stressful life events or one event. Heritability is about 40% for depression in women and 30% for men, according to a Swedish study, which is evidence for a genetic link. A further study found that the serotonin transporter gene had a moderating effect on depression following a stressful life event. It seems possible, therefore, that biological make-up can predispose one person to develop depression where another person in the same situation will not.

Evaluation of the monoamine hypothesis

Strengths

- If the explanation is that there are monoamine deficiencies, and drugs that replace those deficiencies work, then this is evidence for the hypothesis.
- The different monoamines link to the symptoms differently and treatment reflects those differences, again supporting the hypothesis. For example, anxiety, compulsions, and lack of interest, energy or concentration can all be explained by deficiency in monoamines.

Weaknesses

- There are drugs (such as opipramol) that affect depression but whose action is not related to monoamine neurotransmitters, putting the monoamine hypothesis in doubt.
- Experiments where monoamines are depleted do not cause symptoms of depression.
- MRI scans have shown some physical differences in the brain in people with depression as compared to those without, so these might be related to the cause rather than faulty monoamine neurotransmitter functioning. One such brain difference is a smaller hippocampus. It may be that drugs increasing serotonin levels affect depression because those heightened levels act to increase the hippocampal area. This increase in the mass of the hippocampus might lift mood and improve memory. So serotonin level is still a factor in the explanation, but its action affects brain mass not monoamine deficiency.
- A different biological explanation implicates the parts of the nervous system related to stress and includes an increase in levels of cortisol. This also goes against the monoamine hypothesis.

Non-biological approach: the cognitive model of depression

Various biological explanations for depression have been identified above, together with the social elements associated with diathesis–stress. A further explanation is psychological: having accepted that environmental stressors and possibly biological make-up can cause unipolar depression, it has been found that an individual's method of coping can affect the course of the disorder and that thinking processes might, in fact, cause the disorder. It does appear that making changes to thinking patterns can help a patient cope with depression. This suggests that distorted thinking is, at least in part, a cause of depression.

In the 1960s, Beck developed the cognitive model of depression, which considers three aspects of thinking. He looked at cognitive errors that people make about themselves (a negative view of themselves), at faulty patterns of thought and schemata and at distorted processing of information.

Seligman put forward a similar theory when he suggested that depression is a form of **learned helplessness**; this is when people learn to give up trying to put things right because they have experienced only failure. **Cognitive–behavioural therapy (CBT)**, a treatment for depression, arises from such theories and is explained in detail later in this section.

There are three aspects of Beck's cognitive model of depression:

■ the **cognitive triad** — a negative view of self, the world and the future
■ cognitive errors — faulty thinking, along with negative and unrealistic ideas
■ schemata — patterns of maladaptive thoughts and beliefs

The cognitive triad found in people with depression involves the person having negative thoughts about themselves (feeling inadequate and unworthy), about the world (feeling defeated or deprived) and about the future (believing that the suffering will continue).

The main issue concerns how an individual assigns meaning to an event. Genetic factors and early experiences affect thinking and schemata are built up from interactions and experiences. Through such experiences beliefs are built up and these beliefs set up assumptions about the world. A person will adhere to their core beliefs and work on the principle that *if* I do this *then* that will happen. This sort of thinking can involve **negative automatic thoughts**.

Schemata are built up through experiences of the world and involve developing positive and negative beliefs and attitudes to interpret the world. A generalised negative belief pattern will make someone vulnerable to depression. Clark and Beck (1999) explained that the negative belief pattern involves schemata about thinking, emotions, motivations and behaviour. The way to overcome depression, according to the cognitive model, is to change maladaptive interpretations by considering alternative thoughts and interpretations of events. If evidence is presented that there are other interpretations, an individual can change their cognitions.

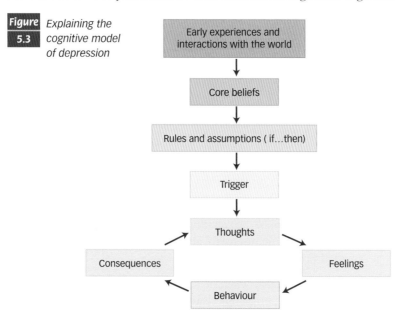

Figure 5.3 *Explaining the cognitive model of depression*

Early experiences and interactions with the world

↓

Core beliefs

↓

Rules and assumptions (if...then)

↓

Trigger

↓

Thoughts

Consequences — Feelings

Behaviour

The likely schemata of a depressed person include:

- cognitive schemata that lead to seeing actual or threatened loss
- affective (emotions) schemata leading to sadness
- physiological (biological) schemata that make someone feel tired and unable to do things
- motivational schemata that lead to helplessness and lack of direction
- behavioural schemata that lead to withdrawal and inactivity

Evidence for the cognitive model for depression

Hollon et al. (2002) report on many attempts to evaluate CBT and found that it performed well in controlled trials. It appears that CBT helps for at least as long as drug treatment. Bothwell and Scott (1997) found that faulty thinking and errors in cognitive processing — especially with regard to needing approval and having low self-esteem — linked with the symptoms of depression continuing after hospital care. Watkins and Baracaia (2002) found that knowing more about mental processes helped to reduce relapse in those with depression and helped to stop them going over thinking in their heads and constantly problem solving (ruminating).

Teichman et al. (2002) looked at relationships between self-concept, hostility between self and partner, a partner's level of depression, involvement in house activities and how severe depression was. They found that self-concept was the most marked link with the severity of the depression. As self-concept involves how people see themselves and what they think about themselves in relation to the outside world, this is evidence for the cognitive model of depression.

Evaluation of the cognitive model of depression

Strengths

- Research has shown that depressed people have negative thoughts and that the cognitive explanation for depression is backed up by both self-report data and other measures. The model is 'evidence-based' because there is a lot of research to support it. Ingram (2001) showed that adverse early experiences relate to later depression, as the model predicts.
- Alloy and Abramson (1999) undertook a longitudinal study of those with depression to evaluate Beck's schema theory and the idea of hopelessness. Some college students were identified as having negative self-schemata. The researchers found that students with negative thought patterns were more at risk from depression, so this study was taken as evidence for the cognitive model — that modes of thinking can cause depression.
- The cognitive model takes into account genes, early experiences and learning and suggests that developmental issues can lead to certain thinking patterns and core beliefs that predispose someone to depression.

Weaknesses

- It is hard to find evidence for the cognitive model's claim that negative thinking actually causes depression, rather than simply being present in those with depression. Negative thinking seems to disappear when the depression stops, which might suggest that faulty thinking comes with depression rather than being a cause of it.

■ It is difficult to distinguish between thinking which *causes* depression and thinking *caused by* depression. The same issue arises with a neurochemical explanation, because depressed thoughts are likely to alter brain chemistry — or brain chemistry could cause depressed thoughts. It is hard if not impossible to test which came first.

Two treatments for unipolar depression

Treatment for depression tends to be carried out in the community, though patients can be hospitalised if they are a risk to themselves or pose a risk to others. The use of psychotherapy and antidepressant drugs is common. Each treatment that you study must come from a different AS approach. In this section biological (drug) treatment and psychotherapy using CBT are the two treatments considered.

Biological approach: drug treatment

Antidepressants are used to treat depression and work on the principle that since low levels of serotonin cause depression, increasing serotonin levels will help. Drugs such as Prozac work in this way. However the fact that Prozac seems to improve depression does not prove that low levels of serotonin are the cause (see weaknesses of the monoamine hypothesis, p. 259). It has also been found that while serotonin levels are quickly raised by drug treatment, improvement in the symptoms of depression may not follow for weeks.

Drugs used in treating depression are called **selective serotonin reuptake inhibitors (SSRIs)**. Examples include Prozac, Fluvoxamine and Citalopram as well as tricyclic antidepressants (older drugs) and **atypical antidepressants** (new drugs which also target other neurotransmitters like norepinephrine and dopamine as well as serotonin). Atypical antidepressants include Burpopion (Wellbutrin), and Trazodone (Desvrel). There are also **monoamine oxidase inhibitors (MAOIs)**. All these drugs have side-effects because neurotransmitters play many roles. Serotonin, for example, is involved in many aspects of physiological function.

Some side-effects of antidepressants

■ SSRIs — nausea, insomnia, anxiety, dizziness, weight change, headaches and fatigue
■ atypical antidepressants — nausea, fatigue, weight gain, nervousness and blurred vision
■ tricyclic antidepressants and MAOIs have more severe side-effects so are only used as a last resort if the others do not work

Withdrawal of antidepressants

Treatment with antidepressants has to be withdrawn gradually to avoid **withdrawal symptoms**, including crying spells, dizziness, insomnia, fatigue, muscle spasms, and aches and pains. These withdrawal symptoms are called antidepressant discontinuation syndrome.

Evidence comparing drug treatment and a form of CBT

A 2008 study (Kuyken et al.) reported that a group-based form of CBT (mindfulness based cognitive therapy — MBCT) is at least as successful in treating depression as medication like Prozac, even in the long term. It was better at preventing relapse, offered a more effective change in quality of life, and was more cost-effective.

The aim of the study (which was carried out by British researchers from Exeter and London universities) was to compare the effectiveness of treatments for depression. It looked at 123 people who had had repeated episodes of clinical depression. The participants were randomly placed in one of two groups. One group carried on with their antidepressant treatment and the other group took part in the MBCT course. The 'MBCT group' was given the choice of whether to stop their medication or not. MBCT targets negative thinking as is explained when CBT is discussed in the next section.

There was an 8-week trial and groups of between 8 and 15 people from the MBCT group attended meetings with a therapist. Group exercises were based on Buddhist meditation techniques and members of the group were taught to focus on the present rather than the past, for example. Many reported greater control over their negative thinking following the group meetings. Over the 15 months after the trial ended, about 47% of the MBCT group had a relapse. However, those who continued the antidepressant treatment without the MBCT had a 60% relapse rate. The MBCT group reported a much better quality of life.

The researchers thought that MBCT had given the participants skills for life, whereas medication did not. This is evidence against the use of drug therapy. Note, however, that some of the MBCT group may have continued with their drug treatment at the same time.

Evaluation of drug treatment for depression

Strengths

- Antidepressants can be prescribed to boost mood so that other therapies like CBT can be used. Although it takes a few weeks for antidepressants to work, this may be necessary where mood is too depressed for an individual to focus on making a change in their thinking.
- Researchers continue to seek more effective antidepressants with fewer side-effects. Atypical antidepressants, for example, have far fewer side-effects than the 'old' tricyclic antidepressants.
- There is theoretical evidence to back the use of antidepressants, in particular the newer ones that consider not only low serotonin levels but also levels of nor-epinephrine (noradrenaline) and dopamine.

Weaknesses

- A government study (2006) showed that less than 50% of those with depression who take antidepressants become symptom-free. Many relapse into depression again even if they keep taking the medication.
- Antidepressants ease symptoms but are not seen as a cure for depression. It is suggested that therapy works just as well and is more likely to prevent relapse. CBT involves the client in learning the triggers for depressive episodes and in acquiring the tools to combat such episodes so it is likely to be better at preventing relapse.

Non-biological approach: cognitive–behavioural therapy (CBT)

Psychotherapy is a broad term for counselling, psychodynamic therapy and other similar forms of therapy. In this section CBT is considered, as it is an evidence-based therapy (having evidence to support it and using evidence within it). It is funded by the government because of studies that show its effectiveness.

CBT developed from Beck's cognitive model of depression. Faulty thinking patterns, including negative automatic thoughts, are regarded as arising from schemata that are built through early experiences. Depression can be treated by helping the individual to focus on their negative automatic thoughts and then to consider new ways of thinking. From a list of possible faulty ways of thinking, the client is encouraged to consider which, if any, apply to them. The CBT practitioner then offers a number of different tools to help cope with negative automatic thoughts, including identifying the triggers for these thoughts so that the cycle can be broken.

The cognitive model suggests some ways of thinking that are found in those who are depressed:

- all-or-nothing thinking — something that goes wrong is taken to indicate that everything will always be wrong
- catastrophising — a single negative event is blown up into the precursor of disaster
- crystal ball thinking — guessing negatively what someone else will do or say or what will happen
- over-generalisation — e.g. loneliness means that you are disliked
- negative mental filter — the negative aspects of a situation are focused upon, while positive ones are 'filtered out'
- disqualifying the positive — when someone gives a compliment and it is brushed to one side
- jumping to conclusions — when something unwanted happens the individual concludes they are worthless or have something wrong with them, rather than seeking another explanation
- magnification and minimisation — exaggeration of the importance of minor problems
- emotional reasoning — a job like cleaning up the house seems overwhelming and hopeless
- 'should' statements — thinking other people should do things and getting worked up about it

- labelling and mislabelling — such as breaking a diet once and thereafter labelling oneself a failure or 'fat pig'
- personalisation — where someone blames themselves for things that are in fact out of their control

How CBT works in practice

A CBT session tends to last about 50 minutes, and the therapist would probably enter a contract to see the client for about six sessions. A review would then take place. The first session involves contracting and setting the scene about what is expected. For example, ethical issues such as confidentiality and privacy have to be discussed, as well as other issues such as the client having to do homework to help themselves to overcome any thinking they feel is faulty.

In each session, an agenda is set with the client so that they decide what issues they would like to raise. Those issues are then focused on. At first the client talks about themselves so that their **frame of reference** can be understood by the therapist. It is important to focus on the client's own words and meanings, as the aim is to help them to uncover their own core beliefs and thinking patterns. The therapist summarises what the client has said to check full understanding, and also works with the client using CBT tools. For example, if a client repeatedly mentions their 'stupidity' in some situations, the therapist can ask what 'stupidity' means to them. David Burns (a therapist central to the development of CBT) developed what he called the **downward arrow technique**, a process by which a negative automatic thought can be investigated. The investigation might start from the thought 'I should have visited my mother at the weekend'. The therapist and client would explore this thought by asking 'if that were true, what would that mean?' The client might say 'I should care about my mother more' and then, on being asked what that would mean, might say 'I am a bad person'. By using such techniques the client and therapist can together uncover core beliefs. Once these are revealed, evidence can be found that the beliefs are not altogether true. For example, the therapist can ask the client if he/she is really a 'bad person' and find evidence that that is not the case.

The therapist can use other tools as well, such as the list of thinking patterns given above. For example, when a client says they are a bad person for not visiting their mother they might be catastrophising (thinking that if they do not visit their mother something really bad will happen to her).

Another tool is to look at self-concept. Clients are asked to talk to family and friends about their views of the client to discover elements of themselves they have not known about before, potentially improving their self-esteem.

Figure 5.3 *The Johari window can help people to see how to use feedback from others to know themselves better, potentially improving their self-esteem particularly in their blindspot*

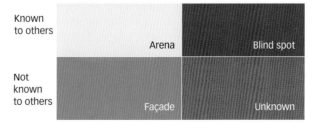

	Arena	Blind spot
Known to others		
Not known to others	Façade	Unknown

Stiles et al. (2006)

Stiles et al. (2006) carried out a study that looked at the effectiveness of CBT as compared to person-centred and psychodynamic therapies, over a 3-year period in 58 NHS settings in the UK. In all, 1309 patients who had received CBT, person-centred therapy or psychodynamic therapy were studied. The researchers used the **clinical outcomes in routine evaluation — outcome measure (CORE-OM)** at the beginning and end of their treatment. The therapists wrote down which therapy was used on an 'end of therapy' form. Clients were divided into six groups. Three groups were treated with one of the three therapies each (CBT, person-centred, psychodynamic) and three groups received one of these therapies and an additional treatment (such as integrative or art therapy). They found that all six groups showed marked improvement and no one group stood out as being more improved. It was concluded that theoretically different approaches tended to have equivalent outcomes, as previous studies have shown.

Evaluation

There was no control group, some data were missing, the clients were not randomly allocated to the groups (the treatment was selected for them) and there was no supervision of the actual treatment. This means there are some limitations with the study.

Evaluation of CBT

Strengths

- This therapy is evidence-based. Kuyken et al. (2008) suggested that a form of CBT was more effective in preventing relapse and in improving quality of life than was the use of antidepressants.
- It is backed by government funding in the UK and is a large part of the initiative to improve access to psychological therapies (IAPT). This might be because it is fairly quick to show results and is relatively cheap to provide.

Weaknesses

- CBT depends for its efficacy on the idea that depression comes from faulty thinking, such as negative automatic thoughts. However, these might be a result of the depression not a cause of it. Some studies have found that when depression is removed so are negative thoughts. This does not mean, however, that there is not a causal relationship between cognitive processing and depression — just that it is hard to demonstrate.
- Many of the data about the effectiveness of CBT come from self-report, and such data are often said to be unreliable. The client might want to please the therapist and say that the therapy is working, for example, which would make the data invalid. Or it might depend on how they were feeling when they completed a questionnaire, which would make the data unreliable.
- Stiles et al. found that, in general, all psychotherapies have the same success rates in spite of their different theories and techniques. It is hard to differentiate between the end result of different therapies. Person-centred therapy focuses on the client's own frame of reference and offers them unconditional positive regard.

Psychodynamic therapy allows the client to examine their early experiences and reveal what could be called core beliefs to help them understand their thinking about themselves and to achieve a more positive self-regard.

Explore Look up more about the UK initiative to improve people's access to psychological therapies and what primary care trusts are doing about it.

Treatment from the psychodyamic and learning approaches

For the A2 course you are required to cover one treatment or therapy from each of the five AS approaches. The alternatives offered by the course are set out in Table 5.7 below; you must choose one for each approach. This chapter has already considered therapy from the biological approach (e.g. drug treatment), from the social approach (e.g. ACT) and from the cognitive approach (e.g. CBT). This section focuses on one psychodynamic therapy and one learning therapy approach.

Table 5.7 *Course requirement alternatives with regard to treatments/therapies*

AS approach	Option 1	Option 2
Social	Family therapy	Care in the community programmes
Cognitive	Cognitive–behavioural therapy	Rational–emotive therapy
Psychodynamic	Free association	Dream analysis
Biological	Drug treatment (chemotherapy)	Electroconvulsive therapy (ECT)
Learning	Token economy programme	Systematic desensitisation

The psychodynamic approach

For the psychodynamic approach you can choose to study either free association or dream analysis. Both these therapies are part of psychoanalysis, which is a therapy used in the treatment of depression and other disorders, so it links well with the mental disorders chosen in this chapter. As dream analysis is the more detailed of the two aspects of psychoanalysis it is considered here.

AS link Review the therapy you chose to study in the learning approach for your AS course and what you learned about psychoanalysis, including free association and dream analysis.

Dream analysis

Freud developed the idea of dream analysis from a dream of his own in 1895. He was worried about a patient called Irma who was not doing well in treatment. Freud blamed himself. He dreamt that he met Irma at a party and examined her. In the dream he saw a chemical formula for a drug that a doctor had given Irma. When he saw this he realised that Irma's condition was caused by a dirty syringe that the other doctor had used. Freud felt relieved and less guilty after this revelation. Freud interpreted his dream as **wish fulfilment**. He wished that Irma's condition was not his fault so he dreamt that it was the fault of another doctor. He proposed that dreams are there to fulfil wishes.

Dream analysis is part of Freud's psychodynamic approach. He suggested that such analysis could uncover unconscious thoughts and wishes, as could free association and slips of the tongue. Freud considered that people's actions are governed to a great extent by unconscious wishes and desires that are not easily accessed and that one way of finding out what is in the unconscious is to analyse someone's dreams. Dreams allow repressed material to leak out, albeit in a disguised, symbolic form; dream analysis therefore involves examining the content of dreams and then looking at that content to uncover symbols that are said to represent unconscious thoughts. The idea is that if unconscious thoughts can be identified they can be acknowledged by the individual and, once acknowledged, dealt with.

Dream work

Everyone's unconscious is unique. The dream therapist needs to know a significant amount about the person's life so that interpretation of dream symbols can be tailored to the individual. The individual can then create an insight into how to solve their problem. The content of the dream is called the **manifest content** and is the story the dreamer tells about what they dreamt. The manifest content is analysed by a psychoanalyst to find underlying meaning. The hidden content of the dream is called the **latent content**. The manifest content is often based on events of the day. **Dream work** is the term for translating the underlying wishes in the dream, using the manifest content. Dream work transforms the unconscious and forbidden wish into a non-threatening form. This reduces anxiety and allows the sleeper to stay asleep. Dream work involves condensation, displacement and secondary elaboration.

- **Condensation** is when two or more ideas are joined into one, so a dream about a man (the manifest content) might be a dream about someone's father and their lover (two ideas).
- **Displacement** is when someone or something that is giving concern is displaced (put) onto someone or something else. For example, someone dreaming about killing a cat might be dreaming about killing a relative. If someone dreamt about killing the relative they would have felt guilt, so they dreamt about killing the cat instead.
- **Secondary elaboration** is when the unconscious mind puts things together so they seem logical when analysed, but this logic might be obscuring further wishes and desires. Freud was not keen on using universal symbols in dreams, such as dancing representing sexual intercourse. The content of the unconscious is personal to the individual and so are symbols. Freud did not agree with dream dictionaries.

How dream analysis is done

Dream analysis would be undertaken as part of psychoanalysis. To become a psychoanalyst a person has to train for a number of years and, as part of the training, they must themselves undergo analysis frequently. This can take place every day during training.

Clients are required to visit the analyst frequently — on average around three times a week — and have to commit time to it. Partly because there are frequent sessions, and because the therapy lasts a long time, psychoanalysis is expensive (around £50 per session) and intensive, especially when compared with CBT.

During the analysis, the psychoanalyst sits slightly behind the client, who lies in a comfortable position on a couch. The analyst is not part of the scene, in so far as that is possible, so that the **analysand** (the person being analysed) is the main focus.

Study hint If you are evaluating dream analysis do not say that it is expensive and takes time without adding some more information to explain your comments. 'Expensive', 'time-consuming', 'cheap' and 'easy' are good evaluation comments only if you expand on the implications of these features.

Features of analysis

Features of analysis (of which dream analysis is a part) include confronting **defence mechanisms** as well as dealing with transference. Defence mechanisms include repression (pushing thoughts and memories into the unconscious so they are not 'known about') and denial, another way of avoiding acknowledging experiences or thoughts. **Transference** refers to the way emotions such as love and hate can be turned onto the analyst; this is thought to be a valuable part of the therapy, indicating that such emotions are starting to be released.

Features of psychoanalysis include topographic theory, which refers to Freud's idea that mental processes are conscious, pre-conscious and unconscious. Conscious thoughts can be immediately accessed but pre-conscious thoughts, though accessible, are not in the consciousness until brought there. Unconscious thoughts cannot be accessed but are powerful influences on behaviour.

Freud also put forward a structural theory for the personality. He suggested that the id (the 'I want' part of personality) was concerned with unconscious thoughts and desires. The superego was concerned with matters of conscience. The role of the ego, the third part of the personality, was to keep the peace between the id's demands and the superego's rules.

AS link

Review your learning about the id, ego and superego from the psychodynamic approach (pp. 188–89).

Theories arising from Freud's ideas

Freud's basic views have given rise to different theoretical ideas informing different therapies. **Conflict theory**, for example, focuses on uncovering conflicts in the unconscious that, once revealed, can be resolved. The work of Abend and Arlow is associated with conflict theory. **Object relations theory** focuses on how early experiences can build up internal representations of the self that might be holding the individual back, causing conflict and problems, including depression. The work of Winnicott is associated with object relations theory. **Interpersonal psychoanalysis** focuses on interactions with other people and how an individual can 'hide' themselves in the way they interact with others. The work of Fromm-Reichman is associated with interpersonal theory.

Evaluation of dream analysis

Evaluation of dream analysis in effect evaluates Freud's psychodynamic approach, because it draws its explanations from that approach.

Strengths

- Freud's ideas question whether a rational scientific approach to understanding people is appropriate (see Fonagy, 1981) and therefore these ideas cannot be criticised simply because they cannot be tested scientifically. Dream theory appears to be a good way of uncovering unconscious thoughts and wishes.
- Freud's ideas about dream analysis and the power of the unconscious have led to many other branches of psychotherapy, including humanistic therapies such as person-centred therapy and recent developments such as CBT, which draw from the cognitive approach to psychology.

Weaknesses

- Shapiro et al. (1991) suggest that psychodynamic therapies are only occasionally successful with depression. This might be because depressed people are not motivated enough to take part in the sessions. In addition, psychoanalysis does not offer a quick cure. The client has to invest time and money, as well as concentration, in the process. This is also a criticism of dream analysis as it is part of psychoanalysis.
- Freud used case studies such as Dora and Little Hans, and case studies are not generalisable because they are about individuals and their unique unconscious thoughts and wishes. The dreams he analysed, such as his own dream about Irma, are not generalisable to others.
- Storr (1987) states that psychoanalysts are bound to use subjective personal opinion in analysis, including dream analysis, so the therapy cannot be called scientific or evaluated scientifically.
- Psychoanalysis creates a power difference between the analyst and the analysand and this entails ethical issues. Masson (1989) discussed such issues.

The learning approach

For a therapy from the learning approach, you can choose to study either token economy programmes or systematic desensitisation. In this section token economy programmes are discussed as they are used in the treatment of schizophrenia.

Token economy programmes

Token economy programmes (TEPs) are based on operant conditioning, the idea that behaviour is repeated if it is rewarded and stopped if it is not rewarded. Token economy programmes are a form of **behaviour modification** because they aim to change behaviour to required or desired behaviour.

> **AS link** Review your learning about operant conditioning principles within the learning approach (p. 343). You may have learned about token economy programmes as well. If so, recall their use as a treatment (p. 337).

Operant conditioning principles

Positive reinforcement is when a reward is given to someone for behaviour and the behaviour is then repeated for that reward. For example, if someone with schizophrenia does not show required social skills — perhaps they fail to clear their tray away after eating, if that is appropriate — they can be rewarded when they do clear their tray, to encourage that behaviour.

If the complete required behaviour is not exhibited immediately, **shaping** can be used: rewarding behaviour that gradually moves nearer to the required behaviour. As the behaviour gets nearer to what is required, rewards are more focused on requirements. For example, if someone with schizophrenia is required to carry out a fairly complex task (e.g. bathing themselves if that is a difficulty), they could be rewarded step by step.

Negative reinforcement is when a person wants to remove something unpleasant so they behave in such a way as to remove the negative issue. For example, if someone has a panic attack when they go shopping they are likely to stop going shopping (or even going out at all) to avoid the negative consequences of the panic attack. Their 'staying at home' behaviour is negatively reinforced in this case.

Punishment is rarely used; it **models** aggressive or negative behaviour and does not help to develop required behaviour, though it might put a stop to undesired behaviour. For example, someone with schizophrenia in a community hostel might not be allowed out to somewhere they wanted to go because they have not adhered to the hostel rules.

> **AS link**
>
> Review your learning about modelling, as explained by social learning theory (p. 341).

TEPs and operant conditioning principles

TEPs follow operant conditioning principles. Tokens are given as rewards for required behaviour and these tokens can be exchanged for something desired. Good behaviour is rewarded with a token. Undesired behaviour is ignored as far as possible so that it is not rewarded, although neither is it punished. Shaping can be used by rewarding desired behaviour, step-by-step.

- **Tokens** are given for desired behaviour instead of direct rewards, partly because they are easier to deal with for those implementing the programme and partly because then they can be saved up for something that is wanted. This might have more value for the individual than a small reward each time.
- People are 'paid' in tokens, which is the '**economy**' part of the programme. They then exchange the tokens for a reward.
- It is a **programme** because there is a plan of what will be rewarded, when, by whom, and of how tokens will be exchanged and for what.

The eight steps of the programme

1 Identify the behaviour or behaviours to be changed. Positive behaviour is usually chosen rather than negative behaviour. For example, tidying dishes away at meal times rather than not leaving things out.

2 Decide the nature of the tokens — points or plastic counters can be used, for example.

3 Decide on the rewards available to be 'bought' with tokens. The individual must desire the rewards that their tokens will buy.

4 Set achievable goals. The individuals must be able to achieve the goals that have been set.

5 Explain the programme to the individuals concerned. They must be able to understand what is required and what the tokens mean.

6 Feedback on progress. Individuals need to know where they are going wrong and why tokens are not being given, for example. **Response cost** can be used, where tokens are taken away or withheld if there is undesirable behaviour.

7 Decide how the rewards are 'bought'. There must be arrangements for when tokens can be exchanged for rewards. There should never be any criticisms of someone who is not 'earning' tokens.

8 Review the programme. Goals should be reviewed, as well as how often tokens are given and how often the exchange takes place. For example, if someone is not making further progress with a particular behaviour, the goal might have to be reviewed.

Evaluation of token economy programmes

Token economy programmes used with long-term schizophrenic patients

Mumford et al. (1975) carried out a TEP with long-term schizophrenic patients. Fourteen institutionalised female schizophrenic patients, whose average length of stay in hospital was 30 years (and whose diagnosis therefore preceded drug treatment for schizophrenia) and who all had a severe version of the illness, were put on a programme where rewards were given for independent behaviour.

It was found that there were both qualitative and quantitative changes in the participants' behaviour but the main focus of the research was on the problems in implementing the programme. It was concluded that such programmes had great potential for rehabilitating long-term patients in psychiatric hospitals. The focus on implementation was to try to build up a version of the programme that was successful and feasible.

In 2008 a programme was carried out and evaluated in Sweden, with 12 chronic (long-term) schizophrenic patients. The patients' activity levels (in areas where change in activity level was desirable) changed in the required direction during the treatment. Activities chosen for two of the patients included lip biting, deficient eye contact and aggressive acts. Then the treatment was stopped as part of the study, and their activity reverted to the undesirable levels. Finally the token economy was reintroduced and their activity levels went back to desirable levels again. Therefore, it was concluded that the treatment programme worked to improve patients' undesirable activity levels. Five of the 12 patients were discharged during the 8 months of the programme and none of those five had been readmitted at the end of the 1-year follow-up on the study.

Studies evaluating the token economy programme

Kazdin (1982) evaluated the TEP and commented that in 10 years since it began in the 1970s the programme had been used with many people and for many behaviours, in circumstances including rehabilitation, education and in community settings. Problems in using the token economy included training of staff, over-coming client resistance, and transferring the programme onto behaviour 'outside' the bounds of the programme, such as outside an institution. Issues also included the integrity of treatment, as there were power issues, and also using the treatment on a large scale, which meant difficulties in ensuring that everyone stuck to the same principles for rewarding behaviour.

McGonagle and Sultana (2008) reviewed the use of token economy in patients with schizophrenia when compared with standard care. They looked at many studies of such programmes to draw conclusions about their effectiveness and chose to draw on data from three controlled trials. One of the studies suggested that token economy was more useful than standard care and showed improvement in negative symptoms of schizophrenia after 3 months. The authors concluded that more evaluation was needed in research that was designed for the purpose. They thought that token economy might have an effect on the negative symptoms of schizophrenia but they could not conclude that such results would apply to others beyond those concerned in the study.

Strengths of token economies

- They appear to be effective, at least to an extent, for long-term schizophrenic patients, and in one study some long-term patients were rehabilitated for at least 1 year.
- The programme rests on clear behaviour-management principles and is under-pinned by a well-researched theory. Research using animals has confirmed the reliability of operant conditioning principles, for example, and studies have been repeated often enough to confirm that positive reinforcement works to give desired behaviour.

Weaknesses of token economies

- There needs to be a strong team using the programme because rewards must be consistent and clear, awarded for the same behaviours and given out at the appro-priate time. This requires a high level of management and commitment from staff, as well as thorough and costly training.
- There is a power issue, in that staff and those administering the programme have the power to reward a patient for their behaviour and the power to demand certain types and levels of behaviour. These are ethical issues that need to be addressed.
- There is possibly a problem in transferring the programme to outside an institu-tion, because the rewards might be associated only with the setting and staff.

Examination-style questions

1 Describe both the statistical definition of abnormality and the social norms definition of abnormality. *(8 marks)*

2 Explain what it means to say that the DSM is not valid. *(3 marks)*

3 Describe cultural issues with regard to diagnosis using the DSM. *(4 marks)*

4 Describe two treatments for schizophrenia. *(8 marks)*

5 Evaluate two treatments for a disorder you have studied, other than schizophrenia. *(8 marks)*

Extension question

Describe and evaluate two explanations for schizophrenia. *(12 marks)*

Studies in detail

For this section you need to look at three studies in detail, the first of which is Rosenhan's study of being sane in insane places. The second study must be about schizophrenia and the third must be about the further mental disorder you studied. In this chapter the focus of discussion has been depression, so the two other studies chosen here concern schizophrenia (Goldstein, 1988) and depression (Brown et al., 1986).

Rosenhan (1973)

Rosenhan 'sent' people into mental hospitals posing as mentally ill patients to see if their sanity would be identified. It was not. The study relates to issues surrounding the use of the DSM and its validity and reliability, as well as issues around defining abnormality.

Background

David Rosenhan (1973) was interested in the difficulty of defining abnormality, including problems with defining 'sane' and 'insane', as well as defining mental disorders such as schizophrenia. If it is hard to define such terms then questions have to be asked about the accuracy of diagnosis. For example, the question of whether 'mental illness' lies in the person, the observer or in the person doing the diagnosis needs to be addressed. The DSM (*Diagnostic and Statistical Manual of Mental Disorders*) offers lists of symptoms which can be matched to those presented by a patient, in order to diagnose a specific illness, thus distinguishing the 'sane' from the 'insane'.

Rosenhan's study placed 'normal' people (who did not have, and had never had, symptoms of a psychiatric disorder) in an institution to see if they could be distinguished from 'the insane context in which they are found' (Rosenhan, 1973, p. 238). The study assumed that the hospital staff were competent, that the individual behaved as they normally did, and that there was no suggestion that they had had any previous mental health problems. Given these factors the study questioned whether their setting alone would be sufficient to lead to the person being accepted as mentally ill.

Aims

The main aim was to see if eight sane people who gained admission into 12 different hospitals would be 'found out' as sane. A further aim was to find out what the experience of being in such an institution was like, and what it feels like to be viewed as 'insane'.

Procedures: study 1

Sample

The sample involved eight **pseudo-patients** (three women and five men) taking part in the study. One was a 20-year-old graduate and the other seven were older and were made up of three psychologists, a paediatrician, a psychiatrist, a painter and a housewife. They all used pseudonyms to avoid any diagnosis giving later embarrassment. Those employed in mental health provided a different occupation to avoid being treated differently. Rosenhan was one of the pseudo-patients; the hospital administrator and chief psychologist where he carried out the research knew about him, but nobody else did. The other seven were unknown.

> **Study hint**   This study helps to illustrate the wide-ranging features of research methods and the difficulty of allocating a specific research method to every study. In some ways Rosenhan's study is like Reicher and Haslam's experimental case study, which you may have studied for AS. There are controls in this study, and some manipulation with regard to what the participants said to doctors and so on; however, there are no conditions as such. The study is in the field, but not in the natural setting of the participants, so it is not quite a field study, while there are features of a case study because of the gathering of in-depth data, both quantitative and (predominantly) qualitative.

Settings

The settings were varied so that the findings could be generalised. The 12 hospitals, for example, were located in five different states in the USA and were varied in character (e.g. old/new, good ratio of staff to patients or not, private or not).

Hospital admission

The pseudo-patients called the hospital for an appointment. Then they arrived at the admissions office saying that they had been hearing voices. The pseudo-patients said the voices were unclear but seemed to be saying 'empty', 'hollow' or 'thud'. These words were chosen because they seemed to place an emphasis on the person's life. Other than that, and changing their name and some of their personal history, the pseudo-patient gave details of their own life. None of their current behaviours or history was pathological.

On being admitted the pseudo-patients stopped simulating symptoms of abnormality in any way. Some were a little nervous, not having believed they would be admitted so easily, but otherwise all behaved as they would 'normally'. They were given medication, which they did not swallow, responded to instructions from staff and chatted to other patients. Each pseudo-patient was told they would have to get out by convincing staff they were sane. All but one wanted to be discharged almost immediately, as hospitalisation was extremely stressful. Therefore they behaved 'sanely' and were 'paragons of cooperation'.

Results: study 1

The pseudo-patients were never detected. All except one were admitted with a diagnosis of schizophrenia in remission. No records or behaviour by hospital staff showed that there were any doubts about the authenticity of the patients. 'Rather, evidence was strong that, once labelled schizophrenic, the pseudo-patient was stuck with that label' (Rosenhan, 1973, p. 241). 'In remission' meant 'able to be discharged' rather than anything else. Between 7 and 52 days were spent in hospital by the 'patients' — on average 19 days.

Factors to note
- The hospitals were considered good or excellent and not to blame for the failure to recognise sanity.
- The pseudo-patients were not carefully observed, so it was not observation of behaviour that led to the label 'schizophrenia'.
- The false diagnosis was not applied because the pseudo-patients did not behave sanely. Visitors, and indeed other patients, felt they were 'sane'; during the first three hospitalisations 35 out of 118 patients on the admissions ward voiced their suspicions, such as 'you're not crazy. You're a journalist or a professor' (this was because of the note-taking). In the study Rosenhan states 'The fact that the patients often recognised normality when staff did not raises important questions' (p. 241).

Rosenhan suggests that, in general, doctors are more likely to err on the side of caution — that is, to call a healthy person sick rather than a sick person healthy. This partly explains the findings. However, psychiatric diagnoses carry stigma, making the implications of misguided psychiatric diagnoses in some ways more serious than medical ones.

Procedures: study 2

Rosenhan wondered whether the diagnosis of 'insane' for 'sane' people could be reversed. Staff at a teaching hospital doubted the findings of the first study. Rosenhan told them that sometime in the next 3 months one or more pseudo-patients would attempt to be admitted. Each staff member was asked to rate patients presenting themselves on a scale of 1 to 10 to reflect the likelihood of them being the pseudo-patient.

Results: study 2

Judgements were given on 193 patients admitted for psychiatric treatment. Forty-one were judged with high confidence by at least one staff member to be pseudo-patients. Twenty-three were considered suspect by at least one psychiatrist and 19 were thought to be pseudo-patients by one psychiatrist and one other staff member. There were, in fact, no genuine pseudo-patients (as far as Rosenhan knew).

Results

'Any diagnostic process that lends itself so readily to massive errors of this sort cannot be very reliable', stated Rosenhan (p. 242). 'Once labelled schizophrenic there is nothing the pseudo-patient can do to overcome the tag', which 'profoundly colours others' perceptions of him and his behaviour' (p. 243). One explanation for the failure to detect sanity is that 'insanity' is a powerful central trait, and therefore all behaviours and characteristics are coloured by the label 'insane', and normal behaviours are thus over-looked.

> **Explore** If you studied sport psychology, consider personality theories and the meaning of concepts such as 'central traits' so that you can use your learning there to extend your understanding. Explore such issues more extensively for yourself.

Rosenhan found that 'normal' family background was interpreted as 'abnormal' in diagnosis. For example, acknowledged changing patterns of closeness between a pseudo-patient and his mother and father over the years was interpreted as 'manifests a long history of considerable ambivalence in close relationships' (p. 244). The records for this pseudo-patient mentioned 'angry outbursts' and 'spankings' of the children (untrue). The facts were unintentionally distorted to 'fit' with a 'popular theory of the dynamics of schizophrenic reaction' (p. 244). Rosenhan also questioned why the extensive note-taking undertaken by the pseudo-patients did not elicit questions from the hospital staff. Three pseudo-patients had their writing diagnosed as an aspect of their pathological behaviour: 'Patient engages in writing behaviour' was recorded.

It is unlikely that someone is insane all the time, just as usually we are not angry or depressed all the time. However, it seems that once a person is labelled 'insane' all their behaviour is understood through that label. Rosenhan suggested that it is perhaps because the state of insanity is not understood that the label is so strong. For instance, schizophrenia cannot be easily understood and so is interpreted as threatening to others, whereas a broken leg is easily understood and is not interpreted as threatening to others. Moreover, mental illness is treated differently from physical illness as it allegedly lasts forever.

Hospital environment

Rosenhan was interested in the hospital environment. The staff and patients were separated, and professional staff had glassed quarters in the corner of a ward, which the pseudo-patients called 'the cage'. Staff emerged from the cage, did their tasks, and then returned. When 'time out of the cage' was measured it was found (in four hospitals) that the average was 11.3% of the whole time. There was little mingling time with the patients. On an average day the nurses came out of the cage 11.5 times per shift. Doctors (especially psychiatrists) were even less available and were rarely seen on the wards. Those with most power had least to do with the patients. Rosenhan wondered if staff learned from their superiors.

Further experiments

The pseudo-patients asked a member of staff a question periodically (such as 'when will I be discharged?'), and always asked politely. In general, staff avoided continuing such contacts. In contrast, a student at Stanford University was attended to and answered when she asked staff there for help, such as how to find an area of the campus. She was helped without exception even when her questions were trivial. However, if she went to the university medical school and asked to see a psychiatrist she was helped less than if she asked to see an internist. So it was concluded that a mental health issue was something that would be avoided by members of the public.

Evaluation of Rosenhan (1973)

Strengths

- The kinds of hospital used were varied, so that there could be generalisation of findings. Twelve hospitals were involved, strengthening the findings and allowing them to be generalised. If just one hospital had been involved it might have been that hospital alone that 'labelled' mental illness.
- The design was simple. The pseudo-patients just had to be themselves, so it is unlikely that any treatment of them was due to their behaviour being similar to someone with a mental illness. The fact that some of the bona fide patients realised that the pseudo-patients were not mentally ill backs this observation up and suggests that their behaviour was validly 'normal'.
- By using eight people in 12 hospitals the study was replicated and the same results were found. The study is therefore regarded as reliable.
- The findings are strong: the labelling was clear, and the idea of people being perceived through the use of such labels was clear as well, and is likely to still be the case, although the study was carried out over 30 years ago.

Weaknesses

- The pseudo-patients said that they heard voices, a standard symptom of schizo-phrenia, so it is perhaps not surprising that they were considered to have schizophrenia. (This does not, however, explain why the patients were not sub-sequently realised to be sane, unless each hospital was being cautious). It is perhaps equally unsurprising that pseudo-patients were wrongly identified in study 2 — staff were wrongly informed that some would be presenting them-selves for treatment. These 'lies' are likely to have guided the results and this means the studies were not natural and, to that extent, not valid.
- In the 30 years since the study was carried out, institutions have changed their working practices considerably and there is a great deal more emphasis on care in

the community, so it might be wrong to conclude that mental illness is still hard to diagnose.

Goldstein (1988)

Goldstein's study is chosen here both because it is about schizophrenia and because she draws on secondary data, the use of which is discussed in the methodology section of this chapter. Her results also illustrate the use of levels of significance and show that many different factors need to be considered when studying mental illness. The study focuses on problems of validity and reliability in the diagnosis of mental disorders, a further focus of this chapter. Finally, it is an illustration of a longitudinal study.

Study hint Note how these studies in detail can be used as examples for many different methodological issues. Use these studies as examples of such issues to show your understanding and to illustrate answers.

Background

This study looks at the question of whether schizophrenic women have a less severe experience than schizophrenic men. It was carried out in 1988, which is an important fact when considering the results, particularly as Goldstein focuses on how DSM-II might have been less precise with regard to diagnosis than DSM-III, which in turn suggests that the current DMS-IV-TR is likely to be different again. However, the conclusions of the study give useful information about issues surrounding diagnosis, gender, social factors and mental health, as well as methodological issues, so the fact that it was carried out over 20 years ago does not make it less worthwhile to study.

Goldstein explains that there are said to be gender differences with regard to schizophrenia in family history, symptom expression, cause of the illness, treatment response and brain abnormalities. She points out that many studies of schizophrenia fail to consider gender differences, and that knowing about gender differences might inform discussion about the illness. Where studies have considered gender differences they have not all looked at the illness from its outset. Goldstein points out that if women have a less severe experience of schizophrenia, they might not be in the sample if the illness is studied some time after the first diagnosis, and that this might mask gender differences. The last point concerns validity — if people with schizophrenia are studied some time after they were first diagnosed and hospitalised this would exclude certain types of schizophrenia or exclude some women. In such cases these studies are not valid if they claim to be schizophrenia studies.

Before carrying out her own study, Goldstein looked at 21 longitudinal studies following patients from first admission; only one showed no gender differences at outcome. In general, studies show that women with schizophrenia experienced fewer re-hospitalisations, shorter hospital stays, better social and work functioning and less severe outcomes. At that time most studies used DSM-II to diagnose schizophrenia and Goldstein suggested that DSM-III would give a different diagnosis for less severe cases. For example, in some cases affective disorder rather than schizophrenia would be diagnosed. This shows that there can be validity problems with diagnosis.

Aims

The aim of the study was to see if there were gender differences with regard to the re-hospitalisation of people with schizophrenia and to the lengths of their hospital stays. The aim was also to look at social factors, mainly factors present before diagnosis, to see if they had an impact on the course of the disorder with regard to gender. Goldstein also aimed to look at DSM-II and DSM-III diagnosis to see if there were differences and to test the DSM for validity and reliability.

Procedures

Sample

The study looked at gender differences in schizophrenic patients diagnosed using DMS-III, who were in the early stages of the disorder and were followed for 10 years. The data were collected in the mid-1970s at a private psychiatric teaching hospital in New York. Patients chosen for the study were those who, between 1972 and 1973:

- had a hospital diagnosis of schizophrenia or acute schizophrenia on admission and on discharge, using DSM-II
- had a hospital stay of less than 6 months
- expected to return to live with their families
- had no other issues with regard to mental health (e.g. brain abnormality)
- had no drug or alcohol misuse
- were aged 18 to 45

Re-diagnosis

Patients were re-diagnosed using DSM-III. The hospital records gave detailed histories for the re-diagnosis and a single blind technique was used, where the psychiatrist was blind to the hypothesis. Goldstein, however, also carried out the re-diagnosis and, since she was not blind to the hypothesis, two other experts were used to undertake a diagnosis of a random sample of the patients to test for reliability. All of the women and some of the men were re-diagnosed. Only some of the men were chosen because out of a random sample of 25 males and 25 females it was found that more than a third of the women were mis-classified compared with one in ten of the men. Out of the original 199 patients who had schizophrenia, acute schizophrenia or schizoaffective disorder according to DSM-II, 169 met the DSM-III criteria for schizophrenia, schizophreniform disorder or schizoaffective disorder.

> **Study hint** You could use this evidence when considering the reliability of the DSM, even though you are considering DSM-IV-TR. You could also use this evidence when considering methodology and testing for reliability.

Testing for reliability of the re-diagnosis

Four males and four females were chosen randomly for the two experts to diagnose, to test for reliability. The experts were given copies of the case histories with names removed and any other information about diagnosis removed. There was a 0.80 agreement and only one case of disagreement with Goldstein's diagnosis. That one case was where Goldstein had diagnosed schizoaffective disorder (depressed) and the expert had diagnosed schizophrenia. However, the expert had said she could not rule out schizoaffective disorder (depressed), so it was thought that the diagnoses were reliable.

Features of the sample

The study looked at first-time admissions and found 52 of them. However, this was thought to be quite a small number for the study, so Goldstein then added those who had had one previous hospitalisation (38 of them), giving a sample size of 90 out of the 169 patients. The sample had a mean age of 24. All had a high level of education, 75 patients had never married, and 97% (87 out of the 90 patients) were non-Hispanic white and middle class.

The diagnoses of the sample included:
- schizophrenia paranoid: 33 (37%)
- schizophrenia non-paranoid: 33 (37%)
- schizophreniform disorder: 13 (14%)
- schizoaffective disorder depressed or manic type: 11 (12%)

Males and females did not differ much in terms of age, education, religion or class but they did differ in job status, with more females in white-collar jobs and employed.

Gathering information about the disorder

The study gathered information about symptoms, functioning before the diagnosis (premorbid functioning) and the course of the illness.

Symptoms

Symptoms were rated by trained interviewers using specially developed questions. They looked at hallucinations, formal thought disorder, paranoia, grandiosity, inappropriate affect (feelings) and behaviour, isolation, withdrawal, anxiety, depressive mood, somatic (physical) complaints, dependency, impulsivity, inability to function, obsessive thoughts and behaviour, and agitation. These give an idea of the characteristics of schizophrenia and related disorders.

Premorbid functioning

Premorbid functioning (before the onset of the illness) was measured by a questionnaire dealing with isolation, peer relationships, and interests from the ages of 6–13 and 14–20. Overall ratings for premorbid functioning were then found. Functioning was also measured by employment and marital status.

Course of the illness

The course of the illness was operationalised by the number of re-hospitalisations and lengths of stay in hospital. Data were obtained over a 10-year period, ending in

1983, with results considered at the 5-year and 10-year stages of the study. Statistical information about re-hospitalisations and lengths of stay were obtained from the New York State Department of Mental Health (secondary data).

Results

The research question was whether men had a higher mean number of re-hospitalisations and longer stays in hospital over the 10-year period of the study than women. It was found that they did. Schizophrenic women had a significantly lower mean number of re-hospitalisations and shorter stays in hospital from 1973 to 1983 than men. The effect is even stronger if the 5-year period is looked at.

Table 5.8 Re-hospitalisation and lengths of hospital stays in a 5-year and 10-year follow-up of 58 male and 32 female schizophrenic patients

Outcomes	Mean	Level of significance
Number of re-hospitalisations		
0–5 years		
Male	1.40	0.0001
Female	0.59	
0–10 years		
Male	2.24	0.03
Female	1.12	
Length of hospital stays in days		
0–5 years		
Male	267.41	0.009
Female	129.97	
0–10 years		
Male	417.83	0.04
Female	206.81	

The **levels of significance** in Table 5.8 show that the findings were significant in all cases, sometimes strongly significant. For both the measures (number of re-hospitalisations and lengths of stay in hospital in days), males had higher numbers than females. This was the case both at 5 years and at 10 years.

To explain the effect of gender over the first 5 years more testing was carried out using complex statistical tests so that different factors could be analysed. The researcher looked at the effects of premorbid functioning and social functioning, as well as the effect of diagnosis, to see if subtypes of schizophrenia affected the findings.

It was found that 13% of the gender effect on re-hospitalisation was due to premorbid functioning. However, premorbid functioning only accounted for 4.3% of the effect of gender on length of stays. Social functioning accounted for the gender effect with regard to re-hopsitalisation only 4.2% more than if premorbid effects were looked at alone. However, with regard to length of stays, social functioning explained 11.3% more of the length of stays than premorbid factors alone. So both premorbid factors and social functioning seemed to be involved in the gender differences to different extents, depending on whether length of stays in hospital or number of re-hospitalisations is looked at.

Goldstein then looked at psychotic and affective (emotional) symptoms to see if different subtypes of schizophrenia affected the gender differences in the findings. They controlled for premorbid history and social functioning and found that clinical status (diagnosis) explained only 1.2% more of the effect of gender on 5-year re-hospitalisations. This was 4.8% more with regard to length of stays.

Conclusions

Females with schizophrenia experienced fewer re-hospitalisations and shorter lengths of stay over a 5- and 10-year period than males. The gender difference is strong enough even when DSM-III (more stringent than DSM-II) was used, even given the relatively small sample. Gender differences seemed to start early in the disorder and premorbid functioning accounted for 50% of the effect of outcome if a 1-year observation was done, though only 1.9% on a 10-year outcome. This means other factors become more prominent than premorbid functioning as the illness progresses. Early studies found that schizophrenic males had poorer premorbid histories than women and the premorbid history was linked with poorer outcomes. This study suggests that schizophrenic males have poorer outcomes than females.

Evaluation of Goldstein (1988)

Strengths

■ Another study carried out in Germany using a larger sample (Angermeyer et al., 1987) produced the same findings, which is evidence to support Goldstein. In addition, her findings supported the many findings that she cites herself, showing that women with schizophrenia in general have a less severe experience than do men.

■ Having other evidence that supports the findings suggests that it is valid to say that there are gender differences in the course of schizophrenia and that premorbid factors appear to be implicated.

■ The study is evidence for the reliability of DSM-III, which suggests that the DSM is useful. Reliability of the hypothesis was checked (two experts who were blind to the hypothesis checked Goldstein's diagnoses).

Weaknesses

■ The sample's age limit of 45 might have affected the findings. Some studies show that the onset of schizophrenia for about 9% of women is after the age of 45 and that this is not the case for men. Late onset for women also tends to involve more paranoia than early onset for males or females. This means the course of schizophrenia for women might be less severe *only* for women under the age of 45.

■ The study used a relatively small sample of people from a limited area (around New York) and a similar cultural background (most were non-Hispanic white). The study was carried out in the 1970s and 1980s using DSM-III. These are limitations that might prevent generalisation to all schizophrenic patients.

Brown et al. (1986)

Brown et al. looked at factors involved in depression and considered only women. They used interviewing to find out how self-esteem and support factors affected the development of depression.

Background

Depression is usually measured using a life-event score rather than looking at a specific life event, and data are usually gathered from the respondent using a standard questionnaire. However, data from semi-structured interviews with a researcher suggest that specific life events are significant in the development of depression. In particular, it is claimed that life events with a severe long-term threat or entailing major difficulties that last 2 years or more can bring about depression. However, only a minority develop depression in such circumstances, suggesting the need to consider vulnerability factors: what causes one person and not another to develop depression in response to the same life event?

Previous research has suggested that vulnerability factors include low self-esteem, lack of close relationships and a woman's relationship with her husband. However, some studies (e.g. Lewinsohn et al., 1981) suggest that self-esteem is not low before depression — it becomes low after the onset of depression, in which case low self-esteem cannot be a cause of depression. When studies look at social support they do not often distinguish core support from general social support, although they show that, in general, social support can protect against depression.

Brown et al. considered such issues and chose to use detailed questioning and investigator-based judgements rather than questionnaires, so that they could find some depth and detail in the data. They chose to look at self-esteem and support factors before the onset of depression in order to investigate causation and they chose to separate social support into two areas: wider social networks and core support/core relationships.

One feature of studies into depression is that they tend to be cross-sectional and to look at depression once it has arisen. When someone is asked after the onset of depression what life events they encountered before they became depressed, the data they give might be affected by the depression. Longitudinal studies that follow a person and gather data about their lives *before* they develop depression are necessary, so that possible causes of developing depression can be identified.

Brown et al. used a **prospective design** so that depressive episodes would not affect the data. They decided on two periods for data collection: 'Time 1' (before any depression) and 'crisis support' (at the time of the depression and afterwards). They took measures at both these times, which were 1 year apart.

Hypotheses

There were a number of hypotheses, including:

- the existence of crisis support protects against the onset of depression, even if there is low self-esteem and lack of general support
- lack of support and low self-esteem are vulnerability factors and they increase the risk of depression given a later provoking agent
- support from a husband, partner or other close relationship (at Time 1 or at the time of crisis) will relate to a reduced risk of depression

Procedure

The study took place in Islington, North London. Women whose husbands were in a manual occupation, who had at least one child under 18 living at home, and who were aged between 18 and 50 were sent a letter by their GP asking if they would be willing to take part in the study. Women who fitted the criteria and all single mothers (who were included because they feature highly in women developing depression) were put into a sample. From this sample a number were randomly chosen for the study. In total, 435 women were found; 91% of them (395) were involved in the first part of the study.

The first part had two phases.

- At first contact (Time 1) measures of self-esteem and personal ties were measured. Psychiatric history was also collected at this point.
- The second phase (12 months later) collected data about any onset of psychiatric disorder in the 12 months following the first contact. Measures of life-event stress and social support were also taken.
- The measures were carried out carefully and by experienced interviewers. There were tests for reliability, with 60 women being interviewed intensively and 21 used in a reliability study. Of these 21, eleven were seen by two interviewers and ten were rated by a second person using tapes of the original interviews. Satisfactory inter-rater reliability was found.

Results

In all, 353 women agreed to a follow-up interview at the end of the year (89% of the original sample). Forty-two of the remaining participants were not followed up and of these, three had moved abroad and two refused because of illness. There were 50 cases of depression at first contact out of the 353 women who agreed to a follow-up interview, so they were excluded. Therefore 303 women were interviewed and their data analysed to see if there was onset of depression over the 12 months after first contact. About half of them (150) had had a severe event or major difficulty in the 12-month follow-up period after the first contact and 32 of the women had the onset of depression.

Life events and onset of depression

Of those who had developed depression in the 12-month follow-up period, 91% (29 out of 32) had experienced a severe event in the 6 months before the onset of depression (involving a loss, failure or disappointment). This compared with 23% of the women with no onset of depression who had experienced a severe event in the 6 months before the interview.

Self-esteem and the onset of depression

Of those who had a provoking agent (life event), 33% of those who developed depression had negative evaluation of self and 13% did not. Table 5.9 shows the relationship of those with negative evaluation of self and those without it set against those with a provoking agent (major life event) and those without one.

Table 5.9 *Vulnerability and onset of depression looking at negative evaluation of self and provoking agent*

Negative evaluation of self	Provoking agent	
	Yes (% of those with onset)	No (% of those with onset)
Yes	33% (18 out of 54)	4% (1 out of 27)
No	13% (12 out of 96)	1% (1 out of 126)

Table 5.9 shows that many more of those participants with a provoking agent developed depression than those without one. It also shows that people with negative evaluation of self were more likely to develop depression following a provoking agent. Those without negative evaluation of self were less likely to develop depression, even in the presence of a provoking agent. Just one person developed depression without a provoking agent and without negative evaluation of self.

Social support

The majority of women with core crisis support (92% or 85 out of 92) saw it as helpful and there was no difference in their perception of support being helpful whether they developed depression or not. It is interesting that where a woman said she had confided in a close tie (core support) at first contact, but not at crisis support and so felt let down, 42% (14 out of 33) developed depression. Of those who had had no support either at first contact or at crisis, 44% (4 out of 9) developed depression.

Conclusions

In general those who were married or had a close tie had a lower chance of the onset of depression, although if they had confided in their husband and were then let down at crisis by not having such support, then the risk of the onset of depression increased. This sort of result clearly shows the complexity of social support situations, where support is given and expectations are aroused but not fulfilled, and someone feels let down. Of course, this is not just about support from a husband, because he might be involved in the situation. An example is a miscarriage or an unplanned pregnancy, where the husband would be involved but is unable to give support. It is possible that self-esteem is an internalisation of social support and that lack of support lowers self-esteem, which is why negative evaluation of self also relates to the onset of depression. A provoking agent seems to be necessary for the onset of depression in most cases.

Evaluation of Brown et al. (1986)

Strengths

- The interviews, both at Time 1 and at crisis support (12 months later) gave the in-depth and detailed data that were required for the analysis of such complex inter-related concepts as self-esteem, core social support and major life events.
- There was inter-rater reliability, which strengthens the results arising from the data.
- The data were likely to be valid, as they were gathered carefully by trained interviewers using a semi-structured interview, allowing detailed information to be explored.
- Sampling was carefully carried out by contacting all eligible women and then carrying out random sampling. This meant that all the women had an equal chance of being chosen, which removes a source of bias.

> **Study hint** If you need to evaluate semi-structured interviews, such as in the final section for your course on issues and debates, use Brown et al. (1986) as an example of their purpose and usefulness.

Weaknesses

- It was hard to separate out the concepts that were scored as numbers and then percentages, because qualitative data were in some cases 'reduced' to quantitative data. For example, the presence or lack of support from a husband at crisis point seemed easy to assess, but then it was shown that such lack of support meant, at least in some cases, that the husband was part of the situation rather than a bystander.
- This was a study of working-class women with at least one child still at home; generalising the findings to all women might not be possible.

Examination-style questions

1 Describe one study of schizophrenia that you have studied in detail. *(6 marks)*

2 Outline the procedure of Rosenhan (1973). *(5 marks)*

3 You have examined two studies in detail, one that looked at schizophrenia and one that focused on another mental disorder. With regard to those two studies, compare them in terms of their methodology. *(6 marks)*

Extension question

Describe and evaluate two studies, one that looks at schizophrenia and one that looks at another mental health disorder. In your answer, focus on both validity and reliability. *(12 marks)*

Key issues

In this section you need to be able to describe one key issue in clinical psychology using the areas covered in this chapter. Suggested key issues include understanding a mental health disorder, supporting someone at home who has a mental health disorder, supporting someone at work who has a mental health disorder, and the way mental illness is portrayed in the media. When choosing a key issue, bear in mind that the practical — which is to develop a leaflet — is related. Therefore, you should choose a key issue about which you would like to develop an information leaflet for a particular audience. With this in mind, and taking into account the material in the content section of this chapter, the issue discussed below is 'understanding a mental health disorder'. Unipolar depression has been chosen, as it is known as the 'common cold' of mental disorders and the audience for the leaflet can, therefore, be a broad one. Other issues are briefly outlined in the online resources supporting this textbook.

Understanding unipolar depression

This chapter has explained unipolar depression in depth, so refer to pp. 257–67 to review your understanding of this area. You need to know enough about it to describe the key issue. Although you will already know the material from your studies of the content section, prepare a description of the material as a key issue. For example, focus on people with unipolar depression and their need to recover, as well as, perhaps, society's need to help people with such a disorder.

Practical: preparing a leaflet

You will have your own ideas about how to develop a leaflet and some ideas are offered here for you to refer to. The aim of planning and preparing a leaflet is to help you understand more about the key issue and to relate it to individuals in daily life, rather than studying it solely as an academic issue. Clinical psychology looks at real human problems and real situations. You will probably remember the material better and understand it more if you can relate it to particular individuals with mental health difficulties. You must use secondary data and focus on a particular audience to whom your leaflet is addressed. It is suggested that you include:

- definitions of terms, including unipolar depression
- symptoms of depression
- features of depression
- two explanations of depression — including some strengths and weaknesses of these explanations
- possible treatments for depression
- one or more case studies of people with depression
- self-help suggestions
- some pictures or diagrams

You could choose as your audience people who think they have unipolar depression, people just diagnosed with unipolar depression, and/or people who live with someone with unipolar depression. Just one of these audiences would be best, unless your leaflet is informative enough to be suitable for all three.

You should add a separate commentary about your leaflet, explaining:

- who the audience is
- why decisions about content were made
- what outcomes are intended

Include reasons for choosing that audience and how the choice affected the planning and design of the leaflet, as well as what was included. Consider the alternative audiences you could have chosen, and explain why you did not. You should mention your reasoning for choosing the material you use (space available, for example). Explain why you chose particular symptoms and the features of those symptoms. You should also comment on why you chose explanations of symptoms and how much depth you chose to go into about them. If you chose to include treatments, comment on why those treatments are appropriate and whether or not you gave contact details for the reader to seek further support. You also need to comment on the level of language you used, and how you defined any technical terms.

If you set out the outcomes then you will find it easier to comment on whether you felt that you achieved them. Be critical of the leaflet. Was there too much information? Was it written at the right language level? Was the leaflet interesting? Would anyone pick it up and want to read it?

Examination-style questions

1 Describe a key issue within clinical psychology, using the areas covered in this chapter. *(5 marks)*

2 When studying clinical psychology you will have prepared a leaflet about a key issue in an area you have studied. Answer the following questions based on your work in producing the leaflet:

(a) Outline the key issue. *(2 marks)*

(b) Outline the audience for your leaflet. *(3 marks)*

(c) Why did you choose that audience? *(3 marks)*

(d) What was the aim of your leaflet? *(2 marks)*

(e) What format did your leaflet take? *(3 marks)*

(f) Outline two limitations with your leaflet, given the audience you chose and the design decisions you made. *(4 marks)*

Extension question

Describe and evaluate your production of a leaflet for a key issue in clinical psychology. In your answer remember to explain the key issue that was the subject of the leaflet. *(12 marks)*

Chapter 6

Issues and debates

This chapter covers the synoptic part of the A2 course, which means that different areas of the course are drawn upon to consider the issues and debates that arise in psychology. For the most part it revisits what has been covered in the AS and A2 course. You are asked to consider the contributions that psychology can make both to society and to methodology, including the ethical issues involved in carrying out research in psychology (the use of animal and human participants). This part of the course involves revising the key issues you have already studied and ensuring that you are able to apply your learning to situations you may not have previously considered. It also includes consideration of debates such as the effect of cultural differences on behaviour, how far psychology is a science, the issue of using psychology in social control, and the consideration of nature and nurture when looking at causes of behaviour.

Summary of learning objectives

Definitions

You are required to know methodological terms (for example, observation, experiment, hypothesis) and evaluation terms (for example, validity, reliability) learnt during your course, as well as others to do with ethical guidelines, confidentiality and competence. A few terms that you may not have already defined are also used, including:

- content analyses
- ethnocentrism
- science
- social control
- practitioner

Contributions to society

You have to know two contributions from each of the five AS approaches you studied (social, cognitive, psychodynamic, biological and learning). You are also required to know one contribution from each of the two A2 applications you studied (from the four applications of criminological, child, health and sport) and one contribution from clinical psychology. In total, therefore, you need to be familiar with 13 contributions that psychology makes to society. Contributions can also be key issues, as well as relating to both an approach and an application, so you will be able to use your material efficiently.

Ethical issues

You are required to know five ethical guidelines that relate to using human participants and five ethical principles that relate to using animals in psychological research. You should then be able to describe and evaluate ethical issues when researching in psychology, as well as describe and evaluate two studies in terms of their ethical considerations.

Research methodology

The research methods you need to know about include the three types of experiment (laboratory, field and natural), observations, questionnaires, interviews, content analyses, correlations and case studies. You also need to be able to describe and evaluate one study for each of these research methods. You should ensure that you are able to plan a study yourself from a given context, including its aim, hypotheses, design, procedure, ethical considerations, analysis of results and evaluation. You must be able to evaluate psychological studies and in addition make suggestions for improving studies, such as changing the method, improving reliability or improving controls.

Key issues

You will have looked at one key issue from each of the five AS approaches, one from each of your two A2 applications and one from clinical psychology. You will therefore have looked at eight key issues and you need to revise these (or prepare others). Remember, key issues can also be contributions, so prepare material appropriately to organise your learning.

Debates

There are four main debates to consider in this section. The first is a new one and considers ethnocentrism — the belief that the particular culture to which you belong is superior to others, or represents 'normality'. If researchers hold such a belief it can lead to bias. This debate includes looking at cultural differences that might affect psychological research, including cross-cultural research. The second debate involves asking to what extent psychology can be said to be a science. You have already considered this when looking at issues of reliability, validity, credibility and objectivity. You must revise these issues and consider what the word 'science' means. The third debate involves looking at how psychological understanding is used in social control, including the use of drug therapy, token economy, classical conditioning and the power of the therapist. The fourth debate is about the relative roles of nature and nurture in shedding light on causes for behaviour.

New situations

You need to be able to use your knowledge and understanding of psychological studies and theories to explain a situation that you might not have come across before. This is to show full understanding and the ability to apply what you have learned.

Table 6.1 *Checklist of what you need to know for issues and debates and your progress*

I need to know about	Done	More work	I need to know about	Done	More work
Defining: content analysis, ethnocentrism, social control, token economy, practitioner			One study each for three types of experiment, observations, questionnaires, interviews, content analyses, correlations and case studies		
Defining: science, nature and nurture			Plan and evaluate psychological studies when given a context		
Two contributions each from social, cognitive, psychodynamic, biological and the learning approaches			One key issue from each of social, cognitive, psychodynamic, biological and the learning approaches		
One contribution each from two applications from criminological, child, health and sport			One key issue from two of criminological, child, health and sport psychology and one from clinical psychology		
One contribution from clinical psychology			Cultural issues in psychology		
Five ethical guidelines when using human participants			The debate about whether psychology is a science		
Five ethical principles when using animals as participants			Psychology and social control including drug therapy, token economy, classical conditioning and the power of the therapist		
Two studies that involve ethical issues			The nature–nurture debate		
The research methods: three types of experiment, observations, questionnaires, interviews, content analyses, correlations and case studies			Applying psychology to new situations		

An introduction to issues and debates

This chapter focuses on summarising material that you have covered over the duration of the course, asking you to revise what you have learnt and using and applying your understanding of psychology. If you wish to use the material on issues and debates chosen here then that will suit the purpose. Use of your own examples is, of course, welcomed.

You need to know the key issues associated with the contributions to society discussed below. You are also required to have knowledge of how psychological understanding can lead to social control procedures like drug therapy, token economy programmes and classical conditioning. Finally, when looking at social control, you need to consider the issue of who has power and who is in control (this could be the therapist).

The four debates may require you to learn some new material, including the research method of 'content analysis' if you have not previously covered it. Apart from this, you will be able to use what you have already studied. For example, you will have covered five ethical guidelines when learning about human participants and you will have prepared eight key issues.

Rather than introduce new material, this chapter often uses the same issues to cover the requirements of your course with regard to contributions to society, key issues and the required areas of social control. Where areas have already been covered, you will find that you are referred back to the relevant section. This means you can strengthen your understanding of one area of psychology, use this to inform other areas of your study of psychology and enable you to enrich your answer to different questions in the examination.

Contributions to society

A contribution to society is anything that has helped society to function well, for instance therapies to support those with mental disorders, ideas for helping people to live in harmony and information about how to control members of society whose antisocial behaviour adversely affects others.

Make sure that you know your information in sufficient detail and can both describe and evaluate the contributions you have chosen. The following sections cover all five AS approaches (each requires two contributions) and all four of the A2 applications (though you will only need contributions from two of them), plus clinical psychology. You need to know 13 contributions in all.

> **study hint** Remember not to focus only on the issue. However, when answering a question on contributions to society, you should conclude any answer with a sentence explaining how the issue you are using contributes to society.

Social psychology

The two contributions chosen are social psychology's explanations for prejudice and for blind obedience.

Helping to reduce prejudice

Social identity theory (Tajfel) explains that people form 'in-groups' and 'out-groups' (such as football teams). One aspect of categorising oneself as part of an in-group is to publicly identify with the group, its members and its norms (for example, by wearing team kit). In order to raise self-esteem an individual will want to see their in-group favourably (for instance, regarding your team as the best) and will tend to look down on any out-groups. The word used to describe this denigration and hostility is **prejudice**.

Another explanation for prejudice that you may have studied is that it stems from realistic conflict (Sherif). Not only do those in an in-group show hostility to out-group members, but the groups tend to be in conflict as well (for instance, the football league). This realistic conflict also fosters prejudice. Social identity theory would suggest that breaking down barriers between in-groups and out-groups would reduce prejudice. Realistic conflict theory suggests that working towards what is called a 'superordinate' goal, which means a goal that everyone has to work together to achieve, is the way to reduce prejudice (such as when football players get together to play for their country and fans then come together to support their country's team). Prejudice — and its resulting conflicts, ranging from football hooliganism to genocide — is something that a society wants to reduce, for both economic and humane reasons, so any theory that suggests a method of reducing people's prejudices is making a contribution to society.

> **AS link** You covered social identity theory in your AS course (pages 54–57) and you might also have covered realistic conflict theory and/or learned about Sherif's Robbers Cave study.

Table 6.2 *Evaluation of explanations for prejudice leading to suggestions for its reduction*

Strengths	Weaknesses
• Studies looking at prejudice (such as Tajfel's and Sherif's studies listed for your AS course) tend to use an experimental method (either laboratory or field) and so tend to have reliability because of the clear controls and the fact that they are replicable.	• Taking one aspect of prejudice such as being in a group means reducing a complex social interaction rather than looking at the whole experience of being prejudiced or being discriminated against. Experiments tend to take a **reductionist** view by necessarily focusing on one aspect so they are not likely to capture the whole explanation of the cause of prejudice. This means findings may not be useful for suggesting ways of reducing prejudice.
• Social identity theory and social conflict theory are not incompatible. Sherif found that the two groups of boys in his well-known Robbers Cave study denigrated one another even before there was any competition, which supports Tajfel's claims.	• When studies take a reductionist view they are likely to lack validity because they do not study the 'real' situation or behaviour. For example, Tajfel's studies used artificially formed groups, which suggests the findings would lack validity.

Explaining blind obedience

Milgram's well-known work looking at obedience (1963) has led to understanding that people will obey orders as agents of society and will then do things that cause them moral strain. Hofling et al. (1966) found the same behaviour. They used a fake doctor to telephone real nurses in their real hospital setting. All but one of the

22 nurses was prepared to administer an apparently dangerous dose of a drug to a patient, on being told to do so over the phone by a doctor they did not know.

Two decades after Milgram's study, Meeus and Raaijmakers (1986) also found that their participants obeyed an instruction to make stressful remarks when someone was, they thought, applying for a job. It seems that people act as agents to authority figures and obey instructions, even when to do so goes against their usual behaviour and understanding of what is right. In Abu Ghraib prison in Iraq in 2004, for example, US soldiers displayed abusive behaviour towards Iraqi prisoners. There was an outcry and a court case was held to try the soldiers involved. Social psychology had by then shown that people *do* blindly obey authority. Zimbardo, who had carried out studies on the relationship of obedience and brutality, was involved in the court case to explain that it was the situation that had caused the US soldiers to act so brutally, not their personality. The argument was lost: the court did not agree that the soldiers bore no responsibility for their brutal behaviour, but perhaps Zimbardo's argument had carried some weight. Social psychology contributed to the defence of soldiers who had seemingly gone beyond their duty, though ethical and moral arguments about responsibility remain.

Explore If you are not familiar with the Abu Ghraib situation look it up to see what was done to the prisoners and also to find the outcome of the court case. You could also research the notorious massacre in the village of My Lai in Vietnam (1968).

Table 6.3 *Evaluation of explanations for blind obedience*

Strengths	Weaknesses
• The three studies mentioned above (Milgram, Hofling et al. and Meeus and Raaijmakers) all use experimental methods, with two of them using laboratory experiments. There are therefore strong controls over extraneous variables and the studies are replicable. Indeed, Meeus and Raaijmakers to a large extent replicated Milgram's studies. The findings are likely to be reliable.	• Meeus and Raaijmaker's study had similar findings to Milgram's but it could be said that the Netherlands is not markedly different from the USA, so generalising findings to a culture that shows significant differences — such as a collectivist culture — might not be appropriate.
• Meeus and Raaijmakers's study was in the Netherlands and over 20 years later than Milgram's, so as they also found blind obedience it appears that findings of such studies can be generalised across different cultures.	• Milgram put forward the agency theory to explain obedience and Zimbardo suggested obedience comes from the situation. Other theories of obedience include theories of social power. So there have been different explanations of obedience, which might affect how theories are used to contribute to society.

Explore Look up the different psychological theories and explanations for obedience, so that you have more to add to the discussion about how such explanations contribute to society.

Cognitive psychology

The two contributions chosen are how understanding of eyewitness memory has contributed to the questioning of eyewitness testimony and the related issue of the use of the cognitive interview to elicit information from witnesses.

Understanding problems with eyewitness memory

If you have studied criminological psychology you will have looked at three studies of eyewitness memory, including the study of Loftus and Palmer (1974), which is covered later in this chapter as an example of a laboratory experiment, as well as in Chapter 1. You may also have looked at Yuille and Cutshall's study (1986), which contradicts Loftus and Palmer's study.

Elizabeth Loftus has carried out many studies in the area of eyewitness memory. Her studies often require participants to watch a film of something happening. In the 1974 study the film involved a car accident; other studies have been about cars at stop signs and scenery in a film. Following the film, participants are asked to complete a questionnaire containing one or more 'leading' questions. The idea is to see to what extent misleading information affects someone's memory of an event. Loftus found that central information was reasonably well recalled but that more peripheral information could be affected by how questions were asked.

Yuille and Cutshall (1986) carried out a field study interviewing people who had witnessed a robbery. They found that the witnesses' memories remained reasonably accurate even after some time had passed, which goes against Loftus's findings. Yarmey has also studied eyewitness memory (2004), finding out that people think eyewitnesses will be better than they often prove to be. These findings about eyewitness memory contribute to how questions are asked in court as well as to how much weight should be placed on witness testimony, considering the possible unreliability of their memory.

If you studied criminological psychology you will have looked at studies of eyewitness testimony. Use information from these both to discuss the contribution to society and to discuss eyewitness testimony as a key issue.

Table 6.4 *Evaluation of how far eyewitness memory is understood*

Strengths	Weaknesses
• Studies in the area of eyewitness memory tend to be experiments, which have good controls of extraneous variables and clearly study an **independent variable** and how it affects a **dependent variable**. Such studies have reliability. This is also evident when it is considered how much their findings support one another.	• Yuille and Cutshall (1986) studied the memory of real witnesses using interviewing and found that their memories were not affected by questioning. Their study suggests that the experiments that studied the same area did not have valid findings.
• Courts have taken a long time to accept psychological evidence that suggests that eyewitness memory is unreliable, partly because experimental evidence is seen as lacking validity. However, there are guidelines now (with regard to line-up procedures, for example), so the findings have been applied. It seems that the findings are now accepted as both valid and reliable, as well as generalisable and objective.	• Ethically it is hard to study the memories of real witnesses: any further questioning by researchers might affect their memories and, therefore, the case. Also, the event may have been traumatic and therefore unacceptably distressing for a witness to go over it all again.

The use of a cognitive interview to elicit correct information

Issues around eyewitness memory include factors likely to affect what people remember when they witness an incident, such as how the presence of a weapon is focused upon over everything else. Loftus has found that what happens between the witnessed incident and the eyewitness being asked to recall it also affects memory. Loftus and Palmer (1974) have shown that leading questions can affect recall. Loftus has also shown that other factors can affect an eyewitness's account of what they have seen, including the length of time of the incident and the length of time before recall.

Reconstructive memory theory (e.g. Bartlett, 1932) suggests that people might interpret what they see to make sense of it, and so add to what they recall or miss things out. It is likely, therefore, that the use of leading questions will alter the responses of a witness. In any case, memory is not like a tape recording and no witness statement is likely to retell what happened with complete accuracy.

Geiselman and colleagues (e.g. Fisher and Geiselman, 1992) developed the cognitive interview technique (CIT) to assist police in obtaining helpful and accurate information from eyewitnesses using information from psychological studies like Loftus's. For example, it is helpful to ask someone to imagine themselves back in the situation they were in as a witness and to start recalling as if in a different place. Witnesses can be helped to set the scene by using cues, such as how they were feeling or what they were planning to do before witnessing the event.

Table 6.5 *Evaluation of the use of the cognitive interview technique (CIT)*

Strengths	Weaknesses
• The CIT rests on strong experimental evidence such as Loftus's and findings are reliable, e.g. the effect of leading questions. Leading questions to witnesses are therefore avoided. • A technique was needed to overcome the issues of unreliability in eyewitness testimony. The cognitive interview was developed using research findings, so is a useful contribution to society. Such a technique was needed from both a moral and ethical point of view.	• Memon et al. (1997) found that asking a witness to recall from different places in the sequence of events, as a cognitive interview would, did not obtain any more information than asking for recall more than once from the start of the witness's involvement. • If memory is affected by existing schemata, as reconstructive theory suggests, then how a witness is questioned after the event will not lead to perfect recall as such recall is not possible — there will have been additions and omissions at the encoding stage.

The psychodynamic approach

Two contributions chosen are the use of psychoanalysis as a therapy and the related contribution of giving an explanation for dreaming.

The use of psychoanalysis as a therapy

Therapies are often instanced when we consider psychology's contributions to society; mental health issues are widespread in society and effective therapies can therefore provide widespread benefit. Economically, a mentally healthy society is more productive, and it could also be claimed that a society is more successful if its people are reasonably happy and fulfilled.

When Freud started out as a doctor he saw that mental disorders were not well understood or well treated. He drew on information from mentally ill, neurotic patients in his practice and built a therapy based on his theories and findings: psychoanalysis, which involves using techniques to trick the unconscious into revealing itself. Psychoanalysis works on the assumption that once unconscious thoughts are made conscious any neurosis will disappear, because finding the energy needed to repress harmful thoughts and desires holds the client back. Much of Freud's evidence for the power of the unconscious, the importance of dreams and the Oedipus complex comes from his in-depth study of Little Hans, which is covered later in this chapter.

During treatment, the psychoanalyst has to sit back from the client and allow them to talk freely about their dreams and their lives. The analyst offers interpretation, but only after sufficient information is available.

Table 6.6 *Evaluation of psychoanalysis as a therapy*

Strengths	Weaknesses
• The therapy is in-depth and thorough, taking time to explore the whole situation, including background, goals, concerns and fears of the individual. It is holistic in this sense (unlike drug therapy, for example, which targets biological aspects), which means a cure is more likely.	• Psychoanalysis rests on evidence from Freud, such as that we are largely governed by unconscious wishes and desires. Such desires are not scientifically measurable and Freud's methods have been said to be subjective and unreliable. This means the therapy is not evidence-based.
• There is evidence from studies (such as the meta-analysis of Bachrach) that psychoanalysis works with some people, such as those who can reflect on their actions and feelings with insight.	• The therapy is expensive and time-consuming because the client is required to attend analysis frequently during the week over many weeks. This means that if the therapy is accepted as useful only certain people can benefit.

> **Study hint**　Remember that you will need to prepare two contributions and one key issue for each approach, as well as evaluation of both the contributions. In this synoptic section you must draw on other areas of your course to make sure you have enough information (such as for an extended essay on the topic).

Explanations for the significance of dreaming

The psychodynamic approach explains that unconscious wishes and desires can be uncovered through analysis of dreams. Dream analysis as a therapy is explained in more detail in Chapter 5. Freud thought that the manifest content of dreams (which is the story that the dreamer recalls) hides a latent content. The latent content is hidden in symbols in the manifest content, and once decoded the symbols give information about unconscious wishes and desires. Once uncovered such unconscious thoughts become conscious and lose their power to influence a person's behaviour and guide their neurosis. According to the psychodynamic approach, therefore, decoding the meaning of dreams is important in treating mental health disorders.

In general, biological explanations for dreaming, such as the **activation synthesis theory**, rest on more evidence than Freud's theory of dreaming. Dreaming takes place during the period of sleep characterised by rapid eye movement (REM sleep), so it is clear when someone is dreaming. Animal studies have been carried out to try to identify the areas of the brain that are active during dreaming. The activation synthesis theory suggests that during dreaming the brain receives no sensory data or movement data to absorb but is still active. The active brain (activation) therefore attempts to make sense of (synthesis) random thoughts in the brain. Such theories help in the approach to treatment of sleep disorders. However, Freud's opposing theory — that dreams have meaning — also contributes to our understanding of sleep and mental health, and offers an alternative explanation.

AS link The debate about whether dreams have meaning is covered in the CD-ROM for the AS textbook and summarised briefly on page 215.

Explore Look up the activation synthesis theory of dreaming (Hobson and McCarley, 1977) — in particular, evidence for it such as Hobson's work with cats.

Table 6.7 *Evaluation of Freud's explanation of dreaming as a contribution to society*

Strengths	Weaknesses
• Freud's work with dreams has the same strength as his therapy psychoanalysis — he gathers a lot of in-depth qualitative information and focuses on them as an individual, taking a holistic view. This is a strength because the explanation is personal and more likely to be both valid and a help to someone.	• Activation synthesis, a biological explanation for dreaming, suggests that dreams do not have meaning. This theory is supported by more scientific evidence, because animal studies can be carried out, as can scanning.
• Freud offers an alternative explanation for dreams, which can explain recurring and upsetting dreams. Activation synthesis cannot explain recurring dreams — though they clearly occur. As the individual is more likely to find that recurring dreams cause anxiety, it might be useful to use Freud's explanation for dreaming for sleep disorders.	• Freud's evidence is not scientific because his concepts are not testable. For example, neither the manifest content nor the latent content of a dream can be tested. An analyst's interpretation is hard to dispute and hard to 'prove'.

Biological psychology

Biological psychology offers many different explanations of human behaviour that can help society to function well. Examples are explaining gender behaviour by looking at incorrect sex assignment and explaining autism by studying brain differences between autistic and non-autistic people. There are other contributions you could choose.

How Psychology Works

Unit 4

Understanding sex assignment and gender behaviour

The biological approach explains how genes provide a blueprint for many human physical (and possibly behavioural) characteristics. An XX pattern of sex chromosomes gives a female and XY gives a male. Research has found other patterns, such as XXY (Klinefelter's syndrome in boys) and XO (Turner's syndrome in girls). Genes trigger the production of hormones and hormones trigger male and female development.

Differences can also occur when hormones are not released 'normally'. During the development of a foetus, for example, secretion of Mullerian inhibiting substance (MIS, which prevents the growth of the uterus and fallopian tubes) might not be supported by androgen secretion (which stimulates the growth of male genitals), in which case the foetus will have neither male nor female internal features. Lack of MIS accompanied by androgen secretion can lead to the development of both male and female structures. Sometimes, though rarely, a baby can be wrongly assigned a sex at birth, and this can cause a great deal of distress for the individual as he or she develops. Understanding of such issues, and of syndromes like Klinefelter's and Turner's, can contribute to society by helping to shed light on the feelings of individuals who feel they are wrongly assigned. Biological solutions, such as the use of hormones, can help such individuals.

> **AS link** You will have studied genes and hormones in the biological approach, as well as how gender development is affected by biology. Both Klinefelter's syndrome and Turner's syndrome are explained in the AS book (pages 271–72).

Table 6.8 *Evaluation of the contribution of the biological approach to understanding sex and gender*

Strengths	Weaknesses
• There is a great deal of evidence about genes and hormones with regard to the development of the human foetus. Evidence comes from animals and from DNA testing of humans. Such evidence is scientific, objective and reliable. • Gene structure predicts the type of development and those with that development type do show the related gene structure: there is predictive validity.	• The biological approach focuses on how nature leads to gender behaviour. However, nurture also has an input and there is probably an interaction between the influence of nature and nurture. • Much gene research has been done using animals. Animals, though showing many similarities, are different from humans and perhaps it is not possible to generalise findings from animal studies to say they are true of humans.

Explaining autism using biological concepts

Autism is a condition that affects male children more than females. General features of autism include social withdrawal, an emphasis on systems and order, and sometimes an extraordinary talent often related to systems and order. For example, an autistic person can have outstanding mathematical, artistic or musical ability, although this does not apply to everyone with autism. Features that might suggest autism in an infant include a lack of eye contact, failure to smile or show affection and (as an older infant) a marked preference for repetitive activities. Some people are much less affected by their autism than others. Asperger's syndrome is at the milder end of the autistic spectrum.

One explanation for autism is that it is related to brain structure, in particular to what is thought of as an 'extreme male' brain. Male brains in general are less lateralised than female brains (this means that females use both sides of the brain more than males do) and produce less empathising ability. Females can have male brains and vice versa, which is why the expression 'male brain' is used here rather than 'males', but in general males have male brains and females have female brains. Simon Baron-Cohen has noted that autistic people seem to have an overemphasis on features that come from a male brain, including systemising ability and lack of empathy with others. Children with autism often require special schooling and need additional understanding and care. Society benefits from an understanding of autism through the availability of effective help for children and parents.

Explore The issue of a biological explanation for autism — that it comes from an extreme male brain — is covered as a developmental issue and a key issue in child psychology. Look up the work of Simon Baron-Cohen, in particular his idea that autism is related to the possession of an extreme male brain.

AS link Autism as an extreme male brain condition was explained in the AS book (pages 293–94).

Table 6.9 *Evaluation of a biological explanation of autism as a contribution to society*

Strengths	Weaknesses
• Scientific evidence can be gathered, for example using scanning techniques to see the different sizes of brain structures. Such research methods are reliable and objective. • The 'extreme male brain' explanation fits with many features of autism and other males (such as males having less empathising ability than females and focusing more on visuo-spatial tasks and systems). The explanation therefore appears to have some validity.	• Scientific study of brain structures is objective but also reductionist. Conditions like autism are complex, involving both nature and nurture issues. It is possible that there are environmental causes for autism and these can occur before birth or during development after birth. • The explanation does not obviously lead to therapy because brain structure is fixed, so the explanation is not as useful as an environmental one, which could suggest ways of improving environment to avoid autism.

The learning approach

The learning approach has made a clear contribution to society, not only through its explanations for behaviour but also through the development of therapies using its concepts. Whether or not a therapy works is a key issue for society, and therefore therapies have been chosen as the contributions to be considered here.

You will have studied one therapy from the learning approach within clinical psychology and one therapy using learning approach principles as part of your AS coverage. The two contributions covered in this section are systematic desensitisation using classical conditioning principles and token economy using operant conditioning principles. This is because you are likely to have covered both of these therapies during your course.

Systematic desensitisation to treat phobias

Classical conditioning principles start from the fact that a stimulus gives a reflexive response, for example a puff of air on the eyeball causing the eyelid to blink, or a hand flinching away from the touch of something hot. Fear can equally be an automatic response to certain stimuli, for instance enclosed spaces or sudden noises. Classical conditioning suggests that if another stimulus is paired with a stimulus that causes an automatic response, then that same automatic response will come to be elicited by the new stimulus. Such principles can explain how phobias are acquired and can also help to cure phobias. If someone has a fear response to enclosed spaces, they may 'learn' (through classical conditioning principles) to fear flying because the aeroplane is an enclosed space and one experience of flying has led to their association between flying and fear. The fear becomes a **phobia** if it prevents someone from flying when they need or want to.

AS link Classical conditioning is explained in the AS book (pages 325–27) and systematic desensitisation later in the same chapter (pages 332–35)

Explore Look up studies that have evaluated systematic desensitisation, such as Capafons et al. (1998).

Systematic desensitisation therapy for phobias works on two fronts. First, the person being treated is asked to write down a hierarchy of fears, for example from getting anxious on seeing a picture of an aeroplane to feeling high levels of fear when getting onto an aeroplane (i.e. they systematise their fears). The second part of the therapy is the 'desensitisation', which involves the person learning a relaxation response. At each stage of the hierarchy they have to relax and replace their fear response with a relaxation response. Gradually (systematically) they will remove their fear until they are relaxed about whatever is at the top of their hierarchy of fears, and the phobia is cured.

Table 6.10 *Evaluation of systematic desensitisation as a therapy and contribution to society*

Strengths	Weaknesses
• Capafons et al. (1998) showed that the therapy worked with fear of flying, and this is evidence for the success of the therapy, at least for phobias. • The therapy is ethical because the individual is involved in the therapy throughout. They devise their own hierarchy of fears and learn to relax in their own way. They have some control over the therapy, unlike other treatments such as the token economy programme for mental health issues.	• Classical conditioning principles on which systematic desensitisation rests come mostly from animal studies. As animals and humans are different it might not be fair to generalise from animal studies to humans (although classical conditioning features reflexive behaviour which is instinctive and not to do with problem-solving). • It is useful for those who can learn to relax and have enough insight into their fears to prepare a hierarchy of them. However, it seems to work mainly for specific phobias and is a therapy that is perhaps not likely to be useful for psychoses such as schizophrenia.

Token economy programmes to aid social control

Token economy programmes (see Chapter 5) can be used to help shape required behaviour, such as in mentally ill people or those in other places where control is desired, such as schools and institutions. Operant conditioning suggests that shaping can be achieved by gradually rewarding behaviour that is required and ignoring other behaviour. Token economy programmes offer tokens of some sort in exchange for required behaviour, which the individual can exchange for something that they desire (a reward). Staff work together to reward the same behaviour(s) and there is careful planning to make sure this happens. Such behaviour modification has been used for those with schizophrenia, offenders in institutions and also in schools (e.g. a 'gold star' system).

Clearly such a widely used application of learning theory contributes to society. It is also relatively cheap and easy to run, because there is a step-by-step programme that staff members can follow with little training. On the other hand, such programmes require careful initial planning and all members of staff have to be equally committed to make it work.

Table 6.11 *Evaluation of token economy as a contribution to society*

Strengths	Weaknesses
• Operant conditioning rests on evidenced-based theory. Animals have been used in many carefully controlled studies and the shaping of behaviour through rewards has been shown to work (e.g. Skinner's work). Such studies are objective and scientific and this means that the therapy rests on reliable evidence.	• There can be a problem when a person trained to behave in a required way goes into another situation, such as going back home if they are in an institution. Shaped behaviour does not always generalise to another situation, possibly because cues in the new situation trigger previously learned behaviours.
• Staff members in an institution can be trained to follow a token economy programme so specialists are not needed, reducing training costs and time. As long as the programme is clearly set out and thoroughly planned a trained therapist is not needed to implement it.	• Evidence comes from animal studies and it might not be possible to generalise findings of such studies to humans. Animals and humans are different in many ways, such as the fact that humans use problem solving and might not respond to rewards as animals do.

Application contributions

You need to know one contribution each from two of the four A2 applications. The following contributions are suggestions. The third contribution you need to know is from clinical psychology.

> **Study hint** Remember that in addition to the contributions, you will be required to prepare one key issue for each of your two chosen applications, as well as one key issue for clinical psychology. In this synoptic section you should draw on other areas of your course to make sure you have enough information (such as for an extended essay on the topic).

Criminological psychology: eyewitness memory

Eyewitness memory and its reliability has been explained earlier in this section as a contribution using concepts from cognitive psychology. Research on eyewitness memory can be used as a contribution and key issue from criminological psychology as well. Remember you need to be able to describe the contribution, describe it as a key issue, evaluate the contribution and explain the key issue using concepts and theories from the application. You should also prepare to use research methods and ethical issues in your explanations and `evaluation. For an evaluation of eyewitness memory as a contribution to society see Table 6.4 (p. 296).

Child psychology: explaining autism or the effects of daycare

One contribution from child psychology has been explained earlier in this section (the 'extreme male brain' explanation for autism). Autism was discussed in Chapter 2 and it was also suggested as a topic for the practical for child psychology. Another possible contribution from child psychology comes from research into daycare, which was also discussed in Chapter 2. Both contributions are briefly outlined here to help you to choose.

Explaining autism

You can use the 'extreme male brain' explanation for autism both as a contribution and a key issue. Remember you need to describe both the key issue and the contribution and to do this you might have to tailor your material to suit the use. You then need to be able to evaluate the contribution and to explain the key issue. Use concepts and theories from child psychology when evaluating, and consider ethical issues as well.

> **AS link**   This issue is also covered in the AS textbook, where it was chosen as a key issue for the biological approach (pages 293–94).

The effects of daycare

If parents are able to use daycare for their children then both parents can work. In economic terms it might therefore be seen as desirable for a society that as many people as possible are able to work. The issue for society is that if daycare leads to antisocial behaviour or affects a child's development negatively in other ways, then that too can be expensive for society, perhaps in terms of criminality. There are moral issues here for society with regard to producing well functioning adults. If you studied child psychology you will have covered research into daycare, including a study that supports daycare and one that suggests it has negative effects.

Research into the effects of daycare therefore contributes to society and the key issue is the debate as to whether daycare is good for a child or not. Make sure you can describe a contribution and a key issue with regard to daycare, as well as being able to evaluate the contribution and explain the key issue. Later in this chapter the study of daycare by Melhuish et al. (1990) is explained in more detail. Use this study when discussing daycare as a contribution and as a key issue.

Health psychology: drug therapy for addiction

If you studied health psychology you will have focused on substance misuse, which is a key issue for society. Research into substance misuse is a contribution. Chapter 3 looked at health psychology and explained how drug treatment can help someone to overcome addiction.

One of the studies for the application was Blättler et al. (2002). This team looked at whether using a methadone treatment programme for heroin addiction would also reduce an addict's use of cocaine. This and other studies suggest that being on a methadone programme can be successful in reducing both heroin and cocaine use. However, if the addict returns to or remains in a situation where peer groups and other environmental cues are present, this can prevent the addict from overcoming his/her addiction.

Such research contributes to society. The economic cost of drug addiction is high in terms of losing people who could work, providing treatment, and family pressures which can lead to ill health in other family members. There are also social, ethical and moral issues involved in overcoming drug addiction. Use the information in Chapter 3 to describe drug treatment both as a key issue for society and a contribution. Remember to prepare enough material to evaluate the contribution and explain the issue. When explaining the issue consider issues such as the research methodology used (e.g. Blättler et al. (2002) used interviewing) and ethical issues (such as the power society has over drug addicts in pressuring them to go for treatment).

Sport psychology: understanding good coaching

If you have studied sport psychology (Chapter 4) you will have covered more than one area that has contributed to, and is a key issue for, society. Sporting success is used to boost the self-esteem of society's members and to that end sport is encouraged in schools, for example to promote the values of working in a team. Good coaching can encourage effective team working, lead to suitable socialisation such as learning social norms and rules, and promote sporting success, which also benefits society through boosting in-group identification.

What makes a good coach? The reason this question is important for society is that sporting success boosts the self-esteem of society's members and leads to stronger identification with the in-group, which in this case is a particular culture or society. Social identity theory was discussed earlier in this section, and you should use this theory to explain how sporting success can lead to good in-group identification. Good coaching includes techniques such as goal-setting and using imagery techniques. Such techniques contribute to society by helping to improve coaching for better sporting performance. You will also have studied the inverted U hypothesis (the effects of levels of arousal on performance). If coaches are aware of such research and the related issues, they can take them into account when coaching. Chapter 4 discusses what makes a good coach, and the qualities and skills are summarised at the end of the chapter.

Sport psychology contributes to society in many ways. For instance, research findings and techniques from sport psychology (such as goal-setting) are used in areas of coaching other than sport, such as in business and people's personal lives.

You will have studied relevant areas, like motivation and personality, so use your knowledge here. Remember to prepare enough information with regard to your chosen contribution and key issue in sport psychology, so that you can describe both the contribution and the key issue, evaluate the contribution and explain, using research, the key issue.

Clinical psychology: token economy programmes

Clinical psychology covers treatments and therapies, so the two contributions for the learning approach that were explained above (systematic desensitisation and token economy programmes) fall within clinical psychology, as does psychoanalysis. As all three of these therapies have been covered earlier, both as contributions and key issues, they are not explained here.

You need to develop your understanding of the token economy programme as a therapy contributing to society. As with issues around eyewitness testimony, remember you need to be able to describe the contribution itself, describe it as a key issue, evaluate the contribution and explain the key issue using concepts and theories from the application. You should also prepare to use research methods and ethical issues in your explanations and evaluation. The token economy programme is explained in more depth in Chapter 5.

Ethical issues

This section describes five ethical guidelines for using humans as participants in psychological research, and five ethical principles when using animals. The ethical issues arising from the use of both humans and animals are then evaluated. Finally, two studies are described and then evaluated in terms of ethical considerations.

Guidelines and principles

Human participants

For the AS course you will have covered the five ethical guidelines of competence, consent, debrief, deceit and right to withdraw. These five guidelines are returned to here.

Table 6.12 *Summary of five ethical guidelines for using humans in psychological research*

Ethical guideline	Description	Evaluation/comment
Competence	Having the qualifications and ability to carry out the study safely and ethically or asking someone else about it.	Ethical committees now would check that someone is competent to carry out the study, so this guideline should be adhered to. Milgram showed competence by researching beforehand what others thought would happen.

Ethical guideline	Description	Evaluation/comment
Consent	Participants have to agree to take part and should be informed as far as possible so that consent is informed. Children and others tend to be special cases.	Often consent is not informed consent because telling a participant all about the study will mean the results will not be useful. If Milgram said the shocks were not real, for example, participants would not be obeying in a real sense.
Debrief	After the study a debrief is carried out to explain everything, and this can cover the problem with obtaining uninformed consent. The debrief should include explanation of the findings.	A debrief is difficult in a naturalistic observation if people are in a public place and not told about the study. They may not be contactable. Otherwise, however, debriefing should not be difficult. Milgram gave a thorough debrief to participants in his studies.
Deceit	Deceit is related to uninformed consent because often a study requires deception. Uninvolved people can be asked if they would mind being involved and from their responses the agreement of uninformed participants could be assumed (presumptive consent) — there are ways to ensure ethical practice even if there is deceit.	A debrief helps with deceit because participants can be informed about what has happened and if they do not agree to their results being used they can withdraw them. Prior consent (participants agree in general to take part without detail) or presumptive consent can contribute to ethical practice. Milgram deceived his participants in more than one way.
Right to withdraw	Participants should have the right to withdraw from a study at any time and must be told about it and reminded. They must also be able to withdraw their results at the end of the study.	It is not usually hard to give the right to withdraw, although naturalistic observations (where participants do not know they are being observed) do not allow the right to withdraw to be given. Right to withdraw the results is given in the debrief and, except for observations, is usually possible.

As well as ethical guidelines and principles there are general ethical issues involved in psychological research. For example, sometimes a study is carried out using a lot of deceit and not giving a clear right to withdraw (e.g. Milgram's). It is necessary to balance the benefit of the findings (to society, for example) against the ethical cost to the participants.

AS link   You will have covered these five ethical guidelines in the social approach (pp. 23–29), so review your learning. There are other ethical guidelines mentioned at AS. For example you will have looked at the issues of confidentiality and privacy when studying the psychodynamic approach (p. 176).

Explore   Look up some examples of other ethical guidelines, including guidelines on distress and the use of children.

Animal participants

The ethical principles laid down for using animals in psychological research are different from the guidelines governing participation of humans. The principles are not voluntary — a Home Office licence is required to carry out research with animals. The Animal and Scientific Procedures Act (1986), for example, sets out principles that must be followed.

Table 6.13 gives some of the guidelines needed when using animals in psychological (and other) research. Other guidelines include giving animals time to recover between experiments and acquiring the animals from approved sources.

Table 6.13	Summary of five ethical principles for using animals in psychological research	
Ethical principle	**Description**	
Care over caging and social environment	Any caging and/or social environment must be suitable for the species	
Avoiding discomfort and stress	Any stress and/or discomfort must be kept to a minimum	
Rules about the use of anaesthetics	Anaesthetics must be used appropriately by someone who knows about them	
Number of animals used	No more animals must be used than necessary	
Look for alternatives	Alternatives to using animals must always be sought, such as using humans or computer simulation	

Describing and evaluating ethical issues

Using human participants

For this section you need to know how to describe and evaluate ethical issues in research regarding humans.

Reasons for the existence of ethical guidelines

It has been recognised from the early years of the twentieth century that people taking part in psychological research need to be protected to ensure that they are not at risk of great distress or other traumatic experience. However, studies were still carried out that would now be frowned upon from an ethical point of view, for example Watson and Rayner's study of Little Albert in 1920 — they wished to instil a phobia in him, and frightened him in order to achieve this. Guidelines have since been strengthened to protect participants from this kind of stress.

Up until the 1970s, participants were known as 'subjects', for example Godden and Baddeley's study of divers and context-dependent memory (1975). It was then recognised that being the 'subjects' of a study gave participants no power or respect. As a result, guidelines like the right to withdraw were strengthened and it was agreed that the term 'participants' would be used. It is possible to argue, from a practical point of view, that, given the large number of participants required for the many different studies being carried out at any one time, the existence of protection ensures that people are more likely to agree to take part.

> **Study hint** The following discussion (of reasons for and against abiding by ethical principles using human participants, and for and against using animal participants) is all about *evaluation*.

> **Study hint** When making points about the ethics (or the methodologies) of studies it is useful to use an example. However, you must say exactly *how* that example illustrates the point you are making.

Reasons for going against ethical guidelines

Research into behaviour in a social setting, such as that by Milgram, Hofling and others into obedience, can be used in society to suggest reasons for obedience. Such findings can help to explain obedience in situations such as at Abu Ghraib prison in Iraq. Milgram's research in particular has been widely criticised for its dubious ethics but there is an argument to be made for his methods being justifiable if his findings are useful for society.

Many studies, in particular laboratory experiments, focus on an independent variable where there are at least two conditions. However, if the participants understand the conditions they may act accordingly, either to help the researcher towards the findings they expect or to hinder them. Either way, such effects come from demand characteristics — the idea that a participant will act differently if they know the purpose of the study. For example, if Milgram's participants 'gave' the shocks to Mr Wallace but knew the shocks were fake, they would not have been obeying the experimenter in the same sense as if they had believed the shocks to be real: their obedience would not have been blind obedience. The findings would not therefore be valid, as they would not be measuring what they claimed to measure. In practice, deceit is often needed to produce valid findings, which is a reason for going against ethical guidelines.

The comments on the ethical guidelines given in Table 6.12 (pp. 306–07) show why these often have to be ignored. A debrief is needed to put these unethical practices right.

Using animal participants

For this section you need to know how to describe and evaluate ethical issues in research regarding animals.

Ethical reasons for using animals

Things can be done to animals in the course of psychological research that cannot be carried out ethically with humans. For example, in various experiments in the 1950s and 1960s, Harry Harlow deprived monkeys of their mothers to see the effect on their development. Animal brains can be given ablations and lesions (tissue damage), helping to reveal the functions of different parts of the brain.

Photo Researchers/SPL

An infant Rhesus monkey with its cloth surrogate mother during an experiment by Harry Harlow into maternal deprivation

6

The idea, first put forward by Ryder (1970), that we ought to do everything we can to find out about and help our own (human) species can be used to support the use of animals in research. Singer (1976) criticised this argument on the grounds that humans are animals and that speciesism is like racism. Both speciesism and racism are ethical arguments.

A third reason in favour of using animals is that from the knowledge gained, animals themselves may benefit. For example, as a result of psychological research more information is revealed about their needs and habits so that zoos can provide better habitats and more suitable care. If animals can benefit, then perhaps the research is ethical.

AS link Check back to the biological approach, where practical and ethical advantages and disadvantages of using animals in research are explored (pp. 257–62).

Study hint When you discuss examples of the use of animals in research, you should refer only to examples from psychology (or possibly biology, if the studies relate to psychology). Do not use research related to medicine or testing cosmetics.

Ethical reasons against using animals

Animals in laboratory experiments are probably confined and in an unfamiliar environment, which is likely to cause them stress. This is why alternatives must always be looked for, such as studying animals in their natural environment. Surgical procedures may be used, which cause discomfort, so unless it is clear that the fewest possible number of animals has been used and that anaesthetic has been considered, then the discomfort might not be justifiable. The decision cube can be used in situations like this (see below).

There are people who object to any use of animals in research and who point to the fact that humans are animals and that animals should not be treated as objects for research any more than humans should. However, Grey (1987) has pointed out that starving animals in studies does not appear to cause them significant distress.

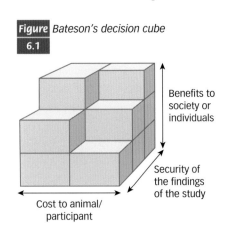

Figure 6.1 Bateson's decision cube

Benefits to society or individuals

Security of the findings of the study

Cost to animal/ participant

Cost–benefit analysis

Bateson (1988) suggested that researchers could use a 'decision cube' when deciding if an animal study is ethical. One dimension of the cube is the ethical cost to the animal participants. Another dimension is the benefit the findings could bring to society or individuals. Finally, there is the scientific dimension (whether the results will stand up to scrutiny with regard to the methodology): if there are flaws in a study and its findings cannot be relied upon, then ethically the study is hard to justify. Although this idea of a 'cost–benefit analysis' applies to animals, it also makes sense to consider it for humans.

Practical reasons for and against using animals

You do not need to consider practical reasons for and against using animals in this particular section but it is worth revising them briefly, so that you can separate ethical and practical reasons.

For

■ Animals are easily handled. This means that many can be studied if appropriate, and that any operations are manageable.

■ Some animals (e.g. mice) have similar brain areas and chromosome patterns to humans. As things can be done to animals (ethically and practically) that cannot be done to humans, animal studies are a practical choice.

■ In general, animals have a short gestation period so different generations can be studied quite quickly, which is useful when looking at the effect of genes on behaviour, for example. It also means that effects (for instance the effects of drug-taking) can be looked at over time and over generations.

Against

■ Animals are not exactly the same as humans — for example, monkeys are similar but do not use the same problem-solving skills and cannot use language in the same way. Rats have similar brain structures but clearly their behaviour is not driven by human cognition. This means that generalising findings of animal studies to say they are true of humans is not appropriate.

■ Areas for study using animals are often specific and reduced to certain behaviours or patterns, whereas humans have more complex experiences and behaviour.

■ Some areas that are studied using animals involve mental disorders, but the actual disorder cannot be induced (e.g. schizophrenia). It is therefore 'represented' by manipulating chemicals in the brain, for example. This is not likely to be measuring what it claims to measure, so the findings of such studies are not valid.

Two studies and their ethical considerations

In the research methods section that follows, examples of studies using each research method are described and evaluated. Two of these studies are briefly referred to here in terms of ethical evaluation. Make sure you can describe the studies you choose for this section in sufficient depth.

Hofling et al. (1966)

The study by Hofling et al. is a prescribed study for the social approach and you are likely to know it well by now. Hofling et al. arranged for 22 nurses in 22 hospitals to be phoned and ordered to give a dosage of a drug to a patient, when the dosage was over the recommended amount. The researchers also asked 22 other nurses whether they would obey such an order. All but one of the 22 nurses surveyed said they would not. However, 21 of the 22 ordered to do so over the phone went on to obey the instruction (they were stopped from actually administering the drug).

Evaluation of the ethics of Hofling et al. (1966)

Ethical strengths

- Nurses were stopped when they went to give the drug and they were then fully debriefed by an observer, so that they were not too distressed. The debrief followed ethical guidelines, because although there was deceit involved, an explanation was subsequently given.
- The study had strong practical applications, so any distress caused to participants might be justifiable, using a cost–benefit analysis. Hospitals found out that nurses would obey a doctor without question rather than refer to their professional training, so they knew there was an issue to address.

Ethical weaknesses

- The participant nurses were not asked if they consented to the study and to being a participant, so did not give consent, let alone informed consent. This can happen in a field study because natural (valid) behaviour is required, and if participants know about the study their behaviour is likely to be affected. The unethical point is that they did not consent.
- The nurses were studied while doing their job and they were asked to go against their training. This might have led to negative repercussions for them. In the event, 21 of the 22 nurses obeyed, so it is not likely that any single nurse would be criticised for obeying. However, if only one had obeyed and 21 disobeyed, the one nurse might have been put into a difficult position.

Melhuish et al. (1990)

Melhuish et al. carried out a study into the effects of different types of daycare on a child's development. The researchers looked at children who experienced four different types of care during the day. Some were cared for by a childminder, some in a nursery, some with relatives and some by the mother at home. In general, those who were at home achieved more in various measures. Those in the nursery seemed to have less satisfactory experiences.

Evaluation of the ethics of Melhuish et al. (1990)

Ethical strengths

- Children were studied in their natural setting and in the type of daycare their parents had chosen, so there was no manipulation of any child's experiences.
- Parents could be asked for permission, given the right to withdraw and given as much information as they wanted. There was no need for deceit, so ethical guidelines could be followed.

Ethical weaknesses

- Parents could access the findings and make choices about daycare accordingly. Findings might appear to be critical of nursery provision, for example, so such criticisms need to be made on a very sound basis. This study appears to have had a sound basis — many different measures were used and carefully operationalised.

However, it was *only* those measures that the findings covered, not every feature of nursery provision. The conclusion that the nursery children seemed to come out at a disadvantage still needs clarification, so there are ethical implications with regard to publishing the findings.

■ This was a large-scale study using different research methods and a high number of families. It is likely that the families involved felt under pressure to participate. In a longitudinal study participants may wish to withdraw, but they may not feel able to do so because of social pressures.

Research methods

For this section you must be able to describe and evaluate the listed research methods: laboratory experiments, field experiments, natural experiments, observations, questionnaires, interviews, content analyses, correlations and case studies. You also need to quote one study as an example of each research method, making sure that you can both describe and evaluate the study. This is to show that you fully understand the research methods. You therefore need to know enough about a study in this section to describe different aspects of it separately (such as the procedure or the results), so make sure you know enough by exploring your chosen studies in detail. Table 6.14 lists studies you may have come across and the research methods used in these studies.

Table 6.14 *Evaluation of research methods*

Study	Research method	Approach/application	Page reference
Loftus and Palmer (1974)	Laboratory experiment	Criminological	p. 39 A2
Milgram (1963)		Social (AS)	p. 36 AS
Tajfel et al. (1970/71)		Social (AS)	p. 68 AS
Craik and Tulving (1975)		Cognitive (AS)	p. 139 AS
Peterson and Peterson (1959)		Cognitive (AS)	p. 136 AS
Scott et al. (2004)	PET scanning	Health	p. 119 A2
Raine et al. (1997)		Biological (AS)	p. 283 AS
Casby et al. (2009)	Animal experiment	Health	p. 114 A2
Skinner (1948)		Learning (AS)	p. 359 AS
Pickens and Thompson (1968)		Learning (AS)	p. 361 AS
Maass and Köhnken (1989)	Field experiment	Criminological	p. 12 A2
Yarmey (2004)		Criminological	p. 29 A2
Rosenthal and Jacobson (1968)		Criminological	p. 23 A2
Isaac (1992)		Sport	p. 194 A2
Hofling et al. (1966)		Social (AS)	p. 58 AS
Godden and Baddeley (1975)		Cognitive (AS)	p. 133

Study	Research method	Approach/application	Page reference
Mellalieu et al. (2006)	Field study	Sport	p. 196 A2
Rosenhan (1973)		Clinical	p. 274 A2
Charlton et al. (2000)	Naturalistic experiment	Issues and debates	p. 319 A2
Parten (1932)	Naturalistic observation	Child	p. 55 A2
Robertson (1948)		Child	p. 70 A2
Melhuish et al. (1990)		Issues and debates	p. 321 A2
Grossman et al. (1985)	Cross-cultural studies	Child	p. 80 A2
Jin Mi Kyoung (2005)		Child	p. 80 A2
Ainsworth (e.g. 1978)	Structured observation	Child	p. 77 A2
Ennett et al. (1994)	Questionnaire	Health	p. 143 A2
Boyd and Munroe (2003)		Sport	p. 198 A2
Brown et al. (1986)	Interview	Clinical	p. 284 A2
Blättler et al. (2002)		Health	p. 138 A2
Hach et al. (2004)		Clinical	p. 221 A2
Goldstein (1988)		Clinical	p. 279 A2
Cohen et al. (2005)		Issues and debates	p. 326 A2
Gottesman and Shields (1966)	Twin study	Clinical	p. 223 A2
Cumberbatch and Gauntlett (2005)	Content analysis	Issues and debates	p. 328 A2
Madon et al. (2003)	Correlation	Criminological	p. 24 A2
Koivula (1995)		Sport	p. 204 A2
NICHD study in the USA	Longitudinal	Child	p. 87 A2
EPPE study in the UK		Child	p. 89 A2
Kim-Cohen et al. (2005)		Clinical	p. 240 A2
Craft et al. (2003)	Meta analysis	Sport	p. 163 A2
Bachrach et al. (1991)		Psychodynamic (AS)	p. 206 AS
Curtiss (1977)	Case study	Child	p. 96 A2
Koluchová (1972)		Child	p. 83 A2
Freud (1909)		Psychodynamic (AS)	p. 196 AS
Axline (1964)		Psychodynamic (AS)	p. 200 AS
Money (1975)		Biological (AS)	p. 279 AS

Study hint   For many of the research methods, you will have looked at more than one study already. For example, with regard to field experiments you have studied Hofling et al. (1966) and Godden and Baddeley (1975), and you may have covered at least one field experiment if you studied criminological psychology.

The laboratory experiment

In this section the laboratory experiment research method and an example of its use are described and evaluated.

Description

- A laboratory experiment takes place in an artificial controlled environment.
- There is an independent variable (IV) that is manipulated and a dependent variable (DV) that is measured, to see the effect of the manipulation of the IV.
- Variables other than the independent and dependent variables are carefully controlled.
- Cause and effect conclusions are drawn and a researcher may claim (depending on the results) that the change in the IV caused the change in the DV.

Methodological terms are included here to remind you of what they mean. You have come across most of them before. Make sure that you are completely sure about their meaning.

Table 6.15 *Evaluation of the laboratory experiment research method*

Strengths	Weaknesses
• Laboratory experiments have careful controls and so are replicable, which means they can be tested for reliability. If a study is carried out again there are likely to be the same findings, meaning that data are reliable.	• In general, laboratory settings involve making a situation unnatural in order to test it, such as removing certain features of a situation to isolate variables for study. If something studied is not as in 'real life', then findings are not likely to be valid.
• A laboratory experiment is well controlled with regard to **extraneous variables** so that there are few **confounding variables** (e.g. there should be no subjectivity arising from the experimenter's interventions and interpretations). Laboratory experiments are therefore both objective and scientific.	• Laboratory experiments usually collect quantitative data, which involve numbers and can be analysed statistically. This is a strength but also a weakness, as the data are likely to lack depth and detail as the laboratory experiment is likely to use a **reductionist** method

If you use reductionism as a criticism of experiments, do not assume that reductionist means bad. Explain why it is a criticism (for example, because by looking at the parts the whole might not be being studied, which reduces validity).

Extraneous variables are those that are not controlled and **confounding variables** are extraneous variables that affected the results.

Reductionism is when something is reduced to a small part in order to study it.

Example of a laboratory experiment: Loftus and Palmer (1974)

Loftus and Palmer (1974) is chosen as the study here because if you have studied the criminological application, you will have covered it. If you chose a different application you might decide to revise a different laboratory experiment for this section. Loftus and Palmer carried out a laboratory experiment to look at the effect of leading questions (or changing the wording of a question) on memory (or judgement) of an event. After watching film of a car accident, participants were asked how fast the cars were going when they 'hit' or 'smashed' (there were other verbs used as well). The results were that use of the verb 'hit' led to estimates of a lower speed than the verb 'smashed'. The researchers' conclusion was that the alteration of just one word in the question affected people's estimate of speed.

Evaluation of a laboratory experiment: Loftus and Palmer (1974)

Strengths

- Loftus and Palmer's study was well controlled so that only the verb in the central question was changed, so the study can be replicated and data are likely to be reliable.
- As extraneous variables were controlled and the researchers did not use interpretation or affect the results, then the findings are objective and scientific.

Weaknesses

- The study asked participants to react to a film, which is not the same as witnessing a real accident. The participants would not have experienced the stress and emotions of a real situation when judging the speed of the car. To this extent, the findings are not valid.
- The situation is reduced to asking for information about the speed of the car rather than about the whole situation, as would be done in a cognitive interview. This laboratory experiment is reductionist rather than holistic, which is a weakness because the whole situation is not studied, meaning there is a lack of validity.

Note that the strengths and weaknesses of the laboratory experiment as a research method and the strengths and weaknesses of the Loftus and Palmer study are the same. In other words, you can evaluate studies using evaluation points from the research method in general.

The field experiment

In this section the field experiment research method and an example of its use are described and evaluated.

Description

- A field experiment takes place in the natural environment of the participant (in the field).
- There is an independent variable (IV) that is manipulated and a dependent variable (DV) that is measured to see the effect of the manipulation of the IV.
- Variables other than the independent and dependent variables are carefully controlled as far as possible, though with a natural setting it is hard to control all the variables.
- Cause and effect conclusions are drawn and a researcher would claim, depending on the results, that the change in the IV caused the change in the DV.

Table 6.16 *Evaluation of the field experiment research method*	
Strengths	**Weaknesses**
• Field experiments have careful controls and so are replicable which means they can be tested for reliability. This means that if a study is done again there are likely to be the same findings so data are reliable.	• In general field experiments involve making a situation unnatural in order to test it, such as by removing certain features of a situation to isolate variables for study. If something studied is not 'real life' then findings are not likely to be valid. So although the setting might be valid the task might not, such as in Hofling et al.'s field study, as explained below.
• A field experiment is well controlled with regard to extraneous variables so that there are few confounding variables (e.g. there should be no subjectivity from the experimenter's interventions and interpretations). Field experiments are therefore objective and scientific.	• Field experiments take place in a natural setting, which means that features of the setting at least are hard to control. Extraneous variables are more likely to affect findings than in a laboratory experiment and there are more likely to be confounding variables.
• A field experiment is done in the participants' natural setting so with regard to the setting at least, if not the task, there is validity. This is known as ecological validity.	

Note that the first two strengths of the field experiment method are also those of a laboratory experiment, showing that similar evaluation points can be made because of methodological similarities.

Example of a field experiment: Hofling et al. (1966)

You should be familiar with the study chosen in this section, Hofling et al. (1966), which you will have covered during the AS course as part of your study of the social approach. It is only briefly described and evaluated here. Hofling et al. carried out a field experiment in different hospitals. Nurses who worked in the hospital were asked over the telephone, by a fake doctor, to administer an overdose of an unknown drug to a patient without proper authorisation. The aim was to see if the nurses would obey the instructions, even when to do so went against the rules. It was found that 21 of the 22 nurses who took part obeyed the instructions. In a different part of the study other nurses were asked if they would obey in such a situation, and they replied on a questionnaire rather than taking part in a study. The findings were that they would not obey. It was concluded that what people say they will do and what they actually do are different — though of course the two parts of the study involved different nurses. It was also concluded that there was blind obedience when the nurses obeyed the doctors.

Evaluation of a field experiment: Hofling et al. (1966)
Strengths
■ Hofling et al. (1966) built in many controls, such as that the study would take place when the nurse was alone on the ward (so he or she could not ask anyone else for advice) and that the 'doctor' used the same script. The study was therefore replicable, and indeed was carried out 22 times with a different nurse in each hospital. This meant the findings were likely to be reliable.

■ The setting was natural for the nurses, as they were working on their own wards in the proper job. This meant there was some ecological validity (even though the phone call was fake, as was the drug and the instructions, which meant that to an extent there was a lack of validity).

Weaknesses

- Hofling et al. (1966) used a fake situation where the 'doctor' was not real, the drug was not real, and there was deliberate organisation for the time of the phone call when nobody else was around for the nurse to consult. This means there was a lack of validity with regard to the task.
- It was hard to control all the variables, although an observer was placed near the ward to check on the timing of the phone call, for example. A confounding variable could have been the presence of the observer. Not being able to control all the variables, as in a laboratory, might have affected the reliability of the findings.

Note that when you are evaluating a particular study you should use general evaluation points of the research method, but also ensure that you link each point to the study explicitly.

The naturalistic experiment

In this section the naturalistic experiment research method and an example of its use are described and evaluated.

Description

- A naturalistic experiment involves a naturally occurring (not manipulated) independent variable (IV).
- Variables other than the independent and dependent variables are carefully controlled insofar as that is possible (though it often is not, because the situation is naturally occurring).
- There is an independent variable (IV) but it is not manipulated and a dependent variable (DV) that is measured to see the effect of the natural change in the independent variable (IV).
- It is likely that the study takes place in the participants' natural setting, as that is likely to be where a naturally occurring IV is found.
- Cause and effect conclusions are drawn and a researcher may claim that the change in the IV caused the change in the DV.

Table 6.17 *Evaluation of the naturalistic experiment research method*

Strengths	Weaknesses
• Naturalistic experiments are the only experiments where the independent variable is naturally occurring and not manipulated by the experimenter. This means that there is validity in the task, and often validity in the setting if the study takes place in the natural setting of the participants.	• As the IV is naturally occurring and often the setting is natural, variables will not be controlled as in a laboratory experiment. It is possible, if not likely, that there are confounding variables because of this lack of control. Therefore, the change in the IV may not have caused the change in the DV.

Strengths	Weaknesses
• There is an attempt to isolate the independent variable and there is still a measurable dependent variable that is operationalised, as in other experiments. There is therefore an attempt to show a cause and effect conclusion — that the change in the IV caused the change in the DV just like any other experiment — and scientific status is claimed for the findings.	• The naturally occurring IV might be hard to isolate as one variable, given that usually situations, behaviour and/or aspects of some-one's personality occur grouped together rather than separately, and this grouping is often complex.

Example of a naturalistic experiment: Charlton et al. (2000)

Charlton et al. (2000) is the study chosen for this section. You may have studied it as part of your coverage of criminological psychology, because the study looks at the effect of television on aggression in children. The researchers carried out a naturalistic study on the remote island of St Helena. Before the introduction of television on the island, children's behaviour in a playground

AS link Experiments (all three types) are explained in detail in the cognitive approach section of the AS textbook, and laboratory experiments are also covered in the biological approach.

was recorded on video. Their behaviour was then recorded again after television had been introduced. The aim was to look at antisocial and prosocial behaviour, to see if there had been any effect from the introduction of television.

Charlton et al. called their study a naturalistic study, not a naturalistic experiment, and the data were gathered by observation of the video recordings. However, as there is a clear independent variable and dependent variable, and as the researchers were looking for a cause and effect conclusion, the study can be called a naturalistic experiment. They found little change in prosocial or antisocial behaviour after the intro-duction of television (9 changes out of 64 compari-sons). It was concluded that watching television did not lead to changes in behaviour, which went against social learning theory.

Explore If you have not covered this study when looking at crimino-logical psychology, then explore it now so that you can describe it in more depth.

Evaluation of Charlton et al. (2000)

Strengths

■ As television was naturally introduced to the island the researchers did not have to affect the participants in any way, except to video their play behaviour, so to that extent this was an ethical study.

■ Charlton et al. (2000) carried out a longitudinal study, and the 'with' and 'without' television behaviour was observed on the same island, so conclusions about the 'before' and 'after' effects could be clearly made. Cause and effect conclusions could reasonably be drawn.

6

Weaknesses

- Being part of a study can affect participants' behaviour. It is possible that the children were 'well behaved' when being video recorded, so the behaviour they exhibited was not natural and the recorded data lacked validity.
- It might be that there were other changes in those 5 years in addition to television being introduced, so it is hard to say that the television made no difference. It might be that there *was* a difference in behaviour as a result of the introduction of television, but not to children's playground behaviour, because this was counter-acted by cultural norms (watching the television may have increased aggression but cultural norms then decreased this effect).

Note that this is the first time in this section that a strength or weakness has included an ethical issue. Ethical strengths and weaknesses, both of studies and of research methods, are often relevant.

Observational research

In this section the observational research method and an example of its use are described and evaluated.

Description

- Observations are usually naturalistic and take place in the participants' natural setting.
- There can be participant observations (where the observer is part of the setting and situation) and non-participant observations (where the observer is not part of the setting and situation).
- There can also be covert observations (where the participants do not know that they are being observed) and overt observations (where the participants are aware that they are being observed).
- Observations can involve categorising behaviours and then tallying to record the number of such behaviours, giving quantitative data.
- Observations can involve video recordings or making detailed notes and transcribing them — giving qualitative data.
- Sometimes observations are structured in an artificial setting and comparisons can be made between the different observations, as in Ainsworth's strange situation studies in child psychology.

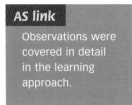

AS link

Observations were covered in detail in the learning approach.

Ensure in an exam answer that you make your point clearly. For example, if you say an observation can be 'overt', make it clear in your answer that you know what that means. You need to show knowledge and understanding in your answer.

Table 6.18	Evaluation of the observational research method	
Strengths	**Weaknesses**
• Naturalistic observations take place in a natural setting and so have ecological validity, in that the setting is the usual one for the participant so their usual behaviour is likely to be observed.	• If the observation is non-participant then the situation may not in fact be natural (because of the 'strange' observer), so there might not be ecological validity.
• If an observation involves categorised behaviour, tallying and more than one observer (so that comparisons can be made) then it might be reliable. Inter-observer reliability can then be tested for.	• Participant observation can be difficult because the individual may find it hard both to record data and take part in the situation, so information is more likely to be missed or selected than if the observation is non-participant.

It is worth considering the strengths and weaknesses of covert, overt, participant and non-participant observations separately so that you are completely clear about the different types of observation and how useful they are.

Example of an observation in psychology: Melhuish et al. (1990)

Melhuish et al. (1990) carried out an observational study of young children to see how far four different types of care during the day affected their behaviour. This observation was part of a longitudinal study that also used interviews and questionnaires. The observational part of the main study is explained here. More detail is provided than with the previous studies in this section, as it is possible that you have not studied an observation in your course.

Aim

The researchers studied 18-month-old children. The aim was to see if different types of care during the day would affect the behaviour of the children.

Procedure

There were four groups, comprising the independent variable. Three groups had parents where there were two earners in the family, and the other group had single-earner families. This last group was made up of a non-working mother with her child looked after at home — this was the home group. The dual-earner families had working mothers and the child was either cared for in a day nursery, with a childminder or with relatives. The study looked at whether the different daycare arrangements affected the children. The data were gathered by observations.

There were 255 families from London used in the study. They were contacted by phone to set up the study and asked to complete a questionnaire giving basic information about themselves. As well as being visited at 18 months, the children were visited at 5 months, 11 months and 36 months of age — this was a longitudinal study. Of the 255 families initially approached, 246 were asked to take part in the study of 18-month-old children. This part of the study made use of interviews and

questionnaires as well as observation, but it is the observation part of the study at 18 months that is focused on here.

There were two separate 1-hour observations of the children in their daycare setting. Observations at home as well as in their daycare setting were made for the children in the nursery, childcare and relative groups. Of the 246 families, 9 refused to take part and in 36 cases the number of staff available was not sufficient to carry out the observation. In 45 cases the child was either not in full-time home care or did not have over 20 hours of one of the three types of daycare, so these children were not included. The study included 44 children 'at home', 34 in a nursery, 59 with a childminder and 19 with a relative.

Observations took place during 'free play' and the observer recorded the child's activity every 10 seconds. The study child was observed and the observer only recorded information about other children if the study child was affected. Some behaviours were 'one-offs' and recorded simply; others were recorded by including their start and end time. If any behaviour had a less than 70% inter-observer agreement it was not included. For the other behaviours there was an 86% inter-observer agreement with regard to adult interactions and an 82% agreement with regard to children's activities. Two observations were made — on two different days — to check for stability of behaviours.

study hint If you need an example of a longitudinal study when discussing methodology, consider using Melhuish et al. (1990).

Children can be observed in their daycare setting to study various aspects of their behaviour

Results

■ Responsiveness: it was found that the home and relatives group showed more responsiveness than the nursery group. The home group was also more responsive than the childminder group.

■ Affection and other emotional behaviours: the researchers put different affection responses together and found the nursery group showed fewer affection responses than the other three groups. An individual child showed less affection to others in the nursery group than in the childminder or home groups.

■ Aggression was greater in nurseries, but low overall.

■ Communication to the study child was also investigated. With regard to language by the child (verbal utterances) the nursery group showed the least use of language when compared with the other three. The childminder group was lower than the home group with regard to utterances as well.

Conclusions

Overall it was thought that the four types of daycare gave different outcomes with regard to specific behaviours, some of which are mentioned here. These are responsiveness, affection, aggression, language to the child, and language by the child. Individual play, crying and gestures did not differ between the four types. Attention, joint play, group activity and language did show differences.

Evaluation of Melhuish et al. (1990)

Strengths

■ There is inter-observer reliability. Where this did not occur the data were not included in the results.

■ The children were observed during free play when they could choose their own activities, which should have led to fair comparisons between the four groups. If the observations were of structured sessions they might have affected the child's behaviour.

Weaknesses

■ The nurseries were privately owned and not well resourced, so other better equipped nurseries may have given different findings.

■ The researchers point out that the observations all watched 18-month-old children, so findings might only generalise to children of that age and not to older or younger children.

Notice that you can evaluate a study by looking at generalisability, reliability, subjectivity or validity, but that there are also evaluation points that are specific to the study, such as the type of nursery. Make sure that your evaluation point relates to the study rather than being a general point about the research method.

Questionnaires

In this section the questionnaire research method and an example of its use are described and evaluated.

Description

- Questionnaires involve asking a set list of questions to a numbezr of participants so that their answers can be compared.
- They usually involve a lot of closed questions, where answers are fixed and there is no freedom for comment.
- Questionnaires may include open questions, where answers are more general and the respondent can elaborate and comment.
- They include questions about personal data because a hypothesis is likely to require some knowledge about the respondent, such as their age, gender or social class, so those questions need to be asked.

AS link Questionnaires are explained in detail in the social approach.

Study hint Check that you understand all the following terms used in this research method: closed questions; open questions; personal data; self-report data; structured/unstructured/semi-structured interview; schedule; cross-sectional/longitudinal study; generalise.

Table 6.19 Evaluation of the questionnaire research method

Strengths	Weaknesses
• Questionnaires are set in one format and are the same for all respondents so that data can be compared between one respondent and another. This helps replicability. • Questionnaires allow for both qualitative and quantitative data to be gathered; analysis is easier with the numbers from closed questions but detail and richness are provided by the open questions.	• Questionnaires have a notoriously low return rate, which is inconvenient and expensive. • The closed questions force a choice of answer from the respondent who may not want to choose any of the responses offered. This may result in a lack of validity.

Example of a questionnaire in psychology: Boyd and Munroe (2003)

Boyd and Munroe (2003) used two questionnaires in their study to look at how climbers (and track and field athletes) use imagery. This study is compulsory for sport psychology in your course, so if you chose that application you will already be familiar with it (see pp. 198–203). The researchers wanted to see if beginner and advanced climbers use imagery in a different way from each other, and also to see if climbers use imagery differently to track and field athletes. The study used 38 track and field athletes and 48 climbers. The track and field athletes used the sport imagery questionnaire (SIQ) and the climbers were given the same questionnaire slightly modified to suit them (the climbers imagery questionnaire or CIQ). On the questionnaires there were 30 statements, each asking for a 7-point rating about how often the respondent uses imagery. A rating of 1 is 'rarely' and 7 is 'very often'. Unusually for a questionnaire, there was a high response rate. It was found that track and field athletes were different to climbers in how they used imagery and the type of imagery they used. However, the researchers did not find much difference in how beginner and advanced climbers used imagery.

Evaluation of Boyd and Munroe (2003)

Strengths

- The questionnaire used (the SIQ) has been used in other situations and studies and this means that findings from such studies can be compared.
- The study allowed for testing to see if the findings were reliable because the questionnaire was fixed and all the statements were rated by everyone. This means the study could be replicated.

Weaknesses

- The CIQ that the climbers used hardly differed from the SIQ that the track and field event athletes used, but the latter were asked about competition and the climbers were asked about climbing. These word changes may have changed how the respondents understood the questions.
- Beginner climbers had some experience and there was only a small point difference between how the researchers separated beginners and advanced. That small point was determined by self-report about their most difficult climb, which may not have been accurate. The difference between beginners and expert climbers was therefore perhaps rather arbitrary.
- The data from the questionnaire were self-report data, which can be unreliable because they might depend on how the respondent feels at the time.

> **Study hint**
>
> You can use any observation or questionnaire method that you have studied, so choose one that you enjoy and know something about.

Interviews

In this section the interview research method and an example of its use are described and evaluated.

Description

- Interviews can be structured — a set of questions is presented to all participants and there is no variation in the questions. The interview uses a questionnaire but is face-to-face and the questions are put directly to the respondent.
- Interviews can be unstructured — there is a schedule that gives the general questions and area for questions but variation is allowed to suit the interviewee, so that particular areas can be explored further.
- Interviews can be semi-structured, which involves a set list of questions but some scope for exploring issues.
- Interviews can involve a schedule — either a formal questionnaire or a loose list of question areas. The schedule is sent to the respondent beforehand so that they are prepared to answer.

> **AS link** Interviews were covered in detail in the social approach.

6

Table 6.20 *Evaluation of the interview research method*

Strengths	Weaknesses
• Unstructured interviews are useful when gathering qualitative data to explore an issue in depth, perhaps to find information to enable a more scientific research method, such as an experiment, to be set up. • Unstructured interviews are likely to gather valid data because they are not restricted and the interviewer can explore the respondent's own 'real life' areas of interest. • Semi-structured interviews are likely to provide both quantitative and qualitative data because some probing can take place around the set questions. Such interviews are therefore likely to be both reliable (the structure can be replicated) and valid ('real life' answers are more likely).	• Unstructured interviews are hard to compare with one another because each one is likely to be unique due to the wide-ranging nature of the responses elicited. • Structured interviews are fixed and so there is no deviation from the set questions. This might limit validity because the respondent is forced to choose certain answers or to talk about certain areas when they do not want to. Forcing a choice can mean forcing the answers, which might then lack validity.

There are three types of interview, each with strengths and weaknesses, so if you are asked to evaluate interviews in general you can choose one type to give a strength or a weakness, which you may find easier than attempting to evaluate interviews in general.

Example of an interview in psychology: Cohen et al. (2005)

An area that is often studied using interviews is depression. As part of your coverage of clinical psychology you may have looked in detail at a study about depression. If this was Brown et al. (1986) then you have already covered an interview and can use that example here. If you have not studied depression, you might like to explore this area looking at the study mentioned here.

Cohen et al. (2005) in Israel interviewed people attending a dermatological clinic (which deals with skin problems) to see what the prevalence of depression was. A standard interview was administered — the mini international neuropsychiatric interview screening tool. The interview was therefore a structured one, using a questionnaire that allowed diagnosis of depression.

It was found that out of the 384 patients who were interviewed, 37 had major depression, 3 had minor depression and 74 had depressive symptoms. This totals 29.7%, which is quite a substantial proportion of the patients. It was found that widow(er)s, divorced and separated people and unemployed patients were the groups with the higher prevalence of depression. This suggests a link with lack of social support. It was also discovered that depression was significantly associated with how much suffering was caused by the skin disease, as well as how severe the patient thought it was. The researchers concluded that when managing skin diseases, depression should be a consideration in deciding upon treatment.

Evaluation of Cohen et al. (2005)

Strengths

- The interview was a structured one using a standardised questionnaire so there is likely to be reliability — the interviewer did not ask different patients different questions, so the findings can be compared with one another (unlike information from unstructured interviews).
- A specific group was targeted — patients suffering from skin disease — and the findings were related directly to that group, so the results are valid in relation to patients with skin disease. It is likely that the results are also valid in relation to depression as a standardised questionnaire was used.

Weaknesses

- The researchers identified as a problem the fact that it was a cross-sectional study (it looked at patients at one moment in time), whereas a longitudinal study would be more useful to check patterns of depression as well as the reliability and validity of the findings.
- The study was carried out in Israel and it was noted that widow(er)s, divorced, separated and unemployed patients were particularly likely to suffer from depression. There are social categories that may be perceived differently in different cultures, so care needs to be taken when generalising.

Content analysis

In this section the content analysis research method and an example of its use are described and evaluated.

Description

- The content that is analysed is from media sources such as magazine articles or television, or any such written or recorded information.
- The aim is to look for themes, categories or behaviours, depending on the purpose of the study.
- Behaviours or examples of the categories are then counted to see how often they appear or are mentioned — this is tallying.
- In this way, quantitative data are gathered.

6

Table
6.21 *Evaluation of the content analysis research method*

Strengths	Weaknesses
• Quantitative data are gathered, which means inferential tests can be carried out on the data to test for the significance of any differences being looked for. For example, if the analysis involves looking at the 'gender' of the roles of boys and girls in children's books, a chi-squared test can be carried out comparing male and female roles with boy and girl characters.	• The categories have to be chosen and defined by the researcher(s), which might bring in subjectivity — someone has to decide what is a 'female' and a 'male' role, and people might differ in their opinions.
• The research method is ethical as it uses secondary sources such as articles in magazines, newspapers and other media or information from television programmes. Participants are not involved and there are few problems with informed consent, for example (although the source for the data must be carefully chosen and consent to use material may be needed).	• The research method is limited to the study of existing articles and media sources, which means it is inflexible and specialist. It is useful on certain occasions but those occasions are limited.
• It could be argued that the data are valid because they are from the secondary source that already exists and the conclusions are about that source. For example, children's roles in children's books are studied with validity with regard to gender.	
• Content analyses are also reliable, because someone else can go to the same source or sources and repeat the analysis, tallying using the same categories.	

Example of a content analysis in psychology: Cumberbatch and Gauntlett (2005)

Aim

Cumberbatch and Gauntlett carried out a content analysis as part of an Ofcom-funded piece of research. Their aim was to find out more about whether smoking, alcohol and drug abuse featured in television programmes watched by 10- to 15-year-olds, and how it was treated.

Procedure

The researchers carried out a content analysis to see how alcohol and drug abuse were depicted. The research focused on the ten programmes most watched by 10- to 15-year-olds and the study was carried out from August to October in 2004. There were 256 programmes involved, with 70% or more of them being soap operas. All were broadcast before the 9 p.m. watershed. Categories that were tallied involved scenes where alcohol, smoking and legal or illegal drugs featured. Overall, 2099 scenes were used. Material that was counted included observed or implied alcohol, smoking or drug-related behaviour, as well as references to alcohol, smoking or drugs. Visual representations of alcohol, smoking or drugs were also recorded (such as a cigarette packet or drink in a scene).

Results

Alcohol featured more than smoking or drugs in the most popular television programmes. Alcohol-related scenes occurred at the rate of about 12 incidences each hour. Smoking-related scenes occurred at about 3.4 incidences each hour and drug-related incidences were half that again, at 1.7 scenes each hour. Just 4%

of the programmes contained none of the target incidences. Both drinkers and smokers had large roles in the scenes; 37% of the major characters were drinkers and 4% were smokers. When considering the type of message rather than just the incidence, it was found that messages about alcohol were more or less neutral (84% of the scenes), 6% of the messages about alcohol were negative, 6% mixed and 4% positive. With smoking, 91% of the messages were neutral, while 57% of the drug scenes carried an anti-drugs message, with 40% neutral and 3% mixed. There were no scenes carrying a positive message about drugs.

Table 6.22	Results of the study of Cumberbatch and Gauntlett (2005)			
Programmes containing target material	Alcohol (%)	Smoking (%)	Drugs (%)
Overt portrayal	84	33	2
Implied portrayal	4	4	6
Discussion/references/visuals	87	53	21
None of the above	7	38	79

Table 6.22 shows that there are more references to alcohol than to smoking or drugs.

Conclusions

Being a content analysis, the results *are* the conclusions, because they are the reason for the content analysis being carried out — to find out about alcohol, smoking and drugs and how they are portrayed in the media. The conclusion is, therefore, the same as the results — that alcohol features quite a lot, whereas smoking is referred to less often and drugs even less. In general, the messages with regard to alcohol and smoking are fairly neutral.

Evaluation of Cumberbatch and Gauntlett (2005)

Strengths

- A content analysis is simply a counting of categories, so there are no ethical issues with regard to using participants.
- Many different programmes and scenes were included so that the analysis was thorough and within the limits of the study (programmes for 10- to 15-year-olds before the watershed). There is generalisability with regard to the findings.
- There was validity in that the programmes were real and broadcast, so the findings were about what children aged between 10 and 15 really watched.

Weaknesses

- The programmes were mainly soap operas (70% or more of the programmes) and so the findings should be generalised to soap operas rather than all television. Also, there was a limitation: all the programmes were shown before the 9 p.m. watershed, so findings should be generalised only to before the watershed.
- The assumption was made that children aged between 10 and 15 would imitate behaviour in their favourite programmes. Social learning theory is accepted, given this

> **Study hint** Make use of what you have learnt about content analysis from your own experience of carrying one out as part of your study of applications. However, when you are asked about a study using content analysis you should discuss a published study, not your own one.

assumption. However, children may also see alcohol, smoking and/or drugs in other situations, such as at home, so it cannot be shown that there is a causal link between alcohol, smoking and/or drugs being shown in a television programme and children using such drugs. A content analysis does not show that causal link.

The correlation research technique

In this section the correlation technique and an example of its use are described and evaluated.

Description

- A correlation is a technique often used in psychology and which can occur with many different research methods, in particular questionnaires — wherever there are quantitative data and those data involve two scores for one person or two scores that may relate.
- The idea is that for a number of people their two scores on the two scales of interest are compared to see if there is a pattern. For example, if one person has a high score on one scale, they might have a high score on the other, and if someone has a lower score on one scale they might have a lower score on the other. This sort of pattern appears to be a correlation — it would be tested to find out.
- A positive correlation means that as scores on one variable rise, they also rise on the other variable. For example, the more time given to learning a list of words, the more words are recalled.
- A negative correlation means that as scores on one variable rise, they fall on the other variable. For example, the higher the anxiety score, the lower the sporting success measure.
- When there is no relationship between two variables a correlational test would give a result of near 0. When there is a positive correlation the test would give a result nearing +1 and when there is a negative correlation the test would give a result close to −1.

> **AS link**
> Correlations were covered in detail in the psychodynamic approach.

Table 6.23 *Evaluation of the correlation research technique*

Strengths	Weaknesses
• Correlational analysis can show a relationship that would not otherwise be noticed. This is useful for starting off an area of research, which might later be followed by a more controlled study to look for a cause for the relationship.	• Correlational techniques might not be valid because two variables have to be operationalised so that quantitative data are found. If the variables are made measurable this might result in a move away from real-life data. For example, sporting success is likely to be measurable and valid but the anxiety score might not be.
• Correlational analysis can be tested for reliability to see if two sets of scores, perhaps taken at a different time, correspond. The quantitative data are often replicable.	• Correlations can show that variables relate to one another but do not show that one causes the other to change. There might be some other reason for the two varying together and this reason cannot be found using correlational analysis. It can be useful to find a relationship between variables, such as anxiety and sporting success, but knowing *why* the two are connected might be more useful if intervention is required.

Note that when the strengths and weaknesses of research methods and methodology are discussed, the statements are often cautious (e.g. 'likely to be measurable'), because in psychology statements are rarely completely true. It is sensible to be careful and to make only cautious general claims.

Example of a correlation in psychology: Craft et al. (2003)

In your course you are likely to have come across more than one study that uses correlational analysis. If you studied sport psychology, you might have looked at Craft et al. (2003), who carried out a meta-analysis looking at the relationship between different types of anxiety and self-confidence. Their study is summarised here.

Craft et al. brought together different studies that looked at types of anxiety and their relationship with sporting performance. They made sure that all the studies had used the same questionnaire — the data were gathered in the same way. Then they used the data from 29 such studies to see how far cognitive anxiety, somatic anxiety and self-confidence were related, both to each other and to sporting performance. Participants had rated themselves on their anxiety and self-confidence, and could be given scores for each type of anxiety. In order to look for a relationship, correlational analysis was carried out. It was found that, in general, it was self-confidence that related to sporting performance rather than anxiety. The two types of anxiety and self-confidence also showed relationships with each other.

Table 6.24 *The relationship between the three different types of anxiety*

Type of anxiety as measured by CSAI-2	Result of correlational test
Cognitive anxiety related to somatic anxiety	$r = 0.52$
Cognitive anxiety related to self-confidence	$r = -0.47$
Somatic anxiety related to self-confidence	$r = -0.54$

It can be seen from Table 6.24 that as cognitive anxiety rises, so does somatic anxiety; the result of the correlational test shows a positive correlation. As anxiety rises, however, self-confidence falls (for both types), as shown by the two negative correlations. This is perhaps what would be expected.

Evaluation of Craft et al. (2003)

Strengths

- Craft et al. (2003) drew on 29 studies, so they had a large amount of data. One of the strengths of a meta-analysis is that more participants' data can be used than is likely in a study using primary data.
- Each participant responded to the questionnaire (a standardised one) in the same way, no matter which study they were involved in, and they were only being compared using their own data. This is not like trying to compare data across different laboratory experiments, where there are likely to have been different situations and variables, for example. The same means of gathering data was used.

Weaknesses

■ Studies can be reliable but without validity. For example, cognitive and somatic anxiety were shown to rise together, but this could have been because the questions were not measuring different types of anxiety but were measuring the same thing. Just because two variables co-vary does not mean they are separate but related. The physical and cognitive (thinking) aspects of anxiety are likely to be related and might not be separable by using different questions.

Study hint Look back through your study of applications (two from criminological, child, health and sport) to see if you can find a correlational analysis. Review the correlation you carried out yourself when studying the psychodynamic approach, but make sure you know a published study as well.

■ The use of other people's data, in studies carried out for different reasons, leaves open the possibility that there are effects from the different studies (such as researcher effects) that have affected the findings. This might mean that data cannot validly be compared. For example, the act of choosing which studies to include may have meant excluding data that went against the findings (unknowingly).

Case studies

In this section the case study research method and an example of its use are described and evaluated.

Description

■ Case studies involve in-depth and detailed research; they usually gather qualitative data, although they can also gather quantitative data.

■ They can involve individuals or small groups.

AS link Case studies were covered in detail in the psychodynamic approach.

■ Many different research methods are used to gather the rich detail including the case history, interviews and questionnaires. Freud used special methods within his case studies, such as dream analysis and clinical interview, as well as free association.

Table 6.25 Evaluation of the case study research method

Strengths	Weaknesses
• In-depth information about one person or a small group gives a researcher the opportunity to uncover information that otherwise might not be found, such as family influences or personal history, and this can lead to new areas of study.	• Case studies cannot easily be repeated to check for reliability. Situations that a case study looks at may not occur again, for example, and even if they do, both the researcher and time are likely to be different.
• The depth of the information is likely to give valid data because information can be checked using different research methods. The individual concerned in the case study can also be asked to check what is recorded, so that validity is ascertained.	• Case studies do not in general yield data that are generalisable, because the depth and detail about one person is personal and may not apply to anyone else. Case studies are therefore not always helpful in building a scientific body of knowledge.

Example of a case study in psychology: Freud's Little Hans case study

For your AS course you will have studied both Freud's case study of Little Hans and the John Money case study of David Reimer. You may also have studied Axline's case study of Dibs. The Little Hans study is summarised here.

Freud gathered evidence from Little Hans's father as well as from the young boy himself and drew from this evidence features of the Oedipus complex. For example, Hans's dream about giraffes was interpreted as Hans wanting his mother and being afraid of his father. Hans's fear of horses was also interpreted as fear of the father. Towards the end of the study, when Hans was playing at 'being' the father with his own mother and with Hans's father 'being' the grandfather, Freud thought that the Oedipus complex was resolved and Little Hans's fear of horses would be removed.

Freud used dream analysis and analysis of the case history to gather a great deal of qualitative data from which to draw his conclusions. He put his suggestions forward for Little Hans to consider (through Hans's father).

Evaluation of Freud's Little Hans case study

Strengths

■ The amount and richness of qualitative data gathered enabled Freud to analyse the information in great detail. For example, he drew on different parts of the story at different times to find an explanation. He drew his conclusions about Little Hans wanting to get rid of his father from a number of incidents, not just one.

■ By referring back to Hans for confirmation of the analysis, Freud was testing his theory for validity. Case studies usually have validity.

Weaknesses

■ The study is not replicable and cannot be tested for reliability.

■ The study is about one boy and so it is hard to generalise its findings to the whole population, although Freud did so.

■ The concepts — such as the Oedipus complex and unconscious desires — are not measurable and so cannot be tested scientifically. Freud tried to be scientific by only using what he felt was 'factual' evidence, such as dreams.

Planning a study

Having followed the A-level psychology course and looked at a lot of studies using many different research methods, you should be ready to plan studies of your own when given a context or area for study.

Drawing out what is to be studied

First, in an exam question, you need to write down the aim of the study, which will come from the context given in the question. Second, where appropriate (and it will usually be appropriate), you should write out both the alternative and the null hypothesis. If a hypothesis is not appropriate, such as in a general case study, you should define the aim. However, it is assumed that the context or area for study will usually lead to a hypothesis. You should work out both the independent and dependent variables when writing the hypothesis (or the variables, if the study is a correlation). Write them down as well. The IV and the DV will need to be operationalised.

Example of a study plan

Context:
A researcher wants to find out if there are gender differences in preference for jobs.

Aim:
To find out if males and females have different preferences for jobs.

Hypothesis:
There are two hypotheses:
(1) Females are more likely to look for jobs that involve caring than males.
(2) Males are more likely to look for jobs that involve mechanics/electronics than females.

IV: gender

DV for hypothesis 1 = preference for jobs that involve caring. Jobs operationalised as nurse, carer, nursery nurse, nanny, doctor or counsellor. Preference operationalised as rating on a scale of 0 (would not like it at all) to 5 (would love to do that job).

DV for hypothesis 2 = preference for jobs that involve mechanics/electronics. Jobs operationalised as car mechanic, civil engineer, electrician, television engineer, computer technician or mechanical engineer. Preference operationalised as rating on a scale of 0 (would not like it at all) to 5 (would love to do that job).

Making design decisions

Decide on the research method if you have not already done so, or if is not specified in the question, and then consider the design — from repeated measures, independent groups, matched pairs or correlation. Alternatively, you could choose a case study and then explain how you will gather the data. Decide on the sampling technique.

Example of design decisions

You need to gather information from both males and females, so the design will be independent groups.

You could devise a questionnaire and ask both male and female participants about their job preferences, making sure questions focus on the list of jobs as well as other issues such as type of work and whether they are keen on a career or not. You could interview both males and females about their job preferences, making sure that questions ask about jobs that involve caring and jobs that involve mechanics. You could set up a test/experiment where a few case studies of individuals in the jobs listed are presented and explain a bit about each job and then you could ask each participant (males and females) to rate all the scenarios for preference. If you can find information about people asking for jobs (such as 'jobs wanted' pages in a newspaper), then you could carry out a content analysis (if you know the gender of the people advertising). You could see if males ask for more mechanical/engineering jobs and females ask for more caring jobs. This would be using secondary data.

Writing out the procedure

Having decided on the best design, you need to write out your procedure. Remember to include the apparatus (what equipment you need, if any), the sample (gender, age, sampling technique, number of participants etc.), and the actual procedure (what would be done).

Example of the procedure

Devise a case study for each of the 12 jobs mentioned in the DVs above. Avoid using a male or female name for the person in the case study. Treat the six jobs for each 'gender' equally, perhaps pairing them up. Give the same information for each pair of case studies, even if in a different order. For example, give age, school background and qualifications as similar for each pair. Then describe some of the work that is done in each of the jobs. Make sure all the case study pairs have the same level of job satisfaction in them (perhaps some things the person likes about the job and some things they do not).

The aim is to produce six case study pairs (six 'female' jobs and six 'male' jobs) that are similar in all respects except for the job title (e.g. carer or electrician). Then find ten male and ten female participants willing to take part. You could use an opportunity sample perhaps, and either set an age for all participants or try to get a range of ages. In this study, choose one age range because there may be cohort differences (for example, there might be different attitudes to the

6

different jobs at different times in history). Give standardised instructions to each participant. Then present all 12 case studies to them and ask them to rate each one on a scale of 0 (I would not like to do this job at all) to 5 (I would love to do this job). Randomise the order of presenting all 12 case studies each time for each participant. Note down the score (preference) for each case study. Each participant rates 12 times.

Noting ethical considerations

Note any ethical considerations, such as problems in giving informed consent or where there is deceit. You should make a note of the fact that there are no ethical issues, if this is the case

Participants must be told the purpose of the study and consent must be gained. However, it cannot be informed consent because if the participants know that their preferences for certain jobs are being measured, this might affect their responses. They could be told that it is a study to find out what they think of each case study. Then, at the end, there should be a full debrief so that the participants are aware that the study is about job choice and gender. Participants must be told that they can withdraw at any time from the study and must be reminded of this during the study. During the debrief, participants must be asked if they wish to withdraw their data. The researchers must be competent to carry out the study — for example, they must have relevant qualifications and be aware of ethical issues such as those given here. The participants will be deceived but a debrief will put this right, and making choices about fictitious case studies is not likely to be stressful. A check could be made beforehand to see if any participant is having problems in trying to get a job, since they may find the questions distressing.

Analysing the data

You will probably need to draw up a table of results and work out some descriptive statistics, such as mean and median. A graph is often required, so describe which type of graph you would use. Consider whether inferential statistics are required and, if so, suggest which test and which probability level.

Example of a data analysis

Data gathered will be in the form of numbers, with 12 numbers from each participant, one rating each for each case study. Tables could be drawn up such as Tables 6.26 and 6.27 (these results are made up).

Table 6.26 Made up results for a study looking at gender and job preferences — female choices

Female participants	The 12 case studies. The first six are for caring jobs and the second six are for mechanics/electrical jobs											
	1	2	3	4	5	6	7	8	9	10	11	12
1	5	4	1	3	4	3	1	2	1	3	2	2
2	4	3	4	5	2	3	2	4	3	2	2	1
3	5	3	5	5	4	4	1	1	3	2	2	2
4	3	2	4	4	3	4	3	4	3	2	2	2
5	3	4	4	3	5	5	2	1	1	1	2	3
6	4	3	3	3	1	3	3	2	2	3	3	2
7	3	3	5	4	4	4	4	3	1	1	2	3
8	2	1	4	4	4	3	4	2	3	1	1	1
9	3	5	2	3	3	1	2	3	2	2	3	1
10	5	4	3	5	5	4	1	1	2	2	1	3
Median	3.5	3	4	4	4	3.5	2	2	2	2	2	2
Mode	3	3	4	3	4	3/4	1/2	1/2	3	2	2	2

Scores are ratings from 1 (would not like the job at all) to 5 (would love to do the job).

Table 6.27 Made up results for a study looking at gender and job preferences — male choices

Male participants	The 12 case studies. The first six are for caring jobs and the second six are for mechanics/electrical jobs											
	1	2	3	4	5	6	7	8	9	10	11	12
1	3	2	1	1	2	2	5	3	3	2	4	3
2	1	2	1	1	1	3	4	3	4	3	2	4
3	3	2	2	1	3	2	5	3	4	5	5	4
4	1	3	2	2	1	1	2	4	3	4	2	5
5	1	2	2	1	3	2	4	3	3	3	2	3
6	2	1	2	3	4	4	5	3	4	2	3	2
7	3	2	4	3	1	1	3	5	2	4	4	3
8	4	1	2	2	1	3	2	4	2	3	5	4
9	2	2	1	1	1	1	4	3	1	1	2	3
10	3	2	3	3	2	2	4	5	3	4	5	2
Median	2.5	2	2	1.5	1.5	2	4	3	3	3	3.5	3
Mode	3	2	2	1	1	2	4	3	3	3/4	2	3

Scores are ratings from 1 (would not like the job at all) to 5 (would love to do the job).

It can be seen from the tables that females have a higher preference for 'female' jobs than 'male' jobs and males have a higher preference for 'male' jobs than 'female' jobs.

A median and a mode can be calculated in each case; a mean average is not suitable because the scores are ordinal and are ratings rather than interval or ratio data.

Each participant could be given an average rating for the male versus the female case studies so that there are two average ratings to compare. A median average is suitable.

Table 6.28 Average (median) rating for each participant for the 'male' and 'female' case studies

Female participants	Case studies for 'female' jobs	Case studies for 'male' jobs	Male participants	Case studies for 'female' jobs	Case studies for 'male' jobs
1	3.5	2	1	2	3
2	3.5	2	2	1	3.5
3	4.5	2	3	2	4.5
4	3.5	2.5	4	1.5	3.5
5	4	1.5	5	2	3
6	3	2.5	6	2.5	3
7	4	2.5	7	2.5	3.5
8	3.5	1.5	8	2	3.5
9	3	2	9	1	2.5
10	4.5	1.5	10	2.5	4

If a statistical analysis is required, a Mann–Whitney U could be carried out since the data are ordinal and the design is independent groups. One of the pairs of case studies could be chosen in each case, so that the ordinal data are the actual rankings rather than a median average.

A graph could be presented.

Evaluating the study

Make some notes about the strengths and weaknesses of your study. You can give standard strengths and weaknesses of the research method or of the design.

Example of an evaluation

A strength of this study is the careful controls, which means that there is replicability. The case studies are carefully prepared, with each pair matching for any features other than the different type of job. There are six of each job type (caring or mechanical/electrical), which means that the study can show whether there is consistency in the gender differences in preferences.

A weakness is that the study uses written out case studies and asks the participants to rate them for preference. This is not a valid way of measuring preferences for jobs as the study may lead to demand characteristics. Participants may guess that the study is about the different job types and they may respond accordingly.

Evaluating psychological studies

You need to be able to evaluate psychological studies, as has been done throughout the course. You must focus on the methodology to evaluate the findings and also to make suggestions for improving studies. Ideas for improving studies can include improving controls, changing the chosen research method or improving reliability or validity, or both. You might be asked to evaluate a study you are given and then asked to make improvements, so practise doing this.

Explore Look up some studies on the internet, evaluate them, and then make at least two suggestions for improving them.

Table 6.29 *Examples of suggestions for the evaluation and improvement of studies*

Study	Evaluation	Improvement
Milgram (1963)	Carried out in a laboratory, so not valid	Carry out in a more natural setting such as a car park, giving out parking tickets
Skinner (1948)	Used pigeons, so cannot generalise to humans	Questionnaire to people about superstitious habits and how they developed
Hofling et al. (1966)	Carried out in 1966 (still valid now?) and with female nurses only, so not generalisable to males	Update, and carry out with male nurses to see if findings are the same
Study above about choice of partner	Not valid, as based on newspaper ads; advertiser might in reality select differently once they meet someone	Interview or use questionnaire to ask people what attracts them about their partner and/or what they would look for

Key issues

Key issues of relevance to today's society

Psychology's contributions to society have been discussed in this textbook. For each contribution, a link is made to it being a key issue to today's society; this section therefore refers you back to the earlier explanations, rather than repeating material here.

You need to be able to describe the key issue itself and to explain it using concepts, theories and/or research, so check that you know enough. An important point to note is that you also need to be able to use your knowledge of research methods and ethical issues when commenting on these issues.

Remember you need to look at key issues for each of the five AS approaches and two of the four applications offered as a choice for your course — two from criminological, child, health and sport psychology. A key issue for clinical psychology is compulsory.

6

Table 6.30	*Suggested key issues related to the five AS approaches and three A2 applications*

Approach or application	Suggested key issue
Social approach	How to reduce prejudice, or explaining blind obedience to authority such as at Abu Ghraib prison
Cognitive approach	The unreliability of eyewitness memory, or how successful the cognitive interview technique is
Psychodynamic approach	When and if psychoanalysis is successful as a therapy, or whether dreams have meaning
Biological approach	Understanding and helping regarding sex assignment (and mis-assignment), or helping to explain autism
Learning approach	The effectiveness of systematic desensitisation to cure phobias, or the effectiveness of token economy programmes to achieve more adaptive behaviour
Criminological psychology	The unreliability of eyewitness memory
Child psychology	The effects of daycare on a child's development
Health psychology	The effectiveness of drug therapy with regard to drug addiction
Sport psychology	How to be a good coach to help with sporting success
Clinical psychology	The effectiveness of token economy programmes

Using research methods to discuss key issues

You will need to be able to describe each key issue as it relates to society. For example, eyewitness testimony is not the key issue as such, but rather the effect of such testimony being unreliable — someone can be found guilty wrongly because of unreliable eyewitness testimony. Then you need to apply concepts, theories and the findings of studies to the key issue to explain how it relates to society. For instance, if it is shown that leading questions can affect the testimony of an eyewitness, the use of such questions should be avoided. You should use the evidence of research findings when making such points and you need to be able to consider the strengths of those findings. For example, Loftus carried out many laboratory experiments that showed the effect of leading questions on recall. However, because they were laboratory experiments the findings could be said to lack validity. You could continue the argument by pointing out that Yarmey carried out field experiments and also found problems with eyewitness memory, so perhaps Loftus's findings are valid after all. When considering key issues and applying findings and psychological concepts to explain the issue, be ready to bring in methodological arguments in this way.

Using ethical issues to discuss key issues

Key issues that affect society are often problems for society. For example, key issues raised in this section include the effectiveness of various therapies (systematic desensitisation, token economy and drug therapy). Society benefits if therapies are effective. However, there are ethical issues raised by the administration of therapies (the power of society to impose therapy on an individual and the effect of the therapy on the individual, or the question of who has the right to control someone else). Such questions (about social control) are considered below. When you are discussing a key issue, remember to consider its ethical issues.

Debates

In this section you are required to consider four debates. This is part of the synoptic element of the course, which asks you to bring various areas of your learning to focus on particular debates. The four debates involve looking at:

- cultural differences between people and the effect of culture on psychological research and on individuals
- the question of whether psychology is a science (which concerns both its subject matter and its methodology)
- social control and how far individuals should be controlled for the sake of society
- the role of nature and nurture in our development

Psychology and cultural differences

In your course you have looked mainly at psychological studies carried out in the UK and the USA. If you covered child psychology then you will have looked at cross-cultural studies of the development of attachments. In health psychology the study of treatment for heroin addiction was part of the Swiss Heroin Project. Boyd and Munroe's study of the use of imagery in climbing was carried out in Canada. If you looked at the work of Pavlov and his development of classical conditioning ideas then you have encountered work from Russia. In clinical psychology you have probably considered how mental illness is differently defined in different countries. However, your view of psychology, having studied a majority of 'Western' views, is likely to be 'ethnocentric'.

Ethnocentrism

Ethnocentrism is a type of bias and it means being focused on one's own culture. The way we construct the world probably means that ethnocentrism is impossible to avoid; this argument links to Bartlett's reconstructive view of memory. Social norms and rules are part of our socialisation and people are likely to understand information and view people using their own cultural understanding and schemata.

Understanding bias in order to avoid it

It is useful to know about ethnocentrism and to attempt to understand someone else's world view so that bias is avoided. Researchers and practitioners need to be aware of their own ethnocentrism. Many therapies such as person-centred therapy, rational emotive therapy and cognitive–behavioural therapy rely on the practitioner having an empathic and non-judgemental relationship with a client, so that the client's world view is the focus rather than the practitioner's. Clinicians also need to be aware of ethnocentrism when diagnosing mental disorders. For example, hearing voices may signify schizophrenia in one part of the world but in another there may be a spiritual explanation.

> **Explore**
>
> Investigate the work of Malinowski in the Trobriand Islands. Some of his work with another culture has been used to criticise Freud's idea of the Oedipus complex.

Bronisław Malinowski is well known for the ethnographic fieldwork he undertook in the early years of the twentieth century, working in Papua New Guinea and the Trobriand Islands. He pioneered the idea of a researcher immersing him- or herself in a culture to gain complete understanding of it and to avoid ethnocentrism.

Malinowski studied the culture of the Trobriand Islanders

A significant problem with anthropology and ethnographic work is that the researcher is unlikely to succeed completely in immersing him- or herself in a different culture. Complete command of the subtleties of a new language, customs and traditions is extremely difficult to achieve.

Cross-cultural research

Research across different cultures can be useful in showing whether a characteristic or ability is universal or unique to a particular culture. A universal ability is likely to come from human nature, whereas something unique to one culture is likely to come from nurture and the environment. Cross-cultural research, therefore, is useful when considering the nature–nurture debate.

The research takes a hypothesis and a methodology and carries out a study in more than one culture. Ainsworth's strange situation test (see pp. 77–79) has been used in this way to find universal attachment types between infants and their caregivers. If, in cross-cultural research, the methodology is the same and the findings are the same, the findings are thought to show a universal characteristic or ability.

An example is a study by Hillary N. Fouts (2008) from the University of Tennessee, looking at the way fathers are involved with children under 4 years of age in the Aka and Bofi foragers in Central Africa. A father's involvement is not the same in all societies. In some societies there are flexible gender roles and a high (equal) regard for both male and female children. In other societies gender roles are more fixed.

In many cultures fathers are not involved until the child is weaned. These are the issues studied by Fouts and findings are awaited.

Evaluation of cross-cultural research
Strengths

Explore Look up the work of Fouts (2008) to see what was discovered, or find other examples of cross-cultural research. Papua New Guinea has many different 'tribes' and they are widely studied.

If a researcher wants to identify differences and similarities between cultures to do with behaviour or characteristics, cross-cultural research is the only way to do this. In this way universal behaviours and characteristics can be uncovered, which can help to shed light on human nature. Cross-cultural research can identify different approaches to certain issues between cultures. What is seen as useful in one culture can be beneficially introduced in another. For example, techniques for improving sporting performance in one society can be transferred and tried in another society (although of course, as in the case of the DSM, in some cases cultural differences will make this transference difficult).

Criticisms

The methodology used for the research might be the same for the studies in different cultures but may be more appropriate or more understood in one culture than another, affecting the findings of the research. This criticism has been made about the strange situation task. The interpretation of cross-cultural research may be biased by the cultural understandings and schemata of the researcher or reader. For example, in the 'strange situation', the idea of secure attachments being best is inferred. However, in another culture, such as Germany, a different type of attachment might be seen as 'good', because children are encouraged to be more independent.

Psychology and science

Throughout the course you will have been looking at how far psychology may be considered a science. The material here will help you to draw conclusions about what science is and how far psychology fits the definition of science.

What is meant by science?
The hypothetico-deductive model

The word 'science' describes a procedure in which a theory is formulated and a suggestion drawn from this theory about what might happen in the world. The suggestion forms a hypothesis, which can then be tested against reality to see if it works. If it does, then more knowledge is added to the theory. If the suggestion does not work the theory is amended, or perhaps even rejected. Through this cycle of testing a theory and amending it, scientific knowledge is built. Karl Popper called this the **hypothetico-deductive** method of reasoning. From the theory a hypothesis is deduced. Testing against reality means gathering **empirical** data – those gathered from the senses through seeing, touching, tasting, hearing or smelling.

6

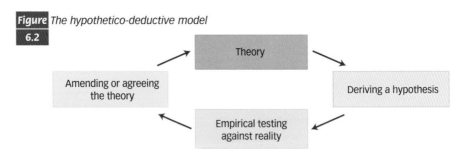

Figure 6.2 *The hypothetico-deductive model*

Relating this idea to psychology

Psychology uses the hypothetico-deductive method a great deal, particularly for experimental research methods and surveys. An idea is drawn from a theory, and a hypothesis put forward. The researcher makes sure that the variables in the hypothesis are measurable and then gathers data to test the hypothesis. From the findings the researcher either concludes that they have supported the theory/idea or not and amends the theory accordingly. A case study, on the other hand, would perhaps have an aim, look at an individual in depth and consider their individual differences; it is thus unlikely to use a hypothetico-deductive method so clearly. Generally, it would seem that psychology is a science with regard to the overall building of knowledge.

Falsification

Popper also emphasised the idea of **falsification**. His point is that nothing can be proved. A well-known example is the idea of testing the hypothesis 'all swans are white'. Someone can find a great many white swans but cannot prove all swans are white, because they cannot ever find and see all swans. However, if they find a black swan they have disproved the hypothesis that 'all swans are white'. Science aims to falsify not to verify. If psychology is a science it also must seek to falsify hypotheses.

Relating this idea to psychology

Relating the idea of falsification to psychology is difficult. For example, social identity theory claims that people act more favourably towards their in-group compared to any out-group member. This could be found many, many times (and has been), but if psychology is a science, just one instance where someone acted more favourably to an out-group member would be enough to disprove social identity theory. However, in psychology any general law or universal law is not 'proved' in this way, because the subject matter involves humans. There are going to be elements of chance and of individual differences to consider. In general, psychology does not try to falsify hypotheses and therefore it is not a science by this definition.

Reductionism versus holism

Science also uses reductionism. To use the hypothetico-deductive method, a hypothesis must be specific and measurable. Sometimes it is hard to make a variable measurable, because it is too broad and too many things affect it. For example, even the task of measuring the temperature of water is affected by air pressure; water boils at a different temperature in an aeroplane than at sea level. So measurement is reduced to one factor or feature. This is an example of reductionism.

Holism means looking at something in its entirety, rather than breaking it down into parts thus losing the 'whole'. By reducing elements of science to one factor the 'whole' situation might not be studied. For example, brain scans usually study and measure one particular area of the brain rather than looking at the working of the brain as a whole. It has been said that the whole is 'more than the sum of its parts'.

Relating this idea to psychology

Psychology does study the parts of human behaviour. Behaviourists study only observable behaviour such as stimulus–response learning. For example, they look at how an association could be made between lifts and fear by transferring a fear of closed spaces to a fear of lifts. Taking a holistic approach to someone with a phobia of lifts might involve looking at their overall functioning to find out how to treat such a fear.

You could argue that case studies take a more holistic view of a behaviour, for example Freud studied Little Hans's development as a whole. Experiments are likely to take a reductionist view, as both the IV and the DV have to be measured clearly. Overall, psychological research does reduce what is being measured to something measurable and testable and so to this extent it would fit the definition of science. Freud, however, did not look at measurable concepts — neither the id nor the unconscious are measurable. There are also areas of psychology that take a holistic view.

Scientific subject matter

Sciences are areas of study where scientific methods are used. In general there is a tendency to call certain subject matter 'scientific' because there are specific sciences such as chemistry, biology and physics. There are other sciences, including environmental science, geology and neuroscience.

Relating this idea to psychology

Psychology at A-level has been called a science because of its use of scientific methods, as argued above. Psychology covers subject matter that is regarded as 'scientific', such as DNA, genes, hormones, neurotransmitters, ideas of evolution, animal experiments, drugs and aspects of mental health disorders. To this extent, psychology is scientific. However, a significant proportion of the subject matter of psychology is less scientific. Theories discussed in the psychodynamic approach are not measurable, for example Freud's concept of 'the unconscious'. As much psychological material is not easily measured, it is therefore often thought of as 'not scientific'. The concepts of obedience, prejudice and learning are not easily operationalised.

> **Study hint** Make a list of areas of psychology where the subject matter could be called 'science' and a list of areas where the subject matter is not scientific.

The paradigm

Thomas Kuhn talked about the need for a **paradigm**, or an overall theory, because hypotheses are deduced from an overall theory in order to build scientific and firm knowledge. It is hard to say what the paradigm in psychology is — it could be said to be pre-paradigmatic. The psychodynamic approach has a paradigm of its own but it is far from being accepted by everyone in psychology. Behaviourism is a paradigm as it has its own set of explanations about behaviour. The cognitive approach links with the biological approach and neuroscience, and it could be said that this is the most accepted and researched area of psychology and could thus be taken as the main paradigm. However, that would be to deny all the other approaches and ideas that are well researched and contribute both to psychology and society. In summary, it is not easy to explain psychology as one area of knowledge, which makes it hard to say it is a science.

> **Explore** Look up the work of Kuhn on paradigms.

Science and the five AS approaches

The question of whether psychology is a science focuses on two aspects — scientific content and scientific methodology. The content, however, links with the methodology because it is content that is measurable, testable and subject to universal laws and therefore considered 'scientific'. Content that is less measurable or about individuals is not considered scientific. It follows that approaches that use scientific methodology are thought of as more scientific than approaches that do not, and have content that is more measurable and universal.

The social approach

The social approach uses a lot of experimentation. Milgram's work is experimental in that he controls variables as independent variables to measure a clearly operationalised dependent variable.

> **Explore** Consider the idea that Milgram's studies are not in fact straightforward laboratory experiments. The issue is that his main variable, which in his main study is setting the procedure up so that participants obey an authority figure, is not in fact an independent variable. This is because there is no other condition (such as having participants 'give' shocks without orders), as this would not be possible given the design. The careful controls and the carefully set up procedure and DV are why the studies are generally called laboratory experiments. Consider other studies you have looked at and think about the research methodology.

Sherif and Tajfel also carried out studies using experimentation. Sherif used field experiments and Tajfel worked in the laboratory. There is much evidence, therefore, to suggest that social psychology is scientific. However, ethnographic studies — for example, looking at differences in gender roles across cultures — involve gathering qualitative data, which is almost the opposite of scientific method. This means a lot of social psychology is not regarded as scientific.

Finally, social psychology looks at concepts that are hard to make measurable, such as obedience and prejudice, as well as behaviour and gender roles. From the point of view of the content, therefore, social psychology is not a science.

The cognitive approach

The cognitive approach uses a lot of experimentation. Concepts such as 'memory' and 'forgetting' are studied by reducing them to parts that can be tested, such as memory for lists of words. For example, Craik and Tulving set up a clear experiment where the same people had to consider words either for their structure, sound or meaning, and it was found that when words were considered for their meaning more were recalled.

The cognitive approach uses case studies as well, but they are case studies of brain-damaged people, where scanning and testing is done to find out how the brain damage has affected cognitive functioning. Such data are gathered scientifically.

Cognitive psychology looks at concepts that are hard to measure. However, as it looks at processing within the brain, there is a lot of biological information used, such as that gathered by scanning the brain to see where there is activity in certain situations. It seems, therefore, that with regard to content, cognitive psychology is close to being scientific.

Study hint Prepare an answer to a question about how scientific each approach is. For each approach, try to find evidence for and against it being scientific so that you are presenting an argument.

The psychodynamic approach

The psychodynamic approach focuses on the unconscious and the idea that a lot of what guides behaviour comes from unconscious wishes and desires. The unconscious by definition is not measurable or testable in a direct way. The personality is made up of the id, ego and superego, none of which is measurable. Freud used case studies — and, within them, research methods such as dream analysis and free association — to uncover unconscious wishes. He gathered data about each individual to interpret their dreams and these data were qualitative. There is little that is scientific in the research methodology. In psychoanalysis there has to be interpretation, which means there could be subjectivity with regard to the data, and science demands objective data from which to draw conclusions.

With regard to content, the psychodynamic approach is not scientific either because the concepts are so hard to measure.

The biological approach

The biological approach is considered to be a scientific one. It uses a lot of experimentation, often on animals. For example, data are gathered by scanning the brain and studying its functions. However, case studies can be carried out non-scientifically, for example twin studies — where MZ (identical) twins are compared with DZ (non-identical) twins — to investigate which characteristics derive from biology and which from the environment. Data are gathered from the twins and questionnaires or interviews may be used, with qualitative data being gathered.

With regard to content, the biological approach is scientific, as it is concerned with genes, hormones, neurotransmitters and brain functioning. Variables can be selected

6

for study in these areas, although not always easily. In all these areas a lot of the functioning is thought to be universal, which helps understanding not only of humans, but also of animals.

The learning approach

The learning approach specifically uses experiments to find out about learning and to separate learning into stimulus and response behaviour without focusing on thought processes that occur. Behaviour is made measurable and reduced to parts, so the methodology can be regarded as scientific. Some parts of learning theory could be called less scientific than others: Bandura's work on social learning theory includes looking at cognitive elements such as motivation, for example. However, the research methods are scientific: the aim is to obtain information about general laws of behaviour through forming a hypothesis and testing it.

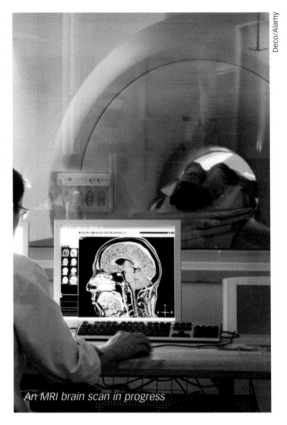

An MRI brain scan in progress

Deco/Alamy

With regard to content, behaviour in general might be thought of as too complex and too individual to be scientifically studied. However, behaviourists have deliberately broken the content down into measurable parts in order to study it scientifically.

Figure 6.3 *Elements of study that make something scientific*

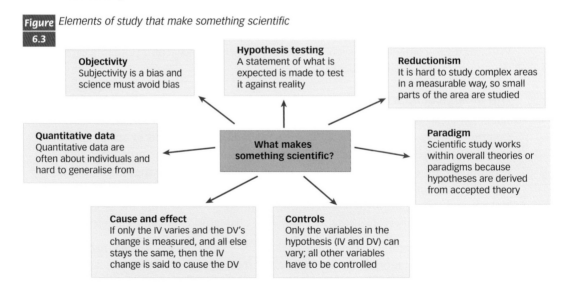

Objectivity
Subjectivity is a bias and science must avoid bias

Hypothesis testing
A statement of what is expected is made to test it against reality

Reductionism
It is hard to study complex areas in a measurable way, so small parts of the area are studied

Quantitative data
Quantitative data are often about individuals and hard to generalise from

What makes something scientific?

Paradigm
Scientific study works within overall theories or paradigms because hypotheses are derived from accepted theory

Cause and effect
If only the IV varies and the DV's change is measured, and all else stays the same, then the IV change is said to cause the DV

Controls
Only the variables in the hypothesis (IV and DV) can vary; all other variables have to be controlled

Table
6.31

The five AS approaches and how far they might be seen as scientific

Approach	Scientific	Not scientific
Social	Experiments, objectivity, cause and effect conclusions	Ethnography, qualitative data, focus on the individual
Cognitive	Experiments, objectivity, scientific subject matter (brain and processing)	Processing hard to measure, some qualitative data (e.g. case studies)
Psychodynamic	Aimed at general (universal) laws	Concepts not measurable, case study method, qualitative data, focus on individual functioning, subjectivity possible (interpretation needed)
Biological	Subject matter (e.g. genes, hormones), experiments, objectivity, universal laws	Twin studies, case studies, subject matter can be hard to measure
Learning	Experiments, cause and effect conclusions, objectivity, measurable	Social learning theory includes cognition such as motivation and attention

Study hint You must be able to compare the approaches with regard to how scientific they are, so practise using these concepts to argue a case for their similarities and differences.

Psychology and social control

This is an important issue in psychology and concerns the use of psychological understanding to control people, for the good of society or for other reasons. This is an ethical issue and concerns questions such as:

- Who should have the power to control someone?
- When (if at all) is control appropriate?
- Who should be controlled?
- What means are appropriate to control someone?

The above questions show that there are both ethical and practical issues involved when considering the use of psychology as a means of social control.

In your course you need to know in particular about four areas of social control. These are:

- the use of drug therapy (such as in health psychology and clinical psychology)
- the use of token economy (such as in criminological, health and clinical psychology)
- the use of classical conditioning (from the learning approach and also used in applications)
- the influence of the practitioner in treatment and/or therapy

These issues have all been covered in this chapter when the contributions of psychology to society were considered, so they are only outlined here. In this section the focus is on the ethical and practical issues that the four areas raise and on the power of the practitioner. Where possible, it is worth considering the areas of social control as they occur in different applications and approaches

The use of drug therapy

Drug therapy was explained in detail in Chapter 3. The overall idea is that someone addicted to a drug can be given a substitute that has fewer side-effects, for example, and that this can help them to come off the drug. Methadone is used as a substitute for heroin and similar substitutes are being developed for other recreational drugs. Drug addiction is thus controlled by drug therapy. Drug therapy is also used for mental disorders, as explaining in Chapter 5 on clinical psychology.

Ethical issues

Ethical issues with regard to drug addiction include social pressure not to take drugs and whether drug taking should be a free choice. A further ethical issue is whether an addict should be allowed to exercise their free will by choosing to continue to take drugs, or be forced to give up drugs because of the harm caused.

With regard to drug addiction, drug treatment itself is time-consuming and invasive. It also means the person is still taking a drug, which may be seen as morally wrong. As drug treatments are developed through experimentation on animals, it could be argued that another ethical issue involves such use of animals.

Practical issues

Looking at drug addiction, one practical issue is whether the addicted person will be prepared to make a commitment to the regular treatment required. The person will also have to invest time in the counselling offered to help him or her to move away from the peer group, which has been shown to influence whether someone gives up the drug or not. The patient may not find it easy to see treatment through.

The power of the therapist/practitioner

Those administering the drug therapy will have power and this includes with regard to addiction to a drug. The therapist has power over the addicted person to an extent, though the individual can choose whether or not to attend the treatment sessions. The power of society might be involved, as the individual may have been put on a treatment programme as a condition of a court case. Many addicts do return to their usual environment and go back to drug use following treatment, which suggests that they (and not the therapist) have ultimate power. In any treatment where drugs are used as therapy, such as antipsychotic drugs, the therapist or clinician is likely to have power over which drug is chosen, and other related issues.

The use of token economy

Token economy has been explained earlier in this chapter and is also dealt with in Chapter 5. The overall idea is that behaviour is managed using operant conditioning principles and tokens are given as rewards for desirable behaviour. The tokens are then exchanged for something the individual wants.

Ethical issues

Behaviour management involves ethical issues because someone has to decide which behaviour is desirable, and token economy programmes are used in cases where the individual's behaviour is considered undesirable. This means that the individual's rights are likely to be infringed, as they are required to change their behaviour for some reward. If the reward is an addition to their usual requirements, this might be seen as ethical. However, if the reward includes what is necessary (such as a meal), then the approach might be considered unethical. In practice, rewards are often items regarded as extras, such as watching television or buying treats like chocolate or cigarettes. There is a fine line here, and the needs of the individual must be considered carefully for token economy treatment to be ethical.

A further ethical issue is that sometimes the treatment is used for those with a mental disorder, which might mean they have little free will over being involved in the programme.

Practical issues

Staff have to be trained to use a token economy programme and must stick to the same reward system for the same behaviours. In practice, this is hard to achieve. A further consideration is that the programme might work in one environment but not in another where the cues and reward structure are not present. This limits the application of the therapy. The programme can be expensive, as rewards must be provided (as well as staff training).

The power of the therapist/practitioner

Staff running and implementing the programme have power over the individual. They can withhold a token at any time, for example, if the programme is not properly supervised. The individual does not have much power because the programme is usually run within an institution, and the individual is likely to have difficulty in giving consent to or withdrawing from the programme.

The use of classical conditioning

Systematic desensitisation, used to treat phobias, is explained earlier in this chapter as well as in Chapter 5. It uses classical conditioning principles as someone learns to associate a previously feared object or situation with a relaxation response instead of a fear response. Aversion therapy also uses classical conditioning principles and is used, for example, to condition an aversive response (such as nausea) to something undesired (such as alcohol).

Ethical issues

Conditioning an adverse response in someone is not something to be undertaken lightly: the therapist has power over the patient. In some situations, such as in prisons and other institutions, it is possible for someone to be pressured into such treatment by removing their power to say no, or by making them feel they cannot

6

refuse. It can be argued, however, that therapies based on classical conditioning have been used to help people. For example, aversion therapy is used to help people to stop smoking or to stop using alcohol. In practice, the therapy involves building a good relationship between the client and the practitioner, including other therapy such as counselling, and deciding on a treatment plan that suits each individual. Classical conditioning is not used in isolation, and the patient/client is usually involved in the treatment — they give informed consent and have the right to withdraw. This is also true of systematic desensitisation.

> **Explore**   Look up systematic desensitisation and aversion therapy to find case histories of people who have undergone such treatments since 2000, as a lot of the studies looking at the effectiveness of such treatments are older ones that are critical of the treatment. Both therapies have evolved over time to give more power to the client and, in general, to be more ethical.

Practical issues

Systematic desensitisation works for specific phobias, where a hierarchy of fears can be set up and worked with. It requires the person being treated to be able to learn the necessary relaxation techniques, so the practical application of systematic desensitisation is limited. On the other hand, it requires little equipment and therefore the cost is low, apart from the practitioner time.

Practical application to daily life is an issue with aversion therapy, for example someone being conditioned to avoid alcohol would still need to drink liquids without feeling sick. There are other practical issues with regard to the therapist: they would need to feel able to work with the client and to build a relationship with them, which might prove harder with some clients than others.

The power of the therapist/practitioner

The therapist conditioning the desired behaviour is in a position of power, as are other therapists. They might be controlling the aversive stimulus in the case of aversion therapy, and with systematic desensitisation they control the hierarchy after it has been decided. However, the client has to agree to the therapy and can withdraw from it, which reduces the power of the therapist.

Different types of power

There are different types of power, according to French and Raven (1960). A therapist possesses most of these types of power.
- Expert power is given to someone who is an expert in the field.
- Reward power is given to a therapist, because they have the power to reward the client either with praise or actual 'gifts' (such as in the case of the token economy programme).
- A therapist has legitimate power, in that society expects people to behave appropriately, and a therapist's role is often to be an agent of society in shaping appropriate behaviour.

- The therapist should not have coercive power, because they will be acting within a set of ethical guidelines and will not be 'allowed' to make someone do something without consent. However, it could be argued that society can make someone do something — for example, a person can be sectioned or ordered to undergo therapy (such as anger management) as part of a court case. In this case, the coercive power of society can be handed down to the therapist, though even then a therapist is required to follow ethical rules when working.
- The fifth type of power is referent power, which is when someone gives someone power because they want to be like them. This type of power includes charisma. A client might transfer feelings of admiration or similar feelings onto a therapist who appears to have knowledge and skills that the client wants (for example, to help them to get better or improve their life).

Use the ideas given above when considering the three types of social control (drug therapy, token economy and classical conditioning) to discuss the power of the practitioner, as well as these ideas about the different types of power.

> **Explore** Look further into the issue of the power of the practitioner. A therapy such as CBT, for example, places great emphasis in its training programmes on the importance of not abusing the power of the therapist.

Psychology and nature versus nurture

You will have studied the nature–nurture debate in both the AS and A2 parts of your course. The basic idea is that some characteristics of human behaviour come from nature and what someone is born able to do, while others come from nurture and the experiences someone has, which then affect them. In practice, the debate is not as clear-cut as this. After conception, for example, the womb is an environment and gives a foetus experiences. A human baby is born ready to mature in certain ways — not only to develop through puberty, but also to develop their thinking processes. Experiences that seem to be about 'nurture' can be driven by maturational processes that are in fact 'nature'. Experiences that seem to be 'nature' (such as from conception onwards) can in fact be 'nurture', because environment has an effect. When someone takes the view that development involves both nature and nurture, this is said to be an **interactionist** view.

How the nature–nurture debate is studied

Twin studies can help to show what (in human behaviour and functioning) is likely to come on the one hand from genetics and on the other from environmental influences. MZ twins share all their genes and DZ twins share 50% of their genes. If MZ twins are more alike than DZ twins in some characteristic, it tends to be claimed that the characteristic is likely to be caused by nature, at least in part.

Adoption studies also look at the nature–nurture debate. For example, if children who have at least one biological parent with schizophrenia are adopted and then develop schizophrenia (but nobody in their adoptive family has the illness), then it is claimed that this is evidence that schizophrenia is at least in part genetic.

6

Animal experiments can help to show what may be genetic inheritance and what derives from nurture — mice can be bred to be genetically identical and their environment varied to see what effect this has.

Cross-cultural studies can also help to show which characteristics in humans are innate (from 'nature'). For example, if attachment patterns between mothers and babies are the same across all cultures, then it might be concluded that human infants have an innate tendency to form an attachment with a caregiver.

Evaluating nature–nurture explanations

When evaluating explanations of behaviour or characteristics that draw on the nature–nurture debate, you can evaluate the research methods used to gather evidence for either nature, nurture or interactionism. For example, there is no characteristic that, if found in one MZ twin, is always found in the other, so there is not 100% agreement, although MZ twins share 100% of their genes. For example, schizophrenia in one MZ twin does not always predict schizophrenia in the other twin. Some of the behaviour must therefore be down to nurture.

Cross-cultural studies are hard to draw conclusions from because it is difficult to become completely immersed in a different culture, and researchers tend to be ethnocentric.

Animal studies can help to draw conclusions about human behaviour, but animals are different from humans in important ways, including the fact that they do not use problem solving to the same extent. It is therefore hard to generalise findings from animal studies to say they are true of humans.

Approaches, applications and the nature–nurture debate

The five AS approaches and the three applications you have studied (two from criminological, child, health and sport, and also clinical psychology) have different views about the nature–nurture debate. Some focus more on one or the other, and some focus on both.

Table 6.32 *How approaches and applications link to the nature–nurture debate*

Approach/ application	Nature	Nurture
Social	Perhaps that people have evolved to act as agents in society	Focuses on how society affects people, including interactions of in-groups
Cognitive	Information processing in the brain takes place in a certain way and brain structures serve different functions with regard to thinking	Cues in the environment are used to help us to remember; how we encode something from the environment can affect forgetting/recall
Psychodynamic	People have the id, ego and superego and are guided by unconscious forces	Parents and society give the superego and conscience and so we learn to fit with society
Biological	Hormones, neurotransmitters, brain structures link with the genetic blueprint, as do maturational processes	The environment from conception onwards affects maturation and development

Approach/application	Nature	Nurture
Learning	Reflexes are innate, as is the tendency to learn by association and reward (how we learn)	What we learn comes from the environment, including all our experiences
Criminological	Can include whether someone is born criminal, perhaps linked to aggression and brain structures (or hormones)	Includes the effect of the environment on becoming criminal, such as the self-fulfilling prophecy
Child	Babies are born with a tendency to form attachments and to develop language, among other features	Environment, such as privation and deprivation, affects development
Health	Drugs affect neuronal transmission at the synapse, for example	Treatments for drug addiction seem to have to include removing environmental cues that might lead to relapse
Sport	Personality such as introvert or extrovert can come from biological make-up; the level of arousal can affect performance	Arousal can come from the environment; other issues such as need for achievement can be learned (or innate?)
Clinical	Mental disorders can come from nature such as schizophrenia and depression, where there might be an element of inherited tendency	Mental health issues seem to be affected by the environment — for example, those with social support seem to be less affected by depression

New situations

You need to be able to apply psychology to any new situations that are explained in the examination and that you may not have considered before. There are no specific preparations for this section, but some general rules apply.

Finding the underpinning approach or application

First, look at the stimulus material that gives you the 'new situation'. Decide which approach or application fits best. For example, anything about interactions between people and groups is within social psychology. Situations involving the processing of information are within the cognitive approach. If a situation involves early childhood experiences or problems in adulthood with functioning that might come from early childhood difficulties, then the psychodynamic approach is useful. Biological issues should be clear, and for many situations about people biological aspects such as the influence of genes or an evolutionary explanation can be considered. Classical conditioning, operant conditioning and social learning principles are often useful as well, in particular the idea of imitation and modelling, and so the learning approach is often useful. If a situation involves crime, children, health or sport the relevant application is useful, and if the situation is about mental health issues then clinical psychology is involved.

Using themes and methodology

There are general overall themes that can help to explain a situation or behaviour:

- Genes and the genetic blueprint underpin much of someone's behaviour, including abilities and characteristics they are born with and maturational processes as they mature.
- Evolution theory is an explanation of many aspects of human nature, including how animal and human behaviour can be compared.
- Themes in social psychology such as obedience and prejudice occur frequently because they are about group behaviour and how individuals behave as social beings.
- How people process information — in particular, how they remember and why they forget — are themes that occur frequently. For example, the idea of being a witness involves cognitive processes, as do revision processes and memory aids.
- The Oedipus complex is a useful theme when considering gender behaviour and problems that might come from early childhood with regard to developing later relationships with the opposite (or same) sex.
- Social learning theory is useful as an explanation of many different behaviours.

> **Study hint** There are many other themes you will be familiar with from the course. Make a list of any theories, concepts or studies you can think of and then alongside the list note down what situations or characteristics they would help to explain. For example, social identity theory helps to explain football violence.

When applying concepts, theories and the findings of studies to a new situation, be ready to evaluate using methodology points. By evaluating a study or theory you are evaluating the explanation of the new situation, which is a useful contribution. For example, when showing how social identity theory explains conflict between groups you can add the point that Tajfel tended to use laboratory experiments to develop the theory, so the findings may lack validity, which in turn might affect how far the theory is accepted as an explanation of the particular situation under discussion.

Examination-style questions

1 Explain what is meant by 'contribution to society'. *(2 marks)*

2 Outline two ethical guidelines when using human participants. *(4 marks)*

3 Explain two weaknesses of one laboratory experiment you have studied in your course. *(4 marks)*

4 Describe one questionnaire study that has been carried out in psychology. *(4 marks)*

5 Compare observations and questionnaires in terms of validity. *(4 marks)*

6 Describe what is meant by social control. *(2 marks)*

7 Distinguish between nature and nurture, using examples. *(4 marks)*

Extension questions

1 Describe and evaluate two contributions to society made by one application of psychology that you have studied. *(12 marks)*

2 Describe and evaluate the claim that psychology should be called a science. *(12 marks)*

A